T0325195

Social Reflections of Human–Computer Interaction in Education, Management, and Economics

Gamze Sart
Istanbul University–Cerrahpasa, Turkey

A volume in the Advances in Systems Analysis, Software Engineering, and High Performance Computing (ASASEHPC) Book Series

Published in the United States of America by
    IGI Global
    Engineering Science Reference (an imprint of IGI Global)
    701 E. Chocolate Avenue
    Hershey PA, USA 17033
    Tel: 717-533-8845
    Fax: 717-533-8661
    E-mail: cust@igi-global.com
    Web site: http://www.igi-global.com

Library of Congress Cataloging-in-Publication Data

CIP Data Pending
 ISBN: 979-8-3693-3033-3
eISBN: 979-8-3693-3034-0

British Cataloguing in Publication Data
A Cataloguing in Publication record for this book is available from the British Library.

All work contributed to this book is new, previously-unpublished material.
The views expressed in this book are those of the authors, but not necessarily of the publisher.

For electronic access to this publication, please contact: eresources@igi-global.com.

Advances in Systems Analysis, Software Engineering, and High Performance Computing (ASASEHPC) Book Series

Vijayan Sugumaran
Oakland University, Rochester, USA

MISSION

The theory and practice of computing applications and distributed systems has emerged as one of the key areas of research driving innovations in business, engineering, and science. The fields of software engineering, systems analysis, and high performance computing offer a wide range of applications and solutions in solving computational problems for any modern organization.

The **Advances in Systems Analysis, Software Engineering, and High Performance Computing (ASASEHPC) Book Series** brings together research in the areas of distributed computing, systems and software engineering, high performance computing, and service science. This collection of publications is useful for academics, researchers, and practitioners seeking the latest practices and knowledge in this field.

Coverage

- Computer Graphics
- Human-Computer Interaction
- Network Management
- Storage Systems

IGI Global is currently accepting manuscripts for publication within this series. To submit a proposal for a volume in this series, please contact our Acquisition Editors at Acquisitions@igi-global.com or visit: http://www.igi-global.com/publish/.

Titles in this Series

For a list of additional titles in this series, please visit:
http://www.igi-global.com/book-series/

Revolutionizing Curricula Through Computational Thinking, Logic, and Problem Solving
Mathias Mbu Fonkam (Penn State University, USA) and Narasimha Rao Vajjhala (University of New York, Tirana, Albania)
Engineering Science Reference • copyright 2024 • 245pp • H/C (ISBN: 9798369319741)
• US $245.00 (our price)

Harnessing High-Performance Computing and AI for Environmental Sustainability
Arshi Naim (King Khalid University, Saudi Arabia)
Engineering Science Reference • copyright 2024 • 401pp • H/C (ISBN: 9798369317945)
• US $315.00 (our price)

Recent Trends and Future Direction for Data Analytics
Aparna Kumari (Nirma University, Ahmedabad, India)
Engineering Science Reference • copyright 2024 • 350pp • H/C (ISBN: 9798369336090)
• US $345.00 (our price)

Advancing Software Engineering Through AI, Federated Learning, and Large Language Models
Avinash Kumar Sharma (Sharda University, India) Nitin Chanderwal (University of Cincinnati, USA) Amarjeet Prajapati (Jaypee Institute of Information Technology, India) Pancham Singh (Ajay Kumar Garg Engineering College, Ghaziabad, India) and Mrignainy Kansal (Ajay Kumar Garg Engineering College, Ghaziabad, India)
Engineering Science Reference • copyright 2024 • 354pp • H/C (ISBN: 9798369335024)
• US $355.00 (our price)

Advancements, Applications, and Foundations of C++
Shams Al Ajrawi (Wiley Edge, USA & Alliant International University, USA) Charity Jennings (Wiley Edge, USA & University of Phoenix, USA) Paul Menefee (Wiley Edge, USA) Wathiq Mansoor (University of Dubai, UAE) and Mansoor Ahmed Alaali (Ahlia University, Bahrain)

701 East Chocolate Avenue, Hershey, PA 17033, USA
Tel: 717-533-8845 x100 • Fax: 717-533-8661
E-Mail: cust@igi-global.com • www.igi-global.com

Table of Contents

Detailed Table of Contents

Chapter 1
Integrating Machine Learning to Enhance Online Learning Student
Performance ....
1

Somdeep Das, Management Development Institute, Murshidabad, India
Pinaki Pratim Acharjya, Haldia Institute of Technology, India

The extensive growth of online learning in recent years has opened the avenues of learning without any physical boundaries. The ultimate aim of online learning is to increase the perimeter of students learning and to achieve this students performance should also be monitored and improved. Online learning integrated LMSs enables capturing and tracking data related to students and courses. The performance of students may highly be impacted by various parameters in online learning environment. This work proposes the study and analysis of student performance which may be enhanced by implementing Machine Learning technologies on the student information mined in the LMSs. It focuses on developing models based on machine learning (ML) to comprehend the multiple factors that influence student success in an online learning environment. Various machine learning classifier algorithms were utilized to train the model.

Chapter 2

Machine Learning (ML)-Based Braille Lippi Characters and Numbers
Detection and Announcement System for Blind Children in Learning ....

> *Kutubuddin Sayyad Liyakat Kazi, Brahmdevdada Mane Institute of Technology, Solapur, India*

Character and number recognition in Braille Lippi is the process by which a computer can recognise language. To read students' and lecturers' Braille Lippi notes, a character recognition system that can read Braille Lippi is being developed. A Braille Lippi character recognition system is developed through a variety of strategies and procedures and concentrates on neural networks (NN). When compared to other computational methods, neural networks are more effective and reliable for recognising Braille Lippi characters. Along with testing and system development findings, the report also describes the Braille Lippi character recognition system's methodology, design, and architecture with an accuracy of 99.09%. The goal is to demonstrate how effective neural networks are to recognise Braille Lippi characters.

Chapter 3

Utilizing Machine Learning to Increase Online Learning Instructors'
Efficiency ....

> *Somdeep Das, Management Development Institute, Murshidabad, India*
> *Pinaki Pratim Acharjya, Haldia Institute of Technology, India*

The online learning management system (OLMS) is one of the fundamental parts of the e-learning framework. As assessment of teachers is referred to as an essential part of education and a helpful contribution to improve the nature of teaching, the Feedback module of the OLMS provides with the facility to collect potential feedback of the teachers. The integration of the feedback module of the system with artificial intelligence (AI), especially machine learning (ML) allows with the ability to investigate vast amounts of data and discover patterns that can be useful in the progression of teaching techniques and ensures a deep analysis of the performance of the teachers. This absolutely underpins educational institutions to undertake noteworthy decisions for the improvement of the teachers and ultimately, the learners. This work proposes that the incorporation of technologies, like machine learning algorithms, with OLMS may facilitate in augmenting teaching efficiency.

The chapter discovers the role of human-computer relations in entrepreneurship. It answers the question of how far AI can influence human beings and how AI fosters entrepreneurial creativity and innovative ideas. The right use of AI and technology would not replace; instead, it would assist humans in making advancements in different fields. It is completely in our hands, whether to let AI overpower us, or keep it under our control. The chapter also emphasizes on approaching entrepreneurship in the form of creative destruction theory. Teachers must employ a variety of pedagogies to cater to entrepreneurial education in students. The education 'about', 'for', and 'through' entrepreneurship is crucial to give the students entrepreneurial exposure through classroom settings. It also talks about the scope of entrepreneurship i.e. the rapid expansion of Entrepreneurship and the use of AI in Entrepreneurship in different countries. Lastly, how AI tools can be used for the automation of finance, managing expenses, and managing supply chains, to sustain the business for a long period of time.

The perception of artificial intelligence among employees is increasingly relevant as artificial intelligence technologies become more prevalent in the workplace. A positive perception of artificial intelligence can lead to improved job performance, as employees may be more willing to embrace and utilize artificial intelligence technologies to enhance their work. Conversely, a negative perception of artificial intelligence can hinder job performance, as employees may resist or feel threatened by artificial intelligence technologies. This study aims to examine the association between attitudes to artificial intelligence and job performance among 500 academicians employed in universities in Istanbul, using structural equation modeling. The findings of the analysis indicate a statistically significant positive relationship ($\beta=0.412$, p<0.01) between artificial intelligence and job performance. It is necessary to emphasize the importance of making academics' attitudes towards artificial intelligence positive.

Ashy Sebastian, Christ University, Bengaluru, India
Veerta Tantia, Christ University, Bengaluru, India

This chapter focuses on the idea of business analytics through AI and aims to address how AI has emerged as a powerful force in augmenting and replacing traditional human-computer interactions in the realm of business analytics. AI-powered analytics can uncover hidden patterns, detect anomalies, and automate decision-making processes, significantly augmenting the efficiency and accuracy of data analysis. Thus, the purpose of this chapter is two-fold. First, the chapter sheds light on business analytics, big data, and big data analytics through AI. It delves into the theories of machine and deep learning and their synergy with big data analytics. Secondly, the authors analyze a case study to substantiate our theory. ML-based prediction models using stock market data are developed to underline the significance of adopting AI-driven approaches for business analytics.

Chapter 7

Emre Yaşar, Isparta University of Applied Sciences, Turkey
İsmail Öztürk, Kırıkkale University, Turkey
Eda Yayla, Bitlis University, Turkey
Erge Tür, Istanbul Esenyurt University, Turkey

This study evaluates the role and impact of ChatGPT in tourism education. According to the study results, the areas of use of ChatGPT in tourism education are preparing course content, curriculum and exams, language learning, and obtaining theoretical knowledge. ChatGPT is suitable for academicians and students within the scope of tourism education. The factors affecting the applicability of ChatGPT in tourism education are the digital skills and technological predispositions of academics and students, ethical and security concerns, and the structural characteristics of tourism education. The positive effects of ChatGPT on tourism students are that it improves their research skills and efficiency, saves time, increases creativity, and provides access to information quickly. The negative effects of ChatGPT on tourism students are the possibility of making them lazy, accessing wrong information, reducing their thinking skills, and making them dependent on technology.

In this study, the QFD approach is used to convert customer requirements into design features for a better mobile phone design. An online survey is conducted with the users to determine their needs. Afterward, technical requirements were identified to meet customer requirements. The relationship between customer requirements and technical requirements is developed to identify the most critical phases. The relationship matrix is then converted into the house of quality (HOQ) matrix. For the analysis part, Apple, Samsung, and Huawei mobile phones are benchmarked, and each step of the QFD is applied to reach a user-centered design for the customers. The results showed that processor and connectivity are the most important factors among the ten different technical features.

In the study, the effects on the design of learning environments were evaluated by considering gender, personality structures and birth order, which are considered as individual differences. Evaluation process eye tracking method was used. In the research, random assignment pattern paired from quasi-experimental research patterns was applied. Nineteen students from a public university participated in the research. To collect the data, a form containing demographic information, the information of the student's gender, age, along with the introverted or extroverted personality structure, and the number of children in the nuclear family were given. Data on eye movements were obtained with the eye tracking tool used while students were studying with materials. As a result of the research, the students have different individual differences, and they have made inferences about the differences in learning with the eye movements they have made in learning materials and various suggestions have been made.

S. C. Vetrivel, Kongu Engineering College, India
K. C. Sowmiya, Sri Vasavi College, India
V. Sabareeshwari, Amrita School of Agricultural Sciences, India
V. P. Arun, JKKN College of Engineering and Technology, India

The advent of advanced technologies has led to a profound transformation in the way humans interact with computers, giving rise to the interdisciplinary field of Human-Computer Interaction (HCI). This chapter explores the multifaceted impact of HCI on the economy, examining its influence on productivity, employment dynamics, market trends, and societal structures. The study synthesizes a comprehensive analysis of the positive and negative implications of HCI, shedding light on its role as a driver of economic growth and a catalyst for socio-economic change. The positive aspects of HCI on the economy are first explored, focusing on increased productivity and efficiency resulting from user-friendly interfaces, intuitive design, and seamless interaction between humans and machines. The adoption of HCI principles has not only streamlined business processes but has also empowered individuals with digital literacy, fostering innovation and entrepreneurship.

Funda Hatice Sezgin, Istanbul University-Cerrahpasa, Turkey

The impact of information technology competence on information management in businesses is extremely important. First of all, information technologies enable businesses to manage data and information more effectively. Thanks to data storage, processing and analysis capabilities, businesses can quickly process large amounts of data and transform it into meaningful information. This enables correct decisions to be made and strategic goals to be achieved more effectively. Additionally, thanks to information technologies, businesses can share information, collaborate and strengthen internal communication. This accelerates the flow of information within the business and increases efficiency. It provides access to accurate and timely information, fast decision-making processes and flexibility. This enables businesses to adapt to market conditions more quickly and gain competitive advantage. The aim of this study is to analyze the situation and make suggestions by considering the effect of information technology competence on information management in businesses from different aspects.

Mohammad Abuturab Zaidi, Christ University, India
Raj Srivastava, Christ University, India
Yashmita Awasthi, Christ University, India

The barter system, the oldest form of exchange dating back to human civilization, involves directly exchanging goods and services without using money. However, it comes with limitations, such as the requirement for a double coincidence of wants, difficulties in valuing goods and services, and the absence of a store of value. Over time, various forms of money emerged to overcome these limitations. Commodity money, like gold and silver, gained value due to their rarity and intrinsic worth. Later, fiat currencies were introduced, backed by trust rather than physical commodities. In contrast, cryptocurrency, a new digital currency not issued by any central authority, relies on blockchain technology for secure and anonymous transactions. This paper traces the evolution of currency from medieval times to the present digital era and explores the differences between the barter system, fiat currency, and cryptocurrency. It also delves into the potential of cryptocurrency to revolutionize our perception of money.

Preface

Welcome to *Social Reflections of Human-Computer Interaction in Education, Management, and Economics,* a comprehensive exploration of the profound impacts that computers and information technologies have had on various aspects of our lives since their widespread adoption in the late 1980s. I'm Gamze Sart from Istanbul University, Turkey, and it is my pleasure to present this edited volume that delves into the intricate and multifaceted relationship between humans and computers.

Since the advent of the digital age, computers have become indispensable in education, households, and businesses. Their ability to efficiently perform and manage a wide range of tasks has significantly increased productivity across numerous fields, including education, business, and healthcare. Today, our interaction with computers is nearly constant, spanning from home to school to the workplace, reflecting the ubiquitous nature of these technologies in our daily routines.

The multidisciplinary field of Human-Computer Interaction (HCI) examines the dynamic interactions between humans and information technologies. It is a critical area of study for any country aiming to enhance its technological prowess and improve the quality of life for its citizens. The objective of this edited book is to explore the social reflections of HCI within the contexts of education, management, and economics. By doing so, we aim to provide insights and foster understanding of how these interactions shape our professional and personal environments.

This book is designed to address the interests and needs of a diverse audience, including professional researchers, individuals, managers, and governmental employees. Given the pervasive use of computers in nearly every aspect of education, business, and domestic life, understanding the implications of HCI is essential for everyone involved in these domains.

The chapters in this book cover a broad spectrum of topics related to HCI. We delve into how HCI principles are integrated into teaching methods and educational environments, exploring strategies for effectively teaching HCI concepts and assessing the role of HCI in enhancing learning experiences. We also examine the practical applications of HCI in educational settings and investigate usability factors that affect HCI.

Further, we explore the implications of HCI for improving teaching practices and its role in increasing business productivity. The influence of HCI on business analytics, manufacturing processes, and innovation is analyzed, shedding light on how these interactions can foster innovation and drive economic growth. Finally, we discuss the economic implications of HCI and its support for entrepreneurship.

Each chapter has been carefully curated to provide a thorough analysis and present the latest research findings in the field. By examining these topics, we hope to shed light on the critical role that HCI plays in shaping our world and driving future advancements.

Thank you for joining us on this exploration of Human-Computer Interaction and its significant social reflections. I trust that this book will serve as a valuable resource for enhancing your understanding of this vital field.

ORGANIZATION OF THE BOOK

Chapter 1: Integrating Machine Learning to Enhance Online Learning Student Performance Authors: Somdeep Das, Pinaki Acharjya

In this chapter, Das and Acharjya explore the burgeoning field of online learning and the critical role that Machine Learning (ML) can play in enhancing student performance. The authors propose a comprehensive study utilizing Learning Management Systems (LMS) to capture and analyze student data. By implementing various ML classifier algorithms, they develop models to identify and optimize the multiple factors influencing student success in online environments. The chapter underscores the potential of ML to transform online education by providing tailored insights and interventions aimed at improving student outcomes.

Chapter 2: Machine Learning (ML) Based Braille Lippi Characters and Numbers Detection and Announcement System for Blind Children in Learning Author: Kutubuddin Kazi

Kazi's chapter delves into the innovative application of ML for assisting blind children in learning. Focusing on the development of a Braille Lippi character recognition system, the author employs Neural Networks (NN) due to their efficacy and reliability. The system is designed to read and announce Braille characters with an impressive accuracy of 99.09%. This work highlights the system's methodology, design, and architecture, demonstrating the profound impact that ML can have on accessibility and education for visually impaired students.

Chapter 3: Utilizing Machine Learning to Increase Online Learning Instructors' Efficiency Authors: Somdeep Das, Pinaki Acharjya

Das and Acharjya return to examine how integrating ML with Online Learning Management Systems (OLMS) can enhance instructors' efficiency. They emphasize the importance of the feedback module in OLMS, which, when combined with ML, can analyze extensive data to uncover patterns and insights. This integration supports educational institutions in making data-driven decisions to improve teaching methods and overall instructor performance, ultimately benefiting learners. The chapter provides a detailed discussion on the potential of ML to revolutionize teaching practices in online learning environments.

Chapter 4: Entrepreneurship Powered by AI: New Age of Business and Education Authors: Pranav Adithya, Srishti Muralidharan

Adithya and Muralidharan explore the intersection of AI and entrepreneurship, discussing how AI can foster entrepreneurial creativity and innovation. They argue that AI should assist, rather than replace, human ingenuity in various business and educational contexts. The chapter also touches on the theory of creative destruction and emphasizes the importance of diverse pedagogies in entrepreneurial education. By examining the global expansion of entrepreneurship and AI's role in automating business processes, the authors provide a comprehensive overview of AI's transformative potential in entrepreneurship.

Chapter 5: The Impact of Attitudes toward Artificial Intelligence on Job Performance Author: Funda Hatice Sezgin

Sezgin investigates the relationship between employees' attitudes toward AI and their job performance. Focusing on a study involving 500 academicians in Istanbul, the chapter reveals a significant positive correlation between positive perceptions of AI and enhanced job performance. The findings highlight the importance of fostering positive attitudes towards AI in the workplace to maximize its benefits. This research underscores the need for strategic initiatives to improve AI-related perceptions among employees to boost productivity and job satisfaction.

Chapter 6: From Data to Decisions: Harnessing AI and Big Data for Advanced Business Analytics Authors: Ashy Sebastian, Veerta Tantia

Sebastian and Tantia discuss the transformative power of AI and big data in business analytics. The chapter highlights how AI-driven analytics can identify hidden patterns, detect anomalies, and automate decision-making processes, significantly enhancing data analysis efficiency and accuracy. Through a detailed case study involving stock market data, the authors demonstrate the effectiveness of ML-based prediction models. This work underscores the importance of integrating AI with big data analytics to drive business insights and strategic decisions.

Chapter 7: The Use and Effects of ChatGPT in Tourism Education Authors: Emre Yaşar, İsmail Öztürk, Eda Yayla, Erge Tür

This chapter evaluates the application of ChatGPT in tourism education, examining its role in preparing course content, curriculum, and exams. Yaşar, Öztürk, Yayla, and Tür identify both the positive and negative effects of ChatGPT on tourism students. While ChatGPT can enhance research skills, efficiency, and creativity, it also poses risks such as promoting dependency on technology and potential misinformation. The study highlights factors affecting the applicability of ChatGPT, including digital skills, ethical concerns, and the structural characteristics of tourism education.

Chapter 8: Designing a User-Centered Mobile Phone: The Quality Function Deployment Approach Author: Muhammet Bulak

Bulak's chapter presents a detailed study on designing a user-centered mobile phone using the Quality Function Deployment (QFD) approach. Through an online survey, customer requirements are identified and translated into technical specifications. The relationship between these requirements is analyzed using the House of Quality (HOQ) matrix. The study benchmarks Apple, Samsung, and Huawei phones to identify critical design features. The results indicate that processor and connectivity are the most crucial factors, providing valuable insights for user-centered mobile phone design.

Chapter 9: Use of Eye Tracking Method According to Individual Differences: A Review from the Perspective of Gender, Personality Structure and Birth Order Authors: Mustafa Alpsülün, Hasan Celal Balıkçı, Müzeyyen Bulut Özek

Alpsülün, Balıkçı, and Özek explore how individual differences such as gender, personality structure, and birth order affect learning environments using eye-tracking methods. The chapter describes a quasi-experimental study involving 19 students, analyzing their eye movements while interacting with learning materials. The findings reveal significant variations in learning based on individual differences, providing insights into how personalized learning environments can be designed. The authors offer suggestions for incorporating these differences to enhance educational outcomes.

Chapter 10: Navigating the Digital Economy: The Crucial Role of Human-Computer Interaction Authors: Vetrivel SC, Sowmiya KC, Sabareeshwari V, Arun VP

This chapter examines the impact of Human-Computer Interaction (HCI) on the digital economy. Vetrivel, Sowmiya, Sabareeshwari, and Arun analyze how HCI principles enhance productivity, influence employment dynamics, and drive economic growth. The chapter discusses both the positive and negative implications of HCI, emphasizing its role in fostering digital literacy, innovation, and entrepreneurship. By streamlining business processes and empowering individuals, HCI is shown to be a pivotal factor in navigating and thriving in the digital economy.

Chapter 11: The Effect of Information Technology Competency on Information Management in Business Author: Funda Hatice Sezgin

Sezgin explores the critical role of information technology (IT) competency in effective information management within businesses. The chapter highlights how IT enables efficient data processing, storage, and analysis, facilitating informed decision-making and strategic goal achievement. Additionally, IT fosters better internal communication and collaboration, enhancing overall business efficiency. The study provides a comprehensive analysis of IT's impact on information management, offering recommendations for businesses to leverage IT competencies to gain a competitive advantage.

Chapter 12: The Evolution of Currency: A Comparative Study of Barter System & Cryptocurrency Authors: Mohammad Zaidi, Raj Srivastava, Yashmita Awasthi

Zaidi, Srivastava, and Awasthi trace the evolution of currency from the barter system to modern cryptocurrency. The chapter explores the limitations of the barter system and the emergence of commodity and fiat currencies. It then delves into the rise of cryptocurrency, highlighting its reliance on blockchain technology for secure transactions. The authors compare these systems, examining how cryptocurrency addresses the shortcomings of traditional currencies and its potential to revolutionize our understanding of money. The chapter provides a historical perspective and a forward-looking analysis of currency evolution.

IN CONCLUSION

As we conclude this edited volume, *Social Reflections of Human-Computer Interaction in Education, Management, and Economics*, I hope the breadth and depth of the topics covered have provided you with valuable insights into the multifaceted nature of Human-Computer Interaction (HCI). Our exploration has spanned the critical areas of education, management, and economics, highlighting the pervasive influence of HCI on our daily lives and societal structures.

The contributions within this book underscore the essential role that HCI plays in enhancing educational experiences, optimizing business processes, and driving economic innovation. By examining how HCI principles are integrated into various domains, we gain a clearer understanding of the dynamic relationship between humans and technology. This understanding is crucial for developing strategies that leverage HCI to foster productivity, creativity, and overall well-being.

The interdisciplinary approach adopted in this volume reflects the complex and interconnected nature of HCI. The insights from diverse fields emphasize the importance of a holistic perspective when studying and implementing HCI solutions. Whether you are a researcher, educator, manager, or policymaker, the discussions presented here are intended to inform and inspire, providing a foundation for future research and practical applications.

In bringing this book to a close, I extend my deepest gratitude to the contributors whose expertise and dedication have made this compilation possible. Their work not only advances our knowledge of HCI but also paves the way for future innovations that will continue to shape the interactions between humans and technology.

Thank you for engaging with this volume. It is my hope that the insights gained will empower you to contribute to the ongoing dialogue and development in the field of Human-Computer Interaction, ultimately enhancing the integration of technology in ways that benefit society as a whole.

Chapter 1
Integrating Machine Learning to Enhance Online Learning Student Performance

Somdeep Das

Management Development Institute, Murshidabad, India

Pinaki Pratim Acharjya

iD https://orcid.org/0000-0002-0305-2661

Haldia Institute of Technology, India

ABSTRACT

The extensive growth of online learning in recent years has opened the avenues of learning without any physical boundaries. The ultimate aim of online learning is to increase the perimeter of students learning and to achieve this students performance should also be monitored and improved. Online learning integrated LMSs enables capturing and tracking data related to students and courses. The performance of students may highly be impacted by various parameters in online learning environment. This work proposes the study and analysis of student performance which may be enhanced by implementing Machine Learning technologies on the student information mined in the LMSs. It focuses on developing models based on machine learning (ML) to comprehend the multiple factors that influence student success in an online learning environment. Various machine learning classifier algorithms were utilized to train the model.

DOI: 10.4018/979-8-3693-3033-3.ch001

INTRODUCTION

Over the last few span of years, online learning has appreciably grown to offer users with the ability to study and develop new skill sets. Online learning pedagogy is based on technologies and with the blend of education, internet, and communication technology played a potential role to transform higher education in the recent times. Learning Management System (LMS) being the part of this technology connects teachers and students by providing an opportunity to not only sharing classroom materials or activities but also enabling teachers and students to communicate outside the classroom, holding conversations across forums easily resulting in saving time as opposed to the classroom studying. LMS manage learners, keeps track of their progress through the system and monitors their attendance. The LMS is responsible for allocating and maintaining learning services such as enrollment, classroom teaching, and other online learning delivery services (Adzharuddin, Nor. 2013; Villegas, W., et al, 2019; Al-Shabandar, R., et al, 2018). LMS platforms produce a huge volume of data regarding a student's emotional, behavioural, and social characteristics.

Educational Data Mining (EDM) is an effective computational tool for collecting meaningful and valuable information from educational data (Dutt, A., et al, 2017; Al-Shabandar, R., et al, 2020; Junejo, K. N., Eet al, 2016). Huge amount of user data, allows using machine learning algorithms to improve students' learning habits. Artificial Intelligence (AI) and Machine Learning (ML) helps in processing these data and providing real-time, actionable data intelligence to enhance students' capabilities (Ghorbani, R., et al, 2020; Altabrawee, H., et al, 2019; Kumari, P., et al, 2018).

For the purpose of improving course design and lesson plan offered to the students, it is important to predict and understand the future behaviour of students so that appropriate support and guidance on the course can be provided to the enrolled students. Data Mining (DM) is useful in this situation. DM methods examine datasets and collect information in order to convert it into usable constructs for future use (Silva, C., et al, 2017; Hussain, M., et al, 2018). However, it was observed that some difficulties like imbalanced educational data may hinder in predicting students' performance (Ghorbani, R., et al, 2020). Fig1 shows simple block diagram of our approach of Model creation process.

Figure 1. Simple model process block diagram

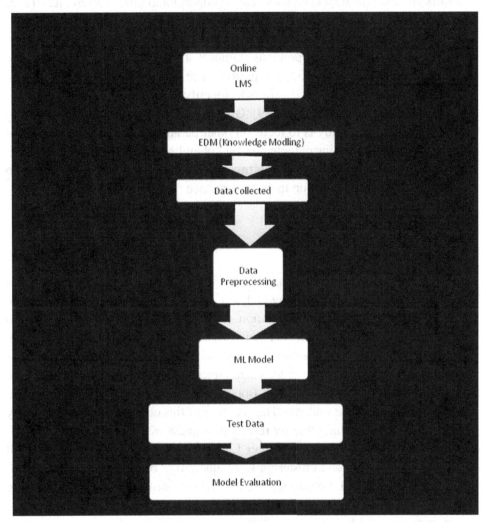

To personalize the information, Machine learning algorithms use pattern recognition for each student.

If a student struggles with a topic during the course, then the platform will change the learning material and include more comprehensive knowledge to assist the student as a result of personalization. According to studies student involvement through online learning has been potentially benefitted by improved impetus and accomplishment as it is self-motivated. However, there are certain factors that impacts academic performance and which are very essential to identify (Lee, J., et al, 02019;

Villegas-Ch, W., et al, 2017). Personality characteristics, class participation, and social network structure have all been shown to be important in previous research. There is currently no method to count the association of these factors and most of these studies were focused on a particular behavioral feature and/or limited sample sizes.

It has been observed from previous studies that a variety of behavioral patterns have been associated with academic performance. These identified traits may be applied to machine learning classifiers to identify student problems and improve their performance (Lee, J., et al, 2019). Other than focusing on only grades of students, the aim of our study is to focus on other parameters that may have a major impact on students' learning outcomes (Abu Zohair LM., 2019), such as attendance, delivery of course by teachers, study time spent, and many others parameters to better understand the impact on their performance.

RELATED WORKS

To improve the student performance, the researchers have conducted many works by implementing machine learning and data mining techniques. Various machine learning techniques such as classification, regression, and clustering where used to analyze and predict future grades or results of students to improve their performance. Researchers in their study identified the internal score, the external score, and the total score as the three features for each subject and then Support Vector, Nave Bayes, Random Forest, and Gradient Booster algorithms were applied to generate an output for each of the students. The accuracy of this output is then calculated by comparing it to the actual semester results (Pushpa, S. K., et al, 2017).

In a study, researchers (Abu Zohair LM., 2019) recommended that for small datasets, visualization and clustering techniques were observed to be much simpler, less complex, and more time efficient He also identified that for forecasting students' success in dissertation projects, grades in courses 1 and 2 are deemed the most important and hence, students' grades in most courses were related to their grades in dissertations.

Authors presented a survey by comparing five models used for the predictive analysis of students' final result in a course namely, "Generalized linear model", "Multilayer Perceptron", "Gradient Boost Model", "Random Forest Model", and "Deep Neural Network" were compared for this survey. Among the all five methods, the Gradient Boost Model has proved to be the most accurate predictor among the four when measured in percent relative performance (Kumar V., et al, 2019).

Other than the grade and results, H et al. identified three student traits that have important associations with academic performance viz. discipline, orderliness, and sleep habits. The researchers determined the prediction outcome by grouping different academic performance-related functions. They built an MTLTR-APP and proposed it. The MTLTR-APP algorithm outperformed other algorithms such as Ridge Regression, Decision Tree, Random Forest, RankSVM, MLP, and XGB in forecasting academic success (Yao, H., et al, 2019).

Rastrollo-Guerrero et al. emphasized on the role of data mining and the application of ML methods for the prediction of student performance. In their survey, the authors also observed that the supervised learning is the most commonly used method for forecasting students' behavior because it produces precise and consistent outcomes. The SVM algorithm, in particular, was the most often used by the authors and made the most reliable predictions (Rastrollo-Guerrero, J. L., et al, 2020).

K et al. suggested that using probabilistic graphical models, increases the accuracy of prediction accuracy considerably. They highlighted that variables like strategies and choices have an effect on the learning outcome. A unique method was adopted to capture the data through an interactive computer-game. In addition, the researchers integrated student information and examination methods into a single model. Besides this, they concluded that, as compared to pure performance models, improved models outperform pure performance models in terms of understanding (Käser, T., et al, 2017).

Buenaño-Fernández et al. conducted a series of experiments with EDM and machine learning applications to find the best correlation between the input variable and the result. The main was to utilize the historical performance of grades of enrolled students in a particular course in an University and Predict the final grades (FGs) (Buenaño-Fernández, D., 2019).

Kassarnig *et al.* suggested the importance of class attendance and social interactions in improving academic performance as opposed to concentrating on only grades as presented in most of the studies. The authors used machine learning techniques, primarily supervised learning models, to assess the importance of various parameters on students' academic success. The model assessed students' performance in terms of classifying them into three categories as low, moderate, or high performers, and discovered that class attendance had the greatest effect on academic performance (Kassarnig, V., et al, 2018).

M et al. compared the results of many ML algorithms used to forecast student engagement during a Virtual Learning Environment (VLE) course and discovered that using an SVM or ANN to predict an individual student's performance is optimal for increasing student engagement. They discovered that the studied model would detect weak students ahead of time, allowing teachers to rethink to augment and customize the course designed (Hussain, M., Zet al, 2018).

F et al. suggested that by offering clear guidance for designing an effective predictive model to detect vulnerable students, both teachers and students will be told ahead of time in order to enhance student performance. On the other hand it was also discovered that pedagogical choices taken by instructors, such as pedagogical style, evaluation process, and grading system guidance, appear to restrict this paradigm to these circumstantial variables and improve student results. However, the efficiency of the Naive Bayes Classifier model was described as the best among the different methods used for the research (Marbouti, F., et al, 2016).

PROPOSED METHODOLOGY

In this article, we present a model of student performance that is based on the parameters which may impact their performances. These parameters can be categorized into student's grades, final grades, demographics, Internet infrastructure, school and family support, academic progress, and educational background. The dataset (Marbouti, F., et al, 2016) has been taken from the public domain and Python 3.7.6 is used for data preprocessing and review.

Data Preprocessing

The raw data available in the dataset may not always be directly used as inputs for Machine Learning model as it may contain noises, missing values, and possibly in an unusable format (Kassarnig, V., et al, 2018). The process to make raw data suitable for a machine learning model is known as data preprocessing. It is the first and most important step in the Machine Learning model development process.

Data Visualization and Feature Selection

Data visualization is a technique that uses different graphs and plots to visualize complex data to ease the discovery of data patterns and helps in machine learning modeling. This is especially useful during the EDA (Exploratory Data Analysis) phase when data patters are to be identified.

Figure 2. Exploration of data by comparing grade with relevant features

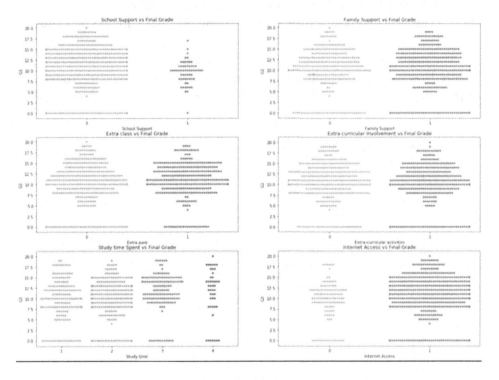

Figure 3. Exploration of social and academic background of student

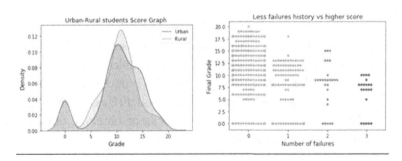

The following has been observed from the visualization in Figure 2.

- Students who do not receive help from their schools have a negative pattern.

- Students who paid for additional courses are experiencing a downward trend.
- Students who have access to the internet perform higher.
- Extracurricular involvement does not show any drastic impact on scores.

The graphs in Figure 3 show that the scores based on location do not vary significantly. However, urban enrollments outnumber rural enrollments. It also indicates that Students who have had less prior failures appear to do well in their grades.

Figure 4. Heatmap plot for correlation

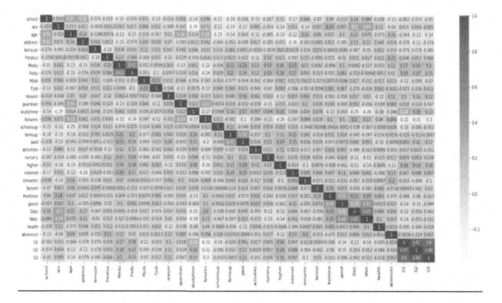

Feature selection is a technique for selecting a subset of attributes from a larger attribute that can adequately represent the input variables. While creating a predictive model reducing the number of input variables reduces the computational cost resulting in enhancing the performance of the model (Hussain, M., Zet al, 2018). In the correlation Heatmap matrix figure 4, it can be observed that columns with the best features are chosen for analysis.

Table 1. Correlation of features

	G1	G2	G3
G1	1.000000	0.865111	0.800971

continued on following page

Table 1. Continued

	G1	G2	G3
G2	0.865111	1.000000	0.884155
G3	0.800971	0.884155	1.000000

Figure 5. Correlation analysis graph

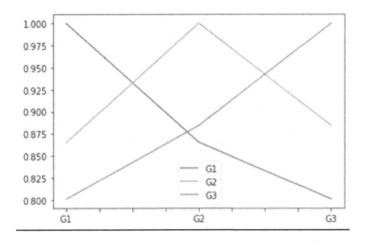

From Table 1 it is clearly visible that G1 and G2 are highly correlated with G3. Figure 5, also visualizes the same correlation through correlation analysis graph.

Machine Learning Model

Machine learning is a subset of AI associated with the creation of algorithms that learn automatically from data and increase their performance over time without being externally programmed to do so. It is focused on analyzing data, which further identifies emerging patterns and takes appropriate action. Figure 6 depicts the various forms of machine learning techniques which are categorized into three types namely, Supervised Machine Learning (SML), Unsupervised Machine Learning (UML), and Reinforcement Machine Learning (RML). These techniques are based on the fundamental concepts of classification (classifying objects), regression (identifying relationships between variables), and clustering (grouping items by similar characteristics).

Figure 6. Machine learning approaches

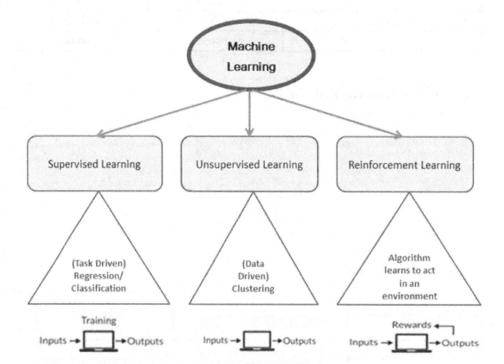

We use many commonly used machine learning algorithms to predict each student's performance in online learning, including Random Forest, Gradient Boosted, Liner Regression, Support Vector Machine, and Baseline. We will recommend the best model for this analysis based on the results of the classifier algorithms.

EVALUATION AND RESULT

We have used two of the most common matrices used in machine learning, first the Root Mean Squared Error (RMSE) and the other one is Mean Absolute Error (MAE).

MAE is a measurement that calculates the average degree of errors in a sequence of predictions without taking into account the position of the errors. It generates a linear value that evenly distributes the weighted individual differences. The model's efficiency improves as the value decreases. The following represents the MAE.

$$MAE = 1/n \sum_{j=1}^{n} |y_j - y_j| \tag{1}$$

The RMSE (Villegas-Ch, W., egt al, 2020) is the most widely used metric for regression. The square root of the average squared difference between the real score and the expected score is used to calculate this. Similar to MAE, the model's performance increases as the value decreases. It represents the following form:

$$RMSE = \sqrt{1/n} \sum_{i=1}^{n} (y_i - y_i^\wedge)^2 \qquad (2)$$

Five benchmark models, Random Forest (RA), Gradient Boosted (GB), support vector machine (SVM), Linear Regression (LR) and Baseline were used for comparative experiments. The choice between these models depends on the data and the purpose. On Evaluation of several Machine Learning models by training on training set and testing on testing set, the result shows in figure 7 that Random Forest is performing the best in both cases with MAE=0.465575 and RMSE=0.798221.

Figure 7. Model evaluation with MAE and RMSE

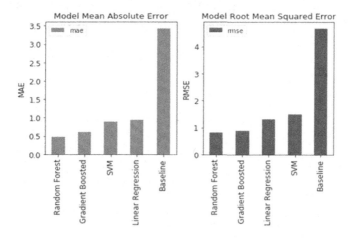

CONCLUSION

Never again will education be the same. In learning and research, online, virtual, or hybrid educational models have taken center stage. Using all available technologies to improve learning is a top goal. It is feasible to enhance learning and lessen issues like high dropout rates and low academic performance rates—which are indicated by the ratio of graduates to admissions—by implementing innovative student-centered educational models. The technology that our research enables can be the perfect helper for educators as well as students. Students' calendars can be managed by them, and events, reminders, and notifications can be generated to let them know what needs to be done. Based on the data collected, the system can also provide ongoing support so that students can perform better. Though it bases this on a detailed examination of all the data the system possesses, the system gives the teacher the ability to ascertain each student's learning condition. The research presented here focused on analyzing factors that affect students using online learning integrated with learning management systems (LMS) as a way to contribute to the online education modality. The primary aim is of the study is designing a machine learning model which could understand the parameters of performance students that may impact on their performance under online environment other than only grade scores of student. The model was trained and validated using various machine learning algorithms with Random Forest appearing as the best performing model. We hope to expand on this work in the near future by using deep learning techniques using larger dataset available. In future research, there is a need to address the imbalance in the data sample and to explore the impact of student–teacher interaction and student-to-student interaction data on student academic performance.

REFERENCES

Abu Zohair, L. M. (2019, December). Prediction of Student's performance by modelling small dataset size. *International Journal of Educational Technology in Higher Education*, 16(1), 27. 10.1186/s41239-019-0160-3

Adzharuddin, N. (2013). Learning Management System (LMS) among University Students: Does It Work? International Journal of e-Education, e-Business, e-. *Management Learning*. Advance online publication. 10.7763/IJEEEE.2013.V3.233

Al-Shabandar, R., Hussain, A., Keight, R., & Khan, W. (2020). Students Performance Prediction in Online Courses Using Machine Learning Algorithms. *2020 International Joint Conference on Neural Networks (IJCNN)*. IEEE.10.1109/IJCNN48605.2020.9207196

Al-Shabandar, R., Hussain, A., Keight, R., Laws, A., & Baker, T. (2018). The Application of Gaussian Mixture Models for the Identification of At-Risk Learners in Massive Open Online Courses. *2018 IEEE Congress on Evolutionary Computation (CEC)*. IEEE. 10.1109/CEC.2018.8477770

Altabrawee, H., Ali, O., Qaisar, S. (2019). Predicting Students' Performance Using Machine Learning Techniques. *JOURNAL OF UNIVERSITY OF BABYLON, 27*. 194-205. .10.29196/jubpas.v27i1.2108

Buenaño-Fernández, D., Gil, D., & Luján-Mora, S. (2019). Application of Machine Learning in Predicting Performance for Computer Engineering Students: A Case Study. *Sustainability (Basel)*, 11(10), 2833. 10.3390/su11102833

Dutt, A., Ismail, M. A., & Herawan, T. (2017). A Systematic Review on Educational Data Mining. *IEEE Access: Practical Innovations, Open Solutions*, 5, 15991–16005. 10.1109/ACCESS.2017.2654247

Ghorbani, R., & Ghousi, R. (2020). Comparing Different Resampling Methods in Predicting Students' Performance Using Machine Learning Techniques. *IEEE Access, 8*, 67899-67911. 10.1109/ACCESS.2020.2986809

Hussain, M., Zhu, W., Zhang, W., & Abidi, S. M. R. (2018). Student Engagement Predictions in an e-Learning System and Their Impact on Student Course Assessment Scores. *Computational Intelligence and Neuroscience*, 2018, 1–21. 10.1155/2018/634718630369946

Hussain, M., Zhu, W., Zhang, W., Abidi, S. M. R., & Ali, S. (2018). *Using machine learning to predict student difficulties from learning session data*. Artificial Intelligence Review. 10.1007/s10462-018-9620-8

Junejo, K. N., & Eman, E. (2016). *Grade Prediction Using Supervised Machine Learning Techniques, 4th Global Summit on Education 2016 At: Malaysia.* http://worldconferences.net/home

Käser, T., Hallinen, N. R., & Schwartz, D. L. (2017). Modeling exploration strategies to predict student performance within a learning environment and beyond. In: *17th International conference on learning analytics and knowledge 2017,* (pp 31–40). ACM. "10.1145/3027385.3027422

Kassarnig, V., Mones, E., Bjerre-Nielsen, A., Sapiezynski, P., Dreyer Lassen, D., & Lehmann, S. (2018, December). Academic performance and behavioral patterns. *EPJ Data Science,* 7(1), 10. 10.1140/epjds/s13688-018-0138-8

Kumar, V., & Garg, M. L. (2019). Comparison of Machine Learning Models in Student Result Prediction. In: Kamal R., Henshaw M., Nair P. (eds) *International Conference on Advanced Computing Networking and Informatics.* Springer, Singapore. 10.1007/978-981-13-2673-8_46

Kumari, P., Jain, P. K., & Pamula, R. (2018). *An efficient use of ensemble methods to predict students academic performance.* 2018 4th International Conference on Recent Advances in Information Technology (RAIT), Dhanbad, India. 10.1109/RAIT.2018.8389056

Lee, J., Song, H., & Hong, A. (2019). Exploring Factors, and Indicators for Measuring Students' Sustainable Engagement in e-Learning. *Sustainability (Basel),* 11(4), 985. 10.3390/su11040985

Marbouti, F., Diefes-Dux, H., & Madhavan, K. (2016). Models for early prediction of at-risk students in a course using standards-based grading. *Computers & Education,* 103, 1–15. 10.1016/j.compedu.2016.09.005

Pushpa, S. K., Manjunath, T. N., Mrunal, T. V., Singh, A., & Suhas, C. (2017). Class result prediction using machine learning. *2017 International Conference On Smart Technologies For Smart Nation (SmartTechCon),* Bengaluru, India. 10.1109/SmartTechCon.2017.8358559

Rastrollo-Guerrero, J. L., Gómez-Pulido, J. A., & Durán-Domínguez, A. (2020). Analyzing and Predicting Students' Performance by Means of Machine Learning: A Review. *Applied Sciences (Basel, Switzerland),* 10(3), 1042. 10.3390/app10031042

Silva, C., Fonseca, J. (2017). *Educational Data Mining: A Literature Review.* Springer. 10.1007/978-3-319-46568-5_9

Villegas, W., Molina-Enriquez, J., Chicaiza-Tamayo, C., Ortiz-Garcés, I., & Luján-Mora, S. (2019). Application of a Big Data Framework for Data Monitoring on a Smart Campus. *Sustainability (Basel)*, 11(20), 5552. 10.3390/su11205552

Villegas-Ch, W., & Luján-Mora, S. (2017). *Systematic Review of Evidence on Data Mining Applied to LMS Platforms for Improving E-Learning.* In Proceedings of the International Technology, Education and Development Conference, Valencia, Spain. 10.21125/inted.2017.1510

Villegas-Ch, W., Román-Cañizares, M., & Palacios-Pacheco, X. (2020). Improvement of an Online Education Model with the Integration of Machine Learning and Data Analysis in an LMS. *Applied Sciences (Basel, Switzerland)*, 10(15), 5371. 10.3390/app10155371

Yao, H., Lian, D., Cao, Y., Wu, Y., Zhou, T. (2019). Predicting Academic Performance for College Students: A Campus Behavior Perspective. *ACM Trans. Intell. Syst. Technol., 1.* DOI:10.1145/3299087

Chapter 2
Machine Learning (ML)–Based Braille Lippi Characters and Numbers Detection and Announcement System for Blind Children in Learning

Kutubuddin Sayyad Liyakat Kazi
https://orcid.org/0000-0001-5623-9211
Brahmdevdada Mane Institute of Technology, Solapur, India

ABSTRACT

Character and number recognition in Braille Lippi is the process by which a computer can recognise language. To read students' and lecturers' Braille Lippi notes, a character recognition system that can read Braille Lippi is being developed. A Braille Lippi character recognition system is developed through a variety of strategies and procedures and concentrates on neural networks (NN). When compared to other computational methods, neural networks are more effective and reliable for recognising Braille Lippi characters. Along with testing and system development findings, the report also describes the Braille Lippi character recognition system's methodology, design, and architecture with an accuracy of 99.09%. The goal is to demonstrate how effective neural networks are to recognise Braille Lippi characters.

DOI: 10.4018/979-8-3693-3033-3.ch002

INTRODUCTION

L. Braille created the Braille Lippi writing or printing method for blind people, which uses combinations of palpable dots or points to form letters, characters, etc. that can be read by touch. People who are blind or partially sighted can read for the rest of their lives if they learn Braille. Learning Braille early on is especially beneficial for literacy because Braille is a considerably more effective medium for comprehending punctuation, grammar, and spelling than audio. Books and publications aren't the only things that are written and typed in Braille. Additionally, it is used to mark commonplace objects like prescriptions as well as door signs, elevator keypads, and restaurant menus in public areas. It is used to make a variety of papers, including bank statements, more easily accessible. For example, three different Braille cells are used to write the word "can" in Alphabetic Braille—one cell for every one of the three letters within the word. If your primary hobbies are making grocery lists, playing board and card games, writing down phone numbers, reading lift buttons and memorizing room numbers, The Frenchman Louis Braille created it in 1824. Each letter uses a different pattern to make up the six dots that make up a Braille "cell," which resembles a domino. Around 250 letters (phonograms), numbers, punctuation, formatting symbols, contractions, and abbreviations make up this language (logograms). Some English Braille characters, like "ch," correlate to several print letters. The Braille cell, also known as the basic Braille character, is composed of six dots arranged in a rectangle shape, three dots high and two dots wide. These six dots can form other symbols in some cases. Known as uncontracted and contracted Braille, Grades 1 and 2 are the two most popular types of Braille. The most fundamental type of Braille is Grade 1, often known as uncontracted Braille or alphabetic Braille.

Due to its usefulness in several daily tasks, Braille character & digits recognitions have gained importance in today's digital environment. The fact that numerous recognition systems are being developed or proposed for use in a variety of sectors at which high categorizing efficiency is necessary in recent years serves as evidence of this. People have the ability to finish more complicated tasks that might otherwise require an extended period of time and become expensive due to the aid of systems that identify Braille Lippi letters, characters, and numerals. The biological Braille networks that enable people to learn and model non-linear and complicated relationships can serve as inspiration for the Braille Lippi recognition systems. Therefore, it is created by using the Artificial Neural Network (ANN) by Liyakat (2023), Liyakat(2024). People can distinguish between various Braille Lippi items, such as numbers, letters, and characters, thanks to their Braille's. Humans can choose to interpret Braille Lippi letters and numerals in a variety of ways because they are biased. On the other hand, impartial computer systems can complete extremely difficult jobs that could demand a lot of time and effort from people to complete them in the same way.

The human visual system is mostly used when reading Braille Lippi characters, letters, words, or numerals. It never seems difficult to read handwriting, but it's not as easy as people believe. Even though everything is done unconsciously, people can still interpret what they see by using the information that their Braille has been taught. Only when trying to build a computer system that can read Braille Lippi does the difficulty of visual pattern recognition become obvious. The best strategy for creating systems that can recognize Braille characters is thought to be the use of ANNs. When reading Braille Lippi in condensed manner, NNs assist in simulation, how human Braille functions. It enables technology to read as well as, if not better than, humans. The ability of a neural network to extract meanings from complex data and find trends from data that are difficult to spot by either other manual techniques or humans makes it the most suitable type of algorithm for the suggested system by Mulani (2019). The major goal of the study is to create a model using the Convolution Neural Network (CNN) concept that will be used to read Braille Lippi numerals, letters, and sentences from an image and proclaim them.

Machine Learning (ML) has revolutionized the way we interact with technology, from voice assistants to self-driving cars. But one area where ML is making a significant impact is in improving the accessibility of information for visually impaired individuals by Kazi K(2024). A recent development in this field is the use of ML-based Braille Lippi characters and numbers detection, which is making it easier for visually impaired individuals to read and access Braille text.

Braille is a system of raised dots that are used by individuals with visual impairments to read and write. It was invented in the early 19th century by Louis Braille, a French educator who himself was visually impaired. The Braille system has been a game-changer for the visually impaired community, providing them with a means of reading and writing independently. However, it can be challenging to learn and master, and this is where ML-based Braille Lippi characters and numbers detection comes in.

Traditionally, visually impaired individuals have to rely on physical Braille books or specialized Braille displays to access written information. These methods can be expensive and limited in terms of the amount of information they can provide. With the advancement of technology, there have been attempts to convert text into Braille using software, but the accuracy of these methods has been a challenge. This is where ML-based Braille Lippi characters and numbers detection comes in, offering a more accurate and efficient solution.

So, what exactly is ML-based Braille Lippi characters and numbers detection? It is a technology that uses machine learning algorithms to detect and convert printed or digital text into Braille characters and numbers. The process involves capturing an image of the text, which is then processed by an ML algorithm trained on thousands of different Braille characters and numbers. The algorithm then identifies the characters and converts them into the corresponding Braille characters and numbers.

One of the key advantages of ML-based Braille Lippi characters and numbers detection is its accuracy. With the use of ML algorithms, technology can detect even the tiniest variations in Braille characters, ensuring that the converted text is as accurate as possible. This is a significant improvement from traditional methods, where errors in character recognition were common.

Another benefit of using ML-based Braille Lippi characters and numbers detection is its speed and efficiency. With traditional methods, visually impaired individuals had to wait for a human transcriber to convert the text into Braille, which could take a significant amount of time. With ML-based technology, the process is much faster, allowing for near real-time conversion of text into Braille. This not only saves time but also increases the accessibility of information for visually impaired individuals.

Moreover, ML-based Braille Lippi characters and numbers detection can be integrated into various devices, making it more convenient for visually impaired individuals to access written information. It can be used in smartphones, tablets, and other digital devices, allowing for on-the-go conversion of text into Braille. This makes it easier for visually impaired individuals to access information from a variety of sources, including emails, books, and online articles.

In addition to improving the accessibility of written information, ML-based Braille Lippi characters and numbers detection also has the potential to increase employment opportunities for visually impaired individuals. With the ability to convert text into Braille accurately and efficiently, visually impaired individuals can take on jobs that require reading and transcribing written information. This can have a significant impact on their economic empowerment and independence.

In all, ML-based Braille Lippi characters and numbers detection is a groundbreaking technology that is changing the game for visually impaired individuals. Its accuracy, speed, and convenience make it a valuable tool for improving the accessibility of written information. As ML technology continues to advance, we can expect further developments in this field, making the world a more inclusive and accessible place for visually impaired individuals.

The following sections include an overview of pertinent work, the theoretical underpinnings, the architecture, the methodology, the experimental results, and the conclusion.

Objectives

The major goal of the study is to extend a ML -based expert system for Braille Lippi character identification. Other goals include: -

- Improving Braille Lippi character identification systems' accuracy by creating a system that makes use of cutting-edge technology to extract Braille Lippi words and characters from visual data.
- To examine and show how neural network technology can be used to create effective Braille Lippi character recognition systems.

Questionnaires

- What different approaches and procedures are used in Braille Lippi character recognition?
- How might artificial neural networks be used to boost Braille Lippi recognition systems' performance?

Target Group

The readers of this paper will be college students and professors who wish to convert their Braille Lippi papers & notes into audio format. Despite the rising use of technology in higher education institutions, Braille Lippi continues to be a part of both students' and teachers' everyday life. While reading from various sources and listening to lectures, students take notes using the Braille Lippi system. Some people write their ideas, plans, and thoughts down in their notes as well. The same is true for professors, who may desire to share Braille Lippi notes with their students. Therefore, goal of study is to build a system which will enable instructors and students to convert their Braille Lippi works into electronic work for preserving and sharing. The fundamental premise of this essay is that instructors and students both require electronic copies of the work they produce and store on their personal computers. Additionally, digital technology cannot completely replace Braille Lippi with pen and paper.

RELATED WORK AND THEORETICAL BACKGROUND

One of research areas in Computer Vision, AI, & pattern recognition is Braille Lippi character recognition. It is possible to assert the fact that a computer's program capable of Braille Lippi recognition can collect and recognize characters from written texts and images. The idea employs clever word recognition as well as optical scanning to retrieve Braille Lippi materials from an entire piece of paper. There are two types of Braille Lippi recognition: Offline recognition and Online recognition. To do offline Braille Lippi recognition, text or characters had to be extracted from an image and converted into computer-usable letter codes. A system receives a Braille Lippi document, reads it, and outputs it in both digital file and audio format. On the other hand, online Braille Lippi identification includes automatically recognizing or converting characters as they are written on specific screens and books. To make sure that computers can read characters from Braille Lippi images and papers, many procedures and strategies are employed. NN, HMM, ML, and SVM are a few of the methods now in use to model and train Braille Lippi character recognition. The HMM, ML, SVM, and AI Networks are the main topics of this article by Machha Babita et al (2022)

Artificial Intelligence

One could argue that the idea of computer systems interpreting Braille Lippi symbols, numerals, and words is an imitation of human beings. It might be argued that such a system reads Braille Lippi from photographs or any other Braille Lippi source using artificial intelligence. Artificial intelligence is the state in which machines display intelligence. A gadget or computer that can mimic "cognitive" processes associated with the human mind is referred to by this term. Artificial intelligence enables a computer to perform tasks that a human can perform, learn from mistakes, and adjust to new inputs. According to Maccha Babita et al. (2022) & Devi (2022) there are three subfields of artificial intelligence: machine learning (ML), neural networks (NN), and deep learning (DL).

Machine Learning

The focus on learning from datasets in psychology and biology serves as an inspiration for machine learning technologies. The fundamental premise is that through studying data, machines may learn how to carry out specific activities. The answer to each occurrence of the problem and training data relevant to the chosen problem domain are delivered to a machine learning model. In this manner, the model gains knowledge about how to resolve particular issues. The model uses learning data to identify the precise digit in an image with a Braille Lippi digit by D. Sreenivasulu et al (2022).

Artificial Neural Network (ANN)

The biological NNs that make up the human brain served as the model for the information processing paradigm known as ANN. Systems are built to process information similarly to the way that animal and human brains do, even though they are not exactly the same as biological neural systems. The networks are composed of many interconnected neurons that cooperate to accomplish particular objectives. ANNs acquire knowledge from examples in a similar manner to humans. Consequently, one can train artificial neural network (ANN)[42] to accomplish a particular task, like character recognition as well as data classification. It is necessary to configure the system to a connection as part of the learning process. An ANN is a network of many simple processors, each with a small amount of local memory. Through unidirectional communication channels, the processors (units) are connected, and have limited access to the processors' local data and input by K K (2022).

Biological Neuron and ANN

As was already said, the biological Brains system serves as the model for artificial neural networks by Karale (2023) & Vahida (2023). Thus, understanding the functioning of organic neurons can aid in understanding artificial neural networks. The three stages of the human body's neurological system are the neural network, receptors, and effectors. The receptor first processes stimuli from internal or external environment before sending data to the Neurons is the first stage. The second stage involves the neural network processing data in order to produce the desired output. Converting electrical impulses into reactions to the environment outside is the third and final stage. One could argue that an ANN is a streamlined version of the Brain. Neurons, which are the structural elements of human Brains, carry out computations including pattern recognition, cognition, and logical inference by Sultanabanu (2023).

The neuron models are depicted in Figure 1; however, they don't perform any tasks that ordinary computers can't. It is just a straightforward illustration of an NN system that can do similar tasks to those of a standard computer. McCulloch and Pitts Model, is more complex than the preceding model since its inputs is "weighted," is shown in Figure 2. That implies that each input has a unique impact on how decisions are made. The quantity that, when multiplied by the input, produces a weighted input is referred to as the weight of an input. The results are then summed, and the neuron fires if the sum exceeds a predetermined threshold value; otherwise, it does not.

Figure 1. Artificial neuron model

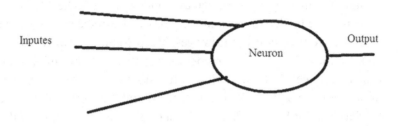

Figure 2. Complicated neuron model

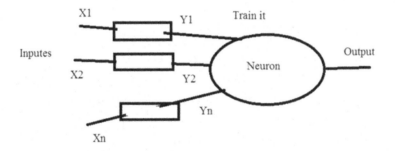

Mathematically, a neuron will only fire if the conditions are met:

$X1.Y1 + X2.Y2 + \ldots > $ Threshold --1

The neuron can modify its weights and/or threshold to adapt to various circumstances. Numerous algorithms can be used to "adapt" neurons, with the most popular methods being Delta Rule and Back-Error Propagation by Abdulllah, M. et al (2018).

Deep NN (Neural Network)

NN is composed of multiple layers of components, every one of which uses a little bit of the value from the layer before it. NN-based structures can calculate inputs within this manner in order to generate the intended output. Similar to how neurons transmit signals throughout the brain, values are transmitted compared to one component in an ANN to a different one to perform the required calculation and generate an additional value to be an output. Layers combine to form a system that begins with imputing layers and progresses to output-producing layers. The layers that exist among input and output layers are referred to as the hidden layer by Kazi K(2024). The Deep Neural Network (Deep NN) utilized for computing the values input in input layer are known as "hidden layers." The "deep" layers of NN are those that are hidden, as seen in Figure 3. To learn the characters that need to be recognized from Braille Lippi images, Deep Neural Networks (DNNs) are employed in Braille Lippi character recognition systems. When sufficient training data is available, a deep NN can perform all tasks intended for neural networks. According to Sara Aqab et al (2020), a Deep Neural Network (NN) can only be considered feasible if it has an adequate number of hidden layers, even if a larger NN is computationally more efficient.

Figure 3. Deep neural network

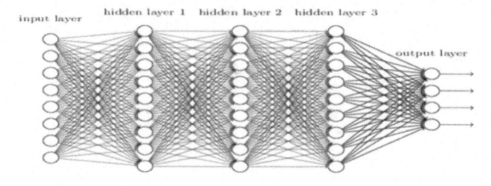

Hidden Markov Models (HMM)

The primary modelling component in a lot of handwriting recognition systems is a Hidden Markov Model (HMM)[48]. It is crucial to examine the theoretical underpinnings of Braille Lippi recognition algorithms in order to completely understand how they function. The statistical Markov model, or HMM, is used in a system that is intended to assume the Markov process. One could argue that it is the most basic dynamic Bayesian network. Given a set of observed variables, a class of probabilistic graphical models called HMM are employed to forecast a sequence of hidden variables. HMMs help systems predict the unknown from the observed, which is why they have been used successfully in speech recognition and character identification applications. According to Dwivedi et al. (2017), HMM is the most widely used model in character recognition.

PROPOSED SYSTEM -

Figure 4. Proposed system

Here we discuss design (Figure 4) and architecture of suggested neural network-based Braillel Lippi character recognition system (figure 4-basic diagram). As depicted in Figure 5, the proposed system consists of preprocessing, NN, and Processed output portions.

Figure 5. Proposed Braille Lippi recognition system (BRS)

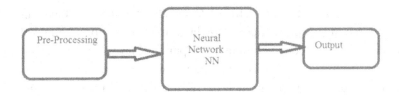

Neural Network Architecture

Figure 6. Neural network architecture

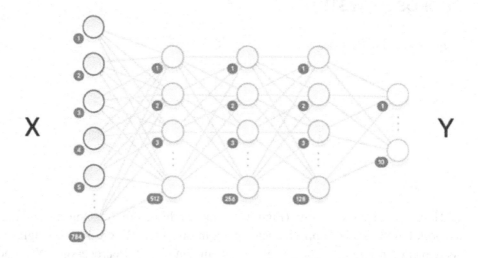

As previously said, neural network architectures are the most effective foundation for BRS systems. Consequently, it is important to comprehend NN architecture. The components that join to form network utilized for Braille Lippi recognition are referred to as NN architecture. A network is made up of layers, which range from the ones in charge of accepting input to the layer in charge of producing values. There is a hidden layer between the output and input level layers that does the majority of processing. From the input photos of handwriting, multiple neural network designs can be used to produce various outcomes. Figure 6 depicts the architecture utilized to distinguish Braille Lippi from pictures. While "Y" denotes the output, "X" displays the input. The task that the system is intended to perform determines the depth of Deep NN layer. However, in the majority of situations, smaller hidden layers that are more computationally efficient can be built to complete the same mission as one that can be completed with an infinitely huge Deep NN. To be able to recognize Braille, Deep NN is supposed to memorize the training data. As a result, optical character recognition systems frequently use deep neural networks.

Convolutional (CNN) Neural Network

The system will make use of CNN, a subclass of Deep NNs employed for character recognition coming from images. Figure 7 shows the CNN architecture which is going to be utilized in the system. Through input layer being the top layer as well as output layer being the bottom layer, the architecture exhibits a variety of layer types. The second layer is called the convolutional layer, and it is followed by pooling layers and convolutional layers. The architecture of CNN is defined as follows:

i) *Input layer:* The input layer is used to feed images containing Braille Lippis into the system. The layer could have RGB values for a color image or be monochrome. The input image's dimensions might be W*H*D, depending on it. The image's dimension, height, as well as depth are represented by the letters W, H, and D, respectively.

ii) *Convolution layer:* This layer serves as the network's base. The bulk of the computation required to identify characters in input is handled by this layer. The parameters of the convolution layer consist of a collection of adaptive filters that comprise the layer.

iii) *Pooling layer:* The pooling layers in a CNN design are situated between convolutional layers. They are responsible for progressively decreasing the spatial size of the network's computational workload. They enable central computing. They achieve this by reducing the dimension that comprises the incoming data by combining the outputs of the neuron clusters. They manage things independently. In this manner, the system can generate the required outcomes.

iv) *Fully connected layer:* Every neuron in the layer that is fully connected is fully connected to every activation in the prevision layer. Consequently, this layer's activations can be computed using matrix multiplication. A system's architecture can determine how many fully connected levels it has.

In all, CNN can be used to solve any pattern recognition issue. The architecture above illustrates the ability of computers based on neural networks to read Braille Lippi. Because they adhere to the hierarchy within which that they function, convolutional networks may be utilized for solving intricate patterns in Braille Lippi inputs. People's ability to discern between different character implements and mentally process what they see is where the concept originated.

Figure 7. Convolutional neural network (CNN) architecture

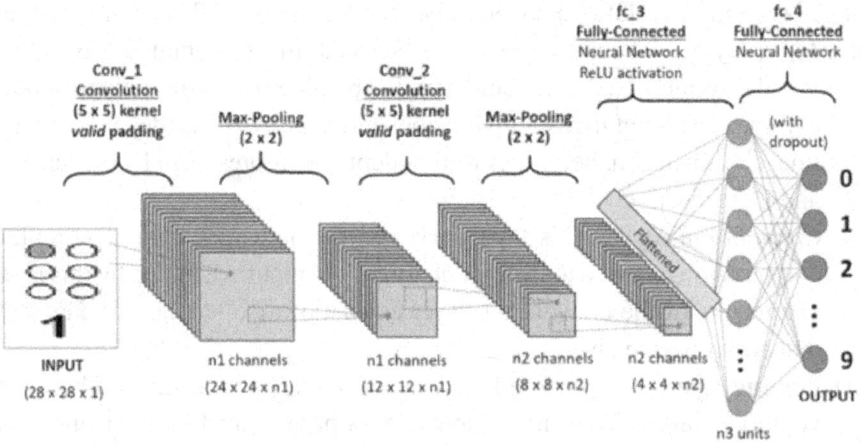

METHODOLOGY

There are five phases after image acquisition in the current system. Image digitization, Preprocessing, Segmentation, Feature Extraction, and Recognition are the stages shown in Figure 8 below.

Image Digitization

Obtaining an input image with Braille is required for the image acquisition stage. In this case, the image needs to be in one of the designated formats, like JPEG or PNG. Images are taken using cameras that are digital, scanning devices, or other appropriate equipment. Conversely, the process of digitization involves converting input paper onto a digital form. The original document must be scanned in order to transform the document into a digital file that may be preserved on a computer's hard drive. A digital file is required for pre-processing.

Figure 8. Stages after braille character acquisition

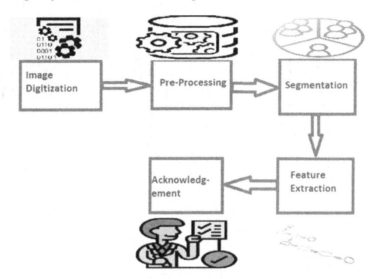

Preprocessing

Figure 9. Preprocessing steps

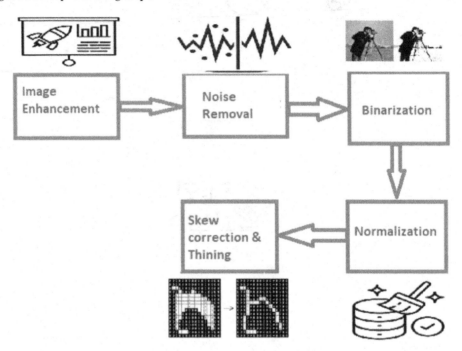

The second step after creating a digital image is preprocessing. The digitized image is checked for skewing after undergoing pre-processing to lower noise. To produce data which optical character recognition structures can process with ease, preprocessing is required. Pre-processing is carried out to make both the foreground and the background clearly distinct from one another, minimize background noise, and highlight areas of interest in the picture. Figure 9 shows the steps of Preprocessing

1) *Image enhancement:* to adjust an image's characteristics in order to improve its suitability and quality; this can be done by increasing contrast, decreasing noise, incorporating image blur, as well as adding additional information. Consequently, it's critical to process an image in a way that improves upon its original state and provides better input to feed automated image enhancement algorithms.

2) *Noise removal*: Different kinds of addictive noises may interfere with visuals. Therefore, noise must be eliminated in order to improve the quality of the image.

3) *Binarization*: By converting a grayscale image to black and white and drastically reducing its information content, this method converts a grayscale image containing multiple grayscale kinds to binary image.

4) *Normalization*: This technique for processing images alters the pixel values' intensity range. Its usual purpose is to convert input images into a range of pixel values which are easier for the senses to identify. By scaling them to a consistent size, images are normalized.

5) *Skew correction and Thinning:* This is one of the initial steps taken on scanned documents when converting them to digital format. Getting a single-pixel width with this method helps with fast character identification.

Segmentation

Character recognition techniques need to perfect the segmentation step, according to Nagare Shweta et al. (2015). Segmenting images is limited to the testing stage. It checks for inclusion errors by contrasting all points with the average distance among segmentation points within the incomplete image. Several areas of the image are created by a process that are known as super pixels. Segmentation's primary objective is to simplify an image's representation so that it can be assessed quickly and easily. It therefore has a positive impact on the recognition rate of the script.

Feature Extraction

Some among the attributes employed to determine the characteristics of the image within this stage are the height of the Braille character, the number of circles, the quantity of horizontal lines, the the amount of dark circles, the dimension of the letter, pixels, positions of different features, and the amount of vertically aligned arcs, to name a few.

Acknowledgment

At this point, NN is used to classify and identify the characters in the picture. Optical character recognition systems most frequently use neural networks based on the MLP-multiplayer perception and Korhonen's Self Organizing Map architectures.

TESTING

The testing and system results are presented in this section. The system's correctness and functioning will be demonstrated in the testing part. The objective is to give important users pertinent information that they may use. The quality of the system is related to the data. On the other hand, the results section highlights indications that the framework was implemented effectively.

Unit Testing

Unit testing was utilized for testing individual system units. The primary focus of the testing is on the modules for image digitization, acquisition, preprocessing, segmentation, feature extraction, and recognition. Any errors in the code can be easily found and fixed thanks to the testing. Finding errors in the source code as quickly as possible is the best way to ensure that the right system is created. It is advantageous to forgo the expenses of fixing a defective system later in the development process. Each unit undergoes testing to make sure the developer intended for it to function as intended.

The functions tested in unit testing are listed as follows:

- Choose the scanned input image of the Braille Lippi (Figure 10)
- Apply pre-processing.
- Segment.
- Extract features.
- Extract digital characters.

Integration Testing

Figure 10. Sample Braille Lippi characters

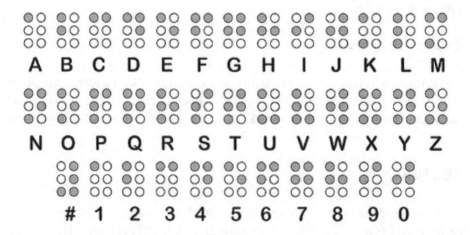

This discrete parts of the systems were combined and tested collectively. Unit-tested input models were the focus of this type of testing. Pointing out problems with the integrated elements' interactions was the main objective. The main focus of integration testing was on connecting components and information flow among combined units. Unit testing was ranked lower in importance than integration connections. The main benefits of integration testing are as follows:

- Making the integration of various system modules simple.
- Making development more rapid and enhancing programmers' confidence.
- Testing is easy to conduct.
- Assists in testing the system in real-world scenarios.
- It facilitates the discovery of problems, such as a malfunctioning database.

AUDIO SYSTEM FOR ANNOUNCEMNT

The recognized characters and number are required to be converted into the audible output. For that, the audio converted system is used, which converts the recognized input by system to the predefined sound output. The pattern of the sound is stored in the system. The designed and preferred system by us is shown in Figure 11 below.

Figure 11. Audio system

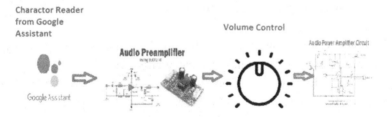

I recently had the opportunity to experience an audio system designed specifically for Braille characters and umber Announcements, and I have to say, it was thoroughly impressed. First of all, the sound quality was exceptional. The speakers produced clear and crisp audio, making it easy to understand every word being spoken. This is crucial for announcements, as it ensures that important information is delivered accurately and effectively.

The system also had a wide coverage range, meaning that no matter where you were in the classroom or rooms, you could hear the announcements loud and clear. This is especially beneficial for larger spaces, where it can be difficult to hear without a proper audio system.

What I found particularly impressive about this system was its ease of use. It was simple to set up and operate, making it a convenient solution for any event or venue. The controls were user-friendly and allowed for adjusting the volume and sound quality easily. It also appreciated the fact that this audio system had multiple input options line Google assistant. This allowed for flexibility in terms of what devices could be connected, whether it be a microphone, music player, or even a laptop for presentations. This made it a versatile system that could cater to various needs.

Furthermore, the system was equipped with features such as echo cancellation and noise reduction, ensuring that the audio remained clear and free from any disruptions. This is crucial for maintaining a professional and polished sound during announcements. Overall, I highly recommend this audio system for any application that requires clear and effective announcements. Its exceptional sound quality, wide coverage range, ease of use, and versatile input options make it a top choice for any situation.

RESULTS AND DISCUSSION

The Braille Lippi characters and numbers are recognized by the suggested system. As was already mentioned, a neural network was used to implement it. The following was what the system was expecting:

- Individual word recognition will be possible thanks to technology. It will demonstrate which the training has been effective.
- The system will show that it can recognize multiple words (sentences). It also shows that the system is operating according to its instructions.
- The recognition accuracy (Table 1) needs to measure no less than 99.09%.
- The display of characters which the system had trouble identifying or that were improperly trained.
- The system will recognize numbers and special characters.

The Braille Lippi characters and numbers are based on a six-dot cell, with various combinations of raised dots representing different letters and numbers. Neural networks have played a crucial role in the development and improvement of Braille Lippi characters and numbers. These networks are trained using large datasets of Braille characters and numbers and are capable of recognizing and classifying them accurately. This has significantly reduced the time and effort required to manually create and input these characters and numbers into Braille devices.

One of the key advantages of using NN in the creation of Braille Lippi characters and numbers is their ability to adapt and learn from new data. This means that as the system is exposed to new characters and numbers, it can quickly incorporate them into its existing database, making it more comprehensive and accurate. This has made it easier to introduce new symbols and characters into the Braille system, providing blind individuals with a wider range of options for reading and writing.

Moreover, the use of NN in the creation of Braille Lippi characters and numbers has also led to improvements in their accuracy and consistency. With traditional methods, manual errors and inconsistencies were common, leading to confusion and difficulties for blind individuals. However, with NN, the characters and numbers are generated and reproduced with precision, ensuring that the Braille text is easily readable and understandable.

In addition to these benefits, the use of NN in the creation of Braille Lippi characters and numbers has also made the process more cost-effective. With the automation of the creation process, the need for manual labor and resources has decreased, making it more accessible and affordable for individuals and organizations. The use of NN in the creation and development of Braille Lippi characters and numbers has revolutionized the Braille system, making it more efficient, accurate, and accessible for blind individuals. With the continuous advancements in technology, it is expected that the Braille system will continue to evolve, providing even more opportunities for the blind community.

Table 1. Predicted and recognized Braille characters

Braille·Lippi·Character	Digit·Prediction	Expected·Output
○● ○● ●● **#**	Correctly·Predicted	#¤
●○ ○○ ○○ **1**	Correctly·Predicted	1¤
●○ ○● ○○ **5**	Correctly·Predicted	5¤
●○ ○○ ○○ **A**	Correctly·Predicted	A¤
●● ●○ ○○ **F**	Correctly·Predicted	F¤
●○ ○○ ●○ **K**	Correctly·Predicted	K¤
●○ ○○ ○○ **A**	Correctly·Predicted	A¤
●○ ○● ●● **Z**	Correctly·Predicted	Z¤
○● ●○ ○○ **I**	Correctly·Predicted	I¤

After Correct Recognition These Corrected/detected characters are announced by means of Announcement system. The accuracy of said work is depicted in Figure 12.

Figure 12. Accuracy of NN classifier

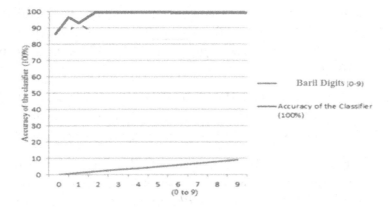

CONCLUSION

The primary goal of this study was to create a system for categorizing and identifying Braille Lippi characters and digits. In today's digital age, character and numeric recognition is essential, especially for businesses that work with Braille Lippi documents that require computer systems for analysis. Organizations and individuals can employ systems for Braille Lippi classification and recognition to complete difficult jobs. The current system processed and read Braille Lippi characters and numerals using neural networks. Neural networks (NN) were advantageous for the system thanks to training data that made it simple to recognize characters and numbers. NN made it possible for the system to be more sensitive to many object features, just like the human visual system. This made it simple to categorize and identify various Braille Lippi characters and numerals using the training data that was saved in the system's database. The use of NN in the creation and development of Braille Lippi characters and numbers has revolutionized the Braille system, making it more efficient, accurate, and accessible for blind individuals. The finished system met the required standards for recognition and accuracy of 99.09%. The current research's findings can be expanded to include announcements in additional languages. The blind students are able to touch and hear the characters and Number by Audio system.

REFERENCES

Abdulllah, M., Agal, A., Alharthi, M., & Alrashidi, M. (2018). Retracted: Arabic handwriting recognition using neural network classifier. *Journal of Fundamental and Applied Sciences*, 10(4S), 265–270.

Aqab, S., & Tariq, M. U. (2020). Handwriting Recognition using Artificial Intelligence Neural Network and Image Processing, (*IJACSA*). *International Journal of Advanced Computer Science and Applications*, 11(7), 137–146. 10.14569/IJACSA.2020.0110719

Chandio, A. A., Leghari, M., & Hakro, D. AWAN, S., & Jalbani, A. H. (2016). A Novel Approach for Online Sindhi Handwritten Word Recognition using Neural Network. *Sindh University Research Journal-SURJ (Science Series),48*.

Chen, L., Wang, S., Fan, W., Sun, J., & Naoi, S. (2015). Beyond human recognition: A CNN-based framework for handwritten character recognition. *3rd IAPR Asian Conference on Pattern Recognition (ACPR)*. IEEE. 10.1109/ACPR.2015.7486592

Ding, S., Zhao, H., Zhang, Y., Xu, X., & Nie, R. (2015). Extreme learning machine: Algorithm, theory and applications. *Artificial Intelligence Review*, 44(1), 103–115. 10.1007/s10462-013-9405-z

Mulani, A. (2019). Effect of Rotation and Projection on Real time Hand Gesture Recognition system for Human Computer Interaction. *Journal of The Gujrat Research Society*, 21(16), 3710–3718.

Dr. J Sirisha Devi, Mr. B. Sreedhar, et al.(2022). A path towards child-centric Artificial Intelligence based Education, *International journal of Early Childhood special Issue,14*(3).

Dwivedi, U., Rajput, P., Sharma, M. K., & Noida, G. (2017). Cursive Handwriting Recognition System Using Feature Extraction and Artificial Neural Network, *Int. Res. J. Eng. Technology*, 4(03), 2202–2206.

El-Sawy, A., Loey, M., & El-Bakry, H. (2017). Arabic handwritten characters recognition using convolutional neural network. *WSEAS Transactions on Computer Research*, 5, 11–19.

Karale Aishwarya A. (2023). Smart Billing Cart Using RFID, YOLO and Deep Learning for Mall Administration. *International Journal of Instrumentation and Innovation Sciences,8*(2).

Kazi, K. (2024). AI-Driven IoT (AIIoT) in Healthcare Monitoring. In Nguyen, T., & Vo, N. (Eds.), *Using Traditional Design Methods to Enhance AI-Driven Decision Making* (pp. 77–101). IGI Global. 10.4018/979-8-3693-0639-0.ch003

Kazi, S. S. L. (2023). Electronics with Artificial Intelligence Creating a Smarter Future: A Review. *Journal of Communication Engineering and Its Innovations*, 9(3), 38–42.

Kazi, V. (2023). Deep Learning, YOLO and RFID based smart Billing Handcart. *Journal of Communication Engineering & Systems*, 13(1), 1–8.

Liyakat, K. K. S. (2023). Machine Learning Approach Using Artificial Neural Networks to Detect Malicious Nodes in IoT Networks. In Shukla, P. K., Mittal, H., & Engelbrecht, A. (Eds.), *Computer Vision and Robotics. CVR 2023. Algorithms for Intelligent Systems*. Springer. 10.1007/978-981-99-4577-1_3

Liyakat, K. K. S. (2024). Machine Learning Approach Using Artificial Neural Networks to Detect Malicious Nodes in IoT Networks. In Udgata, S. K., Sethi, S., & Gao, X. Z. (Eds.), *Intelligent Systems. ICMIB 2023. Lecture Notes in Networks and Systems* (Vol. 728). Springer. https://link.springer.com/chapter/10.1007/978-981-99-3932-9_12, 10.1007/978-981-99-3932-9_12

Sreenivasulu, D. (2022). Implementation of Latest machine learning approaches for students Grade Prediction. *International journal of Early Childhood special Issue,14*(03).

Nair, R. R., Sankaran, N., Kota, B. U., Tulyakov, S., Setlur, S., & Govindaraju, V. (2018). Knowledge transfer using Neural network based approach for handwritten text recognition, *In 2018 13th IAPR International Workshop on Document Analysis Systems (DAS)* (pp. 441-446). Research Gate.

K. K. Sayyad Liyakat. (2022). Nanotechnology Application in Neural Growth Support System. *Nano Trends: A Journal of Nanotechnology and Its Applications,24*(2).

Chapter 3
Utilizing Machine Learning to Increase Online Learning Instructors' Efficiency

Somdeep Das

Management Development Institute, Murshidabad, India

Pinaki Pratim Acharjya

https://orcid.org/0000-0002-0305-2661

Haldia Institute of Technology, India

ABSTRACT

The online learning management system (OLMS) is one of the fundamental parts of the e-learning framework. As assessment of teachers is referred to as an essential part of education and a helpful contribution to improve the nature of teaching, the Feedback module of the OLMS provides with the facility to collect potential feedback of the teachers. The integration of the feedback module of the system with artificial intelligence (AI), especially machine learning (ML) allows with the ability to investigate vast amounts of data and discover patterns that can be useful in the progression of teaching techniques and ensures a deep analysis of the performance of the teachers. This absolutely underpins educational institutions to undertake note-worthy decisions for the improvement of the teachers and ultimately, the learners. This work proposes that the incorporation of technologies, like machine learning algorithms, with OLMS may facilitate in augmenting teaching efficiency.

DOI: 10.4018/979-8-3693-3033-3.ch003

INTRODUCTION

The quick augmentation of online learning has mandated the event of faculty evaluation models focused specifically on the distinctive demands of online learning. Keeping in parity with the rapidly growing online learning programs, the Online Learning Management System serves the twin purpose of mentoring and faculty assessment. In the online learning environment, the faculty evaluation system optimizes the scope of faculty evaluation which would further inspire the consistent growth of faculty and enhances the professional needs of teachers involved in providing online teaching (Adzharuddin, Nor Azura., et al, 2013; Herodotou, C., et al, 2019)). The faculty evaluation module not only plays a critical role in faculty retention, program assessment, and certification but also timely indicates the need of professional development of educators by the Universities.

The OLMS allows students and teachers to communicate beyond the limits of the conventional classroom. The digital environment, basically the software is designed to facilitate as the interface for student participation and provides learning information and services to students (Hussain, M., et al, 2019).

Among the various LMSs, the likes of Moodle, Google Classroom and TalentLMS have gained popularity and installed enormously as Online Learning Management Environments (OLMEs). In Moodle, for example, each course is generated and recorded separately which are broken down into modules that respond on a regular basis (Salekhova, L. L., et al, 2019). The main module of the courses created contains extensive material on the type of study, the subject, and the assigned teacher.

Similarly, students discover the syllabus and lesson guideline, which allow them to fully comprehend the topics to be studied and the tasks to be undertaken (Monllaó Olivé, D., et al, 2019). The module is again subdivided into segments which contain resources, academic events, and relevant information for scheduling an intermittent meeting with the instructor.

In the online learning environment, Learning Management System (LMS) modules can be helpful in measuring and promoting learning. Teachers may use this to collect information about their students and help them understand more about their curriculum and focus more on their own teaching through various instruments available in the survey module (Santiago, B. J., et al, 2020).The Feedback module of LMS makes it easy to build and perform feedback surveys. This includes writing customized questions, instead of selecting from a predefined list of questions. It also allows creating non-graded questions. The teacher evaluation is highly impacted with this activity of Feedback capturing from students.

The Machine Learning integration with LMS plays a significant role in more effective data analysis and automation. Machine Learning allows the LMS to gain access to user data to analyze and identify patterns more quickly in order to enhance the online learning environment. Based on analytical patterns and predefined algorithms, this often defines areas for development (Buenaño-Fernández, D., et al, 2019). In a similar approach this study highlights to assess an online teacher's previous feedback and blend it with new data to forecast the result using ML algorithms integrated with the LMS. This enables the online learners and teachers to set on the proper path based on performance (Al-Shabandar R, et al, 2020) and respective feedbacks to fill the gaps in the available knowledge. All of which is dependent on a number of predetermined parameters. Personalization is one of the characteristics of Machine Learning (ML), and can be used as a mechanism that plays a major role in eLearning. ML offers the prospect to successfully analyzing massive data and identifying patterns that increase the rate of efficiency of teaching (Krendzelak, M., 2014; Dias, S. B., et al, 2020). It also helps in generating more learner-centric statistical data and predictive analytics for the online learning ecosystem.

Feedback can be quantitative as well as qualitative. The Quantitative feedback (QTF) enables the students to provide rating (numerical) based on different parameters depending on the course. But this can only be done with the quantifiable aspect of the parameters. On the other hand Qualitative Feedback (QLF) helps developing an understanding into the reasoning and motivation behind the Quantitative feedback (QTF) i.e. positive or negative feedback.

Here we are analyzing the Qualitative feedback (QLF) for the purpose of enhancing the teachers' efficiency by applying Machine learning for Natural Language Processing (NLP) and text analytics. Machine Learning and NLP are two subfields of AI, which works in conjunction and help in identifying the sentiments or motivation behind the QTF. Natural Language Processing (NLP) being a subset of AI explores how computers and human languages communicate. It is a tool which applies ML algorithms for synthesizing text and determining whether a piece of writing is positive or negative using sentiment analysis (Chaturvedi, S., et al, 2017). Through sentiment analysis, the attitude towards the QLF of teachers expressed in collection of texts can be determined. Sentiment analysis is also termed as opinion mining or emotion analysis which performs analysis on opinions or emotions from text data.

Sentiment analysis determines each person's viewpoint or sentiment with reference to a particular incident. For sentiment analysis, the text that can be analyzed is passed to a model that represents a summarized form of opinion for the given document and allows one to determine if a certain object or service is good, bad, or favored (Kawade, D., et al, 2017). The sentiment analysis took the three point approach namely Lexicon based, Machine learning based and the combined approach. Lexicon based approach is completely NLP based approach, whereas ML based approached combines concepts of NL and ML. Early work in sentiment analysis mostly used lexicon-based (dictionary-based) methods, which do not translate well to various domains or languages and can fail to measure the phrase score if a word is not contained in the dictionary (Hailong, Z., et al, 2014; Rahman, A., et al, 2019). The ultimate approach is the combined approach which combines both the approaches for the development of classification models as shown in Figure 1.

Figure 1. Three approaches for performing the sentiment analysis

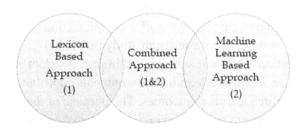

RELATED WORK

The approach of this study is singularly concentrated to analyzing the Qualitative feedback (QLF) of teachers accumulated from LMS for increasing the efficiency of teachers. The sentiment analysis approach is gaining popularity in various areas and adopted for increasing the efficiency of respective areas.

Mugenyi Justice Kintu, et al. have investigated the effectiveness of a blended learning environment through analyzing the relationship between student characteristics/background, design features and learning outcomes. In their study it is aimed at determining the significant predictors of blended learning effectiveness taking student characteristics/background and design features as independent variables and learning outcomes as dependent variables (Kintu, M.J., et al, 2017).

Sanaa Kaddoura, et al. have studied the significance of Machine learning in the entire exam cycle from pre-exam preparation, conduction of examination, and evaluation were studied and discussed. The unsupervised or supervised Machine learning algorithms were identified and categorized in each process. The primary aspects of examinations, such as authentication, scheduling, proctoring, and cheat or fraud detection, are investigated in detail with Machine learning perspectives (Kaddoura, S., et al, 2022).

Seo, K., et al, have done a research work on Artificial intelligence (AI) systems which offers effective support for online learning and teaching, including personalizing learning for students, automating instructors' routine tasks, and powering adaptive assessments. However, while the opportunities for AI are promising, the impact of AI systems on the culture of, norms in, and expectations about interactions between students and instructors are still elusive. In online learning, learner–instructor interaction (inter alia, communication, support, and presence) has a profound impact on students' satisfaction and learning outcomes. Thus, identifying how students and instructors perceive the impact of AI systems on their interaction is important to identify any gaps, challenges, or barriers preventing AI systems from achieving their intended potential and risking the safety of these interactions (Seo, K., et al. 2021).

El-Sabagh, et al, have done a research study on Adaptive e-learning which is viewed as stimulation to support learning and improve student engagement, so designing appropriate adaptive e-learning environments contributes to personalizing instruction to reinforce learning outcomes. The purpose of their study is to design an adaptive e-learning environment based on students' learning styles and study the impact of the adaptive e-learning environment on students' engagement. This study attempts as well to outline and compare the proposed adaptive e-learning environment with a conventional e-learning approach (El-Sabagh, H.A. (2021).

Gligorea, I., et al. have done a study on the rapid evolution of e-learning platforms. In their study, they have pointed that the rapid evolution of e-learning platforms, propelled by advancements in artificial intelligence (AI) and machine learning (ML), presents transformative potential in education (Villegas-Ch, W., et al, 2020). This dynamic landscape necessitates an exploration of AI/ML integration in adaptive learning systems to enhance educational outcomes. Their study aims to map the current utilization of AI and ML in e-learning for adaptive learning, elucidating the benefits and challenges of such integration and assessing its impact on student engagement, retention, and performance (Gligorea, I., et al, 2023).

Hailong, et al. showed that the most accurate machine learning approaches in terms of accuracy are Support Vector Machine (SVM) and Naive Bayes, which can be considered the baseline learning techniques. They also addressed lexicon-based methods as competitive, because they require minimal work in documents which are human-labeled (Hailong, Z., et al, 2014).

Rahman, A., et al. presented that while analyzing the text review data using machine learning classifier, in terms of better accuracy, precision and F-score Multinomial Naive Bayes achieves the best result, while SVM shows higher recall. They conjointly demonstrated that BNB (Bernoulli NB) Classifier achieves higher accuracy than previous experiment (Rahman, A., et al, 2019).

Raza, H., et al, have presented a work which used various machine learning classifiers to present a sentiment analysis system for scientific text. The experiment made by them shows that among the various classifiers, SVM performs the best in terms of evaluation metrics like F1-score, and Accuracy score (Raza, H., et al, 2019).

Nandal et al. have designed a model using ensemble approach to enhance correctness and efficiency of the

Text reviews collected for better sentiment analysis. The researchers used Support vector machines as a classifier for designing the model. This classifier is supervised learning and the three kernels of the classifier i.e. linear, polynomial and radial basis function (RBF) has been used for analysis (Nandal, N., et al, 2020).

Alsaeedi et al. and Hassan, A. have demonstrated that machine learning techniques such as the SVM and MNB produced the best results, particularly when multiple features were used. They also indicated that SVM classifiers may be the traditional learning strategies, but dictionary (lexicon)-based techniques can be very useful in the human-marked archive, requiring little effort (Alsaeedi, A., et al, 2019; Hasan A, et al, 2018).

Francis et al. have applied Naïve Bayes machine learning classifier on a dataset of 3000 words consisting positive and negative words in the ratio 2:1. It was indicated that Naïve Bayes classifiers method is simple to use and comes with computational efficiency, but it does not show the words polarity strength (Balahadia, F., 2016).

As consummately presented above, some of the machine learning techniques like Naïve Byes and Support Vector Machines have been utilized for sentiment analysis. In (Rahman, A., et al, 2019) it was suggested that future researches to be focused on integrating machine learning methods with opinion lexicon methods in order to enhance sentiment classification accuracy and adaptability to different domains and languages.

Chaturvedi et al. in their work presented a review of recent trends in sentiment analysis, their use in various business processes for decision making, and challenges of big data. The researchers also concluded that Sentiment Analysis is a complex task that can have a huge effect on decision-making in any domain and despite the fact that there are multiple machine learning techniques that can be applied to different business domains; there is no widely agreed solution for which technique is best. Researchers attempt one strategy and then repeat it over and over and hence there is no standard approach to be followed (Chaturvedi, S., et al, 2017).

PROPOSED METHODOLOGY

The QLF data are basically textual dataset captured from the LMS containing a collection of texts to detect the feedback associated with a particular teacher or course and depict it as negative or positive accordingly using Machine Learning. Figure 2 depicts the proposed semantic diagram of the methodology used in this study.

NLP involve a collection of statistical techniques for distinctive components of speech, entities, sentiment, and alternative aspects of text. This approach of extrapolation of application of one model to other text conjointly is called supervised machine learning. While applying sentiment analysis to know whether a piece of writing is positive or negative, a weighted sentiment score is assigned to each entity, theme, topic, and category within the document to quantify the data again.

The dataset has been collected from reliable source from an Institution conducting online courses, which basically contains the collection of feedback texts which would be applied upon to detect the sentiment associated with a particular feedback and using ML, determine whether it is negative or positive. The schematic diagram of the proposed model has been shown in Figure 2.

Figure 2. Schematic diagram of the proposed model

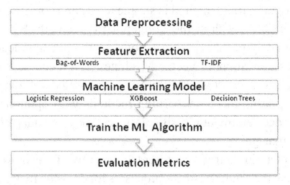

Data Preprocessing

Preprocessing of data includes the process of data cleaning, data integration, data transformation and rata reduction. Four of the most basic natural language processing functions is classification, tokenization, stemming, and lemmatization which are used for preprocessing of the raw feedback data to refined data. The Figure 3 represents the refining feedback as a result of removing special characters.

Figure 3. Obtained refined data by removing special characters

	feedback	id	label	Refined
0	Loving this course!!	1	0.0	Loving this course
1	I did not understand the submitting process ti...	2	0.0	I did not understand the submitting process ti...
2	Excellent to start learning:)	3	0.0	Excellent to start learning
3	It's a great course. The teacher is the best, ...	4	0.0	It s a great course The teacher is the best ...
4	As an introduction course its very helpful. It...	5	0.0	As an introduction course its very helpful It...
5	I've started producing with live in a week. Am...	6	0.0	I ve started producing with live in a week Am...
6	Brilliantly designed course for fundamental un...	7	0.0	Brilliantly designed course for fundamental un...
7	Learned a lot.	8	0.0	Learned a lot
8	Great course !! Won't say anything else... if ...	9	0.0	Great course Won t say anything else if ...
9	Excellent introduction. Very comprehensive, ea...	10	0.0	Excellent introduction Very comprehensive ea...

Data Visualization

After data is being preprocessed, visualization is the most important steps to have an idea of the dataset. Here, WordCloud technique is used for visualization. A WordCloud is a graphic representation in which the most commonly used words are shown in larger font sizes and the less frequently used words are shown in smaller font sizes. Figure 4 shows the WordCloud generated from the feedback dataset.

Figure 4. WordCloud of feedback

Feature Extraction Techniques

A tool for extracting features from text documents is Bag of Words (BoW). Machine learning algorithms can be trained using these features. It provides a vocabulary of all the special terms used in the training set's texts.

TF-IDF is another tool for features extraction. In information processing and text mining, the TF (Term Frequency) and IDF (Inverse Document Frequency) weight is commonly used. This weight is a statistical metric for determining the significance of a term in a list of documents. The value of a word rises in direct relationship with the frequency it appears in the text, but is counterbalanced by its occurrence in the dataset.

TF-IDF(term)=TF(term)*IDF(term)

Tf-idf(t,d)+log(N/df(t)) (1)

Where,
TF(t)= (Number of times term t appears in a document)/(Total number of terms in the document).

IDF(t)= Inverse Document Frequency, which measures how important term is.

Creating Training and Test Dataset

After applying the feature extraction techniques using the BoW and TF-IDF on the feedback dataset, two datasets with different characteristics are obtained, one with the BoW and another with the TF-IDF technique. The next step is to create the training and test datasets from the existing dataset so that our model can be trained and validated. Further, the model is applied to make predictions based on test data that is unseen and unlabeled

Machine Learning Models (MLM) for Training Set

To analyze our dataset and determine which model best suits our dataset, we proceed with the next step to use Machine Learning Models (MLM), and then the model is used to predict test data outcomes. After that, the results of all the models are compared and the best model is selected having the most effective feature extraction technique. The suggested problem falls under the heading of Supervised Machine Learning (SML). In SML, the input variables (X) and output variables (Y) are used to find the mapping output function as $Y = f. (X)$, so that when applied to a new set of input variable (X), the output variables (Y) can be predicted itself with that input variable (X).

In our study, from the feedback dataset, the result needs to be classified into either positive or negative; hence the problem is treated under classification. Feature extraction from the feedback dataset will be done using the BoW and TF-IDF techniques for the selected MLM.

To identify the best model, we normally test verity of models which can be incorporated in our dataset, and then we use that model to predict test data outcomes (Chaturvedi, S., et al, 2017). Regression, XGBoost, and Decision Trees are the three verities of models we have used to identify the best model in our study. Comparing the performance of three different models results in the selection of the best model for predicting results on our test dataset, using the best feature extraction technique

Evaluation Metrics

The performance of the models essentially informs us how likely it is that the input will fall into one of two categories i.e. positive or negative. We use evaluation metric to quantify this. The F1-score is a metric for how accurate a model is on a given dataset. The F1-score, also known as the harmonic mean of the model's precision and recall (Hlioui, F., et al, 2021), is a method of integrating the recall and precision of the model. The following formula constitutes the F1 score metric:

$$F1 = 2*(Precision*Recall)/(Precision+Recall) \quad (2)$$

Table 1. F1 score of models

ML Model	Logistic Regression	XGBoost	Decision Trees
F1 Score_ Bag-of-Words	0.7116551197856655	0.701209171272871	0.6241776937621681
F1 Score_ TF-IDF	0.7286209572172418	0.676651282051281	0.5946937681027287

Figure 5. F1 score of models w.r.t. BoW and TF-IDF

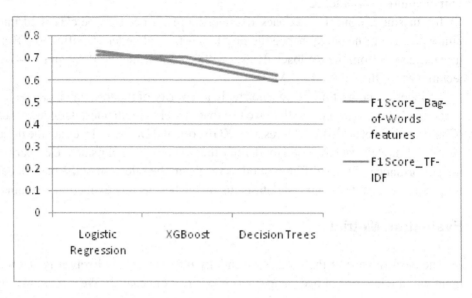

Figure 6. Comparison graph

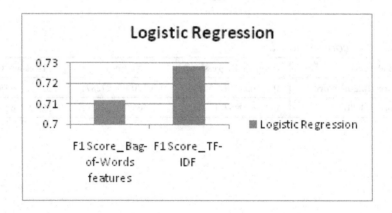

RESULT AND FINDINGS

The result and findings have been done with F1 Score_ Bag-of-Words and F1 Score_ TF-IDF. The comparison among the two has been also done for better understanding of the findings and results of the study. The Logistic Regression Model is used here which is a supervised machine learning algorithm that accomplishes binary classification tasks by predicting the probability of an outcome, event, or observation. This algorithm uses a statistical model to generate a probability between 0 and 1, instead of predicting exactly 0 or 1. It's also known as a logit model, and is often used for classification and predictive analytics.

From graph in figure 5 and table 1,, it is discovered that the Logistic Regression Model which is achieves the best possible F1 Score among the three models in both techniques, i.e. BoW and TF-IDF. Also, TF-IDF technique outperforms BoW technique in the Logistic Regression Model which is evident from figure 5 that shows that in a Logistic Regression model the F1 Score using TF-IDF features (0.728) is more than WoF features (0.711).

CONCLUSION

A part of the academic evaluation process, teacher assessment seeks to monitor and assess the effectiveness of teaching practitioners, which is useful for making judgments about promotions, retention, and other related issues. While there are numerous possible sources of assessment data and feedback on teaching, the most popular and successful method of teacher evaluation is thought to be student feedback.

By embracing computerization, we will be able to achieve our aim of providing accurate and consistent reports in a shorter amount of time. Student feedback is the most prevalent source of information on teaching evaluation, despite the fact that there are many other possible sources of assessment data and feedback. Actually, gathering student reviews is a standard practice at most colleges, and student input is an essential source of evidence regarding the efficacy of a teacher's instruction. As a matter of fact, most colleges have a standard system for gathering student ratings, and student grades are an essential indicator of an instructor's efficacy.

This chapter's research aims to enhance the quality of instruction by utilizing machine learning models on student feedback as a means of teacher evaluation for faculty development as a whole.

We intend to build on this work in the near future by investigating deep learning methods.

REFERENCES

Adzharuddin, N. A. (2013). Learning Management System (LMS) among University Students: Does It Work? International Journal of e-Education, e-Business, e-. *Management Learning*, 3(3), 248–252. 10.7763/IJEEEE.2013.V3.233

Al-Shabandar, R., Hussain, A., Keight, R., & Khan, W. (2020). Students Performance Prediction in Online Courses Using Machine Learning Algorithms. In: *2020 International Joint Conference on Neural Networks (IJCNN)*. Glasgow, United Kingdom: IEEE. DOI:10.1109/IJCNN48605.2020.9207196

Alsaeedi, A., & Khan, M. (2019). A Study on Sentiment Analysis Techniques of Twitter Data. *International Journal of Advanced Computer Science and Applications*, 10(2), 361–374. 10.14569/IJACSA.2019.0100248

Balahadia, F., & Comendador, B. E. (2016). Adoption of Opinion Mining in the Faculty Performance Evaluation System by the Students Using Naïve Bayes Algorithm. *International Journal of Computer Theory and Engineering.*, 8(3), 255–259. 10.7763/IJCTE.2016.V8.1054

Buenaño-Fernández, D., Gil, D., & Luján-Mora, S. (2019). Application of Machine Learning in Predicting Performance for Computer Engineering Students: A Case Study. Sustainability. *Sustainability (Basel)*, 11(10), 2833. 10.3390/su11102833

Chaturvedi, S., Mishra, V., & Mishra, N. (2017). Sentiment analysis using machine learning for business intelligence. *2017 IEEE International Conference on Power, Control, Signals and Instrumentation Engineering (ICPCSI)*. IEEE. 10.1109/ICPCSI.2017.8392100

Dias, S. B., Hadjileontiadou, S. J., Diniz, J., & Hadjileontiadis, L. J. (2020, December). DeepLMS: A deep learning predictive model for supporting online learning in the Covid-19 era. *Scientific Reports*, 10(1), 19888. 10.1038/s41598-020-76740-933199801

El-Sabagh, H. A. (2021). Adaptive e-learning environment based on learning styles and its impact on development students' engagement. *International Journal of Educational Technology in Higher Education*, 18(1), 53. 10.1186/s41239-021-00289-4

Gligorea, I., Cioca, M., Oancea, R., Gorski, A.-T., Gorski, H., & Tudorache, P. (2023). Adaptive Learning Using Artificial Intelligence in e-Learning: A Literature Review. *Education Sciences*, 2023(13), 1216. 10.3390/educsci13121216

Hailong, Z., Wenyan, G., & Bo, J. (2014). Machine Learning and Lexicon Based Methods for Sentiment Classification: A Survey. *2014 11th Web Information System and Application Conference*. 10.1109/WISA.2014.55

Hasan, A., Moin, S., Karim, A., & Shamshirband, S. (2018). Machine Learning-Based Sentiment Analysis for Twitter Accounts. *Mathematical & Computational Applications*, 23(1), 11. 10.3390/mca23010011

Herodotou, C., Rienties, B., Boroowa, A., Zdrahal, Z., & Hlosta, M. (2019, October). A large-scale implementation of predictive learning analytics in higher education: The teachers' role and perspective. *Educational Technology Research and Development*, 67(5), 1273–1306. 10.1007/s11423-019-09685-0

Hlioui, F., Aloui, N., & Gargouri, F. (2021). A Withdrawal Prediction Model of At-Risk Learners Based on Behavioural Indicators. [IJWLTT]. *International Journal of Web-Based Learning and Teaching Technologies*, 16(2), 32–53. 10.4018/IJWLTT.2021030103

Hussain, M., Zhu, W., Zhang, W., Abidi, S. M. R., & Ali, S. (2019). Using machine learning to predict student difficulties from learning session data. *Artificial Intelligence Review*, 52(1), 381–407. 10.1007/s10462-018-9620-8

Kaddoura, S., Popescu, D. E., & Hemanth, J. D. (2022). A systematic review on machine learning models for online learning and examination systems. *PeerJ. Computer Science*, 8, e986. 10.7717/peerj-cs.98635634115

Kawade, D., & Oza, K. (2017). Sentiment Analysis: Machine Learning Approach. *IACSIT International Journal of Engineering and Technology*, 9(3), 2183–2186. 10.21817/ijet/2017/v9i3/1709030151

Kintu, M. J., Zhu, C., & Kagambe, E. (2017). Blended learning effectiveness: The relationship between student characteristics, design features and outcomes. *International Journal of Educational Technology in Higher Education*, 14(1), 7. 10.1186/s41239-017-0043-4

Krendzelak, M. (2014). *Machine learning and its applications in e-learning systems*. 2014 IEEE 12th IEEE International Conference on Emerging eLearning Technologies and Applications (ICETA), Stary Smokovec, Slovakia. 10.1109/ICETA.2014.7107596

Monllaó Olivé, D., Huynh, D. Q., Reynolds, M., Dougiamas, M., & Wiese, D. (2019). A supervised learning framework: Using assessment to identify students at risk of dropping out of a MOOC. *Journal of Computing in Higher Education*. 10.1007/s12528-019-09230-1

Nandal, N., Tanwar, R., & Pruthi, J. (2020). Machine learning based aspect level sentiment analysis for Amazon products. *Spat. Inf. Res.*, 28(5), 601–607. 10.1007/s41324-020-00320-2

Rahman, A., & Hossen, M. S. (2019). Sentiment Analysis on Movie Review Data Using Machine Learning Approach. *2019 International Conference on Bangla Speech and Language Processing (ICBSLP)*. IEEE. 10.1109/ICBSLP47725.2019.201470

Raza, H., Faizan, M., Hamza, A., Mushtaq, A., & Akhtar, N. (2019). Scientific Text Sentiment Analysis using Machine Learning Techniques. *International Journal of Advanced Computer Science and Applications*, 10(12). 10.14569/IJACSA.2019.0101222

Salekhova, L. L., Grigorieva, K. S., & Zinnurov, T. A. (2019). *Using LMS Moodle in Teaching CLIL: A Case Study*. 2019 12th International Conference on Developments in eSystems Engineering (DeSE), Kazan, Russia. 10.1109/DeSE.2019.00078

Santiago, B. J., Ramírez, J. M. O., Rodríguez-Reséndiz, J., Dector, A., García, R. G., González-Durán, J. E. E., & Sánchez, F. F. (2020). Learning Management System-Based Evaluation to Determine Academic Efficiency Performance. *Sustainability (Basel)*, 12(10), 4256. 10.3390/su12104256

Seo, K., Tang, J., Roll, I., Fels, S., & Yoon, D. (2021). The impact of artificial intelligence on learner–instructor interaction in online learning. *International Journal of Educational Technology in Higher Education*, 18(1), 54. 10.1186/s41239-021-00292-934778540

Villegas-Ch, W., Román-Cañizares, M., & Palacios-Pacheco, X. (2020, August 4). Improvement of an Online Education Model with the Integration of Machine Learning and Data Analysis in an LMS. *Applied Sciences (Basel, Switzerland)*, 10(15), 5371. 10.3390/app10155371

Chapter 4
Entrepreneurship Powered by AI:
New Age of Business and Education

Pranav Adithya
PES University, India

Srishti Muralidharan
PES University, India

ABSTRACT

The chapter discovers the role of human-computer relations in entrepreneurship. It answers the question of how far AI can influence human beings and how AI fosters entrepreneurial creativity and innovative ideas. The right use of AI and technology would not replace; instead, it would assist humans in making advancements in different fields. It is completely in our hands, whether to let AI overpower us, or keep it under our control. The chapter also emphasizes on approaching entrepreneurship in the form of creative destruction theory. Teachers must employ a variety of pedagogies to cater to entrepreneurial education in students. The education 'about', 'for', and 'through' entrepreneurship is crucial to give the students entrepreneurial exposure through classroom settings. It also talks about the scope of entrepreneurship i.e. the rapid expansion of Entrepreneurship and the use of AI in Entrepreneurship in different countries. Lastly, how AI tools can be used for the automation of finance, managing expenses, and managing supply chains, to sustain the business for a long period of time.

DOI: 10.4018/979-8-3693-3033-3.ch004

INTRODUCTION

Sam Altman, the CEO of OpenAI, once quoted, "AI will probably most likely lead to the end of the world, but in the meantime, there will be great companies." Although this may seem controversial, this statement makes complete sense. AI has turned into a new revolution and is growing faster in every domain and industry. While it is believed that AI would end up acquiring 80% of the jobs by various researchers, this is not completely true. As human beings, we are responsible for the major developments and advancements in AI and for the same reason, it is we who have the full ability to control the extent of intervention of AI in various fields. Hence, with proper execution and control, AI can be effectively used to create and flourish businesses. Artificial Intelligence is not just merely a technology, it is undoubtedly influencing our daily chores, intervenes with our personal and professional life, but it is to be kept in mind that we have the ability to control this powerful force and we must exert proper control in order to prevent it from overpowering us. (M. Taddeo & L. Floridi, 2018)

On one side, few individuals believe that AI would completely suppress the innovative and creative minds of human beings and demoralize human efforts. On the other hand, it is believed that AI would foster entrepreneurial creativity and innovative ideas in individuals and open up various flourishing businesses. In my opinion, AI can be used as an advantage to create innovation and invoke entrepreneurial creativity in the youth, hence also open ways for research in this field, so that it can be implemented in institutions and companies. If viewed from a holistic perspective, it can be observed that AI does not replace our work, instead it makes repetitive and labor-intensive work simple, which lets individuals focus on new innovations. For example, some people spend a lot of time and energy over managing finances i.e. sales per FY (Financial Year), profit/ gross margin, losses, EBIDTA, etc. If a particular person who is experienced in AI and has extended knowledge on how to use technology for finance management, then the time invested here can be reduced drastically, and the same time and energy can be used by the individual/ group of individuals on how the product itself can be developed, price setting/anchoring based on customer needs and availability, transportation, reach or engagement etc. AI uses applications and tools for finance management, helps in fast processing, tracking policies and approvals and minimizes use of expensive resources. The very famous example is of Amazon. Amazon has mastered the use of AI to dominate Ecommerce – Today, Amazon has reorganized itself to create new innovations and successfully integrate AI into its organization. It is said that AI has played a crucial role in making Amazon one of the most successful Ecommerce Organizations. A live example of how AI can be used to make finance and labor intensive work simple while allowing the founders or entrepreneurs to focus on new innovations and ideas, is clearly studied in the Journey of Amazon – It was started off by Jeff Bezos as an online bookstore in 1994 as a local website and with proper business planning & efficient controllable use of AI, it turned into a successful Ecommerce company providing services such as Amazon Kindle, Amazon Music, Amazon Prime and reached the top in the market. According to statistics; Amazon is at the top of the ecommerce market in US, with a share of 37.8% in the market, making it a No. 1 Ecommerce website, with more than 2 billion visitors per month on the website globally (P. Harrigan, 2023). The World comprises of 25% of youth population and therefore it is important that the younger generation use their potential to the fullest to contribute to the nation. Where internet is booming and expanding drastically, It has been seen by researchers that as many students are getting distracted and carried away due to different forms of addiction. The misuse of internet and social media has led to an increase in IADs and social media addictions which adversely affects the students' health as well (physical and mental health). It has been seen that students struggle with anxiety & depression, eating disorders and inappropriate eating habits. The negative effects can go as far as causing them to be suicidal. Hence, students must be creatively taught entrepreneurship to understand how beautifully AI and internet can be used, for their well-being and betterment of the society. However, there is no universal pedagogy or teaching strategy to inculcate entrepreneurial mindset to students, in fact a completely new set of teaching methodologies would have to be developed or adopted as it is not very objective, but subjective to each individual. The chapter specifically emphasizes these teaching methods which can influence young entrepreneurs to revolutionize the world.

The stigma or notion of entrepreneurship as a "Special Talent" or "Natural Ability" is a result of lack of knowledge on the subject, as well as, the rarity of its success. This is due to the lack of awareness, especially among high school students, and there is the bad influence of internet (social media) to add to the falsehood. Gartner (1985) identified that there are four perspectives/factors which influences a business, these are – The individual and their mindset, activities taken during the creation process, the external environmental and the organizational strategy. Alvarez & Urbano (2011) uncovered that economic, psychological, and sociological approach were the three main approaches in the field of entrepreneurship (A. Quintero, 2019). Hence, we must learn to change and manipulate our own cognition, the surroundings, as well as resort to a completely different way of thinking. In the process of achieving success in any firm or business, the first step is always the hardest and very crucial to the individual. But there is one huge advantage that majority of the people in the world fail to recognize in their lives – Privileges. Privileges do not always have to be money – An individual may have a privilege by birth of being brought up in a rich family, another individual might have the privilege due to his/her social position which is a result of their own hard work, while a few others may have privilege of family business, which helps them gain insights and knowledge about the business world. We often downplay our benefits and do not acknowledge them, which often leads us to think we are not as privileged as we could be to do anything significant. In fact, one should know how much importance is to be given to a privilege such as money and to other privileges such as skill and experience. Amongst this havoc of students who are being controlled by social media, it is seen how committed scholars, realizing the importance of AI and human computer relation, have revolutionized the industries or organizations. One such perfectionist is a young student entrepreneur, Shreyaan Daga. Shreyaan Daga is an 18-year-old entrepreneur from India, who is set out on a mission to empower and educate one billion students, equipping them with essential skills and knowledge for success. This young entrepreneur started an online AI-equipped Learning Platform – OLL to address three problems in terms of education and social skills i.e. lack of awareness of different types of skill acquisition, highly expensive classes & centers, and lack of well-qualified teachers. OLL was started by Shreyaan with a mere investment of 2 lakhs in Indian Rupees, and a moto of "Skill Development for All" catering to the students of grade 1 to grade 10. With the accurate use of AI; live interactive group classes, courses certified by STEM and UNESCO and hiring top 1% teachers to teach the students online (as well as offline) OLL is achieving great heights. In just 28 months, OLL has successfully upskilled 35,000 students over the globe and still counting. Hence, with such an unwavering mindset and a clear goal of reaching 1 billion learners, Shreyaan has successfully created a profitable business, not only for himself, but to educate and upskill the students all over the Globe. Young entrepreneurs are hence more capable than we think they are. If proper learning styles are employed to motivate as well as educate the students, create a goal-oriented practical mindset, create awareness of crucial relationship between AI and entrepreneurship and the different types of entrepreneurships – Young entrepreneurs can achieve great heights of being successful themselves, as well as making a significant contribution to the society. Also, it is not only the students or middle-aged businessmen, even farmers are extensively using AI for agriculture. Farmers in developing countries battle extreme weather conditions and financial problems. In India, The AI for Agriculture Innovation Initiative held workshops to spread awareness of the AI tools that can be used to farm efficiently and as a result, the initiative helped to turn the chili farming for many in Khammam district in India, using bot services, AI-based quality testing and a digital platform to connect buyers and sellers. The famers reported that they doubled their income. Similarly, in countries such as USA, various AI tools such as Crop and soil monitoring, Drones spraying pesticides, AI in aquaculture, etc. have been used efficiently and shown 100% results in terms of improving livelihood of farmers and other small workers. (D. Klosters, 2024)

AI Technology is coming to be extensively used for the purpose of finance and keeping a count of the expenses. Although it might seem to be a minor factor, it plays an important role in any business. Especially in large scale businesses it becomes confusing to handle all financial factors – Equity, Revenue, EBITDA, Valuation, Burn rate, Investment, Margin, Capital, Royalty, Cash flow, Licensing, Gross Margin, Run rate, D2c, Supply chain, Retailers, Proprietary, Market Value etc. A few of the AI tools used for Finance Teams are – Data rails, Domo, Booke.ai, Nanonets Flow, Planful, and Vena – which help in maintain the expenses of a business and provide many more advantages to entrepreneurs. These AI tools help in staying connected to real time data, stores and secures data, better client communication, ease of lease contracts and variety of revenue models. The use of modern statistical techniques or tools has increased, particularly to create stunning visualizations as humans have very good pattern recognition skills. In entrepreneurship, machine learning algorithms – linear regression, logistic regression, neural networks, etc. have been used to effectively make predictions and recognize patterns in the given data. The people are gradually shifting to use of these technologies to their advantage, to increase their expertise and making themselves more efficient.

According to a Forbes Advisor survey, AI have been extensively used to improve business operations, help with cybersecurity & fraud management, customer relationship management, inventory management, accounting assistance & supply chain operations, recruitment & talent sourcing, and audience segmentation. The growth of Artificial Intelligence however, poses certain challenges – AI comes with many biases, it is not transparent sometimes in terms of the information it provides, as there are privacy issues. Hence, we must program AI in such a way that the emotional biases and other restrictions are overcome, ensuring clear and concise generation of information and protect privacy of the users and businesspersons, to run a successful business. History and research of AI in entrepreneurship has shown that the integration of AI into businesses has been minimal, this is because the industries in entrepreneurship are still growing. Although the past statistics shows very minimal contribution of AI, we see a spike in the use of generative artificial intelligence in the last few years. This shows that people are getting more aware of the new technologies that can be used in various business fields, and more research in these aspects can help to increase the growth rate. However, individuals are still resistant to change, which is valid as it involves taking calculated risks. Nevertheless, new technologies specialized with artificial intelligence have come up. If these technologies are integrated into entrepreneurship, it not only leads to holistic development of individual, but also contributes greatly to the economy of the country i.e. enhances team work and leadership skills, makes paperwork simple and allows the entrepreneurs to work on practical work rather than the technical work in a business.

LIMITING AI INFLUENCE ON DAILY LIFE

Artificial Intelligence is advancing by leaps and bounds, present in every part of our lives from professional to personal life. We use AI for reminders and alarms, AI for complex projects and assignments, AI for raising the credibility of our work, AI to automate intensive businesses, AI to manage our finances or expenses, as well as to make our daily chores simpler. While AI has made our lives much simpler and helped flourish businesses, it is very crucial to limit its influence, in order to prevent it from overpowering us humans. Despite the fact that we have discovered Artificial Intelligence, we must be mindful that it can cause havoc if not kept under control. Let us consider that in a few decades, humans develop programs which includes cognitive, as well as emotional intelligence in robots and automated machines. This means that the artificial intelligence technology can work as efficient as us. We, as humans discriminate in various aspects (gender or sex differences, job opportunities, reservations, etc.). The same can be reflected in AI bots. Additionally, ethical issues have been raised in the past concerning the sensitive information that it could generate or also absorb from its surroundings. Consider hypothetically, a fully automated application which is run without human intervention, for job opportunities around the globe. Considering that the bots also develop human-like emotional intelligence, the same discrimination can be seen in terms of recruiting people on the basis of gender, caste, income, etc. Hence, more research must be conducted on how we develop technologies in generative artificial intelligence, to control its influence on our daily lives. It is a very hypothetical situation, yet caution must be taken while using complex technologies as AI forms a major portion when it comes to businesses. Legal and ethical considerations are an important part of any business, that an entrepreneurship must consider. A unique differentiator in very successful businesses is the protection of user or customer privacy. This is important in online businesses, which includes digital communication between the businessperson and the customer. The trust must be maintained to make one's business more appealing and to maintain ethics. This is the main reason that the center of focus of entrepreneurs must not be transforming from human-controlled businesses to AI-automated businesses, instead it should be integration of both i.e. establishing a good human-computer relationship to ensure that we make the best use of modern technology in entrepreneurship, but at the same time, limit its use case in terms of reducing prejudices and discriminations, historical inequalities and to create a more ideal society with a good balance of humans flourishing businesses with the use of AI to ease the complications. Thus, an individual who would start his entrepreneurial journey must use AI mindfully, wherever necessary. Irrespective of any methods employed, human intervention is a must especially in businesses, as we are addressing the global population's needs. As evidence to the proposed ideas, it has been seen in the case of ChatGPT. Although the invention of ChatGPT has revolutionized the work of all the people, the misuse has caused serious ethical problems as well. It is a known fact that ChatGPT was never a final product or innovation. It is an AI tool pack which continuously takes input from every human interaction. It uses these inputs to improve its own functioning overtime. This leads to misinterpretation of information that was provided. It also caused people to get access to information and details of certain confidential aspects over the world. Additionally, ChatGPT revealed certain unethical information which created havoc amongst different groups of people. So, we observe people on two sides of the boat – the ones who support advancements in artificial intelligence, and the other individuals who fear the loss of job opportunities do to the same. This being said, as well as considering the different issues raised with the maladaptive practices using AI, it must be used effectively to automate work to a certain limit, but still other aspects must be addressed by humans which ensures equality of job opportunities and peace in the world.

Creative Destruction: A New Approach to Entrepreneurship

Now with that said, what should be our first step towards human-computer relation (AI) in entrepreneurship? In order to start a business, our first step is to begin with a revolutionary idea. In other words, not very common, neither very specific. A unique approach to entrepreneurship which is talked about minimally is The Creative Destruction Theory. This theory was first proposed by Economist and Economist Historian – Joseph Schumpeter. He described the theory as "process of industrial mutation that incessantly revolutionizes the economic structure from within, incessantly destroying the old one, incessantly creating a new one." Let us try to understand what this means; here the word incessant is used multiple times, which shows that the process of transforming an industry is always a continuous process. Schumpeter emphasizes that "creative destruction" involves industrial mutation i.e. significantly changing the industry, which continuously revolutionizes and changes the economic structure into a completely different economy, to get maximum productivity (Carol M. Kopp, Michael J Boyle & D. Costagliola, 2023). Schumpeter argues that capitalism is continuously growing and not stagnant due to new products and innovations entering the world. For example, in the early 20th century, horse and buggy transportations existed, with small developments for the same, it could be scaled up just a bit i.e. by a considerable amount in the market. However, with the entry of Ford's Model T in 1908, these basic technologies were completely replaced by this innovation. So, this suggests that instead of taking small steps and upgrading on existing technologies, superior innovations completely replace the old ones (such as the replacement of horse & buggy by Model T, and new advancements in different vehicles later replacing the Model T). This model of creative destruction can be seen in technology, retail and finance. Economic development is a result of internal forces of a market and the only motive behind it is opportunity of profit. Here, economics is a dynamic process, equilibrium is no longer the goal, but fluctuating dynamics constantly causes new inventions and innovations (David Adler, 2019). Hence, here we see two models – one is the traditional equilibrium model and the other is the creative destruction model. In my opinion, the creative destruction model is downplayed because of lack of awareness and the tendency to exaggerate its limitations. As an entrepreneur, any individual must have a slightly aggressive approach in order to scale up a business. To become a successful entrepreneur, risky-decision making is an essential trait, yet even this should be accurately measured. This must not be confused with the mechanism of gambling. Consider Mike, a Software Engineer, who has a passion for sustainability. After she finishes her bachelors, she decides to turn her passion for sustainability into a good business. She keeps her goal of modifying automated systems used at homes for different purposes. For instance, she wants to change the high energy and heat bulbs, change the furniture materials, and use eco-friendly systems to run appliances at home. She uses trial and error method and brings the different products that she can think of to the market. Now, if she had followed the traditional method; let us say she would make improvements to LEDs which have already replaced fluorescent lamps/bulbs, which can further reduce heat consumption. Instead, if she uses the creative destruction technique, she would want to completely replace LEDs with CFLs. The challenges she would face are – (1) physical structure – the spiral shape is not as appealing, (2) fixtures – The size and shape is not suited to be fitted in any point, (3) They don't work with dimmer switches. She could overcome these challenges by using her pre-requisite knowledge to modify and change the structure of the CFLs. A very useful technique would be to test it maybe in her own house to check the usability of the appliances. This way she can use her technical skills and experience to good use. Once she starts this business, she could perform a statistical analysis of her data to check the durability of her appliances. Here, persistence is required to keep modifying her inventions, so as to obtain a really good product which is competitive enough as compared to the other ones in the market. Hence, through her determination and hard work, she can launch her products in the market successfully. Hence, here we can say that She has used a creative destruction approach to come up with products completely different from the existing market. The uniqueness of the product would automatically increase the supply and demand for it, convincing Mike that her business is a success. Mike further continues to make new developments using the technologies that she can access. Her continuous persistence allows her to sustain her business for a long period of time. Further she can use statistical analysis to understand which communities living in which parts of the country are facing issues with home appliances and address those issues as well. This would help her to expand her business to other parts of the country, and scale it rapidly. In the above example, we see a combination of Social Entrepreneurship and Technopreneurship i.e. the social issue of overuse of heat and energy consumption is being solved through creative ideas and innovations (with the help of modern technology). Here, where exactly is the intervention of AI necessary? AI is mainly used for creating product designs. For example, 3D visualizations have to be created in order to study the structure of a CFL bulb, so that their size can be reduced and made compact. Mini Tab is a statistical tool pack which can be used here to create stunning 3D visualizations to make accurate modifications to the specific product. AI further helps in creating online webpages for the selling of the products online. The same can be used to obtain feedback and analyze the retention rate of customers, to check the growth of the business. AI and its implications are discussed further in detail.

Pedagogies for AI-Entrepreneurship in Students

In order to help the student entrepreneurs to be able to make calculated risks and accurate decision-making in businesses, they must be properly educated about human-computer relations. As stated in various researches, "Generative artificial intelligence has seen fast paced developments, with it being utilized in numerous contexts, including both entrepreneurship and education" (R. Bell & H. Bell, 2023). Major advantages have been identified by researchers to integrate generative AI into entrepreneurial opportunities. The upcoming technologies could influence teaching methods, assessments and how students can be trained to use modern technology. As AI and technology have grown in quick succession, this integration has been limited and more research & exploration is necessary in this field (R. Bell, 2023). The advancements made in generative AI promotes the need of entrepreneurship educators to adopt to new technologies which develops critical level of thinking, reflective thinking on themselves and a self-assessment of their technical and practical skills. Generative AI plays a huge role in these teaching and assessment techniques. Entrepreneurial education has been mentioned as the "catalyst" in various existing studies in developed and developing countries, as it has been supported and backed by governments and policy makers as a main contribution to long-term sustainable economic growth and development (Singer et al., 2015). Through existing researches and case studies, we see that entrepreneurial education has bought with it certain advantages such as developing entrepreneurial mindsets, preparation for the future, increase in employment opportunities in the AI empowered sectors and to grow a successful business from scratch. One such AI generative tool which has an amazing potential of helping entrepreneurs through these hurdles is ChatGPT, which is shown to have a potential to influence idea production, medium of communication between business and the scaling up of a business through critical analysis of any given input. On one hand, where AI tools have been the key to understanding entrepreneurship and how an individual approaches an ideology with an entrepreneurial mindset, it has raised concerns such as plagiarizing of work, and so it is difficult to categorize between actual work done by student's vs the work that has been copied from the AI tools. Hence, a high level of teaching intervention is required to ensure that the students have actually developed good skills in terms of forming ideologies, critically analyzing a situation they are posed with, to be flexible with the market and to be able to assess where they stand in the society. Contemporary research has shown that entrepreneurial education consists of variance of goals or objectives (Bell, 2021). Three main distinctions were made in entrepreneurial education, they are being 'about', 'for', and 'through' entrepreneurship. (Pittaway & Edwards, 2012: QAA, 2018). These different types of learning provide the learners i.e. the students with distinguished ways of entrepreneurship exposure to prepare them for developing in these areas. First, education 'about' entrepreneurship teaches students to gain general knowledge and information about entrepreneurial settings, managing the people, using generative artificial intelligence to set up finances, etc. This form of learning is influenced with generative AI due to presentation of the information which is being learnt. Although one concern was posed that the educators or teachers may be undermined or that the students may perceive them as less superior due to access to generative artificial intelligence, it has always been that bit more advantageous in supporting learning and allowing the learners to ask questions, review and reflect on themselves and increase engagement and interaction between each other, when this is integrated in the curriculum. So, teaching 'about' focuses on making the key concepts and foundation of entrepreneurship strong. Second, education 'for' entrepreneurship deals with upskilling the students in various business skill areas, in classroom settings itself. With the combination of generative AI, certain entrepreneurial skillsets such as development of unique ideas, evaluation of market, decision-making and communication skills are taught very effectively. Certain classroom activities such as giving them a limited time and see how they come up with ideas for a problem, hackathons are a key for understanding leadership, teamwork and solution-oriented approach to a business. These activities allow the students to understand various concepts of entrepreneurship in classroom settings. Third, education 'through' entrepreneurship is a method of teaching students the business-related skills, by experiencing entrepreneurial activities through its replication in classrooms. This helps students gain better insights into how the work culture, social interactions as well as managing the business would be. Learning is not only through the obtained outputs, but also the feedback that they receive from the people. Entrepreneurial activities such as business simulations, team programs, solutions to real-world problems facilitate group learning and also developing their internal skills for the same, hence leading to holistic development of the Individual. However, the outcomes of the above conducted researches have not been as effective as we would like it to be, simply because it has not been implemented on a large scale in all the countries. In fact, the research mentioned above states that in this era of generative artificial intelligence, it requires new considerations for entrepreneurship educators when developing programs, which have not been explored largely (R. Bell & H. Bell, 2023).

Hence, there is more scope for research in this area, as it is important to understand each student's subjective interpretation of different concepts being taught and to strike a perfect balance between use of AI and effective student-teacher relationship to inculcate entrepreneurial education. Different teaching styles must be employed to cater to the subjective understanding of each student while communicating information. Generative artificial intelligence must be used only in the aspects where complex data is to be analyzed, as using it everywhere would make the learners less creative and lethargic. The main reason being, artificial intelligence generates data based on generalized information and does not consider different situations and perspectives, which could be very misleading. Naturally, the students would lose their critical thinking due to depending too much on AI. For example, consider a classroom setting, in which the learners are being taught how excessive use of social media which causes disorders can be reduced by using technology. To analyze the complex data and perform operations such as ANOVA or time series analysis, AI is necessary. Now, it is the students' job to identify which parts of the analysis is relevant and apply critical analysis to understand the root cause of these problems, considering the current situation. If complex technology is used even for this crucial filtering process, the external environmental factors such as the country from which the vulnerable people come, their subjective experiences, etc. are compromised. Furthermore, the students of the classroom themselves lose their ability to critically analyze data. Hence, the ideal balance must be maintained between AI and human intervention in teaching set-ups, to make the foundation stronger for students. Let us take another case scenario of two different classrooms – One classroom uses AI automated robots to cater to the teaching needs of the students; In order to make the foundation of entrepreneurship stronger, the generative artificial intelligence (bots) generates and presents all the sophisticated information and data that the students need to know about entrepreneurship in the simplest way possible. The new technologies used in artificial intelligence machines, helps it to generate theoretical information easily such as providing wide variety of case studies of incidents in different countries, which students can analyze to get entrepreneurial insights. However, the solutions and techniques that it proposes might not be in line with the present situation in different countries, as it can be very generalized. How much ever accurate and up to date technologies we use, it cannot be completely reliable as the world is constantly changing. Moreover, there is very less practicality in terms of the activities that students are exposed to, giving them very less exposure to entrepreneurial-like settings. A teacher's experience matters a lot in teaching settings which is another limitation here. Now let us consider the other classroom, where teacher(s) teach entrepreneurial education to the students or learners, along with assistance of artificial intelligence to assist the teachers with complex tasks. Here, artificial intelligence can be used to provide theoretical knowledge, whereas the teachers can apply their perspectives to explain the current situation in the world. Different practical experiments and activities such as brainstorming, hackathons, business simulations, case study analysis, group discussions, debates etc. can be implemented within the students or learners, which imbibes various qualities such as leadership, teamwork, self-confidence, creative thinking skills and clarity of entrepreneurial set-ups. Furthermore, AI is used specifically to check every individual's progress and obtain feedback so that the teacher can cater to the needs of specific students and help each learner reach their full potential. In this scenario, students (in case 2) are more likely to be having the capability to turn into great young entrepreneurs than the first classroom. This is achieved due to the perfect strike of balance between theoretical knowledge and practical understanding, which empowers the students to increase their critical thinking and evaluation skills and hence can go on to pursue their entrepreneurship ambitions with confidence.

Scope of Entrepreneurship and Online Businesses

Now that we know how entrepreneurial education can be collaborated with other disciplines to help students achieve their ambitions, it is important that the individuals know about the scope of entrepreneurship. Entrepreneurship is not just a single discipline, but consists of various domains of businesses within itself. In the new era of generative artificial intelligence, the scope for entrepreneurship is growing by leaps and bounds. One main reason for this rapid expansion is that individuals from possibly any field can chose to grow an entrepreneurial business due to the variety of options that it possesses – Technology & Software, Healthcare & Biotechnology, Education & E-Learning, Entertainment & Media, Space & Aerospace Industry, Cybersecurity, Travel & Tourism, Food & Beverage Industry, Agriculture & Agribusiness, Fashion & Apparel, and Home Improvement & Renovation. While there is a high demand for certain entrepreneurial sectors in specific countries, there is a market for almost every other sector in any country. We can categorize these sectors under different domains. For instance, Home Improvement & Renovation, Social Media Platforms, Interactive Business Applications etc. can be categorized under Social Entrepreneurship. Social Entrepreneurship requires an individual to perform detailed analysis of a given social problem, identify the groups being affected or needing the development and to assess consumerism. Philippines has the highest social media usage rate, at over 60% higher than average usage rate of other countries. This also accounts for the various problems such as Internet Addiction Disorders (IAD) and detachment from real world people due to online connections, which are not sufficiently serving their purpose. Hence, here social platforms which can actually engage people and make their lives better can be developed. For example, a user interface app can be made for people of different businesses to meet actual people. This way, the people or individuals can get to know more about other booming businesses around the world and collaborate together. However, for the students or teenagers, interactive learning sessions can be developed to make them aware of their surroundings. Here, this strategy would work perfectly, since the people in Philippines are already using social media excessively. So, they might as well use it for the betterment of their lives, therefore reducing their screen time and spending majority of their time to meet new people and make connections in the real world. Now, we can categorize Technology & Software, Healthcare & Biotechnology, and Education & E-Learning under Technopreneurship. Technology Entrepreneurship is a domain which deals with new technologies in the fields of medication, entertainment, education etc. The high demand for this field is seen in India. Technology and Software are the key pillars of entrepreneurial growth in India. This is because, there is a huge demand in India i.e. many businesses have a thriving need of new technologies, which creates opportunities for these people. India also has the workforce i.e. tech talent who have the expertise and lastly, tech companies in India costs lesser investments. This helps new businesses spend less on technology used for their products, hence contributing to the economy on a large scale. Cyberpreneurship is a domain which is prevalent in many countries such as the United States, Germany, Japan, Canada, China, India etc. Hence, we see that there is a huge scope for entrepreneurship and the different disciplines & domains present in it.

The scope of entrepreneurship itself is large and expanding. In this era of generative artificial intelligence, a new domain has revolutionized small and large businesses – Online business and Trading. Online businesses were not in great flow previously, but with the growth of AI and new technologies, online businesses are much more successful than offline businesses. The different types and most prominent of them are – App Development, Online Blogging, Build Niche Websites, Social Media Platforms and Digital Marketing Agencies. Many companies are in fact, shifting to digital & e-platforms and increased the need for digital marketing services. Even majority of the businesses earn more profits in online than in offline due to accessibility to large public at the ease of their homes or workplace, AI tools which have made managing businesses and business-related finances incredibly easy and fast, and the advantage of being able to connect and collaborate with investors all over the world who can help in the expansion of businesses. Although certain individuals believe that starting an online business is risky, efficiently calculated risks and decisions in these aspects can pretty much produce a high rate of success for the same. This has been sufficiently proven in the history. For instance, Amazon was initially started as an online bookstore, which has now turned out to be the no. 1 e-commerce platform globally, offering different services and all products from A to Z. This could not have been achieved without calculated risks and efficient use of AI and technology. The main reasons for the success were – customer-centric approach, innovations such as individualistic recommendations and continuously changing search engine to always keep the customers engaged and lastly, vast categories of business and services such as Amazon Prime, Amazon mini tv, Amazon Music and Kindle. It leverages data analytics to accurately predict customer behavior and is always evolving to make its user interface better each time. Shopify is another online business which started out very small, but now is one of the leading e-commerce platforms, which helps in managing online stores. Here also, we see the wise use of generative artificial intelligence and technology and calculated risks to turn it into a magnificent business. The major success here is due to its user-friendly interface, customizable templates, and robust features. It helps other businesses to scale up efficiently. Shopify offers a range of integrations, applications, and resources tailored to address the diverse requirements of merchants, spanning marketing, analytics, and inventory control. A similar approach is seen in other OTT channels such as Netflix, whose main highlight is the contrast of colors in its homepage, friendly user interface, attractive animations and a dynamic search engine which makes it a very successful online business.

AI Tools for Financing in Entrepreneurship

Once an individual proposes his ideology, analyzes its place in the market, uses effective strategies to sustain the business and obtains a good retention rate of customers, his journey of entrepreneurship is not over yet. A major process in entrepreneurship, which is necessary for every individual to have expertise in, is finance and investments. Let us consider an individual having set up a great business of selling eco-friendly home furniture online is dealing in profits. But if he or she does not systematically calculate the different financial factors, such as Gross Margin, EBITDA, percentage of B to B (Business to Business) and D to C (Direct to Consumer) distribution, supply chains, etc. could cause this business to turn into a lethal enterprise. First, it is important for any young entrepreneur to learn and be aware of the different factors responsible for finances and expenses in a business, as well as use generative artificial intelligence tools to make the process easier and compact for the individual. Let us see what AI tools are effective in which aspects of entrepreneurship. Data rails is an AI tool used by finance teams, which eases statistical representation of data, empowering the individuals to focus on their strategic value. The advantages of this tool are as follows – It is connected to real time data, i.e. All the decisions can be made by relying on this tool pack, as it provides the most recent and accurate information. The highlight of Data rails is that, it connects all of company's finance integrations and data sources into one. Any datasets entered are always secure. Another important aspect is it provides dashboard and amazing visuals. This is a major add up, as it helps in presenting the calculated statistical data in a very concise and clear manner. Domo is another very efficient AI tool which is mainly used for data analysis and integration. For instance, let us say an individual is successfully running a business of selling chips and drinks. He gets 80% of his revenue from online stores and 20% from offline buying and selling. It is also observed that there is a difference in feedback obtained offline and that of online. There could be various reasons for this, such as packaging, target audience, pricing categories etc. Domo can be used to analyze all these data sets and present the information in a legible manner for the businessperson to take a credible decision. This can help the individual and the investors to identify the gaps in business with utmost ease, as the visual graphs and representations used by Domo to precisely present the data sets helps in easy and quick decision making. It must be noted that Domo software is a connector, and not a data generator. This means that its function is only to integrate a huge chunk of data to a compact space. Booke.AI is a software, which is used for accountancy and finance listing purposes. It helps in having an account of all the sales, different deals and money spent in different areas or gaps of the business. This helps to keep an account of how much is spent in which areas, and so contributes to future planning of the business. The main advantage is its error detection technology which corrects mistakes in calculation of accounts or expenses. Vena helps the finance team in financial planning and sales management i.e. provides assistance in budgeting and predicting, planning of workforce, compensation management, provision of taxes etc. This too uses world class AI technology to integrate different functions. It provides Interactive Dashboards, helps in Predictive Analytics and Anomaly Detection and lastly, Data Analysis Expressions (DAX) i.e. a robust calculation engine (S. Gordon, 2024). Hence, an entrepreneur can only be successful once he develops expertise even in finance matters, as it is the most essential component for investors before investing in any company. We not only see young student entrepreneurs, but also Individuals from distinct areas of work. Even farmers in many countries are increasing their knowledge about finance matters in order to get into entrepreneurship due to the various opportunities present. Entrepreneurship starts with the formation of an ideology, checking the validity of the idea before releasing the specific products into the market, using the gained knowledge and foundation of Entrepreneurship to sustain the business for long period of time, using the appropriate AI tools for organizing the business and to manage finances, finally the individual must have the ambition and spirit to face any challenges throughout his or her entrepreneurial journey that may arise at any stage either with his or her colleagues or any external issues, hence, can become a very successful entrepreneur and compete with various businesses all over the world.

APPROPRIATENESS TO THE AUDIENCE

The different themes proposed above, are inline to the theme of the topic. It is very essential for the teachers to develop or employ different pedagogies to cater to the needs of the students, as well as employ a mix of artificial intelligence and human controlled techniques to give a well-balanced foundation to the students pursuing entrepreneurship. It is found in various research papers that various AI Tools are being used, but there is a need to adopt effective strategies to minimize the time spent on certain aspects in a business. AI tools must only be used wherever necessary. For example, instead of using AI and robots as a replacement for man force in businesses, AI tools should only guide the workforce to make work simple. As discussed above, AI tools can be used to make complex graphs presentable, calculation of multiple variables, to study the impacts of business in specific areas, help in easy financing, etc. Hence, the chapter addresses the students and helps them increase knowledge regarding entrepreneurship, influences teachers to improve education styles used in entrepreneurship education and also calls for more research to be done in this area to improve the lives of young entrepreneurs.

CONCLUSION

Artificial Intelligence is growing by leaps and bounds - AI is largely used in different industries to automate businesses. The ambiguity of where AI would lead us to has resulted in the two thought processes i.e. AI is responsible for making developments & advancements in the society, & AI is a powerful source which will overpower humans in the future. In my opinion, the prudent utilization of Artificial Intelligence ensures that AI is under human control, as well as assists human beings to develop and flourish businesses. In this new era of generative artificial intelligence and booming opportunities in entrepreneurship, AI is used for various inputs – suggestions for innovative ideas or activities based on latest trends in entrepreneurship education. Recommendations such as incorporating interactive simulations, guest speakers, hackathons and real-world case studies help in engaging the students and foster entrepreneurial spirits. The different pedagogies or teaching styles adopted by teachers to cater to the needs of the learners collaborated with artificial intelligence in business simulations, is therefore, crucial for the emergence of young entrepreneurs in the society. Additionally, the chapter emphasizes greatly on 'Creative Destruction Theory', as opposed to the traditional entrepreneurial theories. This approach is required because traditional theories can generate income and contribute to existing norms in the society, but does not lead to any significant growth or make a difference to the way the world functions. The CDT (Creative Destruction Theory) which involves completely replacing existing norms propels the world one step ahead in terms of innovations and discoveries, giving rise to unique perspectives all over the world. This approach also instills a sense of aggressive and daring mindset in the minds of young entrepreneurs and ignites passion to change the world. However, the limitations here can be undermining the practicality in a business setting. Overconfidence-Biases can come into picture, which would affect the mindset of individuals pursuing entrepreneurship. To avoid this, more research must be conducted on the approaches to entrepreneurship, as minimal empirical research has been conducted so far. Entrepreneurship has a broad scope in various domains such as Social, Technical, Environmental and Cyber Security. Additionally, online businesses are flourishing in this era of generative artificial intelligence. Here again, research gaps must be filled i.e. more research is required to understand the risk-taking strategies and decision-making for the same. Lastly, AI plays a very crucial role in managing finances and expenses in entrepreneurship. Differing AI tools such as Data rails, Domo, Booke.AI, and Vena are used for the purposes of stunning visualizations for presentation of data, integration of various data sources into a user-friendly dashboard for effective decision making, managing accountancy, expenses & supply chains, and financial planning & sales management, respectively. In conclusion, entrepreneurship is ever growing due to the different influences that it exerts over various domains of the world, and in this era of generative artificial intelligence, it is that much more important that more empirical researches are conducted to check the validity of existing processes and evaluate them for the future generations. Some of the themes which uses information or includes critical analyses of research papers have been included in the references below. The references are up to date.

REFERENCES

Adler, D. (2019). Schumpeter's theory of creative destruction. *Engineering and Public Policy, 30.*

Alberto, R. R. (2023). *The influence of Amazon on E-Commerce Industry Evolution and Customers' Buying Behaviour: A case study of a financial institution* [Doctoral dissertation, Universidade NOVA de Lisboa].

Bell, R., & Bell, H. (2023). Entrepreneurship education in the era of generative artificial intelligence. *Entrepreneurship Education*, 6(3), 229–244. 10.1007/s41959-023-00099-x

Farmers in India are using AI for agriculture – here's how they could inspire the world. (2024, January 16). World Economic Forum. https://www.weforum.org/agenda/2024/01/how-indias-ai-agriculture-boom-could-inspire-the-world/

Ferrati, F., & Muffatto, M. (2021). Entrepreneurial finance: emerging approaches using machine learning and big data. *Foundations and Trends® in Entrepreneurship, 17*(3), 232-329.

Formica, P. (2002). Entrepreneurial universities: The value of education in encouraging entrepreneurship. *Industry and Higher Education*, 16(3), 167–175. 10.5367/000000002101296261

Gordon, S. (2024, February 12). *8 Best AI Tools for Finance Teams in 2024.* Datarails. https://www.datarails.com/best-ai-tools-for-finance-teams/

Harrigan, P. (2023, January 9). How Amazon Uses AI to Dominate Ecommerce. *Top (Madrid)*, 5.

Quintero, A., Andrade, J. M., & Ramírez, E. (2019). *Entrepreneurship as an area of knowledge: Literature review.*

Shepherd, D. A., & Majchrzak, A. (2022). Machines augmenting entrepreneurs: Opportunities (and threats) at the Nexus of artificial intelligence and entrepreneurship. *Journal of Business Venturing*, 37(4), 106227. 10.1016/j.jbusvent.2022.106227

Stahl, B. C., & Eke, D. (2024). The ethics of ChatGPT–Exploring the ethical issues of an emerging technology. *International Journal of Information Management*, 74, 102700. 10.1016/j.ijinfomgt.2023.102700

Taddeo, M., & Floridi, L. (2018). How AI can be a force for good. *Science*, 361(6404), 751–752. 10.1126/science.aat599130139858

Chapter 5
The Impact of Attitudes Toward Artificial Intelligence on Job Performance

Funda Hatice Sezgin
https://orcid.org/0000-0002-2693-9601
Istanbul University-Cerrahpasa, Turkey

ABSTRACT

The perception of artificial intelligence among employees is increasingly relevant as artificial intelligence technologies become more prevalent in the workplace. A positive perception of artificial intelligence can lead to improved job performance, as employees may be more willing to embrace and utilize artificial intelligence technologies to enhance their work. Conversely, a negative perception of artificial intelligence can hinder job performance, as employees may resist or feel threatened by artificial intelligence technologies. This study aims to examine the association between attitudes to artificial intelligence and job performance among 500 academicians employed in universities in Istanbul, using structural equation modeling. The findings of the analysis indicate a statistically significant positive relationship ($\beta=0.412$, $p<0.01$) between artificial intelligence and job performance. It is necessary to emphasize the importance of making academics' attitudes towards artificial intelligence positive.

DOI: 10.4018/979-8-3693-3033-3.ch005

INTRODUCTION

Artificial intelligence is a technology of great importance for businesses today. Businesses can increase efficiency, streamline business processes, and gain a competitive advantage by using artificial intelligence (Haefner et al., 2021). Artificial intelligence can assist businesses in many areas, especially customer service. Therefore, artificial intelligence is a technology with great potential for businesses and it is important to use it to achieve success in a competitive business environment (Wright and Schultz,2018).

Today, artificial intelligence, which is a source of inspiration for scientists doing research in many different fields, is rapidly advancing and developing with the contribution of information technologies. Artificial intelligence manifests itself in many areas of life and research. This technology is constantly developing and improving with advances in the field of informatics (Budhwar et al., 2022). By using artificial intelligence technologies, employees can perform many tasks that they have been working on more easily and quickly, and can save time by using these technologies in routine and time-consuming tasks (Złotowski et al., 2017).

The widespread use of artificial intelligence technologies may impose new requirements on employees' skills and abilities. These new requirements may affect employees' perception. In today's rapidly changing business world, the impact of technological developments is increasing. Artificial intelligence, which has an important place among these developments, transforms business processes and affects the performance of employees in many areas (Lichtenthaler, 2020). Increasing employee performance in businesses has become one of the important goals of the human resources department. Because employees are the most important capital of businesses. In this regard, certain goals are set for employees in parallel with the goals of the enterprises, and their success or failure in achieving these goals is monitored (Stahl et al., 2021). For this reason, the concept of employee performance should be examined by institutions and organizations on the basis of various types and dimensions, and the necessary guidance and supervision should be carried out to increase performance. Employee job performance plays a critical role in businesses gaining competitive advantage and being successful (Behl et al., 2021). Therefore, the effective use of artificial intelligence technologies in the business world has the potential to increase employee productivity.

The aim of this study is to determine the impact of academics' perceptions of artificial intelligence on their job performance with the help of structural equation model. In the education sector, artificial intelligence offers many important advantages, such as personalizing learning and teaching processes, increasing efficiency and promoting equal opportunities in education. By analyzing students' learning styles, interests, and performance, it can provide customized learning plans and materials for each student. This allows students to learn at their own pace and better respond to their individual needs. It can help academics use their time more efficiently. For example, thanks to automatic evaluation systems, teachers can evaluate exams and assignments faster and spend more time dealing with students one-on-one. AI-powered education platforms can reach students who have limited access to quality educational resources due to geographical or economic barriers. In this way, more equal educational opportunities can be provided for everyone. Artificial intelligence can improve learning processes by providing instant feedback to students. This allows students to quickly correct misunderstandings and achieve learning goals more effectively, allowing the development of innovative approaches and methodologies in education. For example; More interactive and experiential learning environments can be created by integrating with technologies such as virtual reality or augmented reality. The use of artificial intelligence in the education sector can help students have a more effective and personalized learning experience, ease teachers' workload, and provide greater access and equity in education.

CONCEPTUAL FRAMEWORK

Artificial Intelligence

Artificial intelligence is a wide range of algorithms and machine learning tools that can rapidly inject data, identify patterns, and optimize and predict trends. Artificial intelligence algorithms can understand speech, identify photographs, and analyze personal characteristics such as mood and honesty. These algorithms are not "intuitive" like humans, but they are fast. Therefore, they can analyze millions of pieces of information in seconds and quickly associate them with patterns (Thesmar et al., 2019). Statistically, artificial intelligence systems can predict and learn by drawing curves of possible outcomes and then optimizing decisions based on many criteria (Agrawal et al., 2019). Artificial intelligence was developed to enable computers to think logically and work like humans in terms of decision-making (Brougham and Haar, 2018). Artificial intelligence focuses on alleviating and promoting human physical and mental labor through computational models of intelligent behavior, reasoning, learning, decision-making by computer systems, and complex problems that can often only be solved by human professionals. Artificial intelligence has a significant impact on the recruitment process, as well as improving human resources practices (Kim and Bodie,2021).

Today, artificial intelligence is used as a tool by businesses to perform various tasks. Artificial intelligence systems are used in a wide range of areas, such as selecting suitable candidates for positions, making recommendations to customers about financial products, performing financial transactions, insurance, organizing complex logistics processes, diagnosing patients, recommending therapy, predicting technological developments, and tracking criminal activities (Cockburn et al., 2019). The main reasons for the rapid adoption of artificial intelligence by businesses today are; In the last 20 years, there have been developments in science and technology that support artificial intelligence methods (long-term memory units, recurrent neural networks and convolutional neural networks, etc.) and businesses can access these technologies under open source license the increasing effectiveness of information technology in capturing and storing task-related data within the organization, decreasing costs of computer hardware and artificial intelligence compatible chip designs, increasing cloud-based services and making artificial intelligence suitable for businesses at various scales (Makarius et al., 2020).

Contributions of Artificial Intelligence to Businesses

Artificial intelligence is a machine and development algorithm. It is a tool that uses human intelligence in various fields and increases performance. Artificial intelligence helps human resources professionals do their jobs more easily and positively affects the recruitment and orientation process. In addition, artificial intelligence has many other skills. Some of these are as follows (Huang and Rust, 2018; Borges et al., 2021; Gansser and Reich, 2021):

✓ Recruitment and placement: In the future, artificial intelligence will be needed in every organization to recruit the best. Artificial intelligence helps recruiting professionals analyze the resumes received during the recruitment period and compare them with the resumes of existing employees already in the same job role and then select the best candidate. Artificial intelligence is able to process more resumes than humans to find the perfect set of candidates, as well as evaluate a wide pool of talent in light of parameters such as experience, values, skills and performance to perfectly suit the requirements of the processing.

✓ Talent retention: The departure of talented employees is not only an unacceptable drain on business resources, but also a very costly loss of carefully built value. AI can monitor several concrete and even somewhat abstract parameters to retain talent. From identifying employees who should be rewarded through pay raises and bonuses to monitoring work-life balance, AI can help address some of the root causes of talent being dissatisfied with their current jobs and work environments.

✓ Training and performance analysis: Changes in technology and procedure are a demand that a corporate business must constantly meet. Artificial intelligence not only enables human resources departments to develop and organize training programs for entire teams of employees, but it can also automate the process by taking into account the needs, schedules and wishes of individual employees. Artificial intelligence, in general, helps analyze the skills and behavior of specific candidates working at various levels. Customizing the training program using artificial intelligence is very important because different people have different styles and abilities. In addition, these privatization activities act as a bridge between employers and employees.

✓ Conversational AI: AI can gather insights through employee interactions to gather information about employee satisfaction, productivity, and engagement motivation. Artificial intelligence systems based on conversational communication can perform many activities, from collecting input from employees to starting the review process.

Purposes of Artificial Intelligence

The purposes of Artificial Intelligence is to develop computers with human intelligence and make machines that resemble human behavior. Scientists in the field of Artificial Intelligence are interested in developing programs through which similar thinking approaches can be demonstrated by computer systems (Kaplan and Haenlein,2019). "Thinking" is used here to mean that computer programs use human-like approaches when solving problems. In order for a program to gain this ability, it must have sufficient knowledge about the problem area it wants to solve. Therefore, within a narrow problem domain, human-like computer programs can be developed (Bawack et al., 2021). In addition, artificial intelligence is a transition from data processing to information processing, and presenting and processing information in these systems is very important. In this context; It should not be forgotten that information can generally be expressed more easily through symbols and that artificial intelligence should work with symbols rather than numerical data (Nazareno and Schiff, 2021).

The invention, production and purposes of artificial intelligence technology and applications can be examined under three headings. These headings have been determined as scientific purposes, education and development purposes, and innovation and invention purposes in engineering (Tschang and Almirall, 2021).

a) ***Goals of Scientific Concern:*** This aim is to understand and convey the working principles of the human mind and abilities, learning and creative strategies, methods of finding solutions to practical problems, and to use computer models to realize these at the highest possible level (Agrawal et al., 2018).

b) ***Education and Development Objectives:*** It aims to develop education, development and new ways of learning to increase people's hunger and capacity for learning and understanding. Its goal is to enable people to live in harmony with the development of technology and to receive information more continuously in their minds through various applications. Its purpose is to allow people to test and troubleshoot (Huysman, 2020).

c) ***Purposes of Engineering and Finding Innovative Inventions:*** Artificial intelligence studies begin with the instinct of understanding the basic principles of human intelligence and aim to create intelligent programs and robots that can think and decide like humans, and to transfer this complex structure to artificial intelligence. Inspired by this idea, engineers are trying to make people's lives easier with programming and robotic artificial intelligence applications (Kong et al., 2021; Gerlich, 2023).

The Importance of Artificial Intelligence in Education

Artificial intelligence (AI) is increasingly important in education due to its potential to transform teaching and learning processes, enhance educational outcomes, and improve access to quality education. One key area where AI can make a significant impact is personalized learning. AI-powered systems can analyze students' learning styles, preferences, and performance data to tailor educational content and activities to individual needs, enabling more effective and engaging learning experiences (Wu and Shang, 2020; Vrontis et al., 2021).

Furthermore, AI can help address the challenge of limited resources in education. AI-powered tools can automate administrative tasks, such as grading and lesson planning, freeing up teachers' time to focus on providing personalized support and feedback to students. This can help improve the efficiency of educational institutions and ensure that students receive the attention and support they need to succeed (Park and Woo, 2022). Another important role of AI in education is its ability to facilitate access to education for students with diverse learning needs. AI-powered tools can provide support for students with disabilities, such as speech recognition software for students with dyslexia or personalized learning platforms for students with autism. By making education more accessible and inclusive, AI can help ensure that all students have the opportunity to learn and thrive (Kopka and Grashof, 2022).

Moreover, AI can enhance the effectiveness of teaching by providing teachers with valuable insights into student performance and learning patterns. AI-powered analytics tools can analyze large amounts of data to identify trends and patterns in student learning, helping teachers identify areas where students may be struggling and adapt their teaching strategies accordingly (Wijayati et al., 2022). This can lead to more targeted and effective instruction, ultimately improving educational outcomes for students (Makridakis, 2017). In addition to its impact on teaching and learning, AI also has the potential to revolutionize educational research. AI-powered tools can analyze vast amounts of educational data to identify trends, patterns, and correlations that may not be apparent to human researchers. This can help researchers gain new insights into how students learn and how educational systems can be improved, leading to advances in educational theory and practice (Dabbous et al., 2022).

Overall, the importance of artificial intelligence in education lies in its ability to improve the quality, efficiency, and accessibility of education. By leveraging AI technologies, educators can create more personalized learning experiences, improve teaching effectiveness, and ensure that all students have the opportunity to learn and succeed.

Job Performance

Since the impact of job performance is important in achieving the goals of organizations, the concept of employee performance, which is used to measure the outputs of organizations' activities, is widely discussed in the literature. Therefore, effectiveness and identification of job performance are important.

As stated by Griffin et al., (2007), job performance refers to the effort and diligence that employees must show in return for wages. The term "job performance" is a term that refers to an individual's work success, including performing a job in a meaningful way, exerting required effort on the job, and relating to employers or colleagues.

Job performance is a concept that expresses the extent to which an employee fulfills the duties determined by the employer or manager (Grobelna, 2019). Job performance is a multidimensional concept that is not limited to the completion of jobs and tasks. Employees' commitment to the organization should be positive and behaviors that harm the interests of the organization should be avoided. For this reason, performance is evaluated only on outputs, which can sometimes give misleading results. In addition, the concept of performance should include all kinds of behaviors and attitudes carried out in line with the interests of the organization (Buil et al., 2019).

Job performance: It is affected by many factors and is not limited to the physical completion of work. Factors such as employees' abilities, technical and cultural knowledge, and personality traits are important factors that determine performance. In addition, factors such as interest in work, clear determination of goals, receiving feedback, rewarding success, and punishing failure are also important variables that affect employee performance (Anitha, 2014). Job performance is a concept that businesses attach great importance to, and increasing job performance is necessary for businesses in terms of efficiency and continuity of the business. Many factors are effective in the formation of employee performance, but the employee's high motivation is the most important factor. For this high motivation, wages must be sufficient, and promotion and promotion opportunities must be provided on time (Anderson and Stritch, 2016). It is also important to give rewards and bonuses accurately and fairly, provide social rights and respect employees. Giving confidence and initiative, valuing the employee's ideas and giving importance to teamwork are also critical. The higher the employee's performance, the greater his/her contribution to the business will be (Gruman and Saks, 2011).

The most important factor for businesses to achieve their goals in order to be successful is employees. Since the competitive environment in today's business world is intense, businesses need high-performance employees to remain permanent in the market (Riyanto et al., 2017). Having well-equipped, competent, and efficient employees plays an important role in the success of businesses. However, if businesses do not motivate their employees and gain their loyalty to the business, they will not be able to achieve the expected efficiency from these employees (Bratton, 2017).

Employees are the focus of every organization. The success of an organization depends on how well or poorly employees performs their duties. Every organization strives to achieve its own goals, and the most critical factor in achieving these goals is employees (Alfiyah and Riyanto, 2019). Effective employee performance can make a positive contribution to overall organizational performance or otherwise have negative effects. However, effective evaluation of employee performance is demanded in business organizations (Gruman and Saks, 2011).

According to Mondy and Martocchio (2016), performance appraisal is a vital tool for tracking employee performance, providing feedback, and addressing performance deficiencies. It is also emphasized that this process has a positive impact on the career development and motivation of employees. Employee performance evaluation is also a key component of businesses' performance management processes. Dessler (2017) explains that businesses evaluate employees' competencies based on performance evaluation results, set goals, and create development plans to increase performance. This process allows employees to be directed in accordance with the strategic goals of the business and to improve their performance.

Research reveals that an effective employee performance evaluation system provides a number of benefits to businesses. This evaluation enables businesses to better understand the talents and skills of employees and make more accurate decisions in the recruitment process (Campbell and Wiernik, 2015). At the same time, businesses can create reward and incentive systems based on performance evaluation results. In this way, they can increase motivation by rewarding employees with superior performance. Employee performance evaluation is an important tool in increasing the efficiency and effectiveness of businesses. When implemented correctly, this process supports employee development and helps businesses achieve their goals (Baard et al., 2014). However, for a successful employee performance evaluation, it is necessary to determine objective criteria, ensure a fair evaluation process and establish effective feedback mechanisms for employees. These elements are critical to improving employee performance and increasing their motivation (Gitongu et al., 2016).

Performance in academics is crucial for several reasons. Firstly, academic performance is often used as a measure of an individual's knowledge, skills, and abilities in a particular field of study. High academic performance indicates that a student has mastered the content and concepts taught in their courses, which can be important for future academic and career opportunities. Secondly, academic performance can have a significant impact on a student's future prospects. For example, high academic performance can increase the likelihood of being accepted into prestigious universities or graduate programs, which can open up doors to more opportunities in the future (Brew et al., 2021). Additionally, academic performance is often considered by employers when making hiring decisions, as it can be an indicator of a candidate's ability to learn, solve problems, and work effectively. Furthermore, academic performance can have a direct impact on an individual's self-esteem and confidence. Success in academics can boost self-confidence and motivate students to continue working hard and striving for excellence in their studies (Ilomo and Mlavi, 2016). On the other hand, poor academic performance can lead to feelings of inadequacy and frustration, which can have a negative impact on a student's overall well-being. Moreover, academic performance is important for society as a whole. Individuals who perform well academically are more likely to contribute positively to society, whether through groundbreaking research, innovative problem-solving, or leadership in their field (Sothan, 2019). A highly educated workforce can also contribute to economic growth and development, as skilled workers are more likely to secure higher-paying jobs and contribute to innovation and productivity.

In conclusion, performance in academics is important for individuals, as it can impact their future opportunities, self-esteem, and overall well-being. It is also important for society, as it can contribute to economic growth, innovation, and the advancement of knowledge. Therefore, it is essential for students to strive for excellence in their academic pursuits and for educators and policymakers to create environments that support academic success.

STATISTICAL ANALYSIS

The Purpose and the Importance of the Research

The attitude toward artificial intelligence (AI) in human-computer interaction (HCI) is particularly important for academics due to its impact on research directions and methodological approaches. Academics studying HCI often drive innovation in interface design, interaction paradigms, and user experience, and their attitudes toward AI can shape the incorporation of AI technologies into these areas. A positive attitude can lead to the exploration of new AI-driven HCI possibilities, fostering the development of more efficient, intuitive, and personalized interfaces. Conversely, a negative attitude may limit the exploration of AI's potential in HCI, potentially hindering the field's advancement (Pillai and Sivathanu, 2020; Guo and Xu, 2021).

Moreover, the attitude toward AI in HCI among academics can influence educational practices and curricula. As AI becomes increasingly integrated into interactive systems, academics play a critical role in preparing students for the AI-driven future of HCI. A positive attitude can lead to the development of AI-focused coursework that equips students with the skills and knowledge needed to design, implement, and evaluate AI-enhanced interfaces effectively (Kar et al., 2022). Conversely, a negative attitude may result in a lack of emphasis on AI in HCI education, leaving students ill-prepared for the evolving landscape of interactive technology (Schepman and Rodway, 2022; Malik et al., 2022).

Furthermore, the attitude toward AI in HCI can impact interdisciplinary collaborations within academia. HCI research often involves collaboration between experts from various fields, including computer science, psychology, design, and sociology. Academics with a positive attitude toward AI are more likely to engage in interdisciplinary collaborations that leverage AI technologies to address complex HCI challenges. In contrast, a negative attitude may create barriers to collaboration, limiting the potential for innovative solutions that integrate AI into HCI research and practice.

The purpose of this study is to reveal the relationship between attitude toward artificial intelligence and job performance for 500 academicians working in research universities in Istanbul, using structural equation modeling.

Data Collection Tool

General Attitudes to Artificial Intelligence Scale: The scale developed by Schepman and Rodway (2020) was adapted into Turkish by Kaya et al. (2024). The scale consists of two sub-dimensions, negative attitude towards artificial intelligence and positive attitude towards artificial intelligence, and contains a total of 20 items. In the study in which the scale was adapted, it was found that Cronbach Alpha values were between .82 and .88; reliability values were 0.77 for positive attitude and 0.83 for negative attitude. Negative attitude towards artificial intelligence items is reverse coded. The scale is organized in a 5-point Likert scale with 1= Strongly Disagree" and 5= Strongly Agree".

Job performance scale: In the study, the scale developed by Kirkman and Rosen (1999) was used to determine the job performance of academicians. The scale consists of 4 items and is one dimensional. The scale is prepared in 5-point Likert type to measure the frequency of the specified behaviours (1-Never, 2-Rarely, 3-Sometimes, 4-Frequently, 5-Always). There is no reverse item in the scale.

Population and Sample

The population of the study consists of academics working at universities in Istanbul. According to the Higher Education Council 2023 statistics, there are 40,140 academics working at universities in Istanbul. In the sample size table developed by Yazıcıoğlu and Erdoğan (2004), it was determined as 384 people for p=0.50 and q=0.50 for a sampling error of 0.05. In this study, analyses were conducted for 500 academicians. The questionnaire, which was applied by random sampling method, was sent via e-mail as a link. The survey research was conducted between 01.10.2023-20.12.2023.

Research Hypotheses

Given the aforementioned conceptual arguments and empirical evidence, we hypothesize that Attitudes to artificial intelligence has an impact on job performance at universities in Istanbul. The developed hypotheses are presented in Table 1.

Table 1. Research hypotheses

Hypotheses
Attitudes to artificial intelligence and job performance are significantly related
Positive attitude dimension, negative attitude dimension and job performance are significantly related

Statistical Methods

The data acquired from the scale utilized in the study were analyzed via IBM SPSS 27.0 and AMOS 25.0 programs. In the first stage, percentage distributions regarding demographic and general information were presented. In the second stage, exploratory factor analysis (EFA) was applied for the scales, and besides, confirmatory factor analysis (CFA) was performed to test construct validity. In the last stage, correlation analysis and structural equation model estimation results were included in order to identify the relationships.

FINDINGS AND RESULTS

Survey Reliability

For the data obtained from the survey study, Cronbach Alpha, Split, Parallel, Absolute Precise Parallel (strict) tests were carried out as a reliability test. A Cronbach Alpha value above 70% indicates that the survey was successful. Some researchers take this value as 75%. The fact that other criteria are above 70% indicates that the questionnaire has internal consistency and that the results can be trusted (Sart et al., 2018). In this study, the results of the reliability analysis of the questionnaire are Cronbach-Alpha = 0.914, Parallel = 0.913, Split = 0.910-0.917 and Strict = 0.914.

Descriptive Statistics

54.2% of the participants were female, and 45.8% were male. 36.1% of the academician were aged 20-30, 32.4% were aged 31-40, 19.4% were aged 41-50, and 12.1% were aged 51 years and over. In terms of marital status, 56.5% of the individuals were married, while 43.5% were single. Looking at the participants' employment terms, 8.4% worked less than 1 year, 22.7% between 1-5 years, 26.9% between 6-10 years, 29.1% between 11-20 years, and 12.9% worked for 21 years or more. According to their job positions, 18.2% were research assistant, 33.2% assistant professor, 24.7% associate professor, 23.9% professor.

Exploratory Factor Analysis

Factor analysis is a multivariate statistics method intended for finding or discovering a small number of unrelated and conceptually significant new variables (i.e. factors, dimensions) by bringing together p number of interrelated variables. After the suitability of the data set was confirmed by the tests, the "Principal Components

Analysis" approach was applied via the "Oblique" rotation technique as the factor retention method in order to reveal the factor structure.

Table 2. Exploratory factor analysis results

General Attitudes to Artificial Intelligence Scale	PVE	CA	AVE	CR
Positive attitude dimension	38.05%	0.913	0.778	0.895
Negative attitude dimension	31.27%	0.909		
KMO= 0.915; Bartlett $\chi2$= 6834.13 and p= 0.000; Percent of Variance Explained: 69.32%				
Job Performance Scale	**PVE**	**CA**	**AVE**	**CR**
Job Performance	67.45%	0.907	0.743	0.887

KMO= 0.910; Bartlett $\chi2$= 5913.87 and p= 0.000; Percent of Variance Explained: 67.45%

PVE: Percent of Variance Explained, CA: Cronbach's Alpha Coefficient; AVE: Average Variance Extracted; CR: Construct Reliability

As a result of the exploratory factor analysis (EFA); regarding the factor structure, for general attitudes to artificial intelligence scale, 2 factor structure was obtained, which explained 69.32% of the total variance; for the job performance scale 1 factor structure was obtained which explained 67.45% of the total variance. Following the EFA, there was no need to eliminate any questions since there was no item below 0.20 in the inference column and no item with anti-image matrix diagonal values below 0.50.

Confirmatory Factor Analysis

Confirmatory factor analysis (CFA) is utilized to express multivariate statistical analyses containing latent structures denoted by a large number of observable or measurable variables. CFA is a factor analysis technique utilized to question whether the factors revealed as a result of Exploratory Factor Analysis (EFA) are appropriate for the structure of the factors revealed as a result of the hypotheses. While EFA is utilized to examine which variable groups are highly correlated with which factors, CFA is employed to determine whether the variable groups contributing to the k number of identified factors are sufficiently represented by the said factors.

Table 3. CFA model fit indices

Measurement (Fit Statistic)	Good Fit	Acceptable Fit	Research Model Value	Fit Status
General Model Fit				
X^2/df	3	4-5	2.19	Good fit

continued on following page

Table 3. Continued

Measurement (Fit Statistic)	Good Fit	Acceptable Fit	Research Model Value	Fit Status
Comparative Fit Statistics				
NFI	0.95	0.94-0.90	0.919	Acceptable fit
TLI (NNFI)	0.95	0.94-0.90	0.931	Acceptable fit
IFI	0.95	0.94-0.90	0.988	Good fit
CFI	0.97	0.95	0.981	Good fit
RMSEA	0.05	0.06-0.08	0.018	Good fit
Absolute Fit Indices				
GFI	0.90	0.89-0.85	0.946	Good fit
AGFI	0.90	0.89-0.85	0.952	Good fit
Residual-Based Fit Index				
RMR	0.05	0.06-0.08	0.026	Good fit

In Table 3, $X^2/df = 2.19$, a "good fit" decision was made since it met the condition 3. NFI=0.919 resulted in the range of 0.94-0.90, thus an "acceptable fit"; other results were obtained as TLI (NNFI)= 0.931 in the range of 0.94-0.90, thus an "acceptable fit"; IFI= 0.988 was 0.95, a "good fit"; CFI= 0.981 was 0.97, an "good fit"; RMSEA= 0.018 was 0.05, a "good fit"; GFI= 0.946 was 0.90, a "good fit"; AGFI= 0.952 was 0.90, a "good fit"; and RMR= 0.026 was 0.05, thus it was a "good fit".

Structural Equation Modeling

Structural equation modeling (SEM) is a statistical technique used to test models in which causal relationships and correlation relationships between observed variables and latent variables coexist; it is a multivariate method that is formed by combining analyses such as variance and covariance analyses, factor analysis, and multiple regression in order to predict interdependency relationships.

Considering the goodness of fit criteria for SEM, it was found that $X^2/df = 2.79$, a "good fit" decision was made because it met the condition ≤ 3. NFI=0.922 resulted in 0.94-0.90, thus an "acceptable fit"; other results were obtained as TLI (NNFI)= 0.938 was 0.94-0.90, thus an "acceptable fit"; IFI = 0.961 was ≥ 0.95, a "good fit"; CFI= 0.976 was ≥ 0.97, an "acceptable fit"; RMSEA= 0.028 was ≤ 0.05, a "good fit"; GFI= 0.939 was ≥ 0.90, a "good fit"; AGFI= 0.947 was ≥ 0.90, a "good fit"; and RMR= 0.031 was ≤ 0.05, thus it was a "good fit". SEM estimates fit criteria yielded the result "acceptable" for only one criterion; others revealed that a "good fit" was attained and the model was appropriate for interpretation.

Table 4. SEM model estimation results

Structural Relation	Direction	Estimated Coefficient	Std.	t-statistic	p	Result
AI → JP	+	0.412	0.056	7.357	0.000*	Significant relationship
PAI → JP	+	0.382	0.061	6.262	0.000*	Significant relationship
NAI → JP	-	-0.374	0.049	-7.633	0.016*	Significant relationship

*p<0.05, AI: attitudes to artificial intelligence, PAI: Positive attitude dimension, NAI: Negative attitude dimension JP: Job Performance

According to the SEM results, significant relationships were obtained among the variables. AI has a statistically significant positive effect on JP (β=0.412; p<0.01). PAI has a statistically significant positive effect on JP (β= 0.382; p<0.01). NAI has a statistically significant negative effect on JP (β=-374; p<0.01). As the attitude towards artificial intelligence is positive, work performance will increase. If the attitude towards artificial intelligence is negative, work performance will decrease.

The attitude toward artificial intelligence (AI) among academics is crucial due to its pervasive influence on various aspects of academic work and research. Firstly, academics play a pivotal role in shaping the discourse around AI, its capabilities, and its ethical implications. Their attitudes can influence public perception and policy decisions regarding AI development and deployment.

Secondly, academics are at the forefront of AI research and development. Their attitudes toward AI can impact the direction of research, the allocation of resources, and the prioritization of ethical considerations. A positive attitude toward AI can lead to innovative breakthroughs, while a negative attitude may hinder progress and limit the potential benefits of AI.

Thirdly, the attitude of academics toward AI can impact the education and training of future professionals. As AI becomes increasingly integrated into various fields, it is essential for academics to prepare students for a future where AI plays a significant role. A positive attitude can lead to the development of relevant and effective AI-related curricula, ensuring that students are equipped with the necessary skills and knowledge.

Fourthly, academics' attitudes toward AI can affect collaboration and inter-disciplinary research. AI has the potential to transform various disciplines, and a positive attitude can foster collaboration between experts from different fields to harness the full potential of AI. Conversely, a negative attitude may create barriers to collaboration and hinder interdisciplinary progress.

Fifthly, the attitude of academics toward AI can impact public trust and accep-tance of AI technologies. Academics often serve as trusted sources of information, and their attitudes can influence public perceptions of AI's risks and benefits. A positive attitude can help build trust in AI technologies, while a negative attitude may lead to skepticism and resistance.

Lastly, academics' attitudes toward AI can impact their own professional development and job prospects. As AI continues to evolve, academics who embrace AI and adapt their skills and expertise accordingly are more likely to thrive in a rapidly changing academic landscape. A positive attitude toward AI can lead to new opportunities for research, collaboration, and career advancement.

CONCLUSION

Today, artificial intelligence, which is a source of inspiration for scientists doing research in many different fields, is rapidly advancing and developing with the contribution of information technologies. Artificial intelligence manifests itself in many areas of life and research. This technology is constantly developing and improving with advances in the field of informatics. By using artificial intelligence technologies, employees can perform many tasks that they have been working on more easily and quickly, and can save time by using these technologies in routine and time-consuming tasks. The widespread use of artificial intelligence technologies may impose new requirements on employees' skills and abilities. These new requirements may affect employees' perception. In today's rapidly changing business world, the impact of technological developments is increasing. Artificial intelligence, which has an important place among these developments, transforms business processes and affects the performance of employees in many areas.

Increasing employee performance in businesses has become one of the important goals of the human resources department. Because employees are the most important capital of businesses. In this regard, certain goals are set for employees in parallel with the goals of the enterprises, and their success or failure in achieving these goals is monitored. For this reason, the concept of employee performance should be examined by institutions and organizations on the basis of various types and dimensions, and the necessary guidance and supervision should be carried out to increase performance. Employee job performance plays a critical role in businesses gaining competitive advantage and being successful. Therefore, the effective use of artificial intelligence technologies in the business world has the potential to increase employee productivity.

This study aims to examine the association between attitudes to artificial intelligence and job performance among 500 academicians employed in universities in Istanbul, using structural equation modeling. The findings of the analysis indicate a statistically significant positive relationship ($\beta=0.412$, $p<0.01$) between artificial intelligence and job performance. While a positive attitude towards artificial intelligence increases job performance, a negative attitude towards artificial intelligence reduces job performance in academics.

The attitude toward artificial intelligence (AI) in human-computer interaction (HCI) is crucial as it influences how users perceive and interact with AI-powered systems. A positive attitude toward AI can lead to greater acceptance and adoption of AI technologies in HCI. Users who have a positive attitude toward AI may be more willing to use AI-powered systems, explore their capabilities, and provide feedback for improvement. On the other hand, a negative attitude can lead to reluctance, skepticism, and resistance, hindering the effective integration of AI into HCI.

Furthermore, the attitude toward AI in HCI can impact the design and development of AI-powered systems. Designers and developers who have a positive attitude toward AI are more likely to incorporate AI technologies thoughtfully, considering user needs, preferences, and ethical considerations. They may also be more open to exploring innovative ways to leverage AI to enhance user experiences. Conversely, a negative attitude may lead to the neglect of AI technologies or their inappropriate use, resulting in suboptimal HCI outcomes.

Improving the attitude toward artificial intelligence (AI) in academics requires a multifaceted approach that addresses various aspects of research, education, and collaboration. Here are some suggestions:

Promote AI literacy: Encourage AI literacy among academics by offering workshops, seminars, and courses that provide an overview of AI concepts, technologies, and applications. This can help demystify AI and empower academics to engage with AI-related topics more confidently.

Integrate AI into academic curricula: Incorporate AI-related topics into academic curricula across disciplines, including computer science, engineering, social sciences, and humanities. This ensures that students are exposed to AI concepts and applications early in their academic journey, fostering a positive attitude toward AI from the outset.

Foster interdisciplinary collaboration: Facilitate interdisciplinary collaboration between researchers from different fields to explore the intersection of AI and their respective domains. Creating interdisciplinary research groups or centers focused on AI can encourage knowledge sharing, innovation, and the development of cross-disciplinary perspectives on AI-related issues.

Encourage ethical AI research: Emphasize the importance of ethical considerations in AI research and development. Encourage academics to integrate ethical frameworks into their AI-related work, promoting responsible AI practices that prioritize fairness, transparency, accountability, and societal impact.

Support open dialogue and debate: Create forums for open dialogue and debate about AI among academics, practitioners, policymakers, and the public. Encourage discussions about the potential benefits, challenges, risks, and ethical implications of AI, fostering a nuanced understanding of AI-related issues and promoting informed decision-making.

Provide resources and support: Offer resources, funding opportunities, and institutional support for AI research and education initiatives. This can include research grants, scholarships, access to AI tools and datasets, and support for AI-related events and conferences, helping to foster a vibrant AI research community within academia.

By implementing these suggestions, academia can cultivate a more positive and informed attitude toward artificial intelligence, driving responsible AI innovation and promoting the ethical and beneficial use of AI technologies for the betterment of society.

REFERENCES

Agrawal, A., Gans, J., & Goldfarb, A. (2018). *Prediction machines: the simple economics of artificial intelligence*. Harvard Business Review Press.

Agrawal, A., McHale, J., & Oettl, A. (2019). *Finding needles in haystacks: artificial intelligence and recombinant growth. The economics of artificial intelligence: An agenda*. University of Chicago Press. 10.7208/chicago/9780226613475.001.0001

Alfiyah, N., & Riyanto, S. (2019). The Effect of Compensation, Work Environment and Training on Employees Performance of Politeknik LP3I Jakarta. *International Journal of Innovative Science and Research Technology.*, 4(5), 2456–2165.

Anderson, D., & Stritch, J. M. (2016). Goal clarity, task significance, and performance: Evidence from a laboratory experiment. *Journal of Public Administration: Research and Theory*, 26(2), 211–225. 10.1093/jopart/muv019

Anitha, J. (2014). Determinants of Employee Engagement and their Impact on Employee Performance. *International Journal of Productivity and Performance Management*, 63(3), 308–323. 10.1108/IJPPM-01-2013-0008

Baard, S. K., Rench, T. A., & Kozlowski, S. W. J. (2014). Performance adaptation: A theoretical integration and review. *Journal of Management*, 40(1), 48–99. 10.1177/0149206313488210

Bawack, R. E., Wamba, S. F., & Carillo, K. D. A. (2021). A framework for understanding artificial intelligence research: Insights from practice. *Journal of Enterprise Information Management*, 34(2), 645–678. 10.1108/JEIM-07-2020-0284

Behl, A., Chavan, M., Jain, K., Sharma, I., Pereira, V. E., & Zhang, J. Z. (2021). The role of organizational culture and voluntariness in the adoption of artificial intelligence for disaster relief operations. *International Journal of Manpower*, 43(2), 569–586. 10.1108/IJM-03-2021-0178

Borges, A. F. S., Laurindo, F. J. B., Spínola, M. M., Gonçalves, R. F., & Mattos, C. A. (2021). The strategic use of artificial intelligence in the digital era: Systematic literature review and future research directions. *International Journal of Information Management*, 57, 1–19. 10.1016/j.ijinfomgt.2020.102225

Bratton, J. G. (2017). *Human Resource Management, 6th Edition: Theory and Practice*. London: Palgrave.

Brew, E. A., Nketiah, B., & Koranteng, R. (2021). A Literature Review of Academic Performance, an Insight into Factors and their Influences on Academic Outcomes of Students at Senior High Schools. *OAlib*, 8(6), 1–14. 10.4236/oalib.1107423

Brougham, D., & Haar, J. (2018). Smart technology, artificial intelligence, robotics, and algorithms (STARA): Employees' perceptions of our future workplace. *Journal of Management & Organization*, 24(2), 239–257. 10.1017/jmo.2016.55

Budhwar, P., Malik, A., De Silva, M. T., & Thevisuthan, P. (2022). Artificial intelligence–challenges and opportunities for international HRM: A review and research agenda. *International Journal of Human Resource Management*, 33(6), 1065–1097. 10.1080/09585192.2022.2035161

Buil, I., Martínez, E., & Matute, J. (2019). Transformational leadership and employee performance: The role of identification, engagement, and proactive personality. *International Journal of Hospitality Management*, 77, 64–75. 10.1016/j.ijhm.2018.06.014

Campbell, J. P., & Wiernik, B. M. (2015). The modeling and assessment of work performance. *Annual Review of Organizational Psychology and Organizational Behavior*, 2(1), 47–74. 10.1146/annurev-orgpsych-032414-111427

Cockburn, I., Henderson, R., & Stern, S. (2019). The impact of artificial intelligence on innovation. In *The economics of artificial intelligence: an agenda*. University of Chicago Press. 10.7208/chicago/9780226613475.003.0004

Dabbous, A., Aoun Barakat, K., & Merhej Sayegh, M. (2022). Enabling organizational use of artificial intelligence: An employee perspective. *Journal of Asia Business Studies*, 16(2), 245–266. 10.1108/JABS-09-2020-0372

Dessler, G. (2017). *Human Resource Management*. Pearson International.

Gansser, O. A., & Reich, C. S. (2021). A new acceptance model for artificial intelligence with extensions to UTAUT2: An empirical study in three segments of application. *Technology in Society*, 65, 1–20. 10.1016/j.techsoc.2021.101535

Gerlich, M. (2023). The Power of Virtual Influencers: Impact on Consumer Behaviour and Attitudes in the Age of AI. *Administrative Sciences*, 13(8), 178–189. 10.3390/admsci13080178

Gitongu, M. K., Kingi, W., & Uzel, J. M. M. (2016). Determinants of Employees' Performance of State Parastatals in Kenya: Kenya Ports Authority. *International Journal of Humanities and Social Science*, 6(10), 197–204.

Griffin, M. A., Neal, A., & Parker, S. K. (2007). A new model of work role performance: Positive behavior in uncertain and interdependent contexts. *Academy of Management Journal*, 50(2), 327–347. 10.5465/amj.2007.24634438

Grobelna, A. (2019). Effects of individual and job characteristics on hotel contact employees' work engagement and their performance outcomes: A case study from Poland. *International Journal of Contemporary Hospitality Management*, 31(1), 349–369. 10.1108/IJCHM-08-2017-0501

Gruman, J. A., & Saks, A. M. (2011). Performance Management and Employee Engagement. *Human Resource Management Review*, 21(2), 123–136. 10.1016/j.hrmr.2010.09.004

Guo, L., & Xu, L. (2021). The effects of digital transformation on firm performance: Evidence from China's manufacturing sector. *Sustainability (Basel)*, 13(22), 12844. 10.3390/su132212844

Haefner, N., Wincent, J., Parida, V., & Gassmann, O. (2021). Artificial intelligence and innovation management: A review, framework, and research agenda. *Technological Forecasting and Social Change*, 162, 1–18. 10.1016/j.techfore.2020.120392

Huang, M. H., & Rust, R. T. (2018). Artificial intelligence in service. *Journal of Service Research*, 21(2), 155–172. 10.1177/1094670517752459

Huysman, M. (2020). Information systems research on artificial intelligence and work: A commentary on "Robo-Apocalypse cancelled? Reframing the automation and future of work debate". *Journal of Information Technology*, 35(4), 307–309. 10.1177/0268396220926511

Ilomo, O., & Mlavi, B. (2016). The Availability of Teaching and Learning Facilities and Their Effects on Academic Performance in Ward Secondary Schools in Muheza-Tanzania. *International Journal of Education and Research*, 4, 571–581.

Kaplan, A., & Haenlein, M. (2019). Siri, Siri, in my hand: Who's the fairest in the land? On the interpretations, illustrations, and implications of artificial intelligence. *Business Horizons*, 62(1), 15–25. 10.1016/j.bushor.2018.08.004

Kar, A. K., Choudhary, S. K., & Singh, V. K. (2022). How can artificial intelligence impact sustainability: A systematic literature review. *Journal of Cleaner Production*, 1(1), 1–17. 10.1016/j.jclepro.2022.134120

Kaya, F., Aydin, F., Schepman, A., Rodway, P., Yetişensoy, O., & Demir Kaya, M. (2024). The roles of personality traits, AI anxiety, and demographic factors in attitudes towards artificial intelligence. *International Journal of Human-Computer Interaction*, 40(2), 497–514. 10.1080/10447318.2022.2151730

Kim, P. T., & Bodie, M. T. (2021). Artificial intelligence and the challenges of workplace discrimination and privacy. *J Labor Employment Law*, 35(2), 289–315.

Kirkman, B. L., & Rosen, B. (1999). Beyond Self-Management: Antecedents and Consequences of Team Empowerment. *Academy of Management Journal*, 42(1), 58–74. 10.2307/256874

Kong, H., Yuan, Y., Baruch, Y., Bu, N., Jiang, X., & Wang, K. (2021). Influences of artificial intelligence (AI) awareness on career competency and job burnout. *International Journal of Contemporary Hospitality Management*, 33(2), 717–734. 10.1108/IJCHM-07-2020-0789

Kopka, A., & Grashof, N. (2022). Artificial intelligence: Catalyst or barrier on the path to sustainability? *Technological Forecasting and Social Change*, 175, 121318. 10.1016/j.techfore.2021.121318

Lichtenthaler, U. (2020). Extremes of acceptance: Employee attitudes toward artificial intelligence. *The Journal of Business Strategy*, 41(5), 39–45. 10.1108/JBS-12-2018-0204

Makarius, E. E., Mukherjee, D., Fox, J. D., & Fox, A. K. (2020). Rising with the machines: A sociotechnical framework for bringing artificial intelligence into the organization. *Journal of Business Research*, 120, 262–273. 10.1016/j.jbusres.2020.07.045

Makridakis, S. (2017). The forthcoming Artificial Intelligence (AI) revolution: Its impact on society and firms. *Futures*, 90, 46–60. 10.1016/j.futures.2017.03.006

Malik, N., Tripathi, S. N., Kar, A. K., & Gupta, S. (2022). Impact of artificial intelligence on employees working in industry 4.0 led organizations. *International Journal of Manpower*, 43(2), 334–354. 10.1108/IJM-03-2021-0173

Mondy, R. W., & Martocchio, J. J. (2016). *Human Resource Management* (14th ed.). Pearson Education Limited.

Nazareno, L., & Schiff, D. S. (2021). The impact of automation and artificial intelligence on worker well-being. *Technology in Society*, 67, 101679. 10.1016/j.techsoc.2021.101679

Park, J., & Woo, S. E. (2022). Who likes artificial intelligence? Personality predictors of attitudes toward artificial intelligence. *The Journal of Psychology*, 156(1), 68–94. 10.1080/00223980.2021.201210935015615

Pillai, R., & Sivathanu, B. (2020). Adoption of artificial intelligence (AI) for talent acquisition in IT/ITeS organizations. *Benchmarking*, 27(9), 2599–2629. 10.1108/BIJ-04-2020-0186

Riyanto, S., Sutrisno, A., & Hapzi, A. (2017). The Impact of Working Motivation and Working Environment on Employees Performance in Indonesia Stock Exchange. *International Review of Management and Marketing*, 7(3), 342–348.

Schepman, A., & Rodway, P. (2020). Initial validation of the general attitudes towards Artificial Intelligence Scale. *Computers in Human Behavior Reports*, 1(1), 100014. 10.1016/j.chbr.2020.10001434235291

Schepman, A., & Rodway, P. (2022). The General Attitudes towards Artificial Intelligence Scale (GAAIS): Confirmatory validation and associations with personality, corporate distrust, and general trust. *International Journal of Human-Computer Interaction*, 39(13), 2724–2741. 10.1080/10447318.2022.2085400

Sothan, S. (2019). The determinants of academic performance: Evidence from a Cambodian University. *Studies in Higher Education*, 44(11), 2096–3111. 10.1080/03075079.2018.1496408

Stahl, B. C., Andreou, A., Brey, P., Hatzakis, T., Kirichenko, A., Macnish, K., Laulh'e Shaelou, S., Patel, A., Ryan, M., & Wright, D. (2021). Artificial intelligence for human flourishing – beyond principles for machine learning. *Journal of Business Research*, 124, 374–388. 10.1016/j.jbusres.2020.11.030

Thesmar, D., Sraer, D., Pinheiro, L., Dadson, N., Veliche, R., & Greenberg, P. (2019). Combining the power of artificial intelligence with the richness of healthcare claims data: Opportunities and challenges. *PharmacoEconomics*, 37(6), 745–752. 10.1007/s40273-019-00777-630848452

Tschang, F. T., & Almirall, E. (2021). Artificial intelligence as augmenting automation: Implications for employment. *The Academy of Management Perspectives*, 35(4), 642–659. 10.5465/amp.2019.0062

Vrontis, D., Christofi, M., Pereira, V., Tarba, S., Makrides, A., & Trichina, E. (2021). Artificial intelligence, robotics, advanced technologies and human resource management: A systematic review. *International Journal of Human Resource Management*, 1(1), 1–30.

Wijayati, D. T., Rahman, Z., Fahrullah, A., Rahman, M. F. W., Arifah, I. D. C., & Kautsar, A. (2022). A study of artificial intelligence on employee performance and work engagement: The moderating role of change leadership. *International Journal of Manpower*, 43(2), 486–512. 10.1108/IJM-07-2021-0423

Wright, S. A., & Schultz, A. E. (2018). The rising tide of artificial intelligence and business automation: Developing an ethical framework. *Business Horizons*, 61(6), 823–832. 10.1016/j.bushor.2018.07.001

Wu, J., & Shang, S. (2020). Managing uncertainty in AI-enabled decision making and achieving sustainability. *Sustainability (Basel)*, 12(21), 8758. 10.3390/su12218758

Złotowski, J., Yogeeswaran, K., & Bartneck, C. (2017). Can we control it? Autonomous robots threaten human identity, uniqueness, safety, and resources. *International Journal of Human-Computer Studies*, 100, 48–54. 10.1016/j.ijhcs.2016.12.008

ADDITIONAL READING

Holtel, S. (2016). Artificial Intelligence creates a wicked problem for enterprise. *Procedia Computer Science*, 99, 171–180. 10.1016/j.procs.2016.09.109

Kumar, S. P. L. (2017). State of the art-intense review on artificial intelligence systems application in process planning and manufacturing. *Engineering Applications of Artificial Intelligence*, 65, 294–329. 10.1016/j.engappai.2017.08.005

Mikalef, P., & Gupta, M. (2021). Artificial intelligence capability: Conceptualization, measurement calibration, and empirical study on its impact on organizational creativity and firm performance. *Information & Management*, 58(3), 103434. 10.1016/j.im.2021.103434

Raisch, S., & Krakowski, S. (2021). Artificial intelligence and management: The automation–augmentation paradox. *Academy of Management Review*, 46(1), 192–210. 10.5465/amr.2018.0072

KEY TERMS AND DEFINITIONS

Artificial Intelligence: Artificial intelligence is technology that enables computers and machines to simulate human intelligence and problem-solving capabilities.

Jop Performance: Job performance assesses whether a person performs a job well. Job performance, studied academically as part of industrial and organizational psychology, also forms a part of human resources management.

Structural Equation Model: Structural equation modeling is a multivariate statistical analysis technique that is used to analyze structural relationships. This technique is the combination of factor analysis and multiple regression analysis, and it is used to analyze the structural relationship between measured variables and latent constructs.

Chapter 6
From Data to Decisions:
Harnessing AI and Big Data for Advanced Business Analytics

Ashy Sebastian
Christ University, Bengaluru, India

Veerta Tantia
https://orcid.org/0000-0002-8487-5175
Christ University, Bengaluru, India

ABSTRACT

This chapter focuses on the idea of business analytics through AI and aims to address how AI has emerged as a powerful force in augmenting and replacing traditional human-computer interactions in the realm of business analytics. AI-powered analytics can uncover hidden patterns, detect anomalies, and automate decision-making processes, significantly augmenting the efficiency and accuracy of data analysis. Thus, the purpose of this chapter is two-fold. First, the chapter sheds light on business analytics, big data, and big data analytics through AI. It delves into the theories of machine and deep learning and their synergy with big data analytics. Secondly, the authors analyze a case study to substantiate our theory. ML-based prediction models using stock market data are developed to underline the significance of adopting AI-driven approaches for business analytics.

INTRODUCTION

Human-computer interaction (HCI) is "the research area that studies the interaction between people and computers, which involves designing, implementing, and evaluating interactive systems in the context of the user's task and work" (Dix et al.,

DOI: 10.4018/979-8-3693-3033-3.ch006

2004). This can be thought of as an attempt to communicate between two powerful information processing units (a computer and a human) over a narrowband and very limited interface (Tate, 2002). Human cognition, including analytical reasoning and decision-making, is embedded in a computational framework with automated analysis in the human-computer model. It has varied applications for health care (electronic health records, medical imaging systems), education (digital classrooms), gaming platforms (PS4, Xbox One), speech recognition (Alexa, Siri) and in industry and business. HCI has played a crucial role in enhancing business analytics by providing a user-friendly interface that enables professionals to interact with complex data and extract valuable insights. Through intuitive design and interactive visualization tools, HCI has facilitated the interpretation of vast datasets, allowing businesses to make informed decisions and identify patterns that may have otherwise gone unnoticed.

However, the landscape of business analytics has undergone a transformative shift with the advent of artificial intelligence (AI) which enables computers to perform human-like tasks by mimicking cognitive functions such as learning, reasoning, and problem-solving. AI has not only automated many tasks involved in data analysis but has also introduced machine and deep learning algorithms capable of discerning intricate patterns and predicting future trends. This evolution has significantly reduced the reliance on manual interaction in the analytics process, enabling businesses to process and interpret data at an unprecedented speed and scale. While HCI remains crucial for facilitating human understanding and decision-making, AI has emerged as a powerful force in augmenting and, in some cases, replacing traditional human-computer interactions in business analytics. On the other hand, in the information era, huge volumes of data from various sources are accessible to decision-makers. The term "Big data" has been coined to encapsulate this data's unprecedented volume, variety, and velocity, highlighting the need for advanced tools and analytics to derive meaningful insights and make informed decisions in this data-rich landscape.

Fan et al. (2015) introduced a marketing-mix framework aimed at effectively utilising big data for marketing intelligence, offering a structured approach for decision-making in marketing based on insights from big data analytics. A. Sharma et al. (2022) delved into the realm of big data in the healthcare industry, highlighting its wide-ranging impact across various stakeholders such as healthcare systems, insurers, researchers, and governmental bodies. The study emphasized the pivotal role of big data analytics in shaping the future landscape of healthcare delivery, drawing from diverse and abundant data sources, both structured and unstructured. Moreover, Wells et al. (2016) delved into the realm of big data in the healthcare industry, highlighting its wide-ranging impact across various stakeholders such as healthcare systems, insurers, researchers, and governmental bodies. The study emphasized the pivotal role of big data analytics in shaping the future landscape of healthcare delivery, drawing from diverse and abundant data sources, both structured and unstructured. Iqbal et al. (2020) explored the synergistic potential of big data and Computational Intelligence (CI) in addressing real-world challenges in smart cities, identifying numerous areas where innovative applications can be developed by leveraging these powerful tools. Nevertheless, despite these advancements, existing literature lacks research that integrates theories of big data analytics with AI specifically tailored for business analytics.

Hence, this chapter elucidates the imperative of a symbiotic relationship between AI and big data analytics for business decisions. The primary objective of this chapter is to address this current gap in the understanding and application of business analytics, big data, and big data analytics through the integration of AI.

By delving into the theoretical foundations of machine and deep learning and their synergy with big data analytics, the chapter aims to furnish a thorough framework for organizations seeking to harness the full potential of these technological advancements. Our goal is to enlighten businesses regarding the benefits of AI for optimizing operations, improving decision-making processes, and fostering innovation through the incorporation of machine and deep learning techniques. Secondly, in order to provide a more comprehensive understanding of the theories discussed, the study will also include a case study on the implementation of machine learning algorithm on the Indian stock market data.

Furthermore, this chapter contributes to the existing body of literature by seamlessly integrating key concepts from business analytics, big data, and artificial intelligence. By examining the theories of machine and deep learning in conjunction with big data analytics, this chapter presents a comprehensive framework, thereby expanding scholarly understanding and providing practical insights for organizations navigating the complexities of data-driven environments. Consequently, the benefits arising from this wealth of knowledge and information can affect research in numerous ways.

The subsequent order of the chapter is as follows:

First, there is a brief discussion of the method followed. Second, the narrative explains in detail the concept of business analytics and its significance. Third, big data, big data analytics through AI, machine and deep learning are examined. Fourth, the case study is described in detail. Finally, the conclusions are discussed.

METHOD

Within the confines of this chapter, the authors' scholarly inquiry converges upon the intricate interplay among business analytics, big data, and the application of big data analytics through AI. Our scholarly pursuits delve into the underpinning theories of machine and deep learning, unraveling their intricate synergy with the domain of big data analytics. The goal is to explain how these advanced learning theories can transform and improve the way data is analyzed in business. The chapter also includes a case study positioned to empirically substantiate the theoretical framework expounded. This empirical exposition serves to underscore the pragmatic implications and real-world applicability of the synergistic amalgamation of AI, big data, and analytics theories within the contemporary academic discourse on business dynamics.

Business Analytics

The term "analytics" is a relatively recent concept that is rapidly gaining recognition and prominence in both business and academic spheres, unlike anything witnessed in recent history. It can be defined as "the discovery of meaningful patterns – new and novel information and knowledge – in data."

Due to its surging popularity as a buzzword, analytics is now replacing several formerly prevalent terms like intelligence, mining, and discovery. For example, the term business intelligence is now business analytics; customer intelligence is customer analytics, web mining is web analytics, and knowledge discovery is data analytics (Delen & Ram, 2018). Business analytics encompasses all processes that facilitate the transformation of data into actionable insights, contributing to improved and expedited decision-making. It has emerged as one of the most dynamic research domains in both academics and industry or practical contexts.

Why is Analytics Important?

The modern business world comprises incredibly complex systems, which are crucial to science, the economy, and even to daily life. Therefore, the main intellectual and scientific tasks of the 21st Century are to comprehend such complex systems, describe them mathematically, use them for prediction, and finally govern them. (Barabasi, 2016)

Analyzing extensive data samples through analytics unveils and harnesses transformative shifts in business. It enables us to identify what has changed and guides us in determining the appropriate reactions. According to Kohavi et al. (2002) the strategic significance of business analytics has spurred notable advancements in business applications, especially in areas that analyze customers' data. These applications have been used to 'reduce customer attrition, improve customer profitability, increase the value of e-commerce purchases, and enhance the response of direct mail and email marketing campaigns. The application of business analytics in areas like finance, marketing, production, manufacturing, human resources and research and development have also been described in literature (Kohavi et al., 2002; Davenport, 2006; R. Sharma et al., 2010) .Recent studies in business analytics suggests that there is a statistically significant relationship between analytical capabilities and the performance of supply chain operations.(Trkman et al., 2010). Davenport (2006b) opined that organizations will be able to create competitive advantage with the use of business analytics. Likewise, Trkman et al. (2010) argued that the capacity to make lucrative business decisions by leveraging extensive volumes of both internal and external data is feasible exclusively through the application of business analytics. This technology enables the systematic analysis of data collected in substantial quantities on a recurring basis. Analytics empowers managers to make decisions based on statistical facts. These factual insights can guide decisions regarding the future growth of the company by assessing the market and competition over the long term. Through data analysis, managers can incorporate these facts into informed operational decisions.(Niu et al., 2021)

Furthermore, the incorporation of analytics is thought to enhance our ability to generate increasingly dependable information regarding the fundamental relationships among focal variables. This, in turn, enables the production of more pertinent research findings (Breiman, 2003). Consequently, it is crucial for business researchers to integrate analytics into their array of research methods, recognizing it as a novel and promising tool. Hence, it is crucial for business researchers to incorporate analytics as a novel tool to their arsenal of research methods. The predominant focus in business decision analytics research revolves around tasks ranging from developing algorithms to formulating methodologies and constructing applications or solutions.

Big data

Data is the building block upon which any organization thrives. Anything ranging from customer names and addresses to products available, to purchases made, and to employees hired has become essential for day-to-day continuity.

Recently, a notable paradigm shift in data capture and utilization unfolded, primarily driven by the widespread adoption of the Internet. This shift led to the emergence of new channels for data generation, facilitated by expanded storage capacities and diverse data collection methods. Moreover, the decreasing cost of data storage has prompted organizations to maximize the utility of vast data reservoirs This continuous evolution has resulted in an abundance of easily accessible data, generated every second, necessitating analysis for value extraction.

Among the various data sources, social network and media data pose particularly interesting challenges due to their richness in information content and the inherent complexities of analyzing unstructured data. The term 'Big Data' has recently been coined to underscore the unique challenges presented by these new data streams.

Big data is a concept which does not conform to the normal structure of the traditional database. Big data refers to data sets characterized by their extensive scale, distribution, diversity, and/or timeliness, necessitating the application of innovative technical architectures, analytics and tools. These are essential to extract insights that unveil new avenues of business value.

Primarily, three main features characterized big data: volume, variety, and velocity, or the three V's. Recently, two more have been added – veracity and value. Presently, enterprises are delving into extensive datasets with intricate details to unearth previously unknown facts and insights.

Big Data Analytics Through AI

In this digital era, decision-makers now have access to vast volumes of data. Big data are datasets that are challenging to manage with conventional tools and procedures because they are not only large in size but are also highly variable and rapidly changing. Owing to the exponential growth of this type of data, methods for managing and deriving insights and value from these datasets must be investigated and developed. Moreover, decision-makers must be able to draw insightful conclusions from a wide variety of quickly evolving data, including social network data, everyday transactional data, and consumer interactions. Big data analytics, which is the application of sophisticated analytics techniques on big data, can be used to generate such value (Chong & Shi, 2015).

Big data analytics is a fast-growing and influential practice (Russom, 2011).It involves extracting value from vast amounts of data, leading to the creation of new market prospects and optimizing customer retention (Sujitparapitaya et al., 2012). This Big data transcends sheer data volume; it encompasses an unprecedented diversity of data types arriving at varied speeds and frequencies. Through the application of advanced analytics, enterprises can systematically analyze big data to comprehend the present state of their operations and monitor continually evolving facets, including intricate aspects of customer behavior. This analytical approach facilitates the exploration of data hitherto untapped for business intelligence (BI) or analytical purposes, underscoring the transformative potential of big data analytics in fostering strategic decision-making and innovation within academic and scholarly contexts. Big data analytics explores granular details of business operations and customer interactions that seldom find their way into a data warehouse or standard report.(Russom, 2011) .The field of big data analytics delves into minute aspects of consumer interactions and corporate processes that are rarely included in typical reports or data warehouses. In the contemporary landscape, big data empowers business analytics to offer insights that facilitate a deeper understanding of customers, enhance marketing technology, enable personalization, and pinpoint real-time problems and opportunities for companies (Niu et al., 2021).Various methods are employed to extract meaningful insights from vast and complex datasets. One prominent method is the utilization of artificial intelligence (AI), which has emerged as a cornerstone.

Given the sheer scale and complexity of big data, there is a need for advanced analytical tools, and this is where AI excels. Its development has also brought more opportunities to many fields. Especially after the cooperation between AI and business, whether in finance or the Internet industry, it has brought about more possibilities for the development of enterprises (Kell et al., 2018). Machine and deep learning algorithms, subsets of AI, are particularly adept at processing massive datasets, identifying patterns, and making predictions. In turn, the insights generated by AI models contribute to refining and optimizing big data analytics. AI-powered analytics can uncover hidden patterns, detect anomalies, and automate decision-making processes, significantly augmenting the efficiency and accuracy of data analysis. Big data analytics using AI represents a powerful combination that revolutionizes how organizations extract insights from vast and complex datasets.

Machine Learning

Machine learning is a branch of AI that studies how computers can learn without being explicitly programmed. The goal of machine learning is to analyze data structure and fit that into models that users can comprehend. It is also regarded as a combination of algorithms for automatically detecting patterns in data and then using them to forecast future data or complex decisions. Big data analytics have evolved significantly through the utilization of machine learning algorithms and have witnessed growing prominence across a spectrum of application domains, including the realm of stock markets. This is primarily because machine learning algorithms don't need any assumptions about the data and often attain superior prediction accuracy compared to econometric and statistical models (Zhong & Enke, 2019). ML problems are divided into two: supervised and unsupervised techniques.

In supervised machine learning we train the algorithm using labelled data, i.e., the data is already labelled with the correct answer. We have predictors (x) and targets (Y) in supervised learning, and we employ an algorithm to map the relation between them. The purpose is to estimate the mapping function to anticipate the output variables (Y) given new input data (x).

Supervised learning can be bifurcated into classification and regression.

Classification/models are applied in situations where the output variable(Y) is binary or categorical, such as Yes' or' No', 'Defective or non-defective', 'Success' or' Failure'. If the dependent variable is a real value, for instance a distinct number, price, income and height, then regression problems and models are utilized. In unsupervised ML, the model is not trained using labelled data or the output is unknown. It learns to identify patterns and categories data into different clusters on its own.

Deep Learning

Deep learning is a subset of ML which uses artificial neural networks (ANN) to solve problems. They are inspired by the biological neurons that constitute the human brain. Our sensory organs sense the outside environment and give signals or inputs to brains. These signals are sent to our brains via neurons which are the most basic part of our neural system. When the brain receives these signals, it processes and interprets them to give outputs, which enables us to take appropriate actions promptly. When you create a replica of such a system in an artificial environment, we call it ANN, which consists of an input layer, hidden layer and output layer. In one layer, each node is connected to every other node in the next layer. With an increase in the number of hidden layers, it is possible to make the network deeper. Neural networks with multiple hidden layers, enables the creation of deep neural networks (DNNs). The term 'deep' in deep learning refers to the increased depth of the neural network architecture, achieved by incorporating multiple hidden layers between the input and output layers. Figure 1 shows an illustration of a deep neural network:

Figure 1. Illustration of a deep neural network

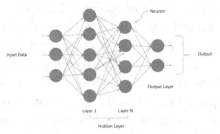

(https://miro.medium.com/v2/resize:fit:1400/1*KHs1Chs6TCJDTIlQVylJxg.png)
Note: Consists of an input layer, two hidden layers and an output layer.

Both ML and DL play crucial roles as integral components of big data analytics. They provide advanced analytical techniques to extract valuable insights, patterns, and predictions from large and complex datasets. This integration represents a paradigm shift, empowering businesses, and researchers to derive deeper, more nuanced insights from the wealth of data available in today's interconnected world. The following are their various use cases in business.

1. Predictive Analytics:

ML and DL algorithms are employed for predictive modelling to forecast future trends and behaviors based on historical data. This is vital for tasks such as predicting customer churn, demand forecasting, and financial market analysis within the context of big data.

2. Classification and Clustering:

Machine learning algorithms, including deep learning models, are used for classification tasks to categorize data into predefined classes. Clustering algorithms help group similar data points. These techniques are applied in areas like customer segmentation, fraud detection, and anomaly identification in big datasets.

3. Feature Extraction:

Deep learning, especially with neural networks, is effective in automatically extracting relevant features from raw and unstructured data. This is particularly valuable in big data analytics when dealing with complex data types like images, audio, and text.

4. Natural Language Processing (NLP):

Machine learning, including deep learning techniques, is extensively used in natural language processing applications within big data analytics. Sentiment analysis, text summarization, and language translation are examples of how NLP can be applied to process and analyze large volumes of textual data.

5. Image and Speech Recognition:

Deep learning models, such as Convolutional Neural Networks (CNNs) for images and Recurrent Neural Networks (RNNs) for speech, are employed in big data analytics for tasks such as image recognition, object detection, and speech-to-text conversion.

6. Recommendation Systems:

ML algorithms, including collaborative filtering and content-based recommendation systems, are utilized in big data analytics to provide personalized recommendations. This is commonly seen in applications like e-commerce, streaming services, and social media.

7. Anomaly Detection:

ML and DL models are employed to detect unusual patterns or outliers within big data sets, aiding in identifying potential fraud, faults, or anomalies. This is crucial in various industries such as finance, cybersecurity and manufacturing.

8. Optimization and Automation:

ML is applied for optimizing various aspects of big data analytics workflows, including model selection, hyperparameter tuning, and data preprocessing. Automated machine learning (AutoML) tools help to streamline the model development process.

9. Scalability:

Both big data technologies and machine learning frameworks need to be scalable. Distributed computing frameworks, such as Apache Spark, and distributed training capabilities in deep learning frameworks, like TensorFlow, enable the parallel processing needed for handling large-scale data.

10. Real-time Analytics:

ML and DL models are increasingly being deployed for real-time analytics applications, enabling organizations to make instant decisions based on streaming data. This is crucial in scenarios such as dynamic pricing, fraud detection, and IoT (Internet of Things) applications.

In summary, machine learning and deep learning are integral components of big data analytics, providing sophisticated techniques to extract meaningful insights, automate decision-making processes, and uncover patterns within vast and complex datasets. The synergy between these technologies has significantly enhanced the capabilities of organizations in various industries.

CASE STUDY

In this case study, the authors delve into the application of AI-powered business analytics within the financial market, seeking to substantiate the previously posited theories. The selection of the financial market as the focal domain for investigation in this study is underpinned by its inherent characteristics that render it a compelling context for the application of advanced analytical methodologies. The financial sector's data-intensive nature, marked by real-time generation of voluminous and dynamic datasets, presents a fertile ground for the deployment of business analytics. Moreover, the complex and fluctuating environment of financial markets necessitates sophisticated tools for risk management, predictive modeling, and decision-making, aligning seamlessly with the capabilities of AI. The financial domain's strategic importance, characterized by its influence on global economies and investment decisions, accentuates the significance of examining the practicality and efficacy of AI-driven business analytics within this context.

Our analysis centers on the profound impact of the recent black swan event, the COVID-19 pandemic, on three prominent Indian monopoly stocks. By meticulously examining the intricate dynamics triggered by this unprecedented event, our study aims to provide a comprehensive understanding of how these stocks were influenced within the volatile financial landscape. Subsequently, the authors propose and implement machine learning-based prediction models, leveraging the capabilities of AI, to forecast and navigate the potential fluctuations in the market. This case study not only serves as an empirical illustration of the theories presented earlier but also underscores the practical application of AI-powered business analytics in enhancing predictive capabilities and decision-making processes within the dynamic realm of financial markets.

What is a Monopoly?

A company is said to enjoy monopoly power when it has a dominant position over an industry or sector in which it can exclude any other viable competitor. In a monopoly market, a single seller controls the price and output. He sells a unique product that has no close substitutes in the market. This makes the entry of any other seller impossible. Monopolies also possess some information that is unknown to other sellers. In finance, monopoly companies are termed MOAT stocks. Moats are either entrance barriers such as large capital, government limitations, or a competitive advantage in which a company has made it difficult for others to compete.

A monopoly or MOAT stock is synonymous with a gold mine for a value investor. MOAT stock will generate significant returns in the long run. However, investors should be cautious because these stocks, like those of other blue-chip businesses, are often overvalued, resulting in reduced returns or losses. Ali & Khan (2018) reported that socio-economic events often affect the variability of stock price returns. The COVID-19 pandemic is one such event that witnessed the downfall of even the major stock market players.

Various studies were undertaken to analyze and study the impact of the pandemic all over the world. In their studies, Dev Mahendra & Sengupta (2020) and Verma & Sinha (2020) analyzed the impact of COVID-19 on the Indian economy. They mentioned that the crisis hit India when its GDP growth slowed down, and unemployment rose due to the economy's subpar recent performance. All major sectors of the economy were severely hit, and equity markets were no exception. "The equity market has been hitting new lows every day since the outbreak of COVID-19. In March 2020, panic selling due to the pandemic shaved off 23% market capitalization of companies listed on the National Stock Exchange (NSE) within just a month."[1]

It is observed from the extant body of studies that the current literature includes research on the impact of COVID-19 on NSE indices but lacks any investigations into monopoly players. Hence, this paper attempts to fill this void by examining the performance of major Indian monopoly stocks after the global pandemic outbreak from January 2020 to March 2022. For our study, the authors choose three monopoly stocks- IRCTC, Nestle India Ltd, and ITC Ltd which enjoy monopoly power in three different sectors.

Methodology

In this section, the authors describe the dual levels of the proposed study. The primary level consists of an analysis of MOAT stocks. The second level involves developing machine learning models for the stocks mentioned above. Figure 2 depicts the flowchart of the proposed methodology.

Analysis of MOAT Stocks

This section analyses the effect of COVID-19 on MOAT stocks and draws inferences. The revenues and profits of previous quarters, from March 2020, are analyzed to learn the impact of the pandemic on the company's' cash flows and revenues.

Develop Machine Learning Models

After analyzing the stocks, the authors build three machine learning models for modelling time series prediction of MOAT stocks' closing price. Each of these models are compared to arrive at the best technique.

Figure 2. Proposed methodology

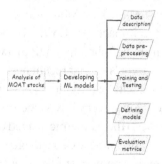

Data description and pre-processing. India's initial COVID-19 case was documented on January 31, 2020. Subsequently, the government opted for a comprehensive, nationwide lockdown from March 25, 2020, the first phase which was regarded as the first wave. This was followed by a more limited lockdown on April 5, 2021, marking the second wave. In January 2023, we witnessed the third wave.

In this regard, the proposed model has taken the historical stock prices of IRCTC, Nestle India Ltd and ITC Ltd from 1 January 2020, the start of the first wave till 31 March 2022, the end of the financial year. The total dataset consisted of 556 trading days. The data was obtained from the official NSE website, and the resulting sample consists of Open, High, Low and Close values. Open, High, and Low values are the input variables and Close value is the output or target variable. The authors choose close price as closing price reflects all the activities of the stock for any day (Adebiyi et al., 2014).

Data quality plays a crucial role in improving prediction accuracy. Hence, it's essential to preprocess raw data before using it for model building. The collected sample consisting of 556 trading days did not have any duplicates and NAN values. The boxplots in Fig. 1 show the distribution of the datasets. The outliers identified with boxplots are removed using the winsorisation technique as followed by Cao & Tay (2001) and Zhong & Enke (2019).

It was observed that the outliers are eliminated, and the distribution of transformed data is more symmetrical and closer to normal after adjustments. After winsorisation the min-max scaler is used to normalize the dataset. This ensures that all values fall within a range of [0,1]. Both these techniques will improve the predictive power of the proposed models.

Training and Testing. Prior to using machine learning algorithms, the cleaned datasets were divided into two categories: training data (80%; 444 samples) and testing data (2%; 112 samples). Scikit-learn library was used to build all the prediction models for both training and testing (Pedregosa et al., 2011).The machine learning models were first fitted on the training data with labelled output, so that the algorithm identifies and learns the relationship between input and output variables. The trained algorithm was then tested on the test data set to predict future stock prices.

Defining ML models. This study attempts to construct Linear Regression, Support Vector Machine and Random Forest for our study.

- *Linear regression*

Linear regression is a popular machine learning algorithm that belongs to the supervised learning technique. This algorithm models the relationship between variables using linear predictor functions, while values for unknown variables are determined using the known variables. A linear regression analysis helps us to assess how much variability of Y is explained by 'x'. The equation is

$$Y = C + b1x1 + b2x2 + b3x3 + \ldots bnxn \quad (1)$$

Where Y is the dependent variable, x is the independent variable, b is the coefficient and c is the intercept.

- *Support Vector Machine*

Support Vector Machines introduced by Vapnik (1999) are supervised learning techniques initially developed for pattern recognition. But their usage has now been extended to solve non-linear regression problems including time series data (Cao & Tay, 2001).

This investigation uses an SVR (Support Vector Regressor) together with RBF (Radial Basis Function) as the kernel function of the SVMs as followed by Meesad & Rasel (2013) and Pyo et al. (2017). SVR focuses on support vectors, which are data points that have the most significant influence on the regression model. The RBF kernel tends to emphasis support vectors in regions with the most complex and changing patterns, which can be particularly valuable for capturing critical turning points or anomalies in stock prices.

- ### *Random forest*

Random Forest is a supervised machine learning technique that relies on the decision tree algorithm. It is applicable for both Classification and Regression problems in machine learning. For building an RF model, the bagging method is employed to select multiple sample data sets from the original training data. This process results in the creation of N distinct training data sets. Next, the primary task involves training N individual decision tree models using these N training data sets. Subsequently, the Random Forest is formed by assembling these N decision trees. In regression scenarios as in our case, the final result is derived by computing the mean of the predicted values from the N decision trees (Prinzie & Van den Poel, 2008; Yuan et al., 2020)

The proposed study will use the above-mentioned machine learning algorithms to predict three monopoly stocks in the Indian market.

Evaluation metrics. Performance evaluation metrics were used to assess the accuracy of the models built. Since our problem is a multi- class regression problem, Root Mean Squared Error (RMSE) and R^2 are used to evaluate the error function (Henrique et al., 2018; Aldhyani & Alzahrani, 2022; Nayak et al., 2022; Lachaab & Omri, 2023). The RMSE is derived by taking the square root of the mean of the squared difference between the predicted and actual target values. R-squared assesses the model's ability to explain the variation in target variables, i.e., it evaluates the quality of the fit. Higher R^2 and lower RMSE indicate higher accuracy.

RESULTS AND DISCUSSIONS

Impact of COVID-19 on MOAT Stocks

IRCTC

Indian Railways Catering and Tourism Corporation (IRCTC) is the only company licensed by Indian Railways to provide online train tickets, operate catering facilities and sell bottled water at all stations and trains in India. They do not have a competitive advantage in terms of a product or business proposition. They enjoy monopoly power since they are regulated by the government which prohibits private players from entering the market.

The revenues slashed to Rs.131.33 Cr from 575.72 Cr after the first lockdown in June 2020 quarter. The June 2021 quarter showed a fall from Rs.338.79 Cr to 243.37 Cr. The net profit also fell to Rs.-24.60 Cr from 135.14 Cr and to Rs.82.52 Cr from 103.79 Cr in June 2020 and June 2021 quarters respectively. The net cash flow fell to Rs. - 252.37Cr in March 2021 from Rs.137.32 Cr in March 2020. Over the last five years, revenue has grown at a yearly rate of -9.62%, vs the industry average of 17.59%.[2]

Figure 3 shows that the stock made a dip during the first COVID wave. Nevertheless, it has been moving sideways post the first wave. It touched an all-time high of 6000 after the second wave, but slashed over 400% by the end of 2021.

NESTLE India Ltd.

Nestlé India Limited is the Indian subsidiary of Swiss multinational Nestlé, the world's largest food and beverages company. It was founded in 1959 and has headquarters in Gurgaon. Nestle holds a monopoly of 96.5% in Cerelac. As of August 2022, it had a market capitalisation of Rs.188,230 Cr, PE ratio of 82 and ROCE 147%. The PE ratio seems to be on the higher side making it an infeasible option to invest. But it is justified by the growth it exhibits in its ROCE.

The net cash flow was Rs. -1223.29 Cr in December 2019, which rose to 177.13 Cr in December 2020 and then had a massive fall to -1704.30 Cr in December 2021. The revenues of June 2020, June 2021 and June 2022 quarters were Rs.3050.48 Cr, Rs.3476.7 Cr and Rs.4036.57 Cr respectively. Comparatively, the revenues have remained consistent without large fluctuations during the pandemic and have been on a rise since December 2021.[3]

It is evident from Figure 4 that the stock has been on an uptrend with higher highs and higher lows. The first COVID wave of 2020 led to a dip, but the stock regained its momentum and touched 18000. The second wave also resulted in a correction, but the stock has been on an uptrend since then breaking the previous highs. Hence, the stock was corrected during the pandemic and recovered soon.

ITC Ltd.

ITC Limited is a multinational conglomerate company based in Kolkata, India, with a diversified presence across various industries such as FMCG, packaging, agribusiness, hotels, cigarettes, paperboards, software and speciality papers. ITC has a near monopoly in the cigarette segment (77%), making eight out of every ten cigarettes sold in India.

The revenues fell to Rs.10478.46 Cr from Rs.11782.16 Cr in June 2020 but, rose to Rs.14342.27 Cr in June 2021 from Rs.13079.72 Cr against the previous quarter of December 2020. The net profit has been on a rise since September 2021. The cashflows fell to Rs.-366.88 Cr from Rs.334.16 Cr in March 2021 and to Rs.-43.48 Cr in March 2022.The revenues again rose to Rs.18489.45Cr from Rs.16555.53 Cr in June 2022 quarter. The company hasn't had a major setback due to the pandemic.[4]

Figure 5 shows that ITC stock prices were slashed once the first wave hit. Thereafter, it gained momentum, and reached 220 before the second wave. The prices fell during the second wave but climbed 40 points thereafter. The stock prices always moved within a range and there was no tremendous change to be pointed out. No new highs were created. ITC played as a defensive stock. It had stable. revenues and had been distributing regular dividends of 5-7%. The valuations also seem fair but regardless of all these the stock price seems to be moving sideways within a range for quite a long time now. Hence there was a question of none, or less capital appreciation.

Despite being monopoly stocks of their sectors, all the above three stocks have varied performance in the stock market during a pandemic. This necessitated the need for a prediction model. Three machine learning models were developed, trained and tested to arrive at the best one.

Figure 3. Average stock price of IRCTC

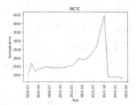

Figure 4. Average stock price of Nestle

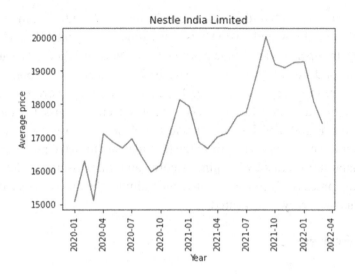

Figure 5. Average stock price of ITC

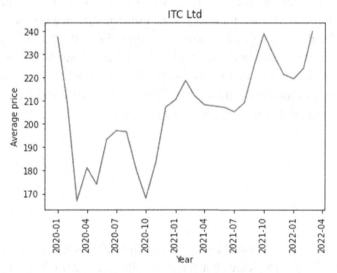

Note: X axis shows the year and y axis shows the average price of the stock.

Developing Machine Learning Models

For the purpose of building machine learning based prediction models, the data was split into training and testing sets consisting of 444 and 112 trading days respectively. In supervised machine learning techniques, an algorithm learns to make predictions or decisions by training on a labelled dataset. Hence, both training and test data were then labelled as 'X' and 'y', with the former corresponding to predictor variables and the latter to target variables. Here, in our study the predictors were the open, high and low values and the close price was the target variable. The model learns to generalise from the training data to make predictions on new, unseen data. It does this by learning patterns and relationships in the data during the training process. Once we complete the training, the model is tested on the test data set and accuracy is measured.

Linear Regression

First, the authors tried to build a linear regression model by employing open, high, and low values of the dataset, as predictor variables to predict close price which was the response variable. OLS (Ordinary Least Square) technique was used for minimising the sum of squared residuals. It was noted that there may be influential data points that affected the predictive power of linear regression models by greatly influencing the regression coefficient. An Influence Index Plot helped to identify and eliminate these influential data points. Further, variance inflation factor (VIF) was used for diagnosing collinearity or multicollinearity. Higher values signify that assessing the predictors' contribution to a model is nearly impossible. Hence, it is necessary to remove them from the prediction model. The authors plotted the Influence Index Plots and computed VIF for all the three stocks before proceeding with the final model. VIF was computed as follows

VIF=

$$\frac{1}{1 - R^2} \tag{2}$$

Figures 6, Figure 7, and Figures 8 show the Influence Index Plots of all three stocks. The Figures depicted that the Rows 456, 229 and 66 are influential data points within the entire dataset. Also, Table I shows high VIF for the opening values. Hence, they were excluded as predictor variables from the study.

The following function was used to build a linear regression model
"import statsmodels.formula.api as smf"

Figure 6. Influence index plot of IRCTC

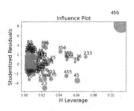

Figure 7. Influence index plots of Nestle

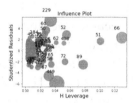

Figure 8. Influence index plots of ITC

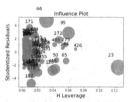

Note: The plot shows the influential data points in the datasets

Table 1. VIF

VIF			
Variables	*IRCTC*	*Nestle*	*ITC*
Open	623.9976	83.300411	120.912548
High	358.2661	62.135159	89.323675

continued on following page

Table 1. Continued

VIF			
Variables	*IRCTC*	*Nestle*	*ITC*
Low	482.6703	64.868894	91.20059 7

Note: Table shows variance inflation factor (VIF) for diagnosing multicollinearity.

The study obtained an RMSE of 3.8%,9.9% and 6% on the test data sets of IRCTC, Nestle India Ltd and ITC Ltd, respectively as against the 3.3%, 9.6% and 8% on train data. The R^2 values demonstrate that 99% of variability in the close values are explained by the high and low values. The Linear Regression Model gave the best results for IRCTC.

SVM

As mentioned in previous sections, the study used an SVR for our study. The parameters were set as kernel= 'rbf', C= 1e2, gamma= 0.1. The gamma value essentially controls the distance of influence of a single training point whereas C is the penalty parameter of the error term. The SVR was fitted on train data and then both train and test data were predicted. Table 3 shows the obtained results. The model obtained a significantly lower RMSE of 3.9%, 6% and 5.8% on the train data set and 4.6%,9% and 5.1% on the test data set. This showed that the actual and predicted values were close. It was also observed that the SVR worked best for IRCTC followed by ITC Ltd.

RF

A random forest regressor with n_estimators = 100 was fitted on the training data and then used for predicting test data. The value n_estimators refer to the number of trees in the forest. The R^2 and RMSE values are given in Table 4. As shown in the Table, the model obtained train RMSE of 4%,3% and 3.3% and test RMSE of 1.4%,10% and 7.4% on our datasets. The results further demonstrated that the random forest regressor gave the best results for IRCTC.

It was observed that all models obtained an R^2 value of 0.99, which suggested that the regression models fit the data extremely well. The vast majority of data points were very close to the regression line, indicating that the models were highly effective at explaining and predicting the behaviour of the dependent variable. Hence, now the criteria for selecting the best model is its RMSE. Figure 9 and Figure 10 show the test and train RMSE of the stocks for all three Machine Learning algorithms. It was observed that the RF models performed well on all the train data, while the SVR models performed well on test data followed by linear regression. This showed that while the RF models performed well on the training data, they might be prone to overfitting, as evidenced by their lower performance on the test data compared to SVR. On the other hand, SVR achieved a better balance between fitting the training data and generalising to unseen data. This suggested that SVR may be a more robust choice for making predictions in a real-world scenario, where the focus is on accurate forecasting of Indian monopoly stock prices during the COVID-19 pandemic. Our results are consistent with the studies of Ou & Wang (2009),Henrique et al. (2018) and Akyildirim et al. (2021) which confirmed the predictive powers of SVR. As reported by Huang et al. (2005) SVM is resistant to the overfitting problem and eventually achieves a high generalisation performance.

It was also observed that all the models gave the best and worst results for IRCTC and NESTLE datasets, respectively. This could be attributed to the variability or spread of the datasets measured in terms of standard deviation. Nestle showed the highest variability among the three datasets. Hence, it can be concluded that variability is inversely correlated to the accuracy of the model. This is consistent with the results of Henrique et al. (2018), who reported that SVR predictions tend to be more accurate and precise during periods characterised by lower price volatility.

By training on historical data, including the impact of the COVID-19 pandemic, the model may learn to recognise patterns and anomalies associated with major disruptions. If a new black swan event occurs, the model can be used to quickly assess its potential impact on Indian monopoly stocks, and act as an early warning system, thus allowing investors to make informed decisions or take preventive measures. Having access to a predictive model can help to restore investors' confidence during turbulent times. While the model may not predict the exact outcome of a black swan event, it can provide data-driven insights and guidance, reducing the level of uncertainty and panic among investors. Hence, it can be concluded that big data analytics through AI techniques like ML helps to take a proactive management approach thus enabling them to anticipate trends, identify patterns, and derive valuable insights from vast datasets.

Table 2. R^2 and RMSE of linear regression model

Company name	R^2		RMSE	
	Train	**Test**	**Train**	**Test**
IRCTC	99.8	99.8	0.033	0.038
Nestle India Ltd	99	99	0.096	0.099
ITC Ltd	99.3	99.4	0.080	0.060

Table 3. R² and RMSE of SVR model

Company name	R²		RMSE	
	Train	Test	Train	Test
IRCTC	99.8	99.7	0.039	0.046
Nestle India Ltd	99.4	99.2	0.060	0.090
ITC Ltd	99.6	99.6	0.058	0.051

Table 4. R² and RMSE of RF model

Company name	R²		RMSE	
	Train	Test	Train	Test
IRCTC	99.9	99.8	0.040	0.014
Nestle India Ltd	99.8	99	0.030	0.100
ITC Ltd	99.8	99.3	0.033	0.074

Figure 9. Test RMSE

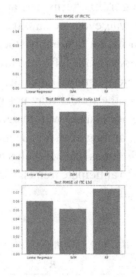

Figure 10. Train RMSE

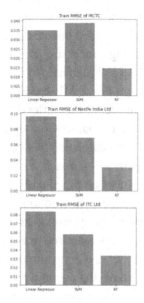

Note: Figures 9 and 10 shows the test and train RMSE of all the three models.

CONCLUSION

Big Data Analytics reflects the challenges posed by data that is extensive, unstructured, and rapidly evolving, surpassing the capabilities of traditional management methods. Across businesses, research institutions, and governments, the generation of unprecedentedly vast and complex data has become routine. Extracting meaningful insights and gaining competitive advantages from such massive datasets is now crucial for organisations worldwide. Effectively deciphering valuable information from these data sources quickly and easily presents a considerable challenge. Consequently, analytics has become indispensable in realising the full value of big data, enhancing business performance, and expanding market share. The tools designed to address the volume, velocity, and variety of big data have significantly improved in recent years, with AI-powered big data analytics emerging as the most advanced solution.

Hence, through this chapter the authors argue how AI augmented and replaced traditional human-computer interactions in the realm of business analytics. This evolution has significantly reduced the reliance on manual interaction in the analytics process, enabling businesses to process and interpret data at an unprecedented speed and scale. This chapter further tries to establish the significance of machine and deep learning for big data analytics with the help of a case study, which not only serves as an empirical illustration of the theories presented but also underscores the practical application of AI-powered business analytics in enhancing predictive capabilities and decision-making processes. The study demonstrates that having access to predictive models like SVR can help to restore investor confidence during turbulent times. Although the proposed ML-based models might not precisely forecast the outcome of unforeseen events, they offer data-driven insights and direction, mitigating uncertainty and investor panic. Consequently, it could be inferred from the case study that employing big data analytics via AI methodologies such as ML facilitates a proactive management approach, enabling the anticipation of trends, recognition of patterns, and extraction of valuable insights from extensive datasets.

Embracing artificial intelligence can lead to increased efficiency, cost savings, and a competitive edge in today's rapidly evolving business landscape. By harnessing the power of AI, organisations can streamline workflows, uncover valuable insights from data, and ultimately pave the way for sustainable growth and success. Moreover, AI-driven analytics platforms have the capability to continuously learn and adapt, allowing organisations to stay ahead in today's dynamic marketplace. In essence, the synergy between big data and AI is reshaping the landscape of business analytics, empowering enterprises to make data-driven decisions with unprecedented speed, accuracy, and agility.

REFERENCES

Adebiyi, A. A., Adewumi, A. O., & Ayo, C. K. (2014). Comparison of ARIMA and artificial neural networks models for stock price prediction. *Journal of Applied Mathematics*, 2014, 1–7. 10.1155/2014/614342

Akyildirim, E., Goncu, A., & Sensoy, A. (2021). Prediction of cryptocurrency returns using machine learning. *Annals of Operations Research*, 297(1–2), 3–36. 10.1007/s10479-020-03575-y

Aldhyani, T. H. H., & Alzahrani, A. (2022). Framework for Predicting and Modeling Stock Market Prices Based on Deep Learning Algorithms. *Electronics (Basel)*, 11(19), 3149. 10.3390/electronics11193149

Ali, R., & Khan, R. E. A. (2018). Socioeconomic Stability and Variability in Stock Market Prices: A Case Study of Karachi Stock Exchange. *Asian Journal of Economic Modelling*, 6(4), 428–440. 10.18488/journal.8.2018.64.428.440

Barabasi, A. L. (2016). *Network science*. Cambridge University Press.

Breiman, L. (2003). Statistical modeling: The two cultures. *Quality Control and Applied Statistics*, 48(1), 81–82.

Cao, L., & Tay, F. E. H. (2001). Financial forecasting using support vector machines. *Neural Computing & Applications*, 10(2), 184–192. 10.1007/s005210170010

Chong, D., & Shi, H. (2015). Big data analytics: A literature review. *Journal of Management Analytics*, 2(3), 175–201. 10.1080/23270012.2015.1082449

Davenport, T. H. (2006). Competing on analytics. *Harvard Business Review*, 84(5), 150.20929194

Delen, D., & Ram, S. (2018). Research challenges and opportunities in business analytics. *Journal of Business Analytics*, 1(1), 2–12. 10.1080/2573234X.2018.1507324

Dix, A. J. F., Abowd, G. D., & Beale, R. (2004). *Human-Computer Interaction*.

Fan, S., Lau, R. Y. K., & Zhao, J. L. (2015). Demystifying Big Data Analytics for Business Intelligence Through the Lens of Marketing Mix. *Big Data Research*, 2(1), 28–32. 10.1016/j.bdr.2015.02.006

Henrique, B. M., Sobreiro, V. A., & Kimura, H. (2018). Stock price prediction using support vector regression on daily and up to the minute prices. *Journal of Finance and Data Science*, 4(3), 183–201. 10.1016/j.jfds.2018.04.003

Huang, W., Nakamori, Y., & Wang, S. Y. (2005). Forecasting stock market movement direction with support vector machine. *Computers & Operations Research*, 32(10), 2513–2522. 10.1016/j.cor.2004.03.016

Iqbal, R., Doctor, F., More, B., Mahmud, S., & Yousuf, U. (2020). Big data analytics: Computational intelligence techniques and application areas. *Technological Forecasting and Social Change, 153*(December 2017), 0–1. 10.1016/j.techfore.2018.03.024

Kaisler, S., Armour, F., Espinosa, J. A., & Money, W. (2013). Big data: Issues and challenges moving forward. *2013 46th Hawaii International Conference on System Sciences*, 995–1004.

Kell, A. J. E., Yamins, D. L. K., Shook, E. N., Norman-Haignere, S. V., & McDermott, J. H. (2018). A Task-Optimized Neural Network Replicates Human Auditory Behavior, Predicts Brain Responses, and Reveals a Cortical Processing Hierarchy. *Neuron*, 98(3), 630–644.e16. 10.1016/j.neuron.2018.03.04429681533

Kohavi, R., Rothleder, N. J., & Simoudis, E. (2002). Emerging trends in business analytics. *Communications of the ACM*, 45(8), 45–48. 10.1145/545151.545177

Lachaab, M., & Omri, A. (2023). Machine and deep learning-based stock price prediction during the COVID-19 pandemic: The case of CAC 40 index. *EuroMed Journal of Business*, 2022. Advance online publication. 10.1108/EMJB-05-2022-0104

Meesad, P., & Rasel, R. I. (2013). Predicting stock market price using support vector regression. *2013 International Conference on Informatics, Electronics and Vision, ICIEV 2013*, (pp. 1–6). IEEE. 10.1109/ICIEV.2013.6572570

Nayak, J., Dash, P. B., Naik, B., Mohapatra, S., & Routray, A. R. (2022). Deep Learning-Based Trend Analysis on Indian Stock Market in COVID-19 Pandemic Scenario and Forecasting Future Financial Drift. *Journal of The Institution of Engineers (India): Series B, 103*(5), 1459–1478. 10.1007/s40031-022-00762-2

Niu, Y., Ying, L., Yang, J., Bao, M., & Sivaparthipan, C. B. (2021). Organizational business intelligence and decision making using big data analytics. *Information Processing & Management*, 58(6), 102725. 10.1016/j.ipm.2021.102725

Ou, P., & Wang, H. (2009). Prediction of stock market index movement by ten data mining techniques. *Modern Applied Science*, 3(12), 28–42. 10.5539/mas.v3n12p28

Pedregosa, F., Varoquaux, G., Gramfort, A., Michel, V., Thirion, B., Grisel, O., Blondel, M., Prettenhofer, P., Weiss, R., & Dubourg, V. (2011). Scikit-learn: Machine learning in Python. *Journal of Machine Learning Research*, 12, 2825–2830.

Prinzie, A., & Van den Poel, D. (2008). Random Forests for multiclass classification: Random MultiNomial Logit. *Expert Systems with Applications*, 34(3), 1721–1732. 10.1016/j.eswa.2007.01.029

Pyo, S., Lee, J., Cha, M., & Jang, H. (2017). Predictability of machine learning techniques to forecast the trends of market index prices: Hypothesis testing for the Korean stock markets. *PLoS One*, 12(11), e0188107. 10.1371/journal.pone.018810729136004

Russom, P. (2011). Big data analytics - TDWI Best Practices Report. *TDWI Best Practices Report. Fourth Quarter*, (August), 38.

Sharma, A., Malviya, R., & Gupta, R. (2022). Big data analytics in healthcare. *Cognitive Intelligence and Big Data in Healthcare*, 2015, 257–301. 10.1002/9781119771982.ch10

Sharma, R., Reynolds, P., Scheepers, R., Seddon, P. B., & Shanks, G. G. (2010). Business Analytics and Competitive Advantage: A Review and a Research Agenda. *DSS*, 187–198.

Sujitparapitaya, S., Shirani, A., & Roldan, M. (2012). Issues in Information Systems. *Issues in Information Systems*, 13(2).

Tate, M. (2002). Human computer interaction: Issues and challenges. *Online Information Review*, 26(5), 348. 10.1016/j.giq.2003.08.006

Trkman, P., McCormack, K., De Oliveira, M. P. V., & Ladeira, M. B. (2010). The impact of business analytics on supply chain performance. *Decision Support Systems*, 49(3), 318–327. 10.1016/j.dss.2010.03.007

Vapnik, V. (1999). *The nature of statistical learning theory*. Springer science & business media.

Wells, T. S., Ozminkowski, R. J., Hawkins, K., Bhattarai, G. R., & Armstrong, D. G. (2016). Leveraging big data in population health management. *Big Data Analytics*, 1(1), 1–14. 10.1186/s41044-016-0001-5

Yuan, H., Tang, Y., Xu, W., & Lau, R. Y. K. (2020). Exploring the influence of multimodal social media data on stock performance: An empirical perspective and analysis. *Internet Research*, 31(3), 871–891. 10.1108/INTR-11-2019-0461

Zhong, X., & Enke, D. (2019). Predicting the daily return direction of the stock market using hybrid machine learning algorithms. *Financial Innovation*, 5(1), 24. 10.1186/s40854-019-0138-0

KEY TERMS AND DEFINITIONS

Artificial Intelligence: It allows computers to perform human-like tasks by mimicking cognitive functions such as learning, reasoning, and problem-solving.

Deep Learning: Deep learning is a subset of ML which uses artificial neural networks to solve problems. They are inspired by the biological neurons that constitute the human brain. Our sensory organs sense the outside environment and give signals or inputs to the brains.

Machine Learning: Machine learning is a branch of AI that studies how computers can learn without being explicitly programmed. The goal of machine learning is to analyze data structure and fit that data into models that users can comprehend.

ENDNOTES

[1] Source: CMIE Economic Outlook, "April 2020 Review of Indian Economy: Financial Market Performance," 5 April, 2020

[2] Source: https://www.screener.in/company/IRCTC/

[3] Source: https://www.screener.in/company/NESTLEIND/

[4] Source: https://www.screener.in/company/ITC/consolidated/

Chapter 7
The Use and Effects of ChatGPT in Tourism Education

Emre Yaşar
https://orcid.org/0000-0003-1573-0930
Isparta University of Applied Sciences, Turkey

İsmail Öztürk
https://orcid.org/0000-0002-1057-7060
Kırıkkale University, Turkey

Eda Yayla
Bitlis University, Turkey

Erge Tür
Istanbul Esenyurt University, Turkey

ABSTRACT

This study evaluates the role and impact of ChatGPT in tourism education. According to the study results, the areas of use of ChatGPT in tourism education are preparing course content, curriculum and exams, language learning, and obtaining theoretical knowledge. ChatGPT is suitable for academicians and students within the scope of tourism education. The factors affecting the applicability of ChatGPT in tourism education are the digital skills and technological predispositions of academics and students, ethical and security concerns, and the structural characteristics of tourism education. The positive effects of ChatGPT on tourism students are that it improves their research skills and efficiency, saves time, increases creativity, and provides access to information quickly. The negative effects of ChatGPT on tourism students

DOI: 10.4018/979-8-3693-3033-3.ch007

are the possibility of making them lazy, accessing wrong information, reducing their thinking skills, and making them dependent on technology.

INTRODUCTION

The emergence of ChatGPT towards the end of 2022 marked a significant development in the realm of artificial intelligence-driven chat tools (Grassini, 2023). Despite its relatively recent introduction, ChatGPT swiftly garnered attention across various sectors, captivating individuals with its innovative capabilities (Demir & Demir, 2023a). Businesses and individuals swiftly embraced ChatGPT, recognizing its potential to decipher complex queries and provide valuable insights (Rathore, 2023). This surge in interest has prompted extensive research endeavors to assess the efficacy of ChatGPT across diverse scientific domains (Demir & Demir, 2023b). Education stands out as one of the focal points for investigating the impact of ChatGPT, with studies delving into its effects on educators and students (Dalgıç et al., 2024). This exploration of ChatGPT's role in education has unveiled a spectrum of outcomes, spanning from beneficial to detrimental trends, thus fueling heightened interest and research efforts in this domain (Dempere et al., 2023).

The impact of ChatGPT on students across various educational levels has been a subject of discussion. ChatGPT offers students many benefits, albeit the extent of these advantages may vary. Nonetheless, there are common perspectives through which these gains can be evaluated. ChatGPT primarily facilitates students' career development by fostering personal growth (Ajlouni et al., 2023; Forman et al., 2023). By providing personalized support, ChatGPT aids students in honing their skills and capabilities, empowering them to navigate their career trajectories more effectively. Moreover, ChatGPT streamlines the process of accessing diverse information sources, enhancing students' learning experiences (Huallpa, 2023; Sharma & Yadav, 2022). This accessibility to a wealth of information empowers students to delve deeper into their studies and broaden their understanding of various subjects. Additionally, ChatGPT serves as a valuable tool for language learning, facilitating students' comprehension and communication skills across different languages (Imran & Almusharraf, 2023). With ChatGPT's language translation capabilities, students can engage with texts and research materials in languages beyond their proficiency, thus expanding their linguistic competence. ChatGPT enables students to approach content creation in novel ways, fostering creativity and innovation (Gill et al., 2024). By providing students with instant access to additional information and ideas, ChatGPT stimulates their innovative thinking, encouraging them to adopt a more creative outlook in their academic endeavors (Kiryakova & Angelova, 2023).

ChatGPT also has negative effects on students. Students' critical and analytical skills are thought to be negatively affected by using ChatGPT (Demir & Demir, 2023c). Since students can make ChatGPT do everything, they do not express and question their thoughts. In this case, students use ChatGPT's information and thoughts as their own. The fact that ChatGPT's access date to information is 2021 is also a subject of criticism (Sallam, 2023). ChatGPT is unaware of the developments and information, especially after 2021. This makes it difficult for students to access up-to-date information. The increase in plagiarism with ChatGPT is also one of the negative issues (Malinka et al., 2023). Having students do their homework on ChatGPT increases the similarity rates, and ethical discussions are experienced.

The discourse surrounding the impact of ChatGPT on students in the field of education is marked by diverse opinions, with no definitive consensus reached thus far. Consequently, research endeavors to unravel the relationship between education and ChatGPT have recently witnessed a surge. This trend is mirrored in tourism education, where scholars have increasingly focused on exploring the ramifications of ChatGPT adoption. In tourism education, studies have delved into various facets of ChatGPT's influence. Some investigations have relied on chat interactions with ChatGPT to infer its potential implications for tourism education (Ali, 2023; Dogru et al., 2023; Iskender, 2023; Ivanov & Soliman, 2023; Ülkü, 2023; Yiğit, 2023). Meanwhile, others have adopted a theoretical lens to elucidate the opportunities presented by ChatGPT within tourism education (Skavronskaya et al., 2023). Moreover, empirical studies have sought to gauge ChatGPT's efficacy in the realm of tourism education, with research probing its utility in examination settings (Göktaş, 2023), educators' perceptions of its applicability (Altun et al., 2024), and its impact on students' learning outcomes, digital literacy (Dalgıç et al., 2024), as well as critical and analytical skills (Demir & Demir, 2023c). Overall, the burgeoning body of literature on ChatGPT and tourism education underscores the growing interest in understanding the potential implications of this technology within the educational landscape, reflecting a broader trend observed across various fields of study.

It is seen that most of the research on ChatGPT in tourism education is theoretical. In tourism education, the positive and negative effects of ChatGPT on students are still undetermined. At the same time, the applicability of ChatGPT in terms of educators, i.e., tourism academicians, has not been adequately investigated. Based on this information, this study aims to determine the potential effects of ChatGPT on tourism students. It also seeks to reveal the applicability of ChatGPT in tourism education.

BACKGROUND

ChatGPT and Education

The application areas and qualities of artificial intelligence technologies are increasing daily due to developments in technologies and digitalization (Ergen, 2020). Due to these developments, this period is expressed with concepts such as the digital age and network society (Robinson et al., 2020). All areas, from culture to art, trade to communication, are sustainable with digitalization, and this process continues to develop daily (Dung & Tri, 2021). Therefore, these technological developments have incorporated the concept of artificial intelligence into our lives over the years. Artificial intelligence is defined as the sum of abilities such as adapting machines to new situations, coping with and solving problems that arise, and performing various functions that require intelligence. Regarding these features, it is possible to say that artificial intelligence is the summit of information technologies and that computers have a share in fulfilling humanoid features (Dwivedi et al., 2021; Lu, 2019).

ChatGPT, a prominent artificial intelligence application developed by OpenAI utilizing GPT language model technology, offers a comprehensive suite of features catering to diverse needs (Dwivedi et al., 2023). Equipped with a robust infrastructure, ChatGPT functions as a sophisticated chatbot capable of performing a multitude of tasks, including answering inquiries, translating text into numerous languages, generating reference materials, providing solutions to complex problems, offering mentorship, and even crafting exam questions (Fraiwan & Khasawneh, 2023; Gürsoy et al., 2023).

In addition to its core functionalities, ChatGPT possesses interactive features that enhance user experience, such as engaging in conversation, maintaining conversational continuity, identifying and rectifying errors, issuing apologies for lacking information, and declining to respond to specific queries (Haleem et al., 2022). Its versatility is further exemplified by its ability to fulfill diverse requests, ranging from coding assistance to content creation, provided the user provides appropriate guidance (Deng & Lin, 2022). By simplifying and expediting processes across various subjects, ChatGPT is a valuable tool for users seeking efficiency and convenience (Demir & Demir, 2023a).

ChatGPT stands out from other artificial intelligence models due to its multifaceted capabilities and user-friendly interface. Since its inception, ChatGPT has garnered significant attention and has been the subject of research and applications across a wide array of fields, including sports, healthcare, tourism, foreign language learning, biology, law, and environmental science (Montenegro-Rueda et al., 2023; Pranada et al., 2023). Undoubtedly, the field of education emerges as a pivotal domain where ChatGPT's transformative impact is particularly prominent.

ChatGPT is a tool with significant potential as an educational incentive (Baidoo-Anu & Ansah, 2023). ChatGPT provides convenience to students, especially in environments where the teacher is inadequate and the lesson time is limited (Kasneci et al., 2023). It is thought to create great convenience in education with its ability to interact at any time of the day (Qadir, 2023). Many tasks, such as summarizing text, editing, writing poetry, translating, clearly expressing complex and difficult-to-understand topics, and creating content on desired topics, are processes that can be performed by ChatGPT (Lo, 2023). With these aspects, it has become a valuable resource for both students and educators in a short time and has a strong potential in the field of education.

The efficacy of ChatGPT-style conversation programs in delivering personalized lessons for students has been highlighted by researchers such as Rejeb et al. (2024). These programs can offer tailored explanations to prevent confusion and facilitate communication at the student's level, as demonstrated by the findings of studies conducted by Gill et al. (2024). Moreover, insights from studies such as that of Liu et al. (2022), which explored the impact of individuals' interactions with chatbots on reading habits, underscore the potential of such interactions to enhance reading engagement. Indeed, the study revealed a notable increase in reading rates among individuals who engaged with chatbots. Given these positive contributions of artificial intelligence applications, particularly ChatGPT, it is anticipated that countries worldwide will ramp up investments in the further development of artificial intelligence technologies. Consequently, as artificial intelligence becomes increasingly integrated into education, we can expect a surge in investments to leverage these technologies to enhance learning outcomes in the years to come.

ChatGPT offers opportunities like asking questions, feedback, reasoning, and educational development through interaction (Javaid et al., 2023). The emergence of ChatGPT-style artificial intelligence not only improves the quality of learning activities but also provides benefits in distributing and controlling educational resources (Rudolph et al., 2023). When we consider education to be self-improvement, career planning, adaptation to society, and benefit, ChatGPT can be used for this purpose (Rasul et al., 2023). Each individual has learning skills with different methods. ChatGPT offers learning methods according to users' preferences (Elbanna & Armstrong, 2024). In addition, ChatGPT-style artificial intelligence applications increase the participation of individuals in education because they have a different experience and are more interesting than traditional learning tools (Alshahrani, 2023). This situation contributes to equality of opportunity and makes education more inclusive (Motlagh et al., 2023).

In addition to its positive attributes, ChatGPT has several notable drawbacks and ethical concerns that merit attention. One prominent issue is the potential for misinformation and ethical dilemmas inherent in its use (Mogavi et al., 2024).

ChatGPT's tendency to generate responses based on learned patterns rather than genuine understanding can lead to inaccuracies and misconceptions (Chinonso et al., 2023). Furthermore, its limited comprehension capacity and inability to grasp complex nuances may result in incomplete or misleading responses (Tian et al., 2024). Moreover, ChatGPT's reliance on pre-existing data may give rise to issues of similarity and lack of originality in responses, posing challenges in academic contexts where plagiarism is a concern (Jarrah et al., 2023). The inability to cite or verify information obtained from ChatGPT further exacerbates these problems, potentially undermining academic integrity.

The ethical implications of ChatGPT's use in education extend to broader concerns such as biased data, information reliability, technology addiction, privacy infringements, and diminished student engagement (Adıgüzel et al., 2023). These issues highlight the importance of establishing clear guidelines and ethical frameworks for integrating artificial intelligence technologies like ChatGPT into educational settings (Liebrenz et al., 2023). Addressing these ethical challenges requires collaboration among educators, policymakers, and developers to ensure the responsible and ethical use of ChatGPT in education (Adeshola & Adepoju, 2023). By implementing safeguards and promoting transparency, stakeholders can mitigate the negative impacts of ChatGPT while harnessing its potential benefits effectively.

ChatGPT and Tourism Education

According to Ivanov and Soliman (2023), ChatGPT is a revolutionary application in tourism education. ChatGPT fulfills most of the things that students need to do. ChatGPT creates assignments, articles, or any text for students. Ivanov and Soliman (2023) predict that digital educators will replace tourism educators with the development of applications such as ChatGPT in the future. Skavronskaya et al. (2023) evaluate the role of ChatGPT in tourism education regarding plagiarism. According to the authors, AI-based applications such as ChatGPT can contribute to tourism education, but new pedagogies need to be created for education with the development of technological applications. Ülkü (2023) states that the texts produced by ChatGPT are adequate in terms of content but emphasizes that this adequacy does not fully meet the expectations for tourism education. To fulfill expectations within the scope of tourism education, applications such as ChatGPT should be further developed.

The literature on ChatGPT's impact on tourism education presents a spectrum of perspectives, highlighting its positive and negative effects on students. Iskender (2023) suggests that ChatGPT holds promise in grading students and fostering brainstorming sessions by exposing them to diverse ideas. However, concerns are raised regarding its potential to diminish students' critical perspectives and impede creativity. Similarly, Demir and Demir (2023c) assert that ChatGPT adversely affects tourism students' critical and analytical skills. Contrastingly, Dalgıç et al. (2024) and Emam (2023) offer a more optimistic view, positing that ChatGPT positively influences students' learning performance and digital literacy, ultimately enhancing their educational outcomes in tourism studies. Ali (2023) and Doğru et al. (2023) acknowledge the positive contributions of ChatGPT to tourism education while emphasizing the importance of addressing its potential drawbacks. Yiğit (2023) underscores the multifaceted contributions of ChatGPT in gastronomy education, spanning from recipe and menu creation to fostering creative ideas and honing presentation techniques. However, Göktaş (2023) expresses reservations regarding the accuracy of ChatGPT, suggesting that while it may excel in specific areas, such as student exams, its efficacy in other realms may still be evolving.

MAIN FOCUS OF THE CHAPTER

Research Method

Positive and negative dimensions characterize the impact of ChatGPT on tourism students. Yet, a comprehensive understanding of these effects remains limited due to a shortage of detailed research in this area. This study aims to address this gap by investigating the potential influence of ChatGPT on tourism students, specifically from the viewpoint of tourism academics. Furthermore, the study assesses the practical feasibility of integrating ChatGPT into tourism education. Given the nuanced nature of individuals' perspectives on this topic, a qualitative research approach was chosen for this study. Qualitative research methodology enables a thorough exploration of participants' thoughts, feelings, and experiences, providing rich insights into the subject matter (Creswell, 2013). By adopting this approach, the study aims to delve deeply into the perceptions of tourism academics regarding the effects of ChatGPT on students and its suitability for integration into tourism education. Through qualitative analysis, this study endeavors to uncover multifaceted insights into the potential benefits and drawbacks of ChatGPT in the context of tourism education.

In this study, the semi-structured interview technique, a qualitative research method, was utilized to learn the thoughts of tourism academics about the effects of ChatGPT on their students. The semi-structured interview technique starts with questions prepared by the researchers and continues according to the participants' responses (Brinkmann, 2014). In this context, an interview form was created. The interview form includes three demographic questions and four questions to learn the effects of ChatGPT on students. These questions were inspired by the studies of

Dalgıç et al. (2024) and Demir and Demir (2023c) to learn the opinions of tourism academics about the effects of ChatGPT on tourism students.

The first question was designed to determine the potential areas of use of ChatGPT in tourism education. The second question was designed to assess the applicability of ChatGPT in tourism education. The third question was intended to learn the potential positive contributions of ChatGPT to students. The fourth question was designed to determine the negative contributions of ChatGPT on students. The questions in the interview form are as follows;

1. What are the potential uses of ChatGPT in tourism education?
2. What factors may affect the applicability of ChatGPT in tourism education?
3. Which specific skills of tourism students can ChatGPT improve?
4. What are the disadvantages of ChatGPT for tourism students?

Sample and Data Collection

Purposive sampling was used in the study. In purposive sampling, it is essential to include participants who align with specific criteria for the research purpose (Bernard, 2017). In this study, there are some criteria for selecting the participants. The academics included in the study are from the field of tourism. Another criterion for including academics in the study is that they have used ChatGPT at least once. Academics who did not use ChatGPT were not included in the study. Within these criteria, interviews were conducted with nine tourism academics. In the qualitative research method, there is no need to increase the number of participants when the interviews continue within an inevitable repetition, and the researcher is convinced that they have reached sufficient data saturation (Miles & Huberman, 1994). Marshall (1996) emphasizes that the interviews should be ended when the participants' responses become repetitive. Creswell (2013) explains that 5-25 participants are sufficient in interviews. Within the scope of this information, the interviews were completed with nine participants.

An online interview form was meticulously designed using Google Forms to facilitate the data collection process for this study. The decision to employ this method was driven by eliciting participants' viewpoints in a manner that offered flexibility and minimized external influences such as time constraints or researcher bias. By opting for an online format, participants could express their candid opinions without feeling pressured or constrained by time limitations. The online interview form was disseminated to potential participants during the period spanning from March 5th, 2024, to March 6th, 2024. This timeframe was chosen to accommodate the participants' schedules while ensuring a timely data collection process. Participants were provided clear instructions and information regarding the research topic within the interview form to ensure transparency and clarity. Importantly, participation in the interviews was voluntary, and participants were not compelled or coerced to participate in the research. This approach was adopted to uphold ethical standards and respect the participants' autonomy. By fostering an environment of voluntary participation, the study aimed to promote genuine engagement and encourage participants to share their honest thoughts and perspectives on the impact of ChatGPT on tourism education. Overall, the online interview form was a convenient and accessible platform for gathering valuable insights from participants, facilitating the comprehensive and inclusive exploration of the research questions.

The responses were analyzed in line with thematic analysis. In thematic analysis, the researcher creates themes and codes aligning with the literature. In this study, themes and codes were determined by utilizing Braun and Clarke (2006). Responses were analyzed by following certain stages. These are recognizing the data, selecting the preliminary codes of the data to explain the content obtained from the data, choosing the recurring themes in the data, finishing the control of the themes, defining and naming the themes, completing the analysis, and preparing the report (Braun & Clarke, 2006). Controls were carried out by an academic who is knowledgeable about the research.

Demographic characteristics of the participants are shown in Table 1. Six of the participants were male and three were female. Participants were from three different departments. All of the participants have previous ChatGPT experience.

Table 1. Demographic characteristics of the participants

Participant	Gender	Department	ChatGPT Usage
P1	Female	Gastronomy And Culinary Arts	Yes
P2	Male	Tourism Guidance	Yes
P3	Male	Tourism Management	Yes
P4	Male	Tourism Management	Yes
P5	Female	Tourism Management	Yes
P6	Male	Tourism Management	Yes
P7	Male	Tourism Guidance	Yes
P8	Male	Tourism Management	Yes
P9	Female	Tourism Management	Yes

Results

Upon analyzing the participants' responses, four primary themes emerged. These encompass the utilization of ChatGPT in tourism education, its applicability in this field, and the positive and negative impacts on students. The main theme regarding the use of ChatGPT in tourism education focuses on elucidating the various domains where participants employ ChatGPT within this educational realm. Sub-themes pertaining to this aspect are detailed in Table 2.

Table 2. The use of ChatGPT in tourism education

Main Theme	Sub Themes
The Use of ChatGPT in Tourism Education	Language learning and translation
	Creating course contents and curriculum
	Preparation of exams
	Obtaining theoretical knowledge about application areas

According to the participants, ChatGPT's utilization in tourism education is primarily categorized into four groups. Firstly, ChatGPT is seen as valuable in language learning and translation within tourism education. Its versatile features enable it to play an educational role in various subjects, with language learning and translation being one such area. For instance, P3 highlighted its potential in language translation, emphasizing its importance in tourism education. According to P3, *"It can also be used in language translation, which is indispensable for tourism education. Thanks to ChatGPT's translation service, language difficulties for students can be reduced."* Similarly, P5 acknowledges ChatGPT's potential in addressing language barriers, stating, *"In addition, the use of ChatGPT to eliminate language problems can be an important element in tourism education."*

Another notable application of ChatGPT in tourism education lies in crafting course content and curricula. Thanks to ChatGPT's capabilities, tourism academics find it convenient to generate content for the courses they oversee. Similarly, faculty administrations can harness artificial intelligence tools like ChatGPT to craft departmental curricula. As expressed by P4, *"We can use it for preliminary preparation in course content."* Additionally, P7 highlights ChatGPT's versatility in various aspects of tourism education, stating, *"ChatGPT can be used in tourism education when creating course content, preparing presentations, or generating exam questions."*

ChatGPT also facilitates the preparation of exam questions in tourism education. By issuing specific commands, *''ChatGPT can generate question suggestions for student exams''*, as noted by P2. Additionally, ChatGPT proves beneficial in providing theoretical insights into practical issues. P3 elaborates on this, stating, *"With ChatGPT, for example, we can obtain theoretical information about applications in the tourism sector. For instance, it can be useful and helpful in creating innovative products in the food and beverage department."*

The main theme of the applicability of ChatGPT in tourism education identifies the factors that are important for its applicability. In Table 3, there is detailed information on the main theme of the applicability of ChatGPT.

Table 3. The applicability of ChatGPT in tourism education

Main Theme	Sub Themes
The Applicability of ChatGPT in Tourism Education	Digital skills of academics and students
	Structural characteristics of tourism education
	Technological aptitude of academics and students
	Ethical and safety concerns

Participants highlight several factors that influence the applicability of ChatGPT in tourism education. One crucial factor is the level of digital skills both academics and students possess. Using and understanding AI tools like ChatGPT may be challenging without adequate digital skills. P2 emphasized, *"Digital skills of academics and students are important. Without digital skills, it can be difficult to use and understand AI tools such as ChatGPT."* Similarly, the technological readiness of academics and students plays a significant role in determining the success of ChatGPT usage. P5 noted, *"Students or academics may have insufficient technological predispositions and may not be able to give the commands required for ChatGPT to provide healthy information."*

Another factor affecting the applicability of ChatGPT in tourism education is its structural characteristics. In other words, tourism education is more prone to practical training rather than theory. It is thought that the fact that the courses in tourism education are taught in an applied manner affects the use of ChatGPT. P3 stated, *"Since tourism is more of an applied field, ChatGPT may not be efficient in practical terms. It can provide enough theoretical support for tourism."* P8 stated, *"Since tourism education is based on practice, it is difficult to digitize it completely through machine learning."* The last factors affecting the applicability of ChatGPT in tourism education are ethical and security concerns. Uncertainty about the confidentiality and reliability of information involves using ChatGPT in tourism education in general. P6 stated, *"Due to ethical and reliability issues, the information obtained from ChatGPT needs to be checked. Therefore, someone who wants to use ChatGPT in tourism education should have all this information."*

With the main theme of the positive effects of ChatGPT on students, it is aimed to learn which skills of students are improved by ChatGPT. Table 4 shows detailed information on the main theme of the positive effects of ChatGPT on students.

Table 4. The positive effects of ChatGPT on students

Main Theme	Sub Themes
The Positive Effects of ChatGPT on Students	Students develop research skills
	Saves students time
	Students' creativity increases
	Obtaining information in a short time
	Students' productivity increases

According to the participants, the first expected positive effect of ChatGPT on students is the development of students' research skills. Students can conduct research by using ChatGPT in their learning processes. Students can obtain the information they desire using ChatGPT and their responsibilities in this process. This situation enables students to develop their research skills. P7 stated, *"ChatGPT can improve tourism students' research skills. When students pose a question to ChatGPT about a research topic, they can analyze the answer more deeply and act with a sense of curiosity."* With ChatGPT, students can access information quickly. Thus, learning processes are accelerated. P4 said, *"It can help them learn information more systematically in a short time"*. At the same time, students save time with ChatGPT. P2 stated, *"It saves time by shortening the time to access information."* P9 said, *"The fact that students do their homework through this application also gives them advantages in terms of saving time and quick access to information."*

P3 thinks that ChatGPT will increase students' creativity. Students who access different information quickly with ChatGPT diversify their thoughts. Students who expand their thought network differentiate their perspectives on issues. P3 stated, *"I think it will improve their creativity."* P1 points out that ChatGPT improves students' questioning skills and increases their research productivity. P1 said, *"It can improve students' ability to ask the right question, which can increase research productivity."*

With the main theme of the negative effects of ChatGPT on students, the negative effects of ChatGPT on students are identified. Table 5 shows detailed information on the main theme of the negative effects of ChatGPT on students.

Table 5. The negative effects of ChatGPT on students

Main Theme	Sub Themes
The Negative Effects of ChatGPT on Students	Makes students lazy
	May increase students' technological dependency
	Can provide misinformation to students
	It weakens students' thinking

The primary negative effect of ChatGPT on students is perceived as fostering laziness. Given its ease of use, students may conduct research effortlessly and swiftly, potentially reducing their motivation for thorough exploration. P1 expressed concern, stating, *"If no limit or quota is set, its excessive use will lead people, especially young people, to research laziness."* Moreover, as the usage of ChatGPT proliferates, there's a likelihood of exacerbating students' technology addiction. P6 highlighted this risk, suggesting, *"In terms of education, it may lead students to technology addiction, and if they are constantly in contact with ChatGPT, a disconnection with real life may occur."* Another issue pertains to the accuracy of information provided by ChatGPT, which may sometimes be erroneous, potentially leading students astray. P3 cautioned, *"The information ChatGPT provides on subjects that are difficult to verify can be misleading. If it is not used and guided correctly, it may provide misinformation."* Finally, increased reliance on ChatGPT might render students passive in the research process, diminishing their critical and analytical thinking skills. P5 remarked, *"ChatGPT can make students lazy and prevent them from thinking in detail because it provides ready-made information."* At the same time, P9 highlighted the risk of stifling the exchange of ideas, stating, *"The use of the application by the students may cause the same answers to emerge, thus eliminating the learning method we call exchanging ideas."*

SOLUTIONS AND RECOMMENDATIONS

The uses of ChatGPT in tourism education emphasize language learning and translation, preparation of course contents and curricula, preparation of exams, and theoretical knowledge. With its natural language processing feature, ChatGPT can understand different languages (Goar et al., 2023). Since ChatGPT is based on artificial intelligence, it has information up to the date it was trained and made available (Lecler et al., 2023). Therefore, it can fulfill many functions. One of them is language learning and translation. Students and academics can consult ChatGPT for grammar, etc., and rules of the language they want to learn (Meyer et al., 2023). They can check ChatGPT in their writing processes (Schmidt-Fajlik, 2023). It is possible to use ChatGPT as a personal assistant in language learning (Kim et al., 2023). ChatGPT can be used for language learning and translating text (Sugiyama & Yamanaka, 2023). For example, a student or an academic whose English is not good can easily translate and understand any text in English with ChatGPT. Ali (2023) also mentions the contributions of ChatGPT in the language education of tourism students.

ChatGPT can be used in tourism education to create course content and curricula. Academicians can ask for help from ChatGPT in course content (Javaid et al., 2023). ChatGPT can also evaluate curricula and identify deficiencies (Lo, 2023). ChatGPT can be used in tourism education to prepare for exams (Ülkü, 2023). In addition, ChatGPT can also take exams instead of students. Göktaş (2023) explains that the success level of ChatGPT is high in multiple-choice exams. ChatGPT can be as successful as a good tourism student in an elective exam. The last use of ChatGPT in tourism education is to provide theoretical knowledge. As in other fields of education, access to theoretical knowledge becomes easier with ChatGPT in tourism education. Ali (2023) mentions that ChatGPT can provide sectoral knowledge to tourism students.

The main factor affecting the applicability of ChatGPT in tourism education is the digital skills of academics and students. With digital skills, using artificial intelligence tools such as ChatGPT gains meaning (Rasul et al., 2023). Because what is essential in the use of tools such as ChatGPT can provide effective and targeted benefits. The realization of this depends on digital skills. The development of digital skills affects the use and meaning of ChatGPT (Nakavachara et al., 2024). Technological aptitude is another critical factor. If academics and students have a technological predisposition, adopting and using ChatGPT accelerates. It is not usual for individuals with a low technological predisposition to follow technological developments. The fact that tourism education continues mainly through practice may limit the use of ChatGPT. It is more possible to benefit from ChatGPT in theoretical courses (AlAfnan et al., 2023). As in other fields, ethical and security issues in tourism education can limit the use of ChatGPT.

The positive effects of ChatGPT on tourism students are that it improves their research skills and increases productivity. Students expand their knowledge level in a short time by using ChatGPT. Thus, their productivity increases. The research skills of students who learn to ask the right questions with ChatGPT also improve. Emam (2023) states that the performance of tourism students increases with ChatGPT. Dalgıç et al. (2024) state that ChatGPT improves students' learning performance. ChatGPT saves students time by quickly accessing information (Huallpa, 2023). Since students access different information with ChatGPT, their creativity can develop (Dai et al., 2023).

The negative effects of ChatGPT on students are often emphasized, and it makes students lazy. Students who perform the research process efficiently with ChatGPT act comfortably. Students with ChatGPT do the research process comfortably and can become lazy (Ngo, 2023; Singh et al., 2023). Frequent use of ChatGPT may increase students' technological addiction. ChatGPT may mislead students with false information. Students may be exposed to false information in a learning process where the information accessed is not controlled (Gravel et al., 2023). The analytical thinking of students who act within the information and suggestions provided by ChatGPT weakens (Demir & Demir, 2023c). Because students have ChatGPT conduct their research processes without thinking. The research process without evaluation and thinking affects students negatively.

Theoretical Implications

This study evaluates the role and impact of ChatGPT in tourism education. Previous studies on ChatGPT and tourism education have addressed the issue from a theoretical perspective based on chat theory. Exceptional studies such as Dalgıç et al. (2024) and Emam (2023) only empirically examined the impact of ChatGPT on tourism students. Therefore, this study is of theoretical importance. With this study, the potential usage areas of ChatGPT in tourism education have been identified. Factors affecting the applicability of ChatGPT in tourism education were identified. The positive and negative effects of ChatGPT on students were also explained. As can be seen, the role and impact of ChatGPT in tourism education have been addressed comprehensively. When the research findings are analyzed, it is seen that ChatGPT has potential contributions to tourism education, but some issues need to be considered. When artificial intelligence tools such as ChatGPT are used in tourism education in a balanced way, positive contributions can be realized intensively.

Practical Implications

This study has several practical contributions. First, ChatGPT has areas of use in tourism education, such as preparing course contents and curricula and creating exams. It is now known that ChatGPT can be used in these areas. Secondly, the main factor affecting the applicability of ChatGPT in tourism education is digital skills. For this reason, studies should be carried out to increase the digital skills of academics and students. At the same time, ethical and security concerns should be addressed. ChatGPT can improve students' research performance and creativity. Therefore, it is necessary to guide students carefully in using artificial intelligence tools such as ChatGPT. Laziness ranks first among the negative effects of ChatGPT on students. It is important to carefully guide students to technological tools to prevent laziness and other negative effects.

FUTURE RESEARCH DIRECTIONS

This study was conducted to determine the role and effects of ChatGPT in tourism education from the perspective of tourism academics. Similar research can be conducted for academics from different fields in future research. The views of academics and students can be compared. This study was conducted using a qualitative research method. Research can be conducted using both qualitative and quantitative methods. Research can be conducted on different positive and negative features of ChatGPT.

CONCLUSION

According to the study results, the areas of use of ChatGPT in tourism education are preparing course content, curriculum and exams, language learning, and obtaining theoretical knowledge. ChatGPT is suitable for academicians and students within the scope of tourism education. The factors affecting the applicability of ChatGPT in tourism education are the digital skills and technological predispositions of academics and students, ethical and security concerns, and the structural characteristics of tourism education. The positive effects of ChatGPT on tourism students are that it improves their research skills and efficiency, saves time, increases creativity, and provides access to information quickly. The negative effects of ChatGPT on tourism students are the possibility of making them lazy, accessing wrong information, reducing their thinking skills, and making them dependent on technology.

REFERENCES

Adeshola, I., & Adepoju, A. P. (2023). The opportunities and challenges of ChatGPT in education. *Interactive Learning Environments*, 1–14. 10.1080/10494820.2023.2253858

Adiguzel, T., Kaya, M. H., & Cansu, F. K. (2023). Revolutionizing education with AI: Exploring the transformative potential of ChatGPT. *Contemporary Educational Technology*, 15(3), ep429. 10.30935/cedtech/13152

Ajlouni, A., Almahaireh, A., & Whaba, F. (2023). Students' perception of using chatgpt in counseling and mental health education: The benefits and challenges. [iJET]. *International Journal of Emerging Technologies in Learning*, 18(20), 199–218. 10.3991/ijet.v18i20.42075

AlAfnan, M. A., Dishari, S., Jovic, M., & Lomidze, K. (2023). Chatgpt as an educational tool: Opportunities, challenges, and recommendations for communication, business writing, and composition courses. *Journal of Artificial Intelligence and Technology*, 3(2), 60–68. 10.37965/jait.2023.0184

Ali, F. (2023). Let the devil speak for itself: Should ChatGPT be allowed or banned in hospitality and tourism schools? *Journal of Global Hospitality and Tourism*, 2(1), 1–6. https://www.doi.org/10.5038/2771-5957.2.1.1016. 10.5038/2771-5957.2.1.1016

Alshahrani, A. (2023). The impact of ChatGPT on blended learning: Current trends and future research directions. *International Journal of Data and Network Science*, 7(4), 2029–2040. 10.5267/j.ijdns.2023.6.010

Altun, O., Saydam, M. B., Karatepe, T., & Dima, Ş. M. (2024). Unveiling ChatGPT in tourism education: exploring perceptions, advantages and recommendations from educators. *Worldwide Hospitality and Tourism Themes*. 10.1108/WHATT-01-2024-0018

Baidoo-Anu, D., & Ansah, L. O. (2023). Education in the era of generative artificial intelligence (AI): Understanding the potential benefits of ChatGPT in promoting teaching and learning. *Journal of AI*, 7(1), 52–62. 10.61969/jai.1337500

Bernard, H. R. (2017). *Research methods in anthropology: Qualitative and quantitative approaches*. Rowman & Littlefield.

Braun, V., & Clarke, V. (2006). Using thematic analysis in psychology. *Qualitative Research in Psychology*, 3(2), 77–101. 10.1191/1478088706qp063oa

Brinkmann, S. (2014). Unstructured and semi-structured interviewing. *The Oxford handbook of qualitative research*. Oxford Press.

Chinonso, O. E., Theresa, A. M., & Aduke, T. C. (2023). ChatGPT for Teaching, Learning, and Research: Prospects and Challenges. *Glob Academic Journal of Humanities Social Sciences*, 5(2), 33–40. 10.36348/gajhss.2023.v05i02.001

Creswell, J. W. (2013). Qualitative inquiry and research design: Choosing among five approaches. *Sage (Atlanta, Ga.)*.

Dai, Y., Liu, A., & Lim, C. P. (2023). Reconceptualizing ChatGPT and generative AI as a student-driven innovation in higher education. *Procedia CIRP*, 119, 84–90. 10.1016/j.procir.2023.05.002

Dalgıç, A., Yaşar, E., & Demir, M. (2024). ChatGPT and learning outcomes in tourism education: The role of digital literacy and individualized learning. *Journal of Hospitality, Leisure, Sport and Tourism Education*, 34, 100481. 10.1016/j.jhlste.2024.100481

Demir, M., & Demir, Ş. Ş. (2023b). Is ChatGPT the right technology for service individualization and value co-creation? evidence from the travel industry. *Journal of Travel & Tourism Marketing*, 40(5), 383–398. 10.1080/10548408.2023.2255884

Demir, M., & Demir, Ş. Ş. (2023c). Reflection of artificial intelligence applications on students' critical and analytical abilities. *Scientific Collection. InterConf*, (184), 459–467.

Demir, Ş. Ş., & Demir, M. (2023a). Professionals' perspectives on ChatGPT in the tourism industry: Does it inspire awe or concern? *Journal of Tourism Theory and Research*, 9(2), 61–76. 10.24288/jttr.1313481

Dempere, J., Modugu, K. P., Hesham, A., & Ramasamy, L. (2023). The impact of ChatGPT on higher education. *Dempere J, Modugu K, Hesham A and Ramasamy LK (2023) The impact of ChatGPT on higher education.Frontiers in Education*, 8, 1206936. 10.3389/feduc.2023.1206936

Deng, J., & Lin, Y. (2022). The benefits and challenges of ChatGPT: An overview. *Frontiers in Computing and Intelligent Systems*, 2(2), 81–83. 10.54097/fcis.v2i2.4465

Dogru, T., Line, N., Hanks, L., Acikgoz, F., Abbott, J. A., Bakir, S., Berbekova, A., Bilgihan, A., Iskender, A., Kizildag, M., Lee, M., Lee, W., McGinley, S., Mody, M., Onder, I., Ozdemir, O., & Suess, C. (2023). The implications of generative artificial intelligence in academic research and higher education in tourism and hospitality. *Tourism Economics*, 13548166231204065, 13548166231204065. 10.1177/13548166231204065

Dung, N. T., Tri, N. M., & Minh, L. N. (2021). Digital transformation meets national development requirements. *Linguistics and Culture Review*, 5(S2), 892–905. 10.21744/lingcure.v5nS2.1536

Dwivedi, Y. K., Hughes, L., Ismagilova, E., Aarts, G., Coombs, C., Crick, T., Duan, Y., Dwivedi, R., Edwards, J., Eirug, A., Galanos, V., Ilavarasan, P. V., Janssen, M., Jones, P., Kar, A. K., Kizgin, H., Kronemann, B., Lal, B., Lucini, B., & Williams, M. D. (2021). Artificial Intelligence (AI): Multidisciplinary perspectives on emerging challenges, opportunities, and agenda for research, practice and policy. *International Journal of Information Management*, 57, 101994. 10.1016/j.ijinfomgt.2019.08.002

Dwivedi, Y. K., Kshetri, N., Hughes, L., Slade, E. L., Jeyaraj, A., Kar, A. K., Baabdullah, A. M., Koohang, A., Raghavan, V., Ahuja, M., Albanna, H., Albashrawi, M. A., Al-Busaidi, A. S., Balakrishnan, J., Barlette, Y., Basu, S., Bose, I., Brooks, L., Buhalis, D., & Wright, R. (2023). "So what if ChatGPT wrote it?" Multidisciplinary perspectives on opportunities, challenges and implications of generative conversational AI for research, practice and policy. *International Journal of Information Management*, 71, 102642. 10.1016/j.ijinfomgt.2023.102642

Elbanna, S., & Armstrong, L. (2024). Exploring the integration of ChatGPT in education: Adapting for the future. *Management & Sustainability: An Arab Review*, 3(1), 16–29. 10.1108/MSAR-03-2023-0016

Emam, R. M. (2023). The effect of using Chat GPT technology as one of the applications of artificial intelligence in tourism education for students of tourism and hotels institutes by using task *Technology fit model, 7*(2), 1-22. 10.21608/mfth.2023.327915

Ergen, F. D. (2020). Artırılmış ve sanal gerçeklik teknolojilerinin Isparta ilinin kültürel miras alanlarında uygulanabilirliği üzerine bir literatür taraması. *Journal of Tourism Theory and Research*, 6(1), 62–74. 10.24288/jttr.673593

Forman, N., Udvaros, J., & Avornicului, M. S. (2023). ChatGPT: A new study tool shaping the future for high school students. *International Journal of Advanced Natural Sciences and Engineering Researches*, 7(4), 95–102. 10.59287/ijanser.562

Fraiwan, M., & Khasawneh, N. (2023). A Review of ChatGPT Applications in Education, Marketing, Software Engineering, and Healthcare: Benefits, Drawbacks, and Research Directions. *arXiv preprint arXiv:2305.00237*. https://doi.org//arXiv.2305.0023710.48550

Gill, S. S., Xu, M., Patros, P., Wu, H., Kaur, R., Kaur, K., Fuller, S., Singh, M., Arora, P., Parlikad, A. K., Stankovski, V., Abraham, A., Ghosh, S. K., Lutfiyya, H., Kanhere, S. S., Bahsoon, R., Rana, O., Dustdar, S., Sakellariou, R., & Buyya, R. (2024). Transformative effects of ChatGPT on modern education: Emerging Era of AI Chatbots. *Internet of Things and Cyber-Physical Systems*, 4, 19–23. 10.1016/j. iotcps.2023.06.002

Goar, V., Yadav, N. S., & Yadav, P. S. (2023). Conversational AI for natural language processing: An review of ChatGPT. *International Journal on Recent and Innovation Trends in Computing and Communication*, 11(3s), 109–117. 10.17762/ ijritcc.v11i3s.6161

Göktaş, L. S. (2023). ChatGPT Uzaktan Eğitim Sınavlarında Başarılı Olabilir Mi? Turizm Alanında Doğruluk ve Doğrulama Üzerine Bir Araştırma. *Journal of Tourism & Gastronomy Studies*, 11(2), 892–905.

Grassini, S. (2023). Shaping the future of education: Exploring the potential and consequences of AI and ChatGPT in educational settings. *Education Sciences*, 13(7), 692. 10.3390/educsci13070692

Gravel, J., D'Amours-Gravel, M., & Osmanlliu, E. (2023). Learning to fake it: Limited responses and fabricated references provided by ChatGPT for medical questions. *Mayo Clinic Proceedings. Digital Health*, 1(3), 226–234. 10.1016/j. mcpdig.2023.05.004

Gursoy, D., Li, Y., & Song, H. (2023). ChatGPT and the hospitality and tourism industry: An overview of current trends and future research directions. *Journal of Hospitality Marketing & Management*, 32(5), 579–592. 10.1080/19368623.2023.2211993

Haleem, A., Javaid, M., & Singh, R. P. (2022). An era of ChatGPT as a significant futuristic support tool: A study on features, abilities, and challenges. *BenchCouncil transactions on benchmarks, standards and evaluations*, 2(4), 100089. 10.1016/j. tbench.2023.100089

Huallpa, J. J. (2023). Exploring the ethical considerations of using Chat GPT in university education. *Periodicals of Engineering and Natural Sciences*, 11(4), 105–115. 10.21533/pen.v11i4.3770

Imran, M., & Almusharraf, N. (2023). Analyzing the role of ChatGPT as a writing assistant at higher education level: A systematic review of the literature. *Contemporary Educational Technology*, 15(4), ep464. 10.30935/cedtech/13605

Iskender, A. (2023). Holy or unholy? Interview with open AI's ChatGPT. *European Journal of Tourism Research*, 34, 3414–3414. 10.54055/ejtr.v34i.3169

Ivanov, S., & Soliman, M. (2023). Game of algorithms: ChatGPT implications for the future of tourism education and research. *Journal of Tourism Futures*, 9(2), 214–221. 10.1108/JTF-02-2023-0038

Jarrah, A. M., Wardat, Y., & Fidalgo, P. (2023). Using ChatGPT in academic writing is (not) a form of plagiarism: What does the literature say. *Online Journal of Communication and Media Technologies*, 13(4), e202346. 10.30935/ojcmt/13572

Javaid, M., Haleem, A., Singh, R. P., Khan, S., & Khan, I. H. (2023). Unlocking the opportunities through ChatGPT Tool towards ameliorating the education system. *BenchCouncil Transactions on Benchmarks. Standards and Evaluations*, 3(2), 100115. 10.1016/j.tbench.2023.100115

Kasneci, E., Seßler, K., Küchemann, S., Bannert, M., Dementieva, D., Fischer, F., Gasser, U., Groh, G., Günnemann, S., Hüllermeier, E., Krusche, S., Kutyniok, G., Michaeli, T., Nerdel, C., Pfeffer, J., Poquet, O., Sailer, M., Schmidt, A., Seidel, T., & Kasneci, G. (2023). ChatGPT for good? On opportunities and challenges of large language models for education. *Learning and Individual Differences*, 103, 102274. 10.1016/j.lindif.2023.102274

Kim, S., Shim, J., & Shim, J. (2023). A study on the utilization of OpenAI ChatGPT as a second language learning tool. *Journal of Multimedia Information System*, 10(1), 79–88. 10.33851/JMIS.2023.10.1.79

Kiryakova, G., & Angelova, N. (2023). ChatGPT—A challenging tool for the university professors in their teaching practice. *Education Sciences*, 13(10), 1056. 10.3390/educsci13101056

Lecler, A., Duron, L., & Soyer, P. (2023). Revolutionizing radiology with GPT-based models: Current applications, future possibilities and limitations of ChatGPT. *Diagnostic and Interventional Imaging*, 104(6), 269–274. 10.1016/j.diii.2023.02.00336858933

Liebrenz, M., Schleifer, R., Buadze, A., Bhugra, D., & Smith, A. (2023). Generating scholarly content with ChatGPT: Ethical challenges for medical publishing. *The Lancet. Digital Health*, 5(3), e105–e106. 10.1016/S2589-7500(23)00019-536754725

Liu, Y., Al-Atawi, A. A., Khan, I. A., Gohar, N., & Zaman, Q. (2022). Using the Fuzzy Analytical Hierarchy Process to Prioritize the Impact of Visual Communication Based on Artificial Intelligence for Long-Term Learning. *Soft Computing*, 27(1), 157–168. 10.1007/s00500-022-07556-0

Lo, C. K. (2023). What is the impact of ChatGPT on education? A rapid review of the literature. *Education Sciences*, 13(4), 410. 10.3390/educsci13040410

Lu, Y. (2019). Artificial intelligence: A survey on evolution, models, applications and future trends. *Journal of Management Analytics*, 6(1), 1–29. 10.1080/23270012.2019.1570365

Malinka, K., Peresíni, M., Firc, A., Hujnák, O., & Janus, F. (2023, June). On the educational impact of chatgpt: Is artificial intelligence ready to obtain a university degree? In *Proceedings of the 2023 Conference on Innovation and Technology in Computer Science Education* V. 1 (pp. 47-53). ACM. 10.1145/3587102.3588827

Meyer, J. G., Urbanowicz, R. J., Martin, P. C., O'Connor, K., Li, R., Peng, P. C., Bright, T. J., Tatonetti, N., Won, K. J., Gonzalez-Hernandez, G., & Moore, J. H. (2023). ChatGPT and large language models in academia: Opportunities and challenges. *BioData Mining*, 16(1), 20. 10.1186/s13040-023-00339-937443040

Miles, M. B., & Huberman, A. M. (1994). Qualitative data analysis: An expanded sourcebook. *Sage (Atlanta, Ga.)*.

Mogavi, R. H., Deng, C., Kim, J. J., Zhou, P., Kwon, Y. D., Metwally, A. H. S., & Hui, P. (2024). ChatGPT in education: A blessing or a curse? A qualitative study exploring early adopters' utilization and perceptions. *Computers in Human Behavior: Artificial Humans*, 2(1), 100027. 10.1016/j.chbah.2023.100027

Montenegro-Rueda, M., Fernández-Cerero, J., Fernández-Batanero, J. M., & López-Meneses, E. (2023). Impact of the implementation of ChatGPT in education: A systematic review. *Computers*, 12(8), 153. 10.3390/computers12080153

Motlagh, N. Y., Khajavi, M., Sharifi, A., & Ahmadi, M. (2023). The impact of artificial intelligence on the evolution of digital education: A comparative study of openAI text generation tools including ChatGPT, Bing Chat, Bard, and Ernie. *arXiv preprint arXiv:2309.02029*. https://doi.org//arXiv.2309.0202910.48550

Nakavachara, V., Potipiti, T., & Chaiwat, T. (2024). Experimenting with Generative AI: Does ChatGPT Really Increase Everyone's Productivity? *arXiv preprint arXiv:2403.01770*. https://doi.org//arXiv.2403.0177010.48550

Ngo, T. T. A. (2023). The perception by university students of the use of ChatGPT in education. *International Journal of Emerging Technologies in Learning*, 18(17), 4–19. 10.3991/ijet.v18i17.39019

Pradana, M., Elisa, H. P., & Syarifuddin, S. (2023). Discussing ChatGPT in education: A literature review and bibliometric analysis. *Cogent Education*, 10(2), 2243134. 10.1080/2331186X.2023.2243134

Qadir, J. (2023, May). Engineering education in the era of ChatGPT: Promise and pitfalls of generative AI for education. In *2023 IEEE Global Engineering Education Conference (EDUCON)* (pp. 1-9). IEEE. 10.1109/EDUCON54358.2023.10125121

Rahman, M. M., & Watanobe, Y. (2023). ChatGPT for education and research: Opportunities, threats, and strategies. *Applied Sciences (Basel, Switzerland)*, 13(9), 5783. 10.3390/app13095783

Rasul, T., Nair, S., Kalendra, D., Robin, M., de Oliveira Santini, F., Ladeira, W. J., & Heathcote, L. (2023). The role of ChatGPT in higher education: Benefits, challenges, and future research directions. *Journal of Applied Learning and Teaching*, 6(1), 1–16.

Rathore, B. (2023). Future of AI & generation alpha: ChatGPT beyond boundaries. *Eduzone: International Peer Reviewed/Refereed Multidisciplinary Journal*, *12*(1), 63-68.

Rejeb, A., Rejeb, K., Appolloni, A., Treiblmaier, H., & Iranmanesh, M. (2024). Exploring the impact of ChatGPT on education: A web mining and machine learning approach. *International Journal of Management Education*, 22(1), 100932. 10.1016/j.ijme.2024.100932

Robinson, L., Schulz, J., Blank, G., Ragnedda, M., Ono, H., Hogan, B., Mesch, G. S., Cotten, S. R., Kretchmer, S. B., Hale, T. M., Drabowicz, T., Yan, P., Wellman, B., Harper, M.-G., Quan-Haase, A., Dunn, H. S., Casilli, A. A., Tubaro, P., Carvath, R., & Khilnani, A. (2020). Digital inequalities 2.0: Legacy inequalities in the information age. *First Monday*, 25(7). 10.5210/fm.v25i7.10842

Rudolph, J., Tan, S., & Tan, S. (2023). War of the chatbots: Bard, Bing Chat, ChatGPT, Ernie and beyond. The new AI gold rush and its impact on higher education. *Journal of Applied Learning and Teaching*, 6(1).

Sallam, M. (2023). The utility of ChatGPT as an example of large language models in healthcare education, research and practice: Systematic review on the future perspectives and potential limitations. medRxiv, 2023-02.

Schmidt-Fajlik, R. (2023). Chatgpt as a grammar checker for japanese english language learners: A comparison with grammarly and prowritingaid. *AsiaCALL Online Journal*, 14(1), 105–119. 10.54855/acoj.231417

Sharma, S., & Yadav, R. (2022). Chat GPT–A Technological Remedy or Challenge for Education System. *Global Journal of Enterprise Information System*, 14(4), 46–51.

Singh, P., Phutela, N., Grover, P., Sinha, D., & Sinha, S. (2023, December). Student's Perception of Chat GPT. In *2023 International Conference on Electrical, Communication and Computer Engineering (ICECCE)* (pp. 1-6). IEEE. 10.1109/ICECCE61019.2023.10442033

Skavronskaya, L., Hadinejad, A., & Cotterell, D. (2023). Reversing the threat of artificial intelligence to opportunity: A discussion of ChatGPT in tourism education. *Journal of Teaching in Travel & Tourism*, 23(2), 253–258. 10.1080/15313220.2023.2196658

Sok, S., & Heng, K. (2023). ChatGPT for education and research: A review of benefits and risks. *Available atSSRN* 4378735.

Sugiyama, K., & Yamanaka, T. (2023). Proposals and Methods for Foreign Language Learning Using Machine Translation and Large Language Model. *Procedia Computer Science*, 225, 4750–4757. 10.1016/j.procs.2023.10.474

Tian, S., Jin, Q., Yeganova, L., Lai, P. T., Zhu, Q., Chen, X., Yang, Y., Chen, Q., Kim, W., Comeau, D. C., Islamaj, R., Kapoor, A., Gao, X., & Lu, Z. (2024). Opportunities and challenges for ChatGPT and large language models in biomedicine and health. *Briefings in Bioinformatics*, 25(1), bbad493. 10.1093/bib/bbad49338168838

Ülkü, A. (2023). Artificial intelligence-based large language models and integrity of exams and assignments in higher education: The case of tourism courses. *Tourism & Management Studies*, 19(4), 21–34. 10.18089/tms.2023.190402

Wang, W., Chen, Y., & Heffernan, N. (2020). *A generative model-based tutoring system for math word problems.* arXiv preprint arXiv:2010.04.

Yiğit, S. (2023). Yapay Zekâ Gastronomi Eğitimine Katkı Sunabilir Mi? ChatGPT Örneği. *Journal of Tourism & Gastronomy Studies.*, 11(3), 1970–1982.

ADDITIONAL READING

Dalgıç, A., Yaşar, E., & Demir, M. (2024). ChatGPT and learning outcomes in tourism education: The role of digital literacy and individualized learning. *Journal of Hospitality, Leisure, Sport and Tourism Education*, 34, 100481. 10.1016/j.jhlste.2024.100481

Demir, Ş. Ş., & Demir, M. (2023a). Professionals' perspectives on ChatGPT in the tourism industry: Does it inspire awe or concern? *Journal of Tourism Theory and Research*, 9(2), 61–76. 10.24288/jttr.1313481

KEY TERMS AND DEFINITIONS

Artificial Intelligence: It is an artificial operating system that exhibits human-like behavior.

ChatGPT: It is an artificial intelligence supported chat robot.

Chapter 8
Designing a User–Centered Mobile Phone:
The Quality Function Deployment Approach

Muhammet Enis Bulak

Uskudar University, Turkey

ABSTRACT

In this study, the QFD approach is used to convert customer requirements into design features for a better mobile phone design. An online survey is conducted with the users to determine their needs. Afterward, technical requirements were identified to meet customer requirements. The relationship between customer requirements and technical requirements is developed to identify the most critical phases. The relationship matrix is then converted into the house of quality (HOQ) matrix. For the analysis part, Apple, Samsung, and Huawei mobile phones are benchmarked, and each step of the QFD is applied to reach a user-centered design for the customers. The results showed that processor and connectivity are the most important factors among the ten different technical features.

INTRODUCTION

User-centered design (UCD) is a design methodology that places paramount importance on the requirements, desires, and actions of end-users from inception to completion. It entails comprehending users' viewpoints, objectives, and obstacles, and incorporating this comprehension into all phases of the design process. The

DOI: 10.4018/979-8-3693-3033-3.ch008

key components of user-centered design include user involvement, iterative design, usability, accessibility, and prototype testing(Fleury, and Chaniaud, 2024).

User-centered design strives to develop products, services, or systems that are intuitive, effective, and pleasurable for their intended users. It highlights the significance of understanding users' requirements and preferences to craft designs that adeptly fulfill those needs (Sudirjo et al., 2024). Designing with users in mind leads to more intuitive and easy-to-use products, reducing the learning curve and allowing users to accomplish tasks more efficiently. Involving users throughout the design process helps identify and address issues early on, reducing the risk of costly redesigns or product failures after launch (Dworschak et al., 2024). When products are designed with users' input and understanding, they are more likely to be adopted and used regularly, leading to higher engagement and retention rates (Lazuardy et al., 2024). Companies that prioritize user-centered design often differentiate themselves from competitors by offering superior user experiences, leading to increased customer loyalty and market share. Investing in user-centered design upfront can save costs associated with fixing usability issues or addressing user dissatisfaction later in the product lifecycle (Dodeja et al., 2024). It is essential for creating products and services that truly resonate with users, driving satisfaction, adoption, and business success.

On the other hand, user-centered design is vital for crafting mobile phone interfaces that are intuitive, effective, and pleasurable to interact with, meeting the diverse requirements of users across different situations, and guaranteeing a favorable user experience (Awan et al., 2024). It is particularly crucial due to the use of a wide range of people with varying levels of technological expertise, preferences, and needs. User-centered design guarantees that mobile phone interfaces address the needs of a varied user demographic, ensuring accessibility and ease of use for all individuals. Mobile phone technology is constantly evolving, with new features, hardware, and software updates being introduced regularly. User-centered design ensures that mobile interfaces evolve alongside user needs and technological advancements, staying relevant and effective over time (Stabile et al., 2024).

This paper aims to define customer requirements to convert design specifications with a quality function deployment (QFD) approach for mobile phones. Customer needs are identified with a survey study of mobile phone users. Technical specifications that meet customer needs are defined, and a correlation matrix is constructed between customer needs and technical specifications. The relationship matrix is then converted into the house of quality (HOQ) matrix. The most critical technical factors are identified which mobile phone companies need to pay attention to improve. A significant part of the QFD is the HOQ. The "whats" part which refers to customer requirements and "hows" refers to technical requirements are combined in HOQ. For the analysis part, Apple, Samsung, and Huawei mobile phones are benchmarked, and each step of the QFD is applied to such products to reach a user-centered design for the customers.

BACKGROUND

Koswara and Alifin (2024) aimed to develop a distinguished approach for designing user interfaces (UI) for CRM systems that align closely with user needs and specifications. Primary data is gathered through direct observation and questionnaires within an IT company to assess and define user requirements and expectations. By integrating Design Thinking and Quality Function Deployment (QFD) methodologies, this study aims to innovate and tailor UI design methods specifically for CRM systems, thereby enhancing the user experience. The research findings demonstrate enhancements in user experience resulting from a user-centric approach to UI design.

Li and Kim (2023) utilized semi-structured interviews, online questionnaire surveys, and expert evaluations to comprehend and prioritize factors influencing user needs and design requirements in the design of handicrafts. Employing the Kano-QFD methodology, a quantitative analysis was conducted to discern the varying impacts of twelve user needs and twenty-three design requirements on the design of handicraft ICH apps. After establishing a correlation matrix between user needs and design requirements, the design requirements for the apps were ranked based on their significance

Aydemir et al. (2023) examined the variance in costs, either surplus or deficit, between the target cost levels attained by evaluating customer expectations across 12 distinct criteria and the current cost levels of smartphone components by employing quality function deployment and Grey System Theory.

Imbesi and Scataglini (2021) outlined a user-centered approach to designing smart garments, focusing on assessing users' acceptance of such clothing. This comparative method resembles a streamlined version of the quality function deployment tool, aiding in evaluating how each garment type responds to various categories of requirements and gauging older users' inclination towards using the developed product. The proposed methodology seeks to integrate a tool into the design process for assessing and contrasting developed solutions, thereby simplifying the complexity often associated with design processes.

Buyukozkan et al. (2020) introduced a novel approach for identifying and ranking the crucial design specifications in customer-centric product design. They preferred the Quality Function Deployment (QFD) tool due to its adeptness in addressing customer needs. Fuzzy logic is integrated to accommodate uncertain data representation. The authors employed a combined fuzzy QFD and fuzzy multi-criteria decision-making (MCDM) method for designing customer-oriented multifunctional power banks.

Han et al. (2019) conducted research that comprised three phases aimed at constructing a quality function deployment (QFD) model, which involved interviewing international tourists and industry professionals, conducting focus groups, and administering questionnaires. Through these phases, key categories, content requirements, function requirements, and user resistance were delineated to identify the necessary specifications. The findings of the research delineate tourist requirements grounded in behavioral and psychological indicators and suggest a methodology for converting them into technical design components for mobile augmented reality applications catering to tourists.

Cerit et al. (2014) utilized the QFD methodology to assist Turkey's top mobile communication operator in designing a smartphone intended for release in the final quarter of 2013. However, locating numerous QFD sample projects within the sector proved challenging, mainly due to the rapid completion of product life cycles. Given the dynamic nature of mobile communication technologies, maintaining a competitive edge necessitates ongoing exploration and adoption of new product development techniques.

METHODOLOGY

Quality Function Deployment (QFD) is a systematic approach employed in product development and design to ensure that customer demands and desires are accurately reflected in precise product attributes and functionalities (Hu et al., 2024). Originating in Japan during the late 1960s, QFD has gained global acceptance among various enterprises. Its principal objective is to synchronize design and manufacturing procedures with customer expectations, thereby enhancing product excellence, customer contentment, and competitive edge (Wang et al., 2024). QFD empowers organizations to methodically integrate customer feedback into their product development procedures, resulting in products that more closely align with customer expectations, enhance competitiveness in the marketplace, and have greater prospects for sustained success (Karasan et al., 2022). The process typically involves the following key steps covering the customer requirements, competitor performance, and key insights gained from the application as indicated in Figure 1 as well.

Figure 1. Research methodology

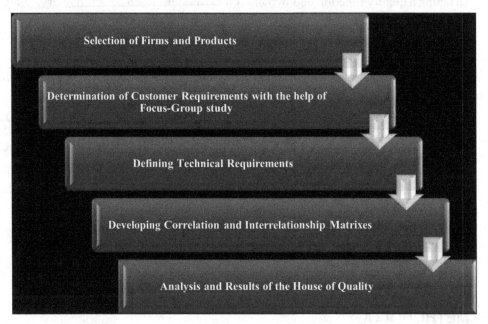

RESULTS AND DISCUSSION

Quality Function Deployment Approach

1. Firm Selection

Apple is a well-established and renowned company in the technology industry, known for its innovative products and strong market presence. It has a track record of delivering high-quality smartphones and has a loyal customer base. Selecting Apple as the firm for the iPhone 14 Pro ensures credibility, reliability, and access to Apple's ecosystem and integration with other devices.

2. Define the customer/user for the product/service that the company provides

The target customer/user for the iPhone 14 Pro can be defined as tech-savvy individuals who value high-performance smartphones with advanced features.

3. Determine 10 important customer requirements by making focus group work

Based on the focus group work, the 10 important customer requirements for the iPhone 14 Pro could include:

Requirement #1 High-resolution display: Deliver a vibrant and sharp display with a high pixel density, excellent color accuracy, and wide viewing angles.

Requirement #2 Powerful and efficient processor: Provide a fast and efficient processor that ensures smooth performance, seamless multitasking, and quick response times.

Requirement #3 Enhanced camera capabilities: Deliver a camera system with high-resolution sensors, advanced image processing, optical image stabilization, and features like low-light performance, portrait mode, and video recording capabilities.

Requirement #4 Long-lasting battery life: Provide a battery that offers extended usage time, optimized power management, and efficient charging capabilities, allowing the iPhone 14 Pro to last throughout the day.

Requirement #5 Fast and reliable connectivity options: Deliver fast and reliable connectivity through features like 5G capability, Wi-Fi 6 or higher, Bluetooth 5.2, and NFC for seamless data transfer, browsing, and communication.

Requirement #6 Intuitive and user-friendly interface: Provide an intuitive user interface (UI) with a user-friendly design, easy navigation, customizable settings, and a smooth user experience.

Requirement #7 storage capacity: Deliver sufficient storage options, including high-capacity variants, to accommodate user data, apps, photos, videos, and other multimedia content.

Requirement #8 Robust security features: Provide advanced security measures such as biometric authentication (e.g., Face ID or Touch ID), encrypted data storage, secure enclave, and regular software updates to ensure user privacy and data protection.

Requirement #9 Seamless integration with other Apple devices: Deliver seamless integration and compatibility with other Apple devices and services, allowing users to easily sync and transfer data, access iCloud services, and benefit from ecosystem features like AirDrop, Handoff, and Continuity.

Requirement #10 Innovative and cutting-edge design Provide a visually appealing and premium design with a slim form factor, high-quality materials, ergonomic considerations, and attention to detail, showcasing Apple's commitment to innovation and aesthetics.

4. Ask customers to define;

-Requirements' importance rate, Firms' rate to meet customer requirements, Comparison between the company and 2 competitor firms

A survey was conducted asking different phone users (iPhone 14 PRO – Samsung S21 – Huawei P60 PRO) to rate the importance of requirements, evaluate our firm's performance in meeting those requirements, and provide a comparison with two competitor firms. Summary of the survey results for customers' opinions about requirements' importance rate, firms' rate to meet customer requirements, and comparison between the company and two competitor firms are as follows:

Requirements' Importance Rate

The highest-rated requirement in terms of importance resulted in "High-resolution display," receiving an average rating of 4.9 out of 5. The second most important requirement is a "Powerful and efficient processor," with an average rating of 4.6. "Enhanced camera capabilities," "Long-lasting battery life," and "Fast and reliable connectivity options" are also deemed highly important, receiving average ratings of 4.8, 4.9, and 4.2, respectively. "Intuitive and user-friendly interface" and "Innovative and cutting-edge design" are moderately important, with average ratings of 3.4 and 4.2, respectively. "Storage capacity," "Robust security features," and "Seamless integration with other Apple devices" are considered important but ranked slightly lower, with average ratings of 3.3, 4.2, and 3.7, respectively.

Firms' Rate to Meet Customer Requirements

Apple received high ratings for meeting customer requirements across various categories, ranging from 4.3 to 5. Samsung and Huawei also performed well, but their ratings were slightly lower compared to Apple, ranging from 2.3 to 4.8 for Samsung and 1 to 4.5 for Huawei. Overall, Apple is perceived as the best performer in meeting customer requirements, with consistently higher ratings compared to the two competitor firms.

Comparison Between the Company and Two Competitor Firms

Apple outperformed Samsung and Huawei in most categories, consistently receiving higher ratings. Samsung had a mixed performance, with some ratings comparable to Apple's but also lower ratings in certain areas. Huawei received lower ratings overall compared to Apple and Samsung, indicating a relatively weaker performance in meeting customer requirements.

Based on these results, it can be concluded that customers highly prioritize requirements such as high-resolution display, powerful processor, enhanced camera capabilities, and long-lasting battery life for the iPhone 14 Pro. Apple is perceived as the leading company in meeting these requirements, outperforming Samsung S21 and Huawei P60 PRO. However, it's important to note that customer opinions may vary, and individual preferences play a significant role in evaluating the importance of different requirements and firms' performance.

5. Defining Technical Requirements

Based on the customer requirements and the performance ratings provided, we can define the specific technical requirements for the iPhone 14 Pro as follows:

1. Display

2. Processor
3. Camera
4. Battery Life
5. Connectivity
6. User Interface
7. Storage
8. Security
9. Integration with Other Devices
10. Design

6. Defining Correlation Matrix

By analyzing this matrix, we can identify the areas that require improvement to better align the technical specifications with the customer requirements as seen in Figure 2. "●" indicates a high relationship with a score of "9", "○" indicates an average relationship with a score of "3" and

" " indicates a low relationship with a score of "1".

As illustrated in Figure 2, "High-resolution display" (Customer Requirement #1) has a positive correlation with the technical specification "Display" (Technical Specification #1). Improving the display will positively impact the high-resolution display requirement. "Intuitive and user-friendly interface" (Customer Requirement #6) does not correlate with most technical specifications, indicating that improvements in the technical specifications may not have a significant impact on the interface's intuitiveness and user-friendliness. "Robust security features" (Customer Requirement #7) have a positive correlation with the technical specification "Security" (Technical Specification #). Enhancing security features will positively impact the requirement for robust security. Based on the relationship matrix, the company can prioritize the technical specifications that have a positive correlation with customer requirements and focus on improving them to enhance customer satisfaction and meet their expectations.

Figure 2. Correlation matrix

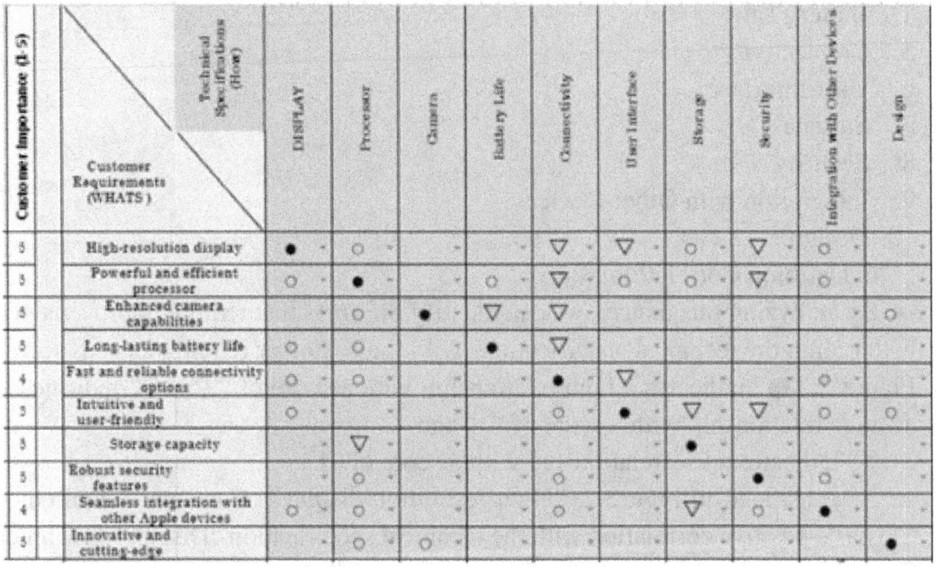

Customer Importance (1-5)	Customer Requirements (WHATS)	DISPLAY	Processor	Camera	Battery Life	Connectivity	User Interface	Storage	Security	Integration with Other Devices	Design
5	High-resolution display	●	○			▽	▽	○	▽	○	
5	Powerful and efficient processor	○	●		○	▽	○	○	▽	○	
5	Enhanced camera capabilities		○	●	▽	▽					○
5	Long-lasting battery life	○	○		●	▽					
4	Fast and reliable connectivity options	○	○			●	▽			○	
3	Intuitive and user-friendly	○				○	●	▽	▽	○	○
3	Storage capacity		▽					●			
5	Robust security features		○			○			●	○	
4	Seamless integration with other Apple devices	○	○			○		▽	○	●	
5	Innovative and cutting-edge		○	○							●

7. Competitor Analysis

The data provided in Figure 3 represents the technical analysis of competitor products, including the iPhone 14 Pro, Competitor 1 (Samsung S21), and Competitor 2 (Huawei P60 Pro). The numbers in the table indicate ratings or scores given to each product based on certain criteria or technical aspects.

Figure 3. Competitor analysis

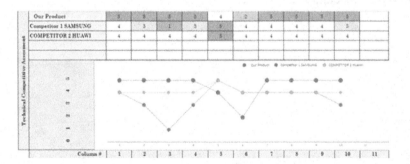

Based on the given data, we can observe the following: For the criteria evaluated in the analysis, the iPhone 14 Pro consistently received high ratings of 5, indicating strong performance or superiority in those aspects compared to the competitors. Competitor 1 (Samsung S21) generally received lower ratings compared to the iPhone 14 Pro, with scores ranging from 1 to 5. This suggests that the Samsung S21 performed moderately well in some areas but lagged in others. Competitor 2 (Huawei P60 Pro) received consistent ratings of 4, indicating a relatively stable performance across the evaluated criteria. However, it is important to note that the ratings are lower than those given to the iPhone 14 Pro. Overall, the data suggests that the iPhone 14 Pro outperforms both competitors in terms of the technical aspects evaluated. It indicates that the iPhone 14 Pro has a competitive advantage and provides a stronger offering in terms of those specific technical features compared to the Samsung S21 and Huawei P60 Pro.

8. Define Target Values for Technical Requirements

The target values for the technical requirements of the product are as follows:

1. Pixel Density (PPI): The target value is set at 600 PPI, indicating a high-resolution display with excellent image clarity and sharpness.

2. Clock Speed (GHz): The target value is set at 3.5 GHz, representing a fast and powerful processor capable of handling demanding tasks and providing smooth performance.

3. Resolution (Megapixels): The target value is set at 24 Megapixels, indicating enhanced camera capabilities with high-resolution image capture.

4. Usage Time (hours): The target value is set at 12 hours, indicating a long-lasting battery life to provide extended usage without frequent charging.

5. Network Speed (Mbps): The target value is set at 1 Gbps, indicating fast and reliable connectivity for seamless internet browsing and data transfer.

6. Responsiveness (ms): The target value is set to be less than 10 ms, indicating a highly responsive user interface with minimal delay or lag.

7. Storage Capacity (GB): The target value is set at 1 TB, indicating a generous amount of internal storage space for storing a large number of files, apps, and media.

8. Security Level: The target value is set as Advanced Facial Recognition, indicating a high level of security using facial recognition technology for device unlocking and authentication.

9. Compatibility with Other Apple Devices: The target value is set to ensure seamless integration and compatibility with other Apple devices, enabling easy data sharing and synchronization.

10. Thinness (mm): The target value is set to be less than 7 mm, indicating a slim and sleek design for a visually appealing and portable device. These target values represent the desired specifications and performance levels that the product aims to achieve for each technical requirement.

9. Defining Interrelationship Matrix

The interrelationship matrix provides insights into the relationships between different technical requirements for the iPhone 14 Pro. "+" indicates the positive relationship, "-" indicates the negative relationship, and "0" indicates the no relationship between the two technical relationships.

Figure 4. Interrelationship matrix

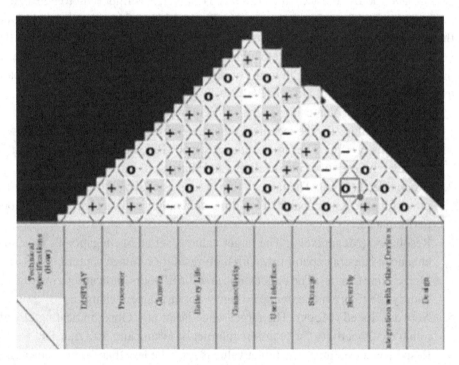

10. Determining Absolute and Relative Importance Values of the Technical Requirements

The importance rate of each technical requirement is found by multiplying the value of the existing relationship between customer requirements and technical requirements with a given customer importance value. "●" indicates a high relationship with a score of "9", "○" indicates an average relationship with a score of "3" and " " indicates a low relationship with a score of "1". Finally, relative importance values are found based on absolute scores. As indicated in Table 1, a higher absolute importance value suggests that the corresponding technical requirement has a greater impact on customer satisfaction and is considered more critical for the success of the product.

Table 1. Absolute and relative importance values

Technical Requirements	Display			Battery Life		User Interface				Design
Absolute Importance	114	149	60	65	138	69	84	72	108	75
Relative Importance(%)	12	16	6	7	15	7	9	8	12	8

The analysis of the 1st House of Quality provides valuable insights into customer opinions and expectations regarding the iPhone 14 Pro. Here is a summary of the comments and suggestions: •Customer requirements: The House of Quality helps identify and prioritize customer requirements, providing insights into what features and attributes are most important to customers. In the case of the iPhone 14pro, customers place high importance on a high-resolution display, a powerful processor, enhanced camera capabilities, long-lasting battery life, and fast connectivity options.

•Competitor comparison: The House of Quality allows for a comparison between the company (Apple iPhone 14 pro) and its competitors (Samsung s21 and Huawei p60 pro) in terms of meeting customer requirements. Apple was perceived as the best performer, consistently receiving higher ratings compared to its competitors.

Figure 5. House of quality

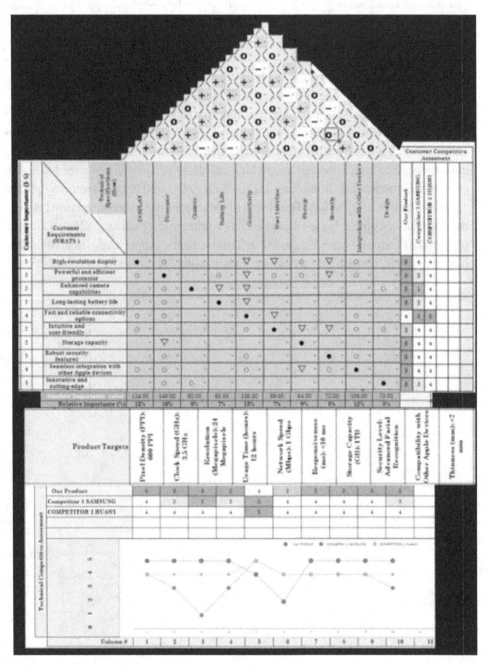

The correlation and interrelationship matrixes provide information on the relationships and correlations between different technical descriptors. Engineers can identify areas that need improvement based on the negative correlations and prioritize actions accordingly. In the case of the iPhone 14 Pro, areas that may require improvement include the battery life-connectivity relationship and the user interface-security relationship.

FUTURE RESEARCH DIRECTIONS

In future research, diverse users of mobile phones could be considered for their input to improve and develop a better design of the product. Also, the data collection process can be different ways such as one-to-one interviews, and observing the users with different usability tests.

CONCLUSION

In this study, the QFD approach is used to convert customer requirements into design features for a better mobile phone design. In this respect, an online survey was conducted with the users to determine their needs. Afterward, technical requirements were identified to meet customer requirements. The relationship between customer requirements and technical requirements was developed to identify the most critical phases. When products are designed with users' input and understanding, they are more likely to be adopted and used regularly, leading to higher engagement and retention rates (Lazuardy et al., 2024). Companies that prioritize user-centered design often differentiate themselves from competitors by offering superior user experiences, leading to increased customer loyalty and market share. Investing in user-centered design upfront can save costs associated with fixing usability issues or addressing user dissatisfaction later in the product lifecycle (Dodeja et al., 2024). The House of Quality also generates valuable comments and suggestions from customers. These suggestions can guide engineers and product developers in making improvements to mobile phones, such as incorporating advanced display technologies, optimizing power efficiency, enhancing camera features, and ensuring seamless integration with other devices.

Overall, the House of Quality enables a systematic approach to understanding customer requirements, comparing with competitors, identifying areas for improvement, and generating suggestions for enhancing the product. It provides valuable insights that can guide the product development process and help ensure that the considered product achieves high levels of customer satisfaction.

REFERENCES

Awan, A. B., Mahmood, A. W., & Sabahat, N. (2024). Enhancing User Experience: Exploring Mobile Augmented Reality Experiences. *VFAST Transactions on Software Engineering*, 12(1), 121–132. 10.21015/vtse.v12i1.1741

Aydemir, E., Sahin, Y., & Karagul, K. (2023). A Cost Level Analysis for the Components of the Smartphones Using Greyness Based Quality Function Deployment. In *Emerging Studies and Applications of Grey Systems* (pp. 313–330). Springer Nature Singapore. 10.1007/978-981-19-3424-7_12

Büyüközkan, G., Güler, M., & Mukul, E. (2020). An integrated fuzzy QFD methodology for customer oriented multifunctional power bank design. *Customer Oriented Product Design: Intelligent and Fuzzy Techniques*, 73-91.

Cerit, B., Küçükyazıcı, G., & Kalem, G. (2014). Quality function deployment and its application on a smartphone design. *Science Communication*, 2, 87.

Dodeja, L., Tambwekar, P., Hedlund-Botti, E., & Gombolay, M. (2024). Towards the design of user-centric strategy recommendation systems for collaborative Human–AI tasks. *International Journal of Human-Computer Studies*, 184, 103216. 10.1016/j.ijhcs.2023.10321638558883

Dworschak, C., Heim, E., Kuhn, N., Schwager, J., Tröster, A., & Maercker, A. (2024). User-centered development of an internet-based CBT intervention for the treatment of loneliness in older individuals. *Internet Interventions : the Application of Information Technology in Mental and Behavioural Health*, 35, 100720. 10.1016/j.invent.2024.10072038328277

Fleury, S., & Chaniaud, N. (2024). Multi-user centered design: Acceptance, user experience, user research and user testing. *Theoretical Issues in Ergonomics Science*, 25(2), 209–224. 10.1080/1463922X.2023.2166623

Han, D. I. D., Jung, T., & Tom Dieck, M. C. (2019). Translating tourist requirements into mobile AR application engineering through QFD. *International Journal of Human-Computer Interaction*, 35(19), 1842–1858. 10.1080/10447318.2019.1574099

Hu, S., Zhang, L., Guo, W., Zhang, D., Jia, Q., Yang, Z., & Guo, M. (2024). Research on the design of smart sleep aid interactive products. *International Journal of Industrial and Systems Engineering*, 46(2), 151–168. 10.1504/IJISE.2024.136413

Imbesi, S., & Scataglini, S. (2021). A user-centered methodology for the design of smart apparel for older users. *Sensors (Basel)*, 21(8), 2804. 10.3390/s2108280433923514

Karasan, A., Ilbahar, E., Cebi, S., & Kahraman, C. (2022). Customer-oriented product design using an integrated neutrosophic AHP & DEMATEL & QFD methodology. *Applied Soft Computing*, 118, 108445. 10.1016/j.asoc.2022.108445

Koswara, R., & Alifin, F. I. (2024). A User-oriented UI/UX Application Design Using The Integration of Quality Function Deployment (QFD) and Design Thinking Methods. *MOTIVECTION: Journal of Mechanical. Electrical and Industrial Engineering*, 6(1), 85–100.

Lazuardy, M. A., Marie, I. A., & Salim, A. (2024). User Interface User Experience Design with User Centered Design Method On Mobile Application For Laundry KK Reservation. *Intelmatics*, 4(1), 52–58. 10.25105/itm.v4i1.18228

Li, J., & Kim, K. (2023). Kano-QFD-based analysis of the influence of user experience on the design of handicraft intangible cultural heritage apps. *Heritage Science*, 11(1), 59. 10.1186/s40494-023-00903-w36974317

Stabile, A. J., Iribarren, S., Sonney, J., Demiris, G., & Schnall, R. (2024). Usability testing of a mobile health application to support individuals with active tuberculosis: A mixed methods study. *Informatics for Health & Social Care*, 1–13. 10.1080/175 38157.2024.233337938529729

Sudirjo, F., Dewa, D. M. R. T., Kesuma, L. I., Suryaningsih, L., & Utami, E. Y. (2024). Application of The User Centered Design Method To Evaluate The Relationship Between User Experience, User Interface and Customer Satisfaction on Banking Mobile Application. *Jurnal Informasi Dan Teknologi*, 7-13.

Wang, J., Yu, L., & Rong, Y. (2024). A new CoCoSo ranking-based QFD approach in Pythagorean fuzzy environment and its application on evaluating design attributes of mobile medical App. *Journal of Intelligent & Fuzzy Systems*, (Preprint), 1-24.

ADDITIONAL READING

Castiblanco Jimenez, I. A., Cepeda García, L. C., Violante, M. G., Marcolin, F., & Vezzetti, E. (2020). Commonly used external TAM variables in e-learning, agriculture and virtual reality applications. *Future Internet*, 13(1), 7. 10.3390/fi13010007

Gündoğdu, F. K., & Kahraman, C. (2020). A novel spherical fuzzy QFD method and its application to the linear delta robot technology development. *Engineering Applications of Artificial Intelligence*, 87, 103348. 10.1016/j.engappai.2019.103348

Kaya, S. K., & Erginel, N. (2020). Futuristic airport: A sustainable airport design by integrating hesitant fuzzy SWARA and hesitant fuzzy sustainable quality function deployment. *Journal of Cleaner Production*, 275, 123880. 10.1016/j. jclepro.2020.123880

Mistarihi, M. Z., Okour, R. A., & Mumani, A. A. (2020). An integration of a QFD model with Fuzzy-ANP approach for determining the importance weights for engineering characteristics of the proposed wheelchair design. *Applied Soft Computing*, 90, 106136. 10.1016/j.asoc.2020.106136

Rubert, C. K., de Carvalho, C. P., de Almeida, M. D. G. D., de Barros, J. G. M., & de Souza Sampaio, N. A. (2023). Development of automotive packaging by applying the QFD method. *Revista de Gestão e Secretariado*, 14(6), 10527–10548. 10.7769/ gesec.v14i6.2391

KEY TERMS AND DEFINITIONS

House of Quality: It is a significant part of the QFD including the "whats" part which refers to customer requirements and "hows" refers to technical requirements.

Mobile Phone: It is known as a cellphone or simply a phone, is a compact electronic device primarily created for long-distance telecommunications.

QFD: It is an approach that can be used for product development and design purposes.

User-Centered Design: It is a design process that places paramount importance on the requirements, desires, and actions of end-users from inception to completion.

Chapter 9
Use of Eye Tracking Method According to Individual Differences:
A Review From the Perspective of Gender, Personality Structure, and Birth

Mustafa Alpsülün
https://orcid.org/0000-0003-2928-218X
Harran University, Turkey

Hasan Celal Balıkçı
https://orcid.org/0000-0002-1539-1863
Harran University, Turkey

Müzeyyen Bulut Özek
Fırat University, Turkey

ABSTRACT

In the study, the effects on the design of learning environments were evaluated by considering gender, personality structures and birth order, which are considered as individual differences. Evaluation process eye tracking method was used. In the research, random assignment pattern paired from quasi-experimental research patterns was applied. Nineteen students from a public university participated in the research. To collect the data, a form containing demographic information, the information of the student's gender, age, along with the introverted or extroverted personality structure, and the number of children in the nuclear family were given. Data on eye movements were obtained with the eye tracking tool used while students

DOI: 10.4018/979-8-3693-3033-3.ch009

were studying with materials. As a result of the research, the students have differ-ent individual differences, and they have made inferences about the differences in learning with the eye movements they have made in learning materials and various suggestions have been made.

INTRODUCTION

For effective learning to occur, material design should be created by considering the individual differences among learners. Individual differences such as learners' perceptions, gender, personality structures, birth order, etc. should be identified, and learning environments should be provided that will enable the learner to dis-cover, interpret, and therefore their learning to occur effectively (Austin, 2009). A useful learning process can be realized through instructional design that is aware of individual differences (Ilgaz et al., 2014). Considering individual differences in learning environments, it is important to identify situations that will reduce students' motivation and prevent effective learning (Gropper, 2015; Kendeou et al., 2014). Based on this necessity, some researchers have put forward exemplary studies on the design of various teaching environments based on individual differences (Akçay & Altun, 2019; Austin, 2009; Lusk et al., 2009; Mazman & Altun, 2012; Schweppe & Rummer, 2014; Uz & Altun, 2014).

The proposition that instructional materials should be adapted taking into account the influence of birth order on attention is supported by research findings showing that there are inherent differences in behavioral and cognitive characteristics between first-borns, middle children, and youngest children.(Leman, 2009)(Rohrer et al., 2015)) In particular, first-born children are often characterized by a high propensity for attention and responsibility, suggesting that they are more likely to benefit from instructional materials that are structured in a detailed and directive manner(Marleau & Saucier, 2002) . In contrast, middle-born children, notable for their adaptability and flexibility, are likely to engage more extensively with materials designed to be exploratory and interactive, in line with their intrinsic characteristics(Sulloway, 1999) .Meanwhile, the youngest children, typically described as more creative and open to new experiences, may find materials that emphasize open-endedness and creativity more suited to their learning style. (Tizard & Hughes, 2008)) Therefore, the preparation of instructional materials requires not only the acknowledgment of these differences in attention and learning preferences by birth order, but also the incorporation of a range of approaches that capitalize on these differences. Thus, by aligning instructional design with the psychosocial developmental dispositions associated with birth position, it becomes possible to optimize educational outcomes.

The argument for adapting instructional materials to accommodate different attention preferences dictated by introversion and extroversion personality traits is well-founded in psychological and educational research. Introverts, characterized by deep, reflective thinking and a tendency towards introspection, naturally benefit from educational content that is enriched with detailed explorations and designed to foster inner reflection.(Herbert et al., 2023) This approach not only aligns with their cognitive styles but also maximizes their engagement and assimilation of knowledge. Conversely, extroverts, who flourish through social interactions and are oriented towards the external world, are more likely to succeed in a learning environment that promotes exploration through dynamic, interactive, and group activities.(Alaskar, 2023) Such differentiation in instructional design not only acknowledges the inherent variability in human attention and processing but also represents a movement towards a more personalized and effective educational paradigm. Educators can optimize the educational experience by tailoring instructional materials according to these personality-based learning preferences, thereby ensuring that both introverted and extroverted students receive education in a manner that best suits their natural tendencies and promotes optimal learning outcomes.(Ramirez et al., 2023)

Eye tracking, traditionally used to analyze the effectiveness of multimedia materials and contrasted with questionnaires or surveys, which have a more subjective nature, provides information that cannot be consciously controlled by students. Eye tracking allows us to collect information about their inferences and preferences, which are more difficult to obtain using traditional techniques (Molina et al., 2018). Learning efficiency is directly related to the understanding and comprehensibility of learning materials. To objectively measure the comprehension of the displayed content, the interpretation of various metrics provided by the eye tracker can be utilized (Hyönä, 2010; Jacob & Karn, 2003; Liu et al., 2011; Mutlu Bayraktar & Bayram, 2017; Park et al., 2015; Scheiter & Eitel, 2017; van Gog et al., 2009; van Gog & Scheiter, 2010). The use of eye-tracking techniques allows us to add physical evidence of quality to the assessment of aspects such as students' comprehensibility and students' visual effort when trying to grasp graphical and textual representations. The use of an eye-tracking device allows us to answer research questions such as "Where do students look when trying to understand and analyze a slide in a multimedia presentation?", "How do they fix their attention?". The contributions of the eye-tracking method in the literature have provided opportunities to design environments according to individual differences (Scheiter & Eitel, 2017). When these studies are examined, it is seen that the eye-tracking method is a suitable evaluation tool for determining the usability of instructional design environments and how the user processes information. Eye-tracking technologies provide data on how information is obtained in different materials, how inferences are made (Chuang & Liu, 2012; Holsanova et al., 2009), how they interact between these materials (Chuang & Liu,

2012), and where students' interests are concentrated (Alpsülün, 2018; Arndt et al., 2015; Holsanova et al., 2009; Tabbers et al., 2008). Although there are studies in the literature on eye movements in learning materials according to different individual differences (Akçay & Altun, 2019; Alpsülün, 2018; Jarodzka et al., 2015; Meira Jr et al., 2018; Mutlu Bayraktar & Bayram, 2017; Schmidt-Weigand, 2009, Gao et al., 2023,Kuperman et al., 2023,Emhardt et al., 2023), there are a limited number of studies based on individual differences of students. Recent research indicates that many parameters related to visual attention obtained through eye-tracking can be used to explain students' information processing processes in educational environments. While the number of fixations made in learning environments is considered as related effort (Tabbers et al., 2008), attention directed to the area of interest is considered as the level of information processing (Jarodzka et al., 2015; Scheiter and Eitel, 2017). Another parameter used to make inferences about the information processing process is the duration of fixations on the visual scene. Fixation duration provides important information about the acquisition of information from the visual scene (Schwonke et al., 2009). A long fixation duration is considered an indicator of difficult understanding of the information and high mental effort, while a short duration is considered an indicator of easy understanding of the relevant information (Majooni et al., 2016). There are also studies that consider this metric as the load of information in memory (Tabbers et al., 2008; van Gog et al., 2009). In this study, it was aimed to examine gender, introverted extrovert personality structure and birth order eye metrics as cognitive individual differences in terms of individual differences.

Research Problems

This study aims to examine the eye metrics of students with individual differences on the material. In this direction, answers to the following questions will be sought on the material of students with individual differences.

Gender, Introversion, and extroversion according to personality structure and birth order:

1. Is there a significant difference between the students' total fixation time on the material?
2. Is there a significant difference between the students' total number of fixations of the material?
3. Is there a significant difference between the focusing time of the students according to the areas of interest of the material?
4. Is there a significant difference between the number of students fixation on the material according to their areas of interest?

METHOD

In this study, paired random assignment design, one of the quasi-experimental research designs, was applied. It is a research design used to compare groups by determining certain individual differences instead of randomly assigning the groups formed in the research (Fraenkel et al., 2012).

Participants

Nineteen associate degree students (9 female and 10 male) from a state university participated in the study. The ages of the participants ranged between 19 and 37. The participants were determined by unbiased purposive sampling method. The characteristics of the participants are given in Table 1.

Table 1. Relevant information on students

f%			
Gender	**Female** **Male**	**9** **10**	**47** **53**
Introverted-Extroverted	Introverted Extroverted	11 8	58 42
Birth Order	First Middle End	5 7 7	26 37 37

When Table 1 is examined, 11 of the students participating in the study have an introverted personality structure and 8 of them have an extroverted personality structure. According to the birth order in the family, 5 students are the first child, 7 of them have a brother or sister, and the last 7 students are the youngest child of the nuclear family.

Data Collection Tools

To collect the data, a demographic information form was used to collect information about the gender and age of the student, as well as which personality type the student felt he/she had, introverted, or extroverted, and the number of children in the nuclear family. The Eye Tribe eye tracking device was used to determine eye tracking metrics. It calculates the user's eye peripheral coordinates with a visual angle accuracy of approximately 0.5 to 1°. Nine calibration locations are recommended by the system to increase the accuracy of the gaze coordinates.

Learning Material

The material used in the study (Figure 1) was prepared based on the principles outlined in Fleming and Levie's (1978) instructional message design book. In this learning environment, it was designed with the aim of focusing attention on the written text, the visual or the headline.

Figure 1. Sample image of the material

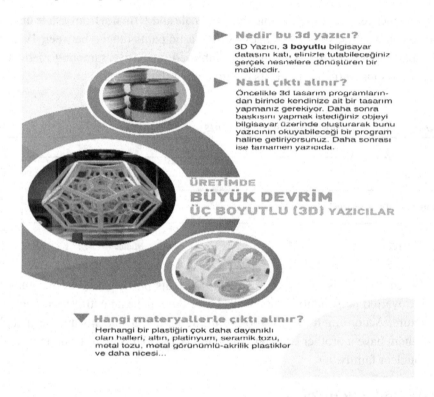

Implementation Phase

In the implementation phase of the study, all volunteer students participating in the study were invited to the computer laboratory between 15:00 and 16:00 on four days. In the first stage of the application phase, students were informed about the application. After the information, a demographic form was applied. After the demographic information of the participants was determined, the students were asked to use the teaching material. Metrics related to the eye movements of the students were obtained with the eye tracking device. This process took an average of nine minutes. The students were thanked for their participation in the study and the session was ended.

Data Analysis

In this study, students' total focusing time, total number of focusing times, total number of focusing times and number of focusing times and number of focusing times on related areas were obtained by OGAMA software. The variables obtained were determined as the dependent variable of the study. The independent variables of the study were students' gender, introverted extrovert personality structures and birth order. Before analyzing the data, the areas of interest were determined on the material as shown in Figure 2.

Figure 2. Sample image of the areas of interest identified in the material

Since the distribution of the research data is not normal and the sample size is small, nonparametric test methods should be used (Altman et al., 1992). In addition to descriptive analysis, Mann Whitney U nonparametric and Kruskal-Wallis test methods were used to compare the groups.

FINDINGS

The data on eye movements obtained within the scope of the research were analyzed with Mann Whitney U nonparametric test methods in the first two research problems, and Kruskal-Wallis test methods were used in the last research problem, and the findings obtained are presented under headings.

Gender, Introversion and Extroversion According to Personality Structure and Birth Order

1. Is there a significant difference between the students' total fixation time on the material?

In the study, students' total focusing time on the material was compared according to gender. It was observed that there was a significant difference between the students in terms of focusing time on the material (U=19.5, Z=-2.094, p(0.036)<.05). Considering the total focusing time, it is understood that the focusing time of females is higher than that of males. This finding can be considered that women analyzed the material more in depth than men.

In the study, the total focusing time of the students on the material was compared according to the personality structure of introversion and extroversion. It was seen that there was no significant difference between the students in terms of the focusing time on the material (U=22, Z=-1.827, p(0.068)>.05).

In the study, students' total focusing time on the material was compared according to birth order. It was observed that there was no significant difference between the students in terms of the focusing time on the material (X2=0.107, df=2, p(0.948)>.05).

2. Is there a significant difference between the students' total number of fixations of the material?

In the study, the total number of students' focusing on the material was compared according to gender. It was seen that there was no significant difference between the students in terms of the number of focusing on the material in terms of focusing time (U=43.5, Z=-.123, p(0.902)>.05).

In the study, the total number of students' focusing on the material was compared according to the personality structure of introversion and extroversion. It was seen that there was no significant difference between the students in terms of the number of focusing on the material in terms of focusing times (U=25, Z=-1.571, p(0.116)>.05).

In the study, the total number of students' focusing on the material according to birth order was compared. It was seen that there was no significant difference between the students in terms of the number of focus on the material (X2=1.103, df=2, p(0.597)>.05).

3. Is there a significant difference between the focusing time of the students according to the areas of interest of the material?

In the study, the focusing times of the students according to the interest areas of the material were compared according to gender. It was seen that there was no significant difference between the students in terms of the focusing time on the text, the first of the three areas of interest in the material (U=24.5, Z=-1.686, p(0.092)>.05). It was seen that there was a significant difference between the focusing times from the areas of interest to the title (U=16, Z=-2.44, p(0.014)<.05). Considering the duration of focusing on the title from the areas of interest, it is seen that women have higher focusing times than men. Lastly, it was observed that there was a significant difference in terms of the time spent focusing on the picture (U=6.5, Z=-3.206, p(0.01)<.05). When the focusing time from the areas of interest to the picture is taken into consideration, it is seen that the focusing time of women is higher than that of men. When the areas of interest were analyzed, it was determined that women focused on points of interest other than the text on the material.

In the study, according to the personality structure of introversion and extroversion, the focusing times of the students according to the areas of interest of the material were compared. It was seen that there was no significant difference between the students in terms of the time of focusing on the text, the first of the three areas of interest in the material (U=28, Z=-1.331, p(0.183)>.05). It was observed that there was no significant difference between the focus on the title among the areas of interest (U=26.5, Z=-1.494, p(0.135)>.05). It was observed that there was no significant difference in the duration of focusing on the picture from the areas of interest (U=34, Z=-.842, p(0.400)>.05).

In the study, the focusing times of the students according to the interest areas of the material were compared according to birth order. It was seen that there was no significant difference between the students in terms of the focusing time on the first of the three areas of interest in the material, the text ((X2=3.159, df=2, p(0.206)>.05). It was seen that there was no significant difference between the focusing times on the title among the areas of interest (X2=.237, df=2, p(0.888)>.05). Lastly, it was seen that there was no significant difference in terms of the focusing times on the picture among the areas of interest (X2=5.473, df=2, p(0.065)>.05).

4. Is there a significant difference between the number of students fixation on the material according to their areas of interest?

In the study, the number of students' focusing on the interest areas of the material was compared according to gender. It was seen that there was a significant difference between the students in terms of the number of focusing on the text, the first of the three areas of interest in the material (U=12.5, Z=-2.674, p(0.008)<.05). It was observed that there was a significant difference between the duration of focusing on the title from the areas of interest (U=16, Z=-2.44, p(0.014)<.05). Lastly, there was a significant difference in the duration of focusing on the picture (U=6.5, Z=-3.218, p(0.01)<.05). When the focusing durations for the areas of interest are taken into consideration, it is seen that the focusing durations of women are higher than those of men. When the areas of interest were analyzed, it was concluded that women examined all areas of interest on the material more in-depth than men.

In the study, according to the personality structure of introversion and extroversion, the focusing times of the students according to the areas of interest of the material were compared. It was seen that there was no significant difference between the students in terms of the time of focusing on the text, the first of the three areas of interest in the material (U=28, Z=-1.331, p(0.183)>.05). It was observed that there was no significant difference between the focus on the title among the areas of interest (U=26.5, Z=-1.494, p(0.135)>.05). It was observed that there was no significant difference in the duration of focusing on the picture from the areas of interest (U=34, Z=-.842, p(0.400)>.05).

In the study, the number of students' focusing on the interest areas of the material according to birth order was compared. It was seen that there was no significant difference between the students in terms of the number of focusing on the first of the three areas of interest in the material, the text ((X2=2.096, df=2, p(0.351)>.05). It was seen that there was no significant difference between the number of focusing on the title among the areas of interest (X2=.237, df=2, p(0.888)>.05). Lastly, it was seen that there was no significant difference in the number of focusing on the picture among the areas of interest (X2=4.727, df=2, p(0.094)>.05).

DISCUSSION AND CONCLUSION

Developing technology has shown its effect in the field of education as in every field and has created differences in the structure of scientific studies in this field. Eye-tracking technology, a product of technological progress, has recently become a popular method for educational studies. This method especially considers the individual differences of students with learning environments and supports the design of classrooms by taking into account individual differences in the learning environment.

The aim of this study is to examine whether individual differences such as gender, introverted extrovert personality structure and birth order cause a difference in eye movements in the learning environment. For this purpose, hypotheses about gender, introverted extrovert personality structure and birth order were established, and these hypotheses were tested.

When the analyses were analyzed, it was found that there was a significant difference between male and female students' focusing time on the learning material and female students focused more on the material. On the other hand, there was no difference in the number of times female and male students focused on the learning material. It was found that there was a significant difference between the focusing time of female and male students on the areas of interest (text, title and picture), except for the text, and female students had more focusing time. According to Eşel (2005), since men and women have different neural structures, their information processing and problem solving abilities are different. Therefore, in general, while men approach events and objects more superficially, women approach them in more detail. On the other hand, this finding supports the results of studies such as Valuch et al. (2015) and Sammaknejad (2017).

There was no statistical difference between students' introversion and extroversion and the duration of focusing on the learning material, the number of focusing on the learning material, and the duration of focusing on the title and picture from the areas of interest. On the other hand, it was determined that there was a difference between students' being introverted or extroverted and their interests. According to Yazıcı (1997), the way of perception of extroverted people is more perceptual, while the way of perception of introverted people is intuitive. Therefore, while extroverted people are interested in more concrete things, introverted people try to understand concepts and events with their imagination. In this context, it is thought that the difference stems from here. On the other hand, while these findings partially support the study of A. Aziz (2010), they contradict the studies of Ellingsen et al. (2019) and Meira et al. (2018).

Finally, birth order and the duration of focusing on the learning material, the number of focusing on the learning material and the duration of focusing on the areas of interest (text, title, and picture) were examined and it was found that there was no statistically significant difference between them. In real terms, each new addition to the family changes the attitude of the family and changes the relationships between family members. In the studies conducted, there are differences between the expectations of the families from the first child and the expectations from the next child. For this reason, while the first children are treated more dominantly, the younger ones are treated less oppressively. This shows that birth order may have an effect on personality (Yılmaz & Kesici, 2014). However, in this study, it was determined that birth order did not make a difference on eye movements.

As a result, when designing a learning environment, it is important to evaluate the information processing processes of students by considering their individual differences to make inferences about the effectiveness of the design. Based on this, it is recommended to re-evaluate the existing design principles by considering different cognitive individual differences and to conduct research on students' information processing processes in these designs.

REFERENCES

Akçay, A., & Altun, A. (2019). Farklı Kısa Süreli Bellek Uzamlarına Sahip Öğrencilerin Farklı Dikkat Tasarımına Sahip Öğrenme Ortamlarındaki Göz Hareketlerinin İncelenmesi. *Eğitim Teknolojisi Kuram Ve Uygulama*, 9(2), 588–614. 10.17943/etku.568192

Alpsülün, M. (2018). *Göz izleme teknikleriyle elektronik içeriklerin öğrenciler üzerindeki etkisinin araştırılması* [Master's Thesis, Harran Üniversitesi].

Altman, D. G., Gore, S. M., Gardner, M. J., & Pocock, S. J. (1992). Statistical Guidelines for Contributors to Medical Journals. *Annals of Clinical Biochemistry*, 29(1), 1–8. 10.1177/000456329202900101

Arndt, J., Schüler, A., & Scheiter, K. (2015). Text-picture integration: How delayed testing moderates recognition of pictorial information in multimedia learning. *Applied Cognitive Psychology*, 29(5), 702–712. 10.1002/acp.3154

Austin, K. A. (2009). Multimedia learning: Cognitive individual differences and display design techniques predict transfer learning with multimedia learning modules. *Computers & Education*, 53(4), 1339–1354. 10.1016/j.compedu.2009.06.017

Aziz, R. A. (2010). *Extraversion-introversion and the oral performance of Koya University EFL Students* [Doctoral dissertation, Bilkent University].

Chuang, H.-H., & Liu, H.-C. (2012). Effects of different multimedia presentations on viewers' information-processing activities measured by eye-tracking technology. *Journal of Science Education and Technology*, 21(2), 276–286. 10.1007/s10956-011-9316-1

Ellingsen, E. F., Drevsjø, S., Volden, F., & Watten, R. G. (2019). Extraversion and focus of attention on facial emotions: An experimental eye-tracking study. *Current Issues in Personality Psychology*, 7(1), 91–97. 10.5114/cipp.2019.85413

Emhardt, S. N., Kok, E., van Gog, T., Brandt-Gruwel, S., van Marlen, T., & Jarodzka, H. (2023). Visualizing a task performer's gaze to foster observers' performance and learning—A systematic literature review on eye movement modeling examples. *Educational Psychology Review*, 35(1), 23. 10.1007/s10648-023-09731-7

Eşel, E. (2005). Kadın ve Erkek Beyninin Farklılıkları. *Klinik Psikofarmakoloji Bulteni, 15*(3).

Fleming, M. L., & Levie, W. H. (1978). *Instructional message design: Principles from the behavioral sciences.* Educational Technology. https://www.google.com/books?hl=tr&lr=&id=qr1u-iLqeE0C&oi=fnd&pg=PR3&dq=Instructional+Message+Design:+Principles+from+the+Behavioral+Sciences+%C3%96n+Kapak+Malcolm+L.+Fleming,+W.+Howard+Levie&ots=Gf_ZnjbcH3&sig=72VkdM2Oh_73MszMV1s-tzXhVB4

Fraenkel, J. R., Wallen, N. E., & Hyun, H. H. (2012). *How to design and evaluate research in education.* McGraw-Hill.

Gao, H., Hasenbein, L., Bozkir, E., Göllner, R., & Kasneci, E. (2023). Exploring gender differences in computational thinking learning in a vr classroom: Developing machine learning models using eye-tracking data and explaining the models. *International Journal of Artificial Intelligence in Education*, 33(4), 929–954. 10.1007/s40593-022-00316-z

Gropper, G. L. (2015). Are individual differences undertreated in instructional design? *Educational Technology*, 55(2), 3–13.

Holsanova, J., Holmberg, N., & Holmqvist, K. (2009). Reading information graphics: The role of spatial contiguity and dual attentional guidance. *Applied Cognitive Psychology*, 23(9), 1215–1226. 10.1002/acp.1525

Hyönä, J. (2010). The use of eye movements in the study of multimedia learning. *Learning and Instruction*, 20(2), 172–176. 10.1016/j.learninstruc.2009.02.013

Ilgaz, H., Altun, A., & Aşkar, P. (2014). The effect of sustained attention level and contextual cueing on implicit memory performance for e-learning environments. *Computers in Human Behavior*, 39, 1–7. 10.1016/j.chb.2014.06.008

Jacob, R. J., & Karn, K. S. (2003). Eye tracking in human-computer interaction and usability research: Ready to deliver the promises. In *The mind's eye* (pp. 573–605). Elsevier. https://www.sciencedirect.com/science/article/pii/B97804445102 0450031110.1016/B978-044451020-4/50031-1

Jarodzka, H., Janssen, N., Kirschner, P. A., & Erkens, G. (2015). Avoiding split attention in computer-based testing: Is neglecting additional information facilitative? *British Journal of Educational Technology*, 46(4), 803–817. 10.1111/bjet.12174

Kendeou, P., van den Broek, P., Helder, A., & Karlsson, J. (2014). A cognitive view of reading comprehension: Implications for reading difficulties. *Learning Disabilities Research & Practice*, 29(1), 10–16. 10.1111/ldrp.12025

Kuperman, V., Siegelman, N., Schroeder, S., Acartürk, C., Alexeeva, S., Amenta, S., Bertram, R., Bonandrini, R., Brysbaert, M., Chernova, D., Da Fonseca, S. M., Dirix, N., Duyck, W., Fella, A., Frost, R., Gattei, C. A., Kalaitzi, A., Lõo, K., Marelli, M., & Usal, K. A. (2023). Text reading in English as a second language: Evidence from the Multilingual Eye-Movements Corpus. *Studies in Second Language Acquisition*, 45(1), 3–37. 10.1017/S0272263121000954

Leman, K. (2009). *The birth order book: Why you are the way you are*. Revell.

Liu, H.-C., Lai, M.-L., & Chuang, H.-H. (2011). Using eye-tracking technology to investigate the redundant effect of multimedia web pages on viewers' cognitive processes. *Computers in Human Behavior*, 27(6), 2410–2417. 10.1016/j.chb.2011.06.012

Lusk, D. L., Evans, A. D., Jeffrey, T. R., Palmer, K. R., Wikstrom, C. S., & Doolittle, P. E. (2009). Multimedia learning and individual differences: Mediating the effects of working memory capacity with segmentation. *British Journal of Educational Technology*, 40(4), 636–651. 10.1111/j.1467-8535.2008.00848.x

Marleau, J. D., & Saucier, J. F. (2002). Preference for a first-born boy in Western societies. *Journal of Biosocial Science*, 34(1), 13–27. 10.1017/S0021932002002000013511814210

Mazman, S. G., & Altun, A. (2012). Individual Differences in Different Level Mental Rotation Tasks: An Eye Movement Study. In *Towards Learning and Instruction in Web 3.0: Advances in Cognitive and Educational Psychology* (pp. 231–243). Springer. 10.1007/978-1-4614-1539-8

Meira, C. D. M.Jr, Moraes, R., Moura, M., Ávila, L. T. G., Tosini, L., & Magalhães, F. H. (2018). Extraversion/introversion and age-related differences in speed-accuracy tradeoff. *Revista Brasileira de Medicina do Esporte*, 24(3), 225–229. 10.1590/1517-869220182403172690

Molina, A. I., Navarro, Ó., Ortega, M., & Lacruz, M. (2018). Evaluating multimedia learning materials in primary education using eye tracking. *Computer Standards & Interfaces*, 59, 45–60. 10.1016/j.csi.2018.02.004

Mutlu Bayraktar, D., & Bayram, S. (2017). Evaluation of multimedia learning environment designed according to different attention types via eye tracking method. *Erzincan Üniversitesi Eğitim Fakültesi Dergisi*, 19(2), 119–138. 10.17556/erziefd.331370

Park, B., Korbach, A., & Brünken, R. (2015). Do learner characteristics moderate the seductive-details-effect? A cognitive-load-study using eye-tracking. *Journal of Educational Technology & Society*, 18(4), 24–36.

Rohrer, J. M., Egloff, B., & Schmukle, S. C. (2015). Examining the effects of birth order on personality. *Proceedings of the National Academy of Sciences of the United States of America*, 112(46), 14224–14229. 10.1073/pnas.150645111226483461

Sammaknejad, N., Pouretemad, H., Eslahchi, C., Salahirad, A., & Alinejad, A. (2017). Gender classification based on eye movements: A processing effect during passive face viewing. *Advances in Cognitive Psychology*, 13(3), 232–240. 10.5709/acp-0223-129071007

Scheiter, K., & Eitel, A. (2017). The use of eye tracking as a research and instructional tool in multimedia learning. In *Eye-Tracking Technology Applications in Educational Research* (pp. 143–164). IGI Global. 10.4018/978-1-5225-1005-5.ch008

Schmidt-Weigand, F. (2009). The influence of visual and temporal dynamics on split attention: Evidences from eye tracking. In *Cognitive Effects of Multimedia Learning* (pp. 89–107). IGI Global. 10.4018/978-1-60566-158-2.ch006

Schweppe, J., & Rummer, R. (2014). Attention, working memory, and long-term memory in multimedia learning: An integrated perspective based on process models of working memory. *Educational Psychology Review*, 26(2), 285–306. 10.1007/s10648-013-9242-2

Schwonke, R., Berthold, K., & Renkl, A. (2009). How multiple external representations are used and how they can be made more useful. *Applied Cognitive Psychology*, 23(9), 1227–1243. 10.1002/acp.1526

Sulloway, F. J. (1999). Birth order. Encyclopedia of creativity, 1, 189-202.

Tabbers, H. K., Paas, F., Lankford, C., Martens, R. L., & van Merriënboer, J. J. G. (2008). Studying eye movements in multimedia learning. *Understanding Multimedia Documents*, 169–184. 10.1007/978-0-387-73337-1_9

Tizard, B., & Hughes, M. (2008). *Young children learning*. John Wiley & Sons.

Uz, C., & Altun, A. (2014). Object Location Memory and Sex Difference: Implications on Static vs. Dynamic Navigation Environments. *Journal of Cognitive Science*, 14(1), 27–56. 10.17791/jcs.2014.15.1.27

Valuch, C., Pflüger, L. S., Wallner, B., Laeng, B., & Ansorge, U. (2015). Using eye tracking to test for individual differences in attention to attractive faces. *Frontiers in Psychology*, 6, 42. 10.3389/fpsyg.2015.0004225698993 van Gog, T., Kester, L., Nievelstein, F., Giesbers, B., & Paas, F. (2009). Uncovering cognitive processes: Different techniques that can contribute to cognitive load research and instruction. *Computers in Human Behavior*, 25(2), 325–331. 10.1016/j.chb.2008.12.021

van Gog, T., & Scheiter, K. (2010). Eye tracking as a tool to study and enhance multimedia learning. *Learning and Instruction*, 20(2), 95–99. 10.1016/j.learninstruc.2009.02.009

Yazıcı, H. (1997). *Karadeniz Teknik Üniversitesi Öğrencilerinin Kişilik Özelliklerinin Eysenck'in Kişilik Kuramına Dayalı Olarak Belirlenmesi*. KTÜ Sosyal Bilimler Enstitüsü Eğitim Bilimleri/Psikolojik Danışma ve Rehberlik.

Yılmaz, M. T., & Kesici, Ş. (2014). Anne baba tutumları ve kardeş sırasının üniversite öğrencilerinin öz-anlayışlarının gelişimine etkisi. *OPUS Uluslararası Toplum Araştırmaları Dergisi*, 4(6), 131–157.

Chapter 10
Navigating the Digital Economy:
The Crucial Role of Human–Computer Interaction

S. C. Vetrivel
https://orcid.org/0000-0003-3050-8211
Kongu Engineering College, India

K. C. Sowmiya
Sri Vasavi College, India

V. Sabareeshwari
Amrita School of Agricultural Sciences, India

V. P. Arun
JKKN College of Engineering and Technology, India

ABSTRACT

The advent of advanced technologies has led to a profound transformation in the way humans interact with computers, giving rise to the interdisciplinary field of Human-Computer Interaction (HCI). This chapter explores the multifaceted impact of HCI on the economy, examining its influence on productivity, employment dynamics, market trends, and societal structures. The study synthesizes a comprehensive analysis of the positive and negative implications of HCI, shedding light on its role as a driver of economic growth and a catalyst for socio-economic change. The positive aspects of HCI on the economy are first explored, focusing on increased productivity and efficiency resulting from user-friendly interfaces, intuitive design, and seamless interaction between humans and machines. The adoption of HCI principles has not

DOI: 10.4018/979-8-3693-3033-3.ch010

only streamlined business processes but has also empowered individuals with digital literacy, fostering innovation and entrepreneurship.

INTRODUCTION

Background and Context

In the rapidly evolving landscape of the digital economy, the intricate relationship between humans and computers has become pivotal for success. Human-Computer Interaction (HCI) emerges as a critical discipline that explores the design and implementation of user interfaces, aiming to optimize the interaction between users and digital systems. The roots of HCI can be traced back to the early days of computing when the focus was primarily on functionality. However, as technology advanced, the emphasis shifted towards creating user-friendly interfaces, acknowledging the significance of human experience in the digital realm (Abras et al., 2004). The digital economy itself represents a paradigm shift, where traditional business models are being reshaped by technology, connectivity, and data. Industries are becoming increasingly digitized, and the reliance on digital platforms for communication, commerce, and information has become pervasive. In this context, HCI plays a central role in ensuring that these digital interactions are not only efficient but also intuitive, engaging, and tailored to the diverse needs and preferences of users (Bainbridge, 2004). The success of digital products and services hinges on the seamless integration of technology with human behavior, making HCI an indispensable aspect of the digital economy. Moreover, the rise of emerging technologies such as artificial intelligence, augmented reality, and virtual reality has further underscored the importance of HCI. As these technologies become more prevalent, designing interfaces that effectively leverage their capabilities while remaining user-friendly becomes paramount. HCI practitioners are at the forefront of developing innovative solutions that bridge the gap between human cognition and the capabilities of advanced digital systems. The convergence of these technologies within the digital economy necessitates a holistic understanding of user behavior, cognitive processes, and the social context in which technology is embedded.

Importance of Human-Computer Interaction (HCI) in the Modern World

Human-Computer Interaction (HCI) plays a crucial role in the modern world for several reasons:

User-Centric Design: HCI emphasizes designing technology with a deep understanding of users' needs, preferences, and behaviors. This user-centric approach ensures that technology is more intuitive, user-friendly, and aligned with the way people think and work.

Enhanced User Experience (UX): HCI aims to create positive and meaningful user experiences. A well-designed HCI results in improved usability, satisfaction, and overall user experience, which is vital for the success and adoption of technology products and services.

Productivity and Efficiency: HCI contributes to the design of systems that enhance productivity and efficiency (Acemoglu, 2012). When interfaces are intuitive and user-friendly, users can perform tasks more quickly and accurately, leading to increased efficiency in various domains such as business, education, healthcare, and more.

Accessibility and Inclusivity: HCI addresses the importance of making technology accessible to people with diverse abilities and needs. Designing interfaces that accommodate individuals with disabilities ensures inclusivity and equal access to information and services for everyone.

Reduced Learning Curve: Well-designed HCI minimizes the learning curve for users. Intuitive interfaces and interaction patterns enable users to quickly understand how to operate and navigate through applications, reducing the time and effort required for training.

Innovation and Adoption: HCI is at the forefront of driving innovation in technology. As new technologies emerge, HCI researchers and designers explore novel ways for humans to interact with these technologies, leading to the development of groundbreaking products and services that are more likely to be adopted by users.

User Satisfaction and Loyalty: Positive user experiences lead to higher levels of satisfaction and user loyalty (Aker & Mbiti, 2010). Satisfied users are more likely to continue using a product or service, recommend it to others, and remain engaged with the technology over the long term.

Ethical Considerations: HCI also addresses ethical considerations in technology design, ensuring that systems respect user privacy, security, and values. This is particularly important in today's digital age where concerns about data privacy and ethical use of technology are prominent.

Cross-Cultural Considerations: With technology reaching a global audience, HCI is essential for designing interfaces that are culturally sensitive and suitable for users from diverse backgrounds. This helps in creating technology that is inclusive and applicable across different regions and demographics.

Continuous Improvement: HCI involves iterative design processes that include user feedback and usability testing (Asongu, 2015). This approach ensures that technology evolves and improves over time, adapting to changing user needs and preferences.

Overview of the Economic Impact

The rapid advancement of technology and the pervasive integration of digital systems have significantly transformed the global economic landscape. As societies navigate the digital economy, the role of Human-Computer Interaction (HCI) becomes crucial in shaping and maximizing economic outcomes. HCI refers to the design and use of computer technologies, emphasizing the interaction between humans and machines. Understanding the economic impact of navigating the digital economy requires a comprehensive exploration of how HCI influences productivity, innovation, and overall economic performance. One key aspect of HCI's economic impact lies in its ability to enhance productivity across various sectors. Efficient and user-friendly interfaces, informed by HCI principles, empower individuals to interact seamlessly with digital tools, thereby streamlining workflows and reducing operational bottlenecks. Businesses that invest in well-designed digital interfaces experience improved employee efficiency and effectiveness, contributing to overall economic productivity gains (Bailetti, 2012). Furthermore, HCI-driven innovations in automation and artificial intelligence contribute to labor productivity by automating routine tasks, allowing human workers to focus on more complex and creative aspects of their roles. In the digital economy, innovation is a driving force behind economic growth, and HCI plays a pivotal role in fostering and sustaining innovation. HCI principles guide the development of user-centric technologies, ensuring that innovations are not only technically advanced but also aligned with human needs and preferences. This alignment fosters the adoption of new technologies, creating a positive feedback loop that encourages further innovation. As businesses leverage HCI to create more intuitive and user-friendly digital solutions, they are better positioned to develop groundbreaking products and services that can disrupt traditional markets and drive economic growth. Moreover, the economic impact of HCI in the digital economy extends beyond individual businesses to influence macroeconomic indicators. Countries and regions that prioritize HCI education and research create a competitive advantage in the global digital landscape. A skilled HCI workforce contributes to a thriving technology sector, attracting investments and fostering a conducive environment for digital entrepreneurship. Consequently, economies that embrace HCI principles experience job creation, increased exports of technology-driven products and services, and enhanced global competitiveness.

EVOLUTION OF HUMAN-COMPUTER INTERACTION

Historical Perspective on HCI

Human-Computer Interaction (HCI) has evolved significantly over the years, with its roots tracing back to the mid-20th century. Throughout this evolution, HCI has evolved from a focus on input devices and usability to a broader consideration of the entire user experience (Bhave, 1994). The interdisciplinary nature of HCI incorporates principles from psychology, design, engineering, and computer science to create more effective and enjoyable human-computer interactions.Here's a brief historical perspective on HCI:

1950s-1960s: Early Computers and Interfaces

- o   The field of HCI began with the advent of computers in the 1950s. Initially, computers were large and complex machines used for scientific and military purposes.
- o   Input and output were primarily through punch cards and printouts. The interaction was limited, and user interfaces were not a focal point.

1970s: Emergence of Graphical User Interfaces (GUI)

- o   Xerox PARC (Palo Alto Research Center) played a pivotal role in the development of GUIs during the 1970s. Researchers like Alan Kay and Douglas Engelbart made significant contributions.
- o   The introduction of the mouse as an input device and the graphical representation of information marked a shift toward more user-friendly interfaces.

1980s: Rise of Personal Computers and HCI Research

- o   The 1980s saw the proliferation of personal computers, such as the IBM PC and the Apple Macintosh. This increased the need for more intuitive and user-friendly interfaces.
- o   Researchers like Ben Shneiderman emphasized the importance of designing interfaces based on human factors and usability principles.

1990s: Internet Boom and Web Interfaces

- The widespread adoption of the internet in the 1990s brought new challenges and opportunities for HCI. The focus shifted to designing interfaces for web applications and websites.
- Jakob Nielsen became a prominent figure, advocating for web usability and introducing principles like "10 Usability Heuristics."

2000s: Mobile Computing and Touch Interfaces

- The rise of mobile devices, particularly smart phones, led to a new era in HCI. Touch screens became a common interaction method, and designers had to adapt to the constraints of smaller screens.
- Gestures and multi-touch interfaces gained prominence, influencing the design of both hardware and software.

2010s: Ubiquitous Computing and User Experience (UX)

- The 2010s witnessed the integration of computing into various aspects of daily life. Wearable devices, smart homes, and the Internet of Things (IoT) expanded the scope of HCI.
- UX design became a central focus, emphasizing the overall experience of users with technology rather than just the usability of interfaces.

2020s and Beyond: AI, Augmented Reality, and Emerging Technologies

- The current era is characterized by the integration of artificial intelligence, augmented reality, and virtual reality into HCI. Natural language processing, machine learning, and adaptive interfaces are shaping the next generation of user experiences.

Theoretical Foundations

1. **Usability Principles:** Usability principles guide the design of interfaces to make them more intuitive, efficient, and satisfying for users. These principles include visibility of system status, match between system and real-world, user control and freedom, consistency, error prevention, recognition rather than recall, flexibility and efficiency of use, aesthetic and minimalist design, and help users recognize, diagnose, and recover from errors.

2. **Cognitive Psychology:** Cognitive psychology provides insights into how humans perceive, process, and remember information. Key concepts include mental models, attention, memory, perception, and problem-solving, all of which influence the design of user interfaces.

Milestones in the Development of HCI

Human-Computer Interaction (HCI) has witnessed significant milestones in its development, shaping the way users interact with technology. One of the earliest milestones occurred in the 1960s with the emergence of interactive computing (Billon et al., 2010). Douglas Engelbart's groundbreaking work at the Stanford Research Institute led to the development of the mouse, graphical user interfaces (GUIs), and the concept of hypertext. These innovations laid the foundation for a more intuitive and user-friendly interaction model. The 1970s marked the advent of touchscreens, thanks to the efforts of researchers like E.A. Johnson and Frank Beck at the Royal Radar Establishment in the United Kingdom. This period also saw the rise of early text-based interfaces, introducing command-line interactions that set the stage for future developments. The Xerox Alto, developed at Xerox PARC in the 1970s, further advanced GUIs by introducing overlapping windows, icons, and menus, shaping the graphical interfaces we use today. In the 1980s and 1990s, HCI experienced a paradigm shift with the rise of personal computing. The widespread adoption of desktop computers and the development of operating systems like Microsoft Windows and Apple's Mac OS brought HCI to the mainstream. The concept of usability gained prominence during this era, with researchers like Jakob Nielsen contributing to the development of usability heuristics and guidelines. The turn of the millennium saw the proliferation of mobile devices, leading to a new era in HCI. The introduction of touchscreens in smartphones, popularized by the iPhone in 2007, transformed the way people interacted with technology. Multi-touch gestures, such as pinch-to-zoom and swipe, became integral to user experiences. Additionally, the field of user experience (UX) design gained prominence, emphasizing a holistic approach to designing products that prioritize the overall user journey. Advancements in HCI continued with the rise of augmented reality (AR) and virtual reality (VR) in the 2010s. Technologies like Oculus Rift and Microsoft HoloLens brought immersive experiences, expanding the possibilities of human-computer interaction beyond traditional screens. Gesture-based interfaces, voice recognition, and natural language processing further diversified the ways users could interact with devices (Bloodgood et al., 1996; Bouwman et al., 2008). Looking forward, ongoing research in artificial intelligence, machine learning, and neurotechnology holds the promise of even more seamless and intuitive human-computer interactions. As HCI continues to evolve, these milestones represent crucial steps in creating technology that aligns with human capabilities and enhances user experiences across various platforms and devices.

FRAMEWORKS AND MODELS IN HUMAN-COMPUTER INTERACTION

Overview of HCI Frameworks

Human-Computer Interaction (HCI) frameworks play a crucial role in designing and understanding the interaction between humans and computers. These frameworks provide a structured approach to analyze, design, and evaluate user interfaces. The following paragraphs offer an overview of some prominent HCI frameworks within the broader category of Frameworks and Models in Human-Computer Interaction:

One notable HCI framework is the "User-Centered Design" (UCD) model. UCD places the user at the core of the design process, emphasizing iterative design and user feedback (Braun & Clarke, 2006). This framework involves phases such as understanding user needs, creating design solutions, and conducting usability evaluations. UCD aims to ensure that the final product is both efficient and user-friendly by actively involving users throughout the design lifecycle.

Another significant framework is the "Activity Theory." Originating from the field of psychology, Activity Theory views human-computer interaction as a system of interconnected activities. It explores the relationship between users, their goals, and the tools they use, emphasizing the social and cultural aspects of interaction. Activity Theory is particularly useful in understanding complex interactions and the impact of technology on broader social contexts. The "Cognitive Walkthrough" is a model that focuses on the cognitive aspects of user interaction. It involves evaluators systematically walking through the user interface and evaluating it based on the users' likely thought processes. This framework is valuable for identifying potential usability issues and improving the cognitive efficiency of the interface. Additionally, the "Model-View-Controller" (MVC) architecture is a widely adopted framework in software engineering that has implications for HCI. MVC separates the application into three interconnected components: Model (data and business logic), View (user interface), and Controller (input and user interactions) (Brewer et al., 2005). This separation enhances maintainability, scalability, and flexibility in designing user interfaces and is particularly prevalent in web application development.

Furthermore, the "Persuasive Technology" framework explores the design of interactive technologies aimed at changing users' attitudes or behaviors. Developed by B.J. Fogg, this framework leverages principles of psychology and human behavior to design systems that encourage specific actions or attitudes, making it relevant in areas like health, education, and sustainability.

Theoretical Models Guiding HCI Design

Human-Computer Interaction (HCI) design is guided by various theoretical models that help designers understand and address user needs and interactions with technology. These theoretical models serve as frameworks for understanding user behavior, cognitive processes, and the social context, allowing designers to create more effective and user-friendly interfaces (Cantwell, 2009). Designers often integrate multiple models depending on the specific goals and context of the HCI project. Here are some key theoretical models influencing HCI design:

User-Centered Design (UCD):

- o Principles: Focuses on designing products and systems based on the needs, preferences, and behaviors of end users.
- o Application: Involves users throughout the design process, including requirements gathering, prototyping, and testing.

Activity Theory:

- o Principles: Views human activities as central to the design process, emphasizing the context and social aspects of interactions.
- o Application: Helps designers understand how users perform tasks within a specific context and how technology can support these activities.

Cognitive Walkthrough:

- o Principles: Evaluates the usability of a system by simulating the thought processes of users as they interact with an interface.
- o Application: Designers step through tasks to identify potential usability issues from the user's perspective.

Information Processing Model:

- o Principles: Draws from psychology, focusing on how humans process information and make decisions.
- o Application: Informs interface design by considering cognitive processes such as attention, memory, and problem-solving.

GOMS Model (Goals, Operators, Methods, and Selection rules):

o   Principles: Analyzes user tasks by breaking them down into sub-tasks and specifying the cognitive processes involved.

o   Application: Helps designers optimize task performance by identifying areas where the interaction can be streamlined.

Affordance Theory:

o   Principles: Introduced by Donald Norman, it emphasizes the perceived and actual properties of an object that determine how it can be used.

o   Application: Designers aim to create interfaces where users can easily perceive the functions and actions available to them.

User Experience (UX) Design:

o   Principles: Encompasses various factors such as usability, accessibility, aesthetics, and emotional aspects to create a positive overall experience for the user.

o   Application: Focuses on the holistic experience, considering both functional and emotional aspects of user interaction.

Social-Technical Systems Theory:

o   Principles: Explores the interaction between technical systems and the social context in which they are used.

o   Application: Guides designers in creating systems that align with social structures and support collaboration and communication.

Persona-Based Design:

o   Principles: Involves creating fictional characters (personas) representing different user types to guide design decisions.

o   Application: Provides a human-centered approach, helping designers empathize with and design for specific user needs and characteristics.

Ecological Interface Design:

   º Principles: Takes inspiration from ecological psychology, focusing on the fit between the user and the environment.

   º Application: Aims to create interfaces that support users in adapting and maintaining awareness within complex and dynamic environments.

Application of Models in Economic Contexts

In economic contexts, the application of theoretical models plays a crucial role in understanding and predicting various phenomena, guiding policy decisions, and informing strategic planning. Economic models, such as the classical, Keynesian, and neoclassical models, provide frameworks for analyzing factors like production, consumption, investment, and employment. These models help economists and policymakers make sense of complex economic systems, identify potential outcomes of policy interventions, and assess the impact of various factors on overall economic health (Day & Schoemaker, 2016). Additionally, behavioral economic models integrate psychological insights into economic decision-making, offering a more realistic portrayal of human behavior. Game theory models help analyze strategic interactions among rational decision-makers, while input-output models assist in understanding the interdependencies among different sectors of an economy. The application of these models contributes to evidence-based policymaking, facilitates economic forecasting, and enhances the comprehension of economic dynamics, ultimately supporting efforts to achieve sustainable and equitable economic development.

THE ROLE OF USER EXPERIENCE (UX) IN ECONOMY

Definition and Importance of UX

User Experience (UX) is a multidimensional concept that encompasses the overall interaction a user has with a product, service, or system. It refers to the user's perceptions, emotions, and responses that result from the use or anticipated use of a particular product. UX design aims to enhance user satisfaction by improving the usability, accessibility, and pleasure provided in the interaction with the product. It involves a combination of elements such as user interface design, information architecture, usability testing, and user research to create a seamless and enjoyable experience for the user. In the context of the economy, the role of User Experience is crucial for several reasons (Del Vitto, 2008). Firstly, a positive user experience can lead to increased customer satisfaction and loyalty. When users find a product or service easy to use and enjoyable, they are more likely to become repeat customers, contributing to the sustained success of businesses. Conversely, a poor user experience can result in frustration and dissatisfaction, leading users to abandon a product or service, which can have detrimental effects on a company's bottom line. Secondly, UX plays a pivotal role in differentiating products and services in a competitive market. As consumers have an abundance of choices, businesses need to stand out by offering superior user experiences. A well-designed and intuitive user interface, coupled with thoughtful user-centered design principles, can set a product apart from its competitors and create a distinct brand identity. Thirdly, the efficiency and effectiveness of digital products are directly tied to the quality of their user experience. A seamless and intuitive design reduces the learning curve for users, making products more accessible to a broader audience. This accessibility is particularly important in today's globalized economy, where diverse user demographics and cultural backgrounds must be considered in the design process.

Economic Implications of Positive and Negative User Experiences

User Experience (UX) plays a crucial role in shaping economic outcomes, as both positive and negative user experiences can have profound implications on various economic dimensions. Positive user experiences contribute to increased consumer satisfaction and loyalty, fostering economic growth through repeat business and positive word-of-mouth recommendations. When users find products or services easy to use, enjoyable, and effective, they are more likely to engage in transactions, leading to higher sales and revenue for businesses. This positive feedback loop enhances the overall economic performance of industries and businesses that prioritize and invest in delivering exceptional user experiences. On the contrary, negative user experiences can have detrimental effects on the economy (Donovan & Donner, 2010; Eisenhardt, 1989). Dissatisfied users are more likely to abandon products or services, resulting in decreased sales and revenue for businesses. Moreover, negative user experiences can lead to reputational damage, affecting brand image and trust. In today's interconnected world, where information spreads rapidly through social media and online reviews, a single negative user experience can have a cascading effect, impacting the economic prospects of a company on a larger scale. This interconnectedness highlights the importance of investing in UX to mitigate potential economic losses. From an economic perspective, positive user experiences contribute to job creation and innovation. As businesses thrive due to satisfied users, they are more likely to expand their operations, hire additional staff, and invest in research and development. This positive economic cycle stimulates innovation, as companies strive to stay ahead by continually improving and adapting their products or services to meet user needs. This innovation, in turn, can lead to the emergence of new markets, industries, and job opportunities, contributing to overall economic development. Conversely, negative user experiences may stifle innovation and limit economic growth. When companies face declining sales and financial challenges due to poor user feedback, they may become hesitant to invest in new technologies, research, or expansion. This cautious approach can hinder progress and limit the creation of new economic opportunities. In essence, the role of UX in the economy is not just confined to individual transactions but extends to broader economic dynamics, influencing innovation, employment, and overall economic prosperity (Eisenmann et al., 2012). As such, businesses and policymakers alike need to recognize the economic implications of positive and negative user experiences and strategically prioritize user-centric approaches to drive sustainable economic growth.

Case Studies Highlighting the Economic Impact of UX Design

These case studies demonstrate that investing in UX design can lead to improved user satisfaction, increased engagement, reduced support costs, and ultimately contribute to the economic success of businesses and organizations.

Airbnb:

- Challenge: Airbnb faced the challenge of ensuring that users could easily find and book accommodations on their platform.
- Solution: The company invested heavily in UX design to improve the overall user experience, focusing on intuitive navigation, appealing visuals, and simplified booking processes.
- Results: After the UX redesign, Airbnb reported a significant increase in user engagement and a 30% increase in bookings. This improvement directly contributed to the economic success of the platform.

Intuit (QuickBooks):

- Challenge: QuickBooks, an accounting software, needed to simplify complex financial processes for small businesses and freelancers.
- Solution: Intuit invested in UX research and design to create an intuitive and user-friendly interface, making financial management more accessible to a non-accounting audience.

- Results: The UX improvements resulted in a 15% increase in user engagement and a 32% reduction in customer support calls. This positively impacted the company's bottom line by increasing user satisfaction and loyalty.

Government Digital Service (GDS) - UK:

- Challenge: The UK government faced challenges in delivering digital services that were user-friendly and efficient for citizens.
- Solution: GDS focused on UX design principles to redesign government websites and services, making them more accessible and user-centric.
- Results: The improved user experience led to a 70% increase in online transactions and a substantial decrease in the cost of delivering government services, showcasing the economic benefits of investing in UX for public sector projects.

IBM Design Thinking:

- Challenge: IBM sought to transform its design approach to better meet user needs and enhance product development processes.
- Solution: IBM embraced design thinking and invested in UX design methodologies to create user-centered products and services.
- Results: The adoption of UX design principles contributed to a 300% ROI (Return on Investment) for IBM. The company experienced increased customer satisfaction and reduced development time and costs.

HCI IN BUSINESS AND PRODUCTIVITY

Integration of HCI in Business Processes

The integration of Human-Computer Interaction (HCI) in business processes has become increasingly crucial in the digital age, as organizations recognize the significance of creating seamless and user-friendly interfaces for both employees and customers. HCI involves designing and implementing systems that facilitate effective communication between humans and computers, ensuring optimal user experience and productivity (Freudenthaler, 2015; Ghemawat, 2001). One key area where HCI plays a pivotal role in business processes is in the development of user interfaces for enterprise software. Whether it's a customer relationship management (CRM) system, an enterprise resource planning (ERP) solution, or a project management tool, the design of intuitive and user-centric interfaces is paramount. HCI principles guide the creation of interfaces that enhance user engagement, reduce cognitive load, and streamline workflows, ultimately boosting efficiency and effectiveness in various business tasks. Moreover, HCI integration extends beyond traditional desktop applications, encompassing mobile applications and web platforms. As businesses increasingly rely on mobile devices and online platforms for their operations, HCI ensures that these interfaces are responsive, adaptive, and accessible. This is particularly important for remote work scenarios, where employees may interact with business applications across a variety of devices and environments. In customer-facing processes, HCI becomes a critical factor in creating positive user experiences. E-commerce platforms, online banking systems, and other digital services leverage HCI principles to simplify navigation, personalize interactions, and anticipate user needs. A well-designed user interface enhances customer satisfaction, encourages user engagement, and can lead to increased loyalty and repeat business (Ghemawat, 2007). Furthermore, the integration of HCI in business processes involves ongoing user feedback and iterative design. User testing, usability studies, and feedback mechanisms are integral components of HCI methodologies. This iterative approach allows businesses to adapt and refine their interfaces based on real-world user interactions, ensuring continuous improvement and alignment with evolving user needs.

Impact on Productivity and Efficiency

The integration of Human-Computer Interaction (HCI) in business processes has a profound impact on productivity and efficiency across various domains. By prioritizing user experience and interface design, organizations can realize several benefits that directly contribute to improved operational effectiveness. One key impact is the reduction of learning curves and task completion times. Well-designed interfaces based on HCI principles are intuitive and user-friendly, enabling employees to quickly grasp the functionality of software applications. This leads to faster onboarding of new personnel, increased efficiency in daily tasks, and a decrease in errors associated with complex or confusing interfaces (Griffith & Zhao, 2015). HCI integration also plays a crucial role in enhancing overall employee satisfaction and engagement. A positive user experience contributes to a more enjoyable and efficient work environment, boosting morale and motivation. When employees find it easy to interact with digital tools and systems, they are more likely to embrace technology in their daily workflows, leading to increased productivity and a higher quality of work output. Efficiency gains are particularly evident in streamlined workflows. HCI principles guide the design of interfaces that minimize unnecessary steps and simplify complex processes. This not only saves time but also reduces the cognitive load on users, allowing them to focus on the core aspects of their tasks. Consequently, organizations experience increased efficiency in project execution, decision-making, and collaborative efforts. Moreover, the integration of HCI contributes to a reduction in errors and rework. Interfaces designed with user-centric considerations help prevent misunderstandings and mistakes, leading to a decrease in the need for corrections and revisions. This has a direct impact on the overall quality of work, as well as resource utilization, contributing to improved efficiency in business processes. In customer-facing scenarios, HCI integration directly influences customer satisfaction and loyalty. Interfaces that are easy to navigate and understand contribute to a positive user experience, resulting in increased customer engagement and repeat business. This, in turn, positively affects the efficiency of sales and support processes, as satisfied customers are more likely to complete transactions and recommend the business to others.

Cost-Benefit Analysis of Implementing HCI in Businesses

A cost-benefit analysis (CBA) for implementing Human-Computer Interaction (HCI) in businesses involves evaluating the costs associated with implementing HCI against the benefits it brings (Guesalaga & Marshall, 2008). Below is a simplified example with hypothetical figures in Indian Rupees (INR):

Cost-Benefit Analysis for Implementing HCI in Alok Corporation

Table 1. Costs

Cost Component	Description	Estimated Cost (INR)
HCI Software and Tools	Purchase of necessary software and HCI tools	5,00,000
Employee Training	Training programs for staff on HCI	2,00,000
Infrastructure Upgrade	Hardware and network upgrades for HCI implementation	8,00,000
Integration and Implementation	Cost of integrating HCI into existing systems	3,00,000
Maintenance and Support	Ongoing support and maintenance costs	1,50,000 per annum
Total Implementation Costs		19,50,000

Table 2. Benefits

Benefit Component	Description	Estimated Benefit (INR)
Improved Productivity	Efficiency gains due to streamlined interfaces	15,00,000
User Satisfaction	Enhanced user experience leading to customer loyalty	10,00,000
Error Reduction	Minimized errors and rework, saving time and resources	8,00,000
Competitive Advantage	Differentiation in the market through advanced HCI	12,00,000
Total Expected Benefits		45,00,000

Net Benefit

Net Benefit =Total Expected Benefits−Total Implementation Costs
Net Benefit =45,00,000−19,50,000 =25,50,000

The implementation of HCI in Alok Corporation is expected to yield a net benefit of INR 25,50,000. This indicates a positive return on investment, suggesting that the implementation is financially viable. However, it's important to consider non-monetary factors like improved employee satisfaction, enhanced reputation, and long-term strategic advantages that may not be directly quantifiable.

E-COMMERCE AND CONSUMER BEHAVIOR

Influence of HCI on Online Shopping Behavior

Human-Computer Interaction (HCI) plays a crucial role in shaping and influencing online shopping behavior. The design and usability of online platforms directly impact how users navigate, search for products, and ultimately make purchase decisions. A user-friendly interface can significantly enhance the overall online shopping experience, leading to increased user satisfaction and loyalty. One of the key aspects of HCI in online shopping is the importance of intuitive and responsive design. Websites and mobile applications that are easy to navigate and provide a seamless browsing experience contribute to positive user perceptions. Clear and well-designed interfaces reduce cognitive load, making it easier for users to find products, compare options, and make informed decisions. This can lead to higher conversion rates as users are more likely to complete their purchases without frustration. HCI also influences the personalization of online shopping experiences (Harris, 2016). Through the use of data analytics and user profiling, online platforms can tailor recommendations and content to individual preferences. This personalized approach enhances user engagement, as customers feel that the platform understands their needs and preferences. The implementation of features like personalized recommendations, targeted advertisements, and dynamic content significantly influences users' choices and purchasing behavior. Moreover, the integration of interactive elements, such as chatbots and virtual assistants, contributes to the overall user experience in online shopping. These tools provide real-time assistance, helping users with queries, offering product recommendations, and guiding them through the purchase process. By simulating human-like interactions, these HCI-driven features enhance user engagement and build trust, ultimately impacting purchasing decisions positively. Social factors also come into play, with HCI influencing the integration of social media features on e-commerce platforms. Social sharing, user reviews, and recommendations create a sense of community and trust among online shoppers. Positive interactions within the platform, facilitated by HCI, can lead to increased brand loyalty and influence the purchasing decisions of potential customers who rely on social validation.

Economic Consequences of User-Friendly E-Commerce Platforms

The economic consequences of user-friendly e-commerce platforms are substantial and far-reaching, impacting various stakeholders in the online business ecosystem. Here are several key economic implications:

Increased Sales and Revenue: User-friendly e-commerce platforms tend to attract more visitors and convert them into customers (Hertzum, 2010). A seamless and intuitive interface, along with easy navigation, encourages users to explore products and make purchases. As a result, businesses experience higher sales and increased revenue, directly contributing to economic growth. Reduced Abandonment Rates: User-friendly designs can help reduce cart abandonment rates. When customers find the shopping process easy and enjoyable, they are more likely to complete transactions. This reduction in abandoned carts leads to a higher conversion rate, positively impacting the bottom line for e-commerce businesses.
Enhanced Customer Loyalty: A positive user experience fosters customer loyalty. Users are more likely to return to a platform that provides a seamless and enjoyable shopping experience. Repeat business and loyal customers contribute significantly to the long-term economic success of an e-commerce venture, as it reduces customer acquisition costs and increases customer lifetime value.

Cost Savings in Customer Support: User-friendly platforms can decrease the need for extensive customer support. When customers can easily find information, navigate the website, and complete transactions without issues, the demand for customer service decreases. This leads to cost savings for businesses, allowing them to allocate resources more efficiently.

Market Expansion: User-friendly platforms enable businesses to reach a broader audience. As more people find the platform accessible and easy to use, there is potential for market expansion beyond traditional boundaries. This increased reach can result in a larger customer base, driving economic growth for the e-commerce industry.

Positive Brand Image: A user-friendly e-commerce platform contributes to a positive brand image. Customers associate a seamless online experience with a well-established and trustworthy brand. This positive perception can lead to increased brand value, customer trust, and, consequently, higher economic value for the business.

Innovation and Technological Advancements: The demand for user-friendly interfaces encourages ongoing innovation in the e-commerce sector (Hudson, 2009). Businesses invest in technological advancements to stay competitive, leading to the development of new features and tools that further improve the user experience. This continuous cycle of innovation drives economic growth in the tech industry.

Job Creation: As e-commerce businesses expand and thrive due to user-friendly platforms, there is a potential for job creation. Positions related to website development, customer support, logistics, and digital marketing may see increased demand, contributing to overall employment in the e-commerce sector.

Security and Trust in Online Transactions

Security and trust are paramount in fostering a positive environment for online transactions. The increasing prevalence of e-commerce activities highlights the critical importance of protecting sensitive information and building confidence among users. Here are key considerations regarding security and trust in online transactions:

Secure Payment Gateways: Implementing secure payment gateways is crucial for protecting users' financial information during online transactions. These gateways use encryption technologies to secure sensitive data, ensuring that payment details are transmitted safely between the user and the merchant.

SSL/TLS Encryption: Secure Sockets Layer (SSL) or Transport Layer Security (TLS) encryption protocols are essential for securing the communication channel between a user's browser and the website (Iyer et al., 2006). This encryption helps prevent unauthorized access and eavesdropping, assuring users that their data is transmitted securely.

Two-Factor Authentication (2FA): Implementing two-factor authentication adds an extra layer of security by requiring users to provide additional verification, such as a code sent to their mobile device, in addition to their password. This reduces the risk of unauthorized access, enhancing trust in the transaction process.

Data Protection Regulations: Compliance with data protection regulations, such as the General Data Protection Regulation (GDPR) or the Payment Card Industry Data Security Standard (PCI DSS), instills confidence in users. Adhering to these standards demonstrates a commitment to safeguarding user information and respecting privacy.

Transparent Privacy Policies: Clearly communicated privacy policies build trust with users. E-commerce platforms should provide detailed information about how user data is collected, used, and protected. Transparent communication regarding data practices helps users make informed decisions and reinforces trust in the platform.

Trust Seals and Certifications: Displaying trust seals and certifications from reputable security providers can instill confidence in users. These symbols indicate that the website has undergone security assessments and meets certain standards, assuring users that their transactions are secure.

User Education: Educating users about safe online practices, such as creating strong passwords, recognizing phishing attempts, and understanding security features, empowers them to actively contribute to their own online safety. Informed users are more likely to trust the online transaction process.

Prompt Customer Support: Offering responsive and effective customer support can enhance trust. In the event of any issues or concerns, users should feel confident that they can quickly and easily reach out to the e-commerce platform for assistance.

Regular Security Audits and Updates: Conducting regular security audits and keeping software and systems up-to-date with the latest security patches are crucial. This proactive approach demonstrates a commitment to maintaining a secure environment for online transactions.

Fraud Detection and Prevention: Implementing robust fraud detection mechanisms helps identify and prevent fraudulent transactions. Advanced analytics and machine learning algorithms can analyze patterns and detect anomalies, adding an extra layer of security.

INNOVATION AND ENTREPRENEURSHIP IN HCI

HCI as a Driver of Innovation

Human-Computer Interaction (HCI) serves as a pivotal driver of innovation, re-shaping the way individuals interact with technology and influencing the design and functionality of digital systems. HCI focuses on enhancing the user experience by studying the intersection of humans and computers, emphasizing intuitive interfaces and seamless interactions. Innovations in HCI have propelled the development of touchscreens, voice recognition, gesture controls, and augmented reality, revolutionizing how people engage with devices and applications. The user-centric approach of HCI promotes inclusivity, accommodating diverse user needs and preferences (Jack et al., 2013). As technology becomes more integrated into daily life, HCI plays a crucial role in shaping responsive and adaptive interfaces, ensuring that technological advancements are not only cutting-edge but also accessible and user-friendly. The ongoing evolution of HCI continues to drive innovation across various industries, from healthcare and education to entertainment and beyond, by fostering creativity, efficiency, and a deeper connection between humans and technology.

Startups and Businesses Focused on HCI

Human-Computer Interaction (HCI) has emerged as a pivotal field in the tech industry, fostering the development of startups and businesses dedicated to enhancing user experiences and interface design. These companies recognize the critical role that seamless interactions between humans and computers play in the success of digital products and services. Many startups in the HCI space are leveraging innovative technologies such as augmented reality (AR), virtual reality (VR), natural language processing, and gesture recognition to create intuitive and user-friendly interfaces. They often prioritize user research, employing methodologies like user testing and feedback loops to refine their designs continuously (James & Versteeg, 2007; Johanson & Vahlne, 2009). Furthermore, these businesses frequently collaborate with psychologists, anthropologists, and other experts to gain deeper insights into user behavior and preferences. By focusing on HCI, startups aim to revolutionize how individuals interact with technology, making it more accessible, efficient, and enjoyable. As the demand for intuitive and user-centric designs continues to rise, the HCI sector is becoming a hotbed for entrepreneurial endeavors, driving innovation and shaping the future of digital experiences.

Economic Opportunities and Challenges for Entrepreneurs in HCI

Human-Computer Interaction (HCI) presents a dynamic landscape for entrepreneurs, offering a plethora of economic opportunities alongside notable challenges. On the positive side, the increasing integration of technology into our daily lives has opened up avenues for entrepreneurs to create innovative solutions that enhance user experiences. As the demand for seamless interactions between humans and computers continues to rise, entrepreneurs in HCI can capitalize on designing user-friendly interfaces, developing novel interaction techniques, and creating intuitive user experiences across various platforms. Moreover, the growing emphasis on user-centric design and the rising adoption of emerging technologies such as augmented reality (AR) and virtual reality (VR) create fertile ground for entrepreneurs to explore and pioneer new applications (Jones et al., 2017). Entrepreneurs can find opportunities in sectors like healthcare, education, and entertainment by developing solutions that leverage HCI principles to improve accessibility, learning experiences, and immersive entertainment. However, alongside these opportunities, entrepreneurs in HCI face certain challenges. The fast-paced evolution of technology requires entrepreneurs to stay abreast of the latest advancements to remain competitive. Additionally, the complexity of human behavior and preferences poses a challenge in creating universally appealing and user-friendly interfaces. Entrepreneurs must invest in user research and testing to ensure their HCI solutions meet the diverse needs of the user base (Kalanick, 2016). Moreover, the ethical considerations surrounding user data privacy, security, and the potential societal impact of HCI innovations add another layer of complexity. Entrepreneurs need to navigate regulatory landscapes and adopt responsible practices to address these concerns and build trust among users.

WORKPLACE TRANSFORMATION THROUGH HCI

Impact on Remote Work and Collaboration

Workplace Transformation through Human-Computer Interaction (HCI) has had a profound impact on remote work and collaboration, revolutionizing the traditional office environment. HCI, which focuses on optimizing the interaction between humans and computer systems, has facilitated a seamless integration of technology into the fabric of remote work. The implementation of HCI principles has enhanced user experiences, making communication and collaboration more intuitive and efficient. With the advent of advanced collaboration tools and platforms driven by HCI, teams can now collaborate in real-time, irrespective of geographical locations, fostering a more inclusive and dynamic work environment. The integration of augmented reality (AR) and virtual reality (VR) technologies through HCI has further blurred the lines between physical and virtual workspaces, enabling immersive and engaging collaboration experiences. Moreover, HCI has played a pivotal role in addressing ergonomic concerns, ensuring that remote workers have access to user-friendly interfaces and devices, ultimately enhancing productivity and well-being. In essence, Workplace Transformation through HCI has redefined the landscape of remote work, making it more accessible, interactive, and conducive to effective collaboration.

Economic Implications of Flexible Work Arrangements

Workplace transformation through Human-Computer Interaction (HCI) has ushered in a paradigm shift in the way organizations structure their work environments, particularly through the adoption of flexible work arrangements. This evolution holds profound economic implications that ripple through various facets of the business landscape. Firstly, the implementation of flexible work arrangements, facilitated by HCI technologies, enables organizations to tap into a global talent pool, breaking geographical barriers and potentially reducing labor costs. Additionally, by promoting remote work and providing employees with tools for seamless collaboration, organizations can enhance productivity and efficiency, translating into economic gains (Kamppuri et al., 2006). However, there are also challenges to consider, such as the need for significant investments in technology infrastructure and potential disparities in access to flexible arrangements among different employee groups. Overall, the economic impact of flexible work arrangements under workplace transformation through HCI is multifaceted, encompassing cost savings, productivity enhancements, and potential challenges that require careful consideration for a balanced and sustainable approach.

Trends in HCI for Enhancing Workplace Dynamics

Workplace transformation through Human-Computer Interaction (HCI) is a dynamic and evolving field that seeks to optimize the interaction between humans and technology within work environments. Several trends in HCI are significantly enhancing workplace dynamics, fostering a more efficient and collaborative atmosphere. One notable trend involves the integration of augmented and virtual reality (AR/VR) technologies to create immersive workspaces. This allows employees to collaborate seamlessly across geographical boundaries, enhancing remote work experiences. Additionally, the rise of gesture-based interfaces and natural language processing facilitates more intuitive and user-friendly interactions, reducing the learning curve for employees using advanced technologies. Another pivotal trend is the incorporation of adaptive and personalized interfaces, tailoring the user experience based on individual preferences and work habits. This not only boosts productivity but also contributes to a more positive and inclusive work environment (Khanna et al., 2005). Furthermore, the emphasis on user well-being is evident in the integration of ergonomic designs and the implementation of technologies that promote a healthy work-life balance, such as intelligent scheduling systems. Overall, these trends in HCI for workplace transformation signify a shift towards more collaborative, adaptable, and user-centric environments, ultimately enhancing workplace dynamics in the modern era.

ETHICAL CONSIDERATIONS IN HCI AND ECONOMY

Privacy Concerns in the Digital Age

In the digital age, privacy concerns have become a prominent issue within the realm of Human-Computer Interaction (HCI) and the broader economic landscape. As technology continues to advance, the collection and analysis of personal data have become integral components of digital services and platforms. However, this trend raises ethical considerations regarding user privacy. Users are often unaware of the extent to which their personal information is collected, stored, and shared, leading to a potential erosion of their privacy rights. HCI, as a field focused on designing interactive technologies, faces the ethical challenge of balancing usability and functionality with user privacy. Design choices, such as default privacy settings and data access permissions, can significantly impact user privacy (Liu & Vrontis, 2017; Lohmann et al., 2006). Ethical considerations in HCI involve ensuring transparent communication with users about how their data will be used, giving them control over their privacy settings, and implementing privacy-preserving design principles. Striking a balance between user experience and privacy protection is crucial to building trust in digital interactions. From an economic perspective, the monetization of personal data has become a driving force behind many digital business models. Companies often engage in extensive data collection to target advertisements, personalize user experiences, and optimize services. However, the commodification of personal information raises ethical questions about the fair exchange of value between users and service providers. Users may unwittingly become the product, as their data is traded and sold without their explicit consent, posing challenges to the ethical foundations of digital economies. Moreover, concerns arise about the potential for discriminatory practices based on the analysis of personal data, leading to issues of algorithmic bias. In an economy driven by data, there is a risk that certain demographics may be disproportionately affected by biased algorithms, reinforcing existing inequalities. Ethical considerations in the digital age, therefore, extend beyond individual privacy to encompass broader societal implications, necessitating a holistic approach to responsible technology development and deployment (London & Hart, 2004). Addressing privacy concerns in the digital age within the realms of HCI and the economy requires a multidisciplinary approach. Ethical guidelines, regulatory frameworks, and user education play essential roles in promoting responsible data practices. Balancing technological innovation with ethical considerations is imperative to ensure that the benefits of the digital age are realized without compromising individual privacy and societal well-being.

Economic Consequences of Ethical and Unethical HCI Practices

Ethical considerations in Human-Computer Interaction (HCI) play a crucial role in shaping the economic consequences of technology development and use. Ethical HCI practices can positively impact the economy by fostering trust, user satisfaction, and long-term sustainability. When designers and developers prioritize user privacy, data security, and accessibility, it can lead to increased user confidence, resulting in higher adoption rates and market success. Moreover, ethical HCI practices contribute to a positive corporate image, which can attract investors and customers who value socially responsible business conduct (Masiero, 2013). Conversely, unethical HCI practices can have detrimental economic consequences. For instance, the misuse of user data, privacy breaches, or the development of technologies that exploit vulnerable populations can lead to legal challenges, loss of customer trust, and damage to a company's reputation. These negative outcomes can result in financial losses, decreased market share, and difficulty in attracting and retaining talent. In the long run, companies engaged in unethical HCI practices may face regulatory scrutiny and fines, further impacting their economic stability. In the broader economic context, the societal repercussions of unethical HCI practices can be profound. For example, if technology is designed without considering inclusivity, it may exacerbate existing social inequalities, leading to exclusionary practices that limit access to benefits and opportunities (McHenry & Welch, 2018; Meyer, 2004). This not only has ethical implications but also economic consequences, as it can hinder the overall economic development of communities and countries. On the positive side, embracing ethical HCI practices can foster innovation and sustainability. Technologies developed with a focus on social and environmental responsibility can lead to the creation of new markets and industries, contributing to economic growth. Additionally, ethical considerations in HCI can stimulate a culture of responsible innovation, encouraging businesses to prioritize the well-being of users and society over short-term profits.

This can lead to the development of products and services that better meet the needs of diverse user groups, enhancing overall economic productivity and resilience.

GOVERNMENT POLICIES AND REGULATION

Regulatory Frameworks Related to HCI

Human-Computer Interaction (HCI) is a field that focuses on the design and use of computer technologies, ensuring that they are user-friendly and effective. Regulatory frameworks related to HCI play a crucial role in shaping the development and deployment of interactive systems. These frameworks encompass guidelines, standards, and regulations that aim to ensure the safety, accessibility, and usability of technology for diverse user groups. In many regions, there are specific laws and standards that mandate businesses and developers to adhere to established HCI principles (Meyer et al., 2011). For instance, regulations may dictate accessibility features to accommodate individuals with disabilities, privacy considerations to protect user data, and security measures to safeguard against potential risks. Additionally, regulatory frameworks often evolve to keep pace with technological advancements, addressing emerging challenges such as artificial intelligence and virtual reality. Compliance with these regulations is essential for companies to not only meet legal requirements but also to enhance user satisfaction and trust in the digital landscape. As technology continues to advance, regulatory frameworks related to HCI play a pivotal role in shaping an ethical and user-centric approach to the design and implementation of interactive systems.

FUTURE TRENDS AND CHALLENGES

Emerging Technologies in HCI

Human-Computer Interaction (HCI) is an ever-evolving field, and several emerging technologies are shaping its future. One notable trend is the integration of Virtual Reality (VR) and Augmented Reality (AR) into HCI systems. These immersive technologies offer new ways for users to interact with digital content, creating more engaging and realistic user experiences. VR, in particular, enables users to enter virtual worlds, while AR overlays digital information onto the real world, both presenting exciting possibilities for HCI applications in various domains, such as gaming, education, and healthcare. Another significant development is the increasing use of Artificial Intelligence (AI) in HCI (Miettinen et al., 2016). AI technologies, including machine learning and natural language processing, empower systems to understand and respond to user behavior more intelligently. This leads to the creation of adaptive interfaces that can personalize user experiences based on individual preferences, habits, and contextual information. As AI continues to advance, HCI systems are expected to become more intuitive, anticipating user needs and providing seamless interactions. The Internet of Things (IoT) is also playing a crucial role in shaping the future of HCI. With the proliferation of connected devices, HCI is expanding beyond traditional computing platforms to encompass a wide range of smart devices. This trend presents new challenges in designing interfaces that seamlessly integrate and manage interactions across diverse IoT devices. HCI researchers and practitioners are exploring ways to create cohesive and user-friendly experiences in this interconnected ecosystem, ensuring that users can interact with various devices effortlessly. In addition to these technological advancements, the integration of biometric technologies is another notable trend in HCI. Biometrics, such as facial recognition, fingerprint scanning, and voice recognition, are becoming more prevalent in authentication and user identification (Nielsen, 1994). These technologies enhance the security and convenience of user interactions, but they also raise ethical concerns related to privacy and data protection. Striking a balance between usability and privacy will be a key challenge in the incorporation of biometric technologies into HCI systems. While these emerging technologies hold great promise, they also bring forth several challenges. One of the main challenges is the need for standardization and interoperability. As diverse technologies converge in HCI systems, establishing common standards will be crucial to ensuring compatibility and a seamless user experience across different platforms. Additionally, addressing ethical considerations, such as privacy, security, and the responsible use of AI, is essential to building trust among users and mitigating potential risks associated with these technologies.

Anticipated Economic Shifts Due to HCI Advancements

Anticipated economic shifts due to Human-Computer Interaction (HCI) advancements are expected to be profound, reshaping various industries and fostering unprecedented growth opportunities. As HCI technologies continue to evolve, businesses are likely to witness increased efficiency and productivity through streamlined workflows and enhanced user experiences. The integration of advanced AI-driven interfaces, augmented reality (AR), and virtual reality (VR) into daily operations could lead to significant cost savings and improved decision-making processes (Nobel, 2011). Additionally, the demand for skilled professionals in HCI-related fields is anticipated to surge, fostering a new job market. However, the digital divide may widen, posing challenges for those who struggle to adapt to rapidly advancing technologies. Furthermore, the rise of HCI could fuel innovation in sectors like healthcare, education, and entertainment, opening up novel revenue streams and market dynamics. Governments and businesses will need to adapt policies and strategies to harness the full economic potential of HCI while addressing associated challenges to ensure inclusive growth and sustained economic development.

Challenges and Potential Solutions

The rapid advancements in Human-Computer Interaction (HCI) bring forth a set of challenges that need careful consideration for a seamless integration into society and the economy. One primary challenge is the potential exacerbation of existing inequalities, known as the digital divide (Parente & Prescott, 1994). As HCI technologies become more sophisticated, disparities in access and proficiency may widen, leaving certain demographics at a disadvantage. Another significant challenge is the ethical implications of AI-driven interfaces and data privacy concerns, raising questions about user consent, surveillance, and the responsible use of technology (Patterson et al., 2009). Additionally, the fast-paced nature of HCI development may outpace regulatory frameworks, creating legal uncertainties. To address these challenges, potential solutions involve proactive measures such as investing in digital literacy programs to bridge the digital divide, implementing robust data protection regulations, and fostering a collaborative approach between technology developers, policymakers, and the public to ensure ethical considerations are prioritized (Petersen et al., 2000). Furthermore, establishing international standards and guidelines can contribute to a more cohesive and secure global adoption of HCI technologies, promoting innovation while safeguarding societal values and inclusivity.

Future Scope

The future scope of Human-Computer Interaction (HCI) holds immense promise as technology continues to evolve and integrate into every aspect of our lives. Emerging technologies such as augmented reality (AR), virtual reality (VR), artificial intelligence (AI), Internet of Things (IoT), and wearable devices present new opportunities and challenges for HCI research and practice. HCI researchers will explore innovative ways to create seamless and intuitive interfaces that adapt to users' needs and preferences, leveraging AI algorithms for personalized interactions and anticipatory design. As computing becomes increasingly embedded in our environment, HCI will extend beyond traditional screens to encompass spatial computing, tangible interfaces, and immersive experiences, reshaping how we interact with information and each other. Moreover, HCI will play a crucial role in addressing ethical concerns such as privacy, security, and digital well-being, ensuring that technology serves humanity's best interests. Collaborations across disciplines, including psychology, sociology, design, and engineering, will be essential to tackle these complex challenges and unlock the full potential of HCI in shaping the future of human-computer interaction.

CONCLUSION

In conclusion, navigating the digital economy hinges upon the crucial role of Human-Computer Interaction (HCI), acting as the linchpin between individuals and the rapidly evolving technological landscape. As our world becomes increasingly interconnected and reliant on digital interfaces, the effectiveness of HCI in shaping user experiences and facilitating seamless interactions becomes paramount. The synergy between human intuition, creativity, and technological innovation is essential for harnessing the full potential of the digital economy. By prioritizing user-centric design, fostering interdisciplinary collaboration, and staying attuned to the evolving needs of individuals in the digital realm, we can build a more inclusive, intuitive, and sustainable digital future. The success of navigating the digital economy ultimately rests on our ability to strike a harmonious balance between human insights and technological advancements through the lens of Human-Computer Interaction.

REFERENCES

Abras, C., Maloney-Krichmar, D., & Preece, J. (2004). *User-centered design*. CiteSeer.

Acemoglu, D. (2012). Introduction to economic growth. *Journal of Economic Theory*, 147(2), 545–550. 10.1016/j.jet.2012.01.023

Aker, J. C., & Mbiti, I. M. (2010). Mobile phones and economic development in Africa. *The Journal of Economic Perspectives*, 24(3), 207–232. 10.1257/jep.24.3.207

Asongu, S. (2015). The impact of mobile phone penetration on African inequality. *International Journal of Social Economics*, 42(8), 706–716. 10.1108/IJSE-11-2012-0228

Bailetti, A. J. (2012). What technology startups must get right to globalize early and rapidly. *Technology Innovation Management Review*, 2(10), 5–16. 10.22215/timreview/614

Bainbridge, W. (2004). *Encyclopedia of Human-Computer Interaction*. Sage Publications.

Bhave, M. P. (1994). A process model of entrepreneurial venture creation. *Journal of Business Venturing*, 9(3), 223–242. 10.1016/0883-9026(94)90031-0

Billon, M., Lera-Lopez, F., & Marco, R. (2010). Differences in digitalization levels: A multivariate analysis studying the global digital divide. *Review of World Economics*, 146(1), 39–73. 10.1007/s10290-009-0045-y

Bloodgood, J. M., Sapienza, H. J., & Almeida, J. G. (1996). The internationalization of new high-potential US ventures: Antecedents and outcomes. *Entrepreneurship Theory and Practice*, 20(4), 61–76. 10.1177/104225879602000405

Bouwman, H., de Vos, H., & Haaker, T. (2008). *Mobile service innovation and business models*. Springer Science & Business Media. 10.1007/978-3-540-79238-3

Braun, V., & Clarke, V. (2006). Using thematic analysis in psychology. *Qualitative Research in Psychology*, 3(2), 77–101. 10.1191/1478088706qp063oa

Brewer, E., Demmer, M., Du, B., Ho, M., Kam, M., Nedevschi, S., Pal, J., Patra, R., Surana, S., & Fall, K. (2005). The case for technology in developing regions. *Computer*, 38(6), 25–38. 10.1109/MC.2005.204

Cantwell, J. (2009). Location and the multinational enterprise. *Journal of International Business Studies*, 40(1), 35–41. 10.1057/jibs.2008.82

Day, G. S., & Schoemaker, P. J. H. (2016). Adapting to Fast-Changing Markets and Technologies. *California Management Review*, 58(4), 59–77. 10.1525/cmr.2016.58.4.59

Del Vitto, C. (2008). Cross-Cultural" soft skills" and the global engineer: Corporate best practices and trainer methodologies. *Online Journal for Global Engineering Education*, 3(1), 1.

Donovan, K., & Donner, J. (2010). A note on the availability (and importance) of pre-paid mobile data in Africa. *Proceedings of M4D 2010*, 263–267.

Eisenhardt, K. M. (1989). Building theories from case study research. *Academy of Management Review*, 14(4), 532–550. 10.2307/258557

Eisenmann, T. R., Ries, E., & Dillard, S. (2012). Hypothesis-driven entrepreneurship: The lean startup. *Harvard Business School Entrepreneurial Management Case*, (812–095). Harvard Press.

Freudenthaler, D. (2015). Product Development for Emerging Markets: Towards a Framework for Integrating Contextual Information Into the Design Process. *Proceedings of the 2008 Academy of Marketing Science (AMS) Annual Conference*, (pp. 179–183). Research Gate.

Ghemawat, P. (2001). Distance Still Matters. The Hard Reality of Global Expansion. *Harvard Business Review*, 79(8), 137–147.11550630

Ghemawat, P. (2007). *Redefining global strategy: Crossing borders in a world where differences still matter*. Harvard Business Press.

Griffith, D. A., & Zhao, Y. (2015). Contract specificity, contract violation, and relationship performance in international buyer—Supplier relationships. *Journal of International Marketing*, 23(3), 22–40. 10.1509/jim.14.0138

Guesalaga, R., & Marshall, P. (2008). Purchasing power at the bottom of the pyramid: Differences across geographic regions and income tiers. *Journal of Consumer Marketing*, 25(7), 413–418. 10.1108/07363760810915626

Harris, R. W. (2016). How ICT4D research fails the poor. *Information Technology for Development*, 22(1), 177–192. 10.1080/02681102.2015.1018115

Hertzum, M. (2010). Images of usability. *Intl. Journal of Human--Computer Interaction*, 26(6), 567–600.

Hudson, W. (2009). Reduced empathizing skills increase challenges for user-centered design. *Proceedings of the SIGCHI Conference on Human Factors in Computing Systems*, (pp. 1327–1330). Research Gate. 10.1145/1518701.1518901

Iyer, G. R., LaPlaca, P. J., & Sharma, A. (2006). Innovation and new product introductions in emerging markets: Strategic recommendations for the Indian market. *Industrial Marketing Management*, 35(3), 373–382. 10.1016/j.indmarman.2005.02.007

Jack, W., Ray, A., & Suri, T. (2013). Transaction networks: Evidence from mobile money in Kenya. *The American Economic Review*, 103(3), 356–361. 10.1257/aer.103.3.356

James, J., & Versteeg, M. (2007). Mobile phones in Africa: How much do we really know? *Social Indicators Research*, 84(1), 117. 10.1007/s11205-006-9079-x20076776

Johanson, J., & Vahlne, J.-E. (2009). The Uppsala internationalization process model revisited: From liability of foreignness to liability of outsidership. *Journal of International Business Studies*, 40(9), 1411–1431. 10.1057/jibs.2009.24

Jones, M., Robinson, S., Pearson, J., Joshi, M., Raju, D., Mbogo, C. C., Wangari, S., Joshi, A., Cutrell, E., & Harper, R. (2017). Beyond yesterday's tomorrow: Future-focused mobile interaction design by and for emergent users. *Personal and Ubiquitous Computing*, 21(1), 157–171. 10.1007/s00779-016-0982-0

Kalanick, T. (2016). Uber China Merges with Didi Chuxing. Retrieved August 9, 2019, from https://www.uber.com/newsroom/uber-china-didi/

Kamppuri, M., Bednarik, R., & Tukiainen, M. (2006). The expanding focus of HCI: case culture. *Proceedings of the 4th Nordic Conference on Human-Computer Interaction: Changing Roles*, (pp. 405–408). Research Gate. 10.1145/1182475.1182523

Khanna, T., Palepu, K. G., & Sinha, J. (2005). Strategies that fit emerging markets. *Harvard Business Review*, 83(6), 4–19.15938439

Liu, Y., & Vrontis, D. (2017). Emerging-market firms venturing into advanced economies: The role of context. *Thunderbird International Business Review*, 59(3), 255–261. 10.1002/tie.21900

Lohmann, J. R., Rollins, H. A., & Joseph Hoey, J. (2006). Defining, developing and assessing global competence in engineers. *European Journal of Engineering Education*, 31(1), 119–131. 10.1080/03043790500429906

London, T., & Hart, S. L. (2004). Reinventing strategies for emerging markets: Beyond the transnational model. *Journal of International Business Studies*, 35(5), 350–370. 10.1057/palgrave.jibs.8400099

Masiero, S. (2013). *Innovation and best practice in mobile technologies for development*. Economic and Private Sector Professional Evidence and Applied Knowledge Services.

McHenry, J. E. H., & Welch, D. E. (2018). Entrepreneurs and internationalization: A study of Western immigrants in an emerging market. *International Business Review*, 27(1), 93–101. 10.1016/j.ibusrev.2017.05.008

Meyer, K. E. (2004). Perspectives on multinational enterprises in emerging econo-mies. *Journal of International Business Studies*, 35(4), 259–276. 10.1057/palgrave. jibs.8400084

Meyer, K. E., Mudambi, R., & Narula, R. (2011). Multinational enterprises and local contexts: The opportunities and challenges of multiple embeddedness. *Journal of Management Studies*, 48(2), 235–252. 10.1111/j.1467-6486.2010.00968.x

Miettinen, S., du Preez, V., van Dugteren, J., Moalosi, R., Molokwane, S., & Lu-ojus, S. (2016). *Service design with communities in Africa: the case of UFISA.* Academic Press.

Nielsen, J. (1994). *Usability engineering.* Elsevier.

Nobel, C. (2011). Teaching a 'Lean Startup' Strategy. *HBS Working Knowledge*, (pp. 1–2). Research Gate.

Parente, S. L., & Prescott, E. C. (1994). Barriers to technology adoption and devel-opment. *Journal of Political Economy*, 102(2), 298–321. 10.1086/261933

Patterson, D. J., Sim, S. E., & Aiyelokun, T. (2009). Overcoming blind spots in interaction design: A case study in designing for African AIDS orphan care com-munities. *Information Technologies & International Development,5*(4).

Petersen, B., Welch, D. E., & Welch, L. S. (2000). Creating meaningful switching options in international operations. *Long Range Planning*, 33(5), 688–705. 10.1016/ S0024-6301(00)00076-5

Chapter 11
The Effect of Information Technology Competency on Information Management in Business

Funda Hatice Sezgin
https://orcid.org/0000-0002-2693-9601
Istanbul University-Cerrahpasa, Turkey

ABSTRACT

The impact of information technology competence on information management in businesses is extremely important. First of all, information technologies enable businesses to manage data and information more effectively. Thanks to data storage, processing and analysis capabilities, businesses can quickly process large amounts of data and transform it into meaningful information. This enables correct decisions to be made and strategic goals to be achieved more effectively. Additionally, thanks to information technologies, businesses can share information, collaborate and strengthen internal communication. This accelerates the flow of information within the business and increases efficiency. It provides access to accurate and timely information, fast decision-making processes and flexibility. This enables businesses to adapt to market conditions more quickly and gain competitive advantage. The aim of this study is to analyze the situation and make suggestions by considering the effect of information technology competence on information management in businesses from different aspects.

DOI: 10.4018/979-8-3693-3033-3.ch011

INTRODUCTION

Businesses have to use the raw data obtained from the internal and external environment by transforming them into information. In order to sustain the activities, information is constantly created, this information is protected, renewed and recorded. In this way, as an important process for information management, it will be possible to ensure that information is produced consciously and for a common purpose for the enterprise and can be shared and used by those concerned in all processes.

The increase in the volume of financial transactions with technological developments has also increased the importance of information technologies. At this point, the performance of enterprises that can adapt information technologies to corporate processes will increase; new services, products, business areas, working systems and ways of obtaining information will be taken into consideration in this respect (Costa and Monteiro, 2016).

The benefits that can be provided with information technologies; in a corporate structure; facilitating the reporting of the work done, making the control period of the work effective and increasing business opportunities. In the economic dimension, e-commerce can lead to changes in the way of marketing, no use of intermediaries, new marketing and advertising techniques, the possibility of finding new business partners and making agreements, reduction of costs in internal transactions and positive improvement in the management of relations between customers and suppliers (Gonzalvez et al., 2014).

Today, businesses that thrive are those capable of updating their knowledge to keep pace with economic changes, leveraging more innovative and competitive insights than their rivals. Neglecting technological progress can quickly render existing knowledge obsolete, reducing its ability to enhance a company's competitiveness (Pirola et al., 2020). Thus, it has become essential for businesses aiming to boost and sustain their competitive edge to not only seek out new and novel information sources but also to efficiently manage large volumes of information by processing it swiftly.

A key goal of knowledge management is to foster the creation of more knowledge through the synergy of knowledge sharing among employees. Sharing knowledge involves making all types of information readily available at the right time and place. It goes beyond merely acquiring or transferring knowledge from one unit to another; it includes the transformation that occurs when knowledge is processed and integrated across different units (Kolyasnikov and Kelchevskaya, 2020). Another aim of knowledge sharing is to disseminate information promptly, allowing it to be transformed into a usable form while retaining its relevance.

The aim of this study is to emphasise the importance of information technologies used by enterprises and the information management they apply, to evaluate the relationship between these two concepts and their effects on increasing the competitiveness of companies.

CONCEPTUAL FRAMEWORK

Information Technologies and Their Importance in Business

Technology is an essential aspect of all areas of social life, continually advancing and evolving. These technological advancements enhance the speed and quality of research and development, transportation, and communication, impacting every stage from production to consumption. Generally, technology can be described through concepts such as innovation, methods, change, and development.

Information technologies transform the collected data into usable and meaningful information for businesses. It also ensures that data is stored and transmitted from one user to another through networks (Azma et al., 2012). Information Technology has radically changed the communication style of employees. For example, it has significantly improved a manager's ability to monitor individual and team performance, allowing employees to have more information to make faster decisions and providing employees with more opportunities for information sharing and co-operation (Yaghoubi et al., 2011). Furthermore, information technology has made employees fully available 24 hours a day, 7 days a week, regardless of where they are. Employees are no longer required to be at their desks with their computers in order to communicate with other employees. Three developments in information technology have had a significant impact on current managerial communication. These are Network Based Computer Systems, Wireless Communication Facilities and Information Management Systems (Spirin, 2013).

Information technologies enable activities to be conducted with clear data and greater speed, leading to significant savings in time and resources. This allows managers and staff to focus on generating information related to their primary tasks beyond routine work. In today's information society, computers are a fundamental tool applicable across all fields. The system created by computers and other hardware accelerates work in every sector, including science and technology. In essence, information technologies are a key driver of the recently transformed economic structure. Businesses engage in global competition by reducing costs through the speed and flexibility provided by information technologies (Jafari and Ramalingam, 2015).

Information technology competence is defined by Tippins and Sohi (2003) as "the degree to which an organisation uses information and information technologies efficiently, including software, hardware and related personnel etc. to manage information". According to Bhatt and Grover (2005), "information technology competence is how an organisation uses these technologies to manage its information effectively". Information technologies are basically used to refer to electronic and technology products such as computers, hardware, software, telecommunications, internet. However, the concept of information technology competence is broader than the concept of information technology. It refers to organising and using the flow of information to meet the needs of customers.

Achieving success in the global competitive market, where the market environment loses its clarity, technology changes rapidly, and the transformation times of products are shortened, does not only depend on obtaining information belonging to customers or consumers. In addition, it is necessary to obtain information from inside or outside the business in an efficient and up-to-date manner, to produce new information consistently, to disseminate it widely throughout the business and to use it rapidly with new technology (Hwang et al., 2015).

The important point in establishing the adaptation between knowledge management and communication technology is to recognise that computers, technology and people do good things and not to confuse them. The effectiveness of the technology dimension for knowledge management also depends on the type of knowledge. In the case of explicit information, technical infrastructure is functional in terms of access, storage and communication, while in the case of implicit information, the development of technical infrastructure is not important for the enterprise (Mills and Smith, 2011).

Today, most of the business widely use the Internet for internal and external communication within and outside the organisation, as well as e-commerce transactions with customers and business partners over the Internet. The use of the internet system will reduce many costs and enable small and medium business to participate in e-commerce platforms. However, the effective use of the internet system in this form will create security problems. These problems can be prevented by using passwords (Chakravarty et al., 2013). It is very important to be innovative in today's conditions. In today's conditions of information economy, businesses are constantly making efforts to eliminate the difficulties they face and to capture and secure competitive advantages in their organisational structures. From the perspective of knowledge management, tough competition conditions determine consumer preferences, developing technologies and new business models force businesses to rethink their environment and their processes and practices, including them (Nowacki and Bachnik, 2016).

Information technologies provide and facilitate users' access to the information they need and to the people or sources of information. It is a set of technologies that enable people to disseminate information within the organisation. Electronic mail, voice and video call tools, internet, in-house intranet and extranet structures, web-based tools and portals are the primary examples of this field (Ngah et al., 2016). The development in information technologies has a continuous effect on business operations in terms of cost, time, quality and service and leads to changes in these factors. In particular, the development in information technologies leads to radical changes in the organisational structure and provides unique methods for business to enter new markets, to present their products and services, to increase process efficiency, and to obtain customer acquisition and loyalty (Seleim and Khalil, 2011).

It should be known that the information technologies used are important in increasing productivity, reducing operating costs and improving quality, increasing the efficiency of the internal and external information process. However, measuring the impact of information technologies on businesses involves difficulties due to the fact that these technologies affect almost all of their operations (Alavi and Leidner, 2001). The development in information technologies, licence usage rights related to these technologies and technological infrastructure and the change in the competitive structure in the market with the reduction of costs arising from the lack of labour force and the provision of competitive advantage provide new opportunities. By actively using information technologies, business can increase productivity, reduce costs, develop new products, services and processes and become superior to their competitors (Boh, 2014).

It is important to have the necessary technical infrastructure for knowledge management in business, but the essence of this importance stems from the benefits and speed provided by the technical infrastructure in accessing, storing and disseminating information. The realisation of knowledge management should be evaluated not only at the level of knowledge but also at the level of culture, organisational roles and responsibilities, concentration on the content of knowledge, strategy, technology and economy (Davison et al., 2013). Although technology and technical structure is a very important tool for knowledge management, it is not sufficient alone. Organisations that have technology and technical structure fall into the misconception that this alone will be sufficient.

Innovations and benefits provided by information technologies for businesses the benefits and innovations provided by the use of information technologies for the business processes of businesses can be listed as follows (Löfsten, 2014; Hwng et al., 2015; Pirola et al., 2020):

✓   Information technologies facilitate access to the data needed.

✓ The information networks used support the formation of synergy by facilitating internal communication and thus co-operation. Advances in information systems will significantly affect business in structural, technological and cultural dimensions.

✓ The increasing prevalence of information systems will also change the hierarchy within the organisation. Since today's modern information systems do not overlap with the classical command understanding, it will enable the emergence of a lean and flexible management structure in business.

✓ Information systems used between business eliminate distances and ensure continuous communication between employees, suppliers and customers as users. Thus, businesses can seize opportunities in the rapidly changing competitive market.

✓ Keeping information in a wide area accessible to every employee will enable the business structure to respond more quickly to constantly changing conditions.

✓ Information technologies will expand strategic partnerships between different business and make it possible for them to work together.

✓ It offers alternative ways for businesses to enter new markets where they can compete, to offer their products and services in these markets, to increase business efficiency, to gain new customers and to maintain customer loyalty.

✓ Changes in information technologies continuously affect business activities in terms of quality, cost and time. For businesses, information systems first and foremost provide a non-permanent competitive advantage. Strong and permanent information system infrastructure is of strategic importance for this business to ensure their long-term survival.

Knowledge Management

Knowledge management is a broad process that covers data, information and knowledge and analyses their acquisition, distribution, interpretation and application. Knowledge management is a series of technological and cultural processes that are carried out in order to collect, organise and transform registered or unregistered organisational data and accumulations based on personal knowledge and experience into useful information, to make them accessible at the right times, by the right people, from anywhere, to increase the intellectual property of the organisation, to ensure that all repetitive work is done with technological tools and to achieve positive business results (Haider and Kayani, 2020). From another perspective, knowledge management is defined as "a discipline that enables individuals, teams and the whole organisation to create, share and apply knowledge collectively and systematically in order to achieve organisational goals in a better way" (Chu et al., 2019).

In the information age, the only element that increases the market value of business and provides competitive advantage is knowledge and all values that are extensions of knowledge. In an economic order dominated by uncertainty, the only reliable source of continuous competitive advantage is information itself. When markets change, technological developments increase, competitors increase and products become obsolete in a short time, the business that succeed in being successful will be the ones that consistently create new knowledge, disseminate this knowledge widely throughout the organisation and use it rapidly in new technologies and products (Attia and Salama, 2018).

In this context, knowledge management is one of the most important items of the day for businesses today. Knowledge management is also an important management field that treats mental capital as a manageable value. In this process, factors such as organisational dynamics of business, management models and technology are accepted as important tools in knowledge management. These tools aim to control the acquisition of data and information by an enterprise, the development of the information obtained, their transfer to individuals with specific tasks, their organisation and use (Daňa et al., 2020). The need for information management for businesses includes the necessity to prevent unnecessary information production, especially the compelling effects of the global competitive environment. Today, the amount of internal and external information has reached excessive levels. For this reason, managers also complain of being confronted with too much information. At the same time, having the right information at the right time is an important need for every business. The approach here is to show the ability to separate the important information required for the organisation from the less important ones (Friedrich et al., 2020).

Figure 1. Information technology and business environment

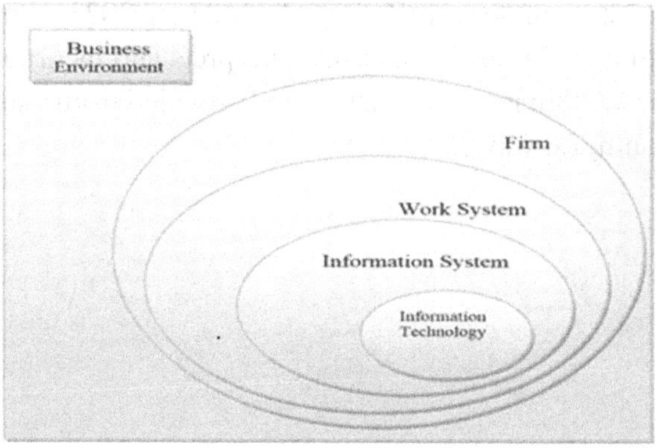

In knowledge management, how knowledge can be created, acquired, used, and managed to achieve organisational goals is addressed in a systematic process. Knowledge management includes the efficient adaptation of knowledge to technological applications, the definition and modelling of processes and the action plan for the use of knowledge in line with the objectives of the organisation. All kinds of information sources in the organisation from database, websites, company employees to business partners are the subject of knowledge management (Diab, 2021). In this process, knowledge is used as a production factor to create value. Knowledge management is an issue that should be handled strategically for organisations. Knowledge management strategy is also a reflection of the organisation's competitive strategy. How value is created for customers, how employees contribute to this value and how the value generated supports the economic model is revealed through knowledge management strategies (Manesh et al., 2021).

In knowledge management, organisations should be managed in the understanding of "learning organisation" and "knowing organisation". "Knowledge management", which supports learning and change throughout the organisation and changes the traditional management approach, cannot be established only by creating databases and "networks". Information technology investment can only create the technological infrastructure of knowledge management, but this does not mean transition to knowledge management. Making knowledge-based management an organisational culture is an important element for the success of knowledge management (Wang and Wan, 2021).

Rapidly developing technology has provided convenience in terms of analysing, storing, transmitting, classifying and presenting information to users in the most appropriate way. The importance of this structure for businesses depends on how successful the managers are depending on their experience. Therefore, in order to find the clearest answer to the question of what is the importance of information management for businesses, the concept of information management should be defined in the most accurate way (Zafar and Alsabban, 2023). Knowledge Management is a system that classifies, analyses, interprets and incorporates the data that the enterprise has within its own structure and provided from outside the enterprise in the most meaningful way.

Figure 2. Information management cycle

Information management typically consists of four major components:

Data: Data is the raw material of information management. It can be structured (organized in a predefined way, such as in a database) or unstructured (like text documents or multimedia files). Data needs to be collected, stored, and maintained effectively to ensure its quality and usefulness.

Information: Information is the processed and organized data that provides context, relevance, and purpose. It is created by analyzing, interpreting, and summarizing data. Information should be accurate, timely, and relevant to be valuable to users.

Knowledge: Knowledge is the insight and understanding derived from information. It involves the application of information to make decisions, solve problems, and create new ideas. Knowledge is often embedded in processes, practices, and people within an organization.

Technology: Technology refers to the tools, systems, and software used to manage, process, store, and transmit data and information. This includes databases, data warehouses, document management systems, and collaboration tools. Technology plays a crucial role in enabling efficient and effective information management.

Effective information management involves the integration of these components to ensure that data is transformed into valuable information, which, in turn, contributes to the creation of knowledge that drives decision-making and innovation within an organization.

In today's intense competitive environment, information has become the most important value for businesses. The concept of information and management, which provides advantage to businesses in competitive conditions, has recently become one of the most important issues to be emphasised. It can be said that the most important asset of business is the knowledge possessed by employees. For such reasons, businesses should focus on how they can improve their knowledge accumulation by focusing on human capital in addition to their normal capital (Shahzad et al., 2021). In today's intensely competitive environment, it is an important problem to determine how to use knowledge with a certain discipline in addition to factors such as quality and time, and thus to determine how business will provide competitive advantage (Ismail and Al-Assa'ad, 2020). In addition to the development and increasing importance of knowledge, human capital, which is one of the basic assets of organisations, has also become important. The wealth of businesses in the upward trend is similar to the acquisition of human capital arising from knowledge (Balouei and Ghasemian, 2014).

In a global world, one of the issues that organisations, which are trying to prepare their businesses for the future and trying to ensure their continuity by providing competitive advantage, have to pay attention to is to manage the knowledge that emerges in the organisation and cannot be imitated by other organisations in the best way. It is a difficult task to directly relate the benefits provided by information management and to measure how much benefit it brings (Farhan and Karim, 2019). However, thanks to the information, it is a good indicator in many important issues such as the calculation of the factors that make up the costs in all units in the business and experience. These transactions can be evaluated and monitored to a close extent, if not completely. The benefits of information management for business can be listed as follows.

Relationship Between Information Technologies (IT) and Information Management in Businesses

IT systems can be expressed as systems that are used in producing information, obtaining it from different data and using it. When information technologies are viewed in this way, it is seen that they form the structure of all information systems and information management process for business. IT alone is not sufficient for a good knowledge management process. Thanks to IT, data can be transformed into information very easily. However, technology may be insufficient in the transformation of information into meta-information in order to present the information to the top management (Ashchaulov, 2016).

Processing, analysing and interpreting the information can only be performed by people. For this reason, human demands and thoughts should definitely be taken into consideration when designing systems for knowledge management. Because human can be characterised as the person who knows the effect of the subject by seeing or predicting its effect on business (Balle et al., 2016). Today, IT has become a strategic element for management in all business and organisations have started to follow the developments by making serious investments in these technologies in order to provide strategic superiority in the globalised competitive environment of competitors (Naqshbandi and Jasimuddin, 2018).

Information systems are also known as systems that maximise the benefits expected from information management with the spread of computer, telecommunication and communication technologies. By revealing the superiorities of the aforementioned technosystems, it is ensured that information is rapidly produced, rapidly shared and thus the information management process is activated and the result is achieved more effectively (Sartori et al., 2022). IT covers the whole of a system. IT system is defined as a concept that consists of various hardware tools and provides information sharing with special programmes and software developed to be used in this hardware. As it can be understood from the definitions, IT systems are not a single application, but systems that bring all applications and systems together in harmony and provide functionality (Sousa and Rocha, 2019).

The need for information in business is shaped according to the state of the organisation, production and service activities. Establishing the most appropriate information network in business ensures that the information need is used at the right place and time (Zhao et al., 2022). Information and technology also provide integration services that help better control critical business areas (Shadi, 2017). Since information management systems are available in most of the business today, it is possible to develop an information management system within themselves. Thus, information can be accessed by the relevant people at any time and from any place. For such a situation, knowledge management systems provide a connection to the entire business information system for everyone with the help of IT (Rafi et al., 2021).

When the ability of information technologies and information management systems come together under the most ideal conditions, it is likely that businesses will reach the best efficiency. People who manage these systems are more aware of the value of data. The management of information is very important for the stakeholders of the relevant units as well as the people who manage these systems. Because this information is the most important element of the enterprise such as human beings and is important for the future (Rehman et al., 2021). Therefore, information management and information technology systems will be more effective in the compatibility of the corporate culture that understands the necessity of this rather than being a system based entirely on technology.

CONCLUSION

Today's business aim to achieve their goals in the fastest and most effective way possible through the information they try to obtain with their resources such as manpower, technology and finance. It is obvious that the flow of this required information between all departments within the enterprise can be possible with an effective information and information system management. In today's competitive environment, similar

The ability of all business to effectively manage their internal processes, to access information that can provide competitive advantage in all processes and to internalise this information is a situation that can only arise as a result of making use of the information technologies that they can keep and develop within their structure.

In today's world, where technological change cannot even be fully followed due to its speed, it is an obligation for businesses to update themselves technologically as well as in every aspect. As with every change, new technologies, which bring along a resistance and anxiety in employees, bring about a change in the ways of doing business, business processes, communication channels and even organisational structures.

One of the most important conditions of being an information society is to be able to obtain information in all areas of life, individuals, society, businesses, government, etc., to use this information and to create new information based on this information. Business should be supported by public institutions; the state should take the necessary measures to minimise the information deficit and should direct all kinds of investments to improve the capacity of business to produce and use information.

The first of the information technologies dimensions included in the research is information technologies knowledge. The knowledge of information technologies will provide an advantage by supporting more effective use of internal resources. Businesses that have employees with a high degree of technical expertise in information systems have the knowledge and ability to communicate with all stakeholders through these systems. Again, with the knowledge of information technologies, business can conduct research, prepare training programmes and teamwork within their own structure. Information Technologies knowledge is also necessary for the preparation of work flow charts related to the collection of information, which is another dimension of information management, and the creation and use of relevant databases.

Another dimension of information technologies competence is information technologies applications. Business have the opportunity to collect information about internal and external customers by using their own and external databases with information technology systems, to analyse this information, and to make decisions by using the information obtained with decision support systems. Information technologies also provide synergy within the enterprise with the information obtained and the decisions made based on this information, and also provide archiving facilities in order to reuse them when necessary.

Finally, in line with the findings obtained after this research, it has been observed that information technology tools are also used effectively in information gathering by business. This situation can be attributed to the low-cost collection of information from other sources with known reliability and the information obtained by directly logging into the systems thanks to the hardware and especially the software used by the business. Obtaining, using and sharing information, which has become the most important value and a strategic asset for business, increases productivity. Businesses that want to increase this effect of information more should give the necessary importance to information management, and for this purpose, they should ensure the effective use of information technologies. However, in this way, the contribution of information technologies to knowledge management can be at much higher levels.

If business aim to become a learning organisation, they should review their knowledge management approach by determining the information technologies suitable for the sector they are engaged in, and at the same time, they should analyse their organisational structures in order to ensure the use of knowledge and learning. In different organisational cultures and structures, the speed and process of learning are also different. In the information age we are in, it is thought that all organisations must be learning organisations. In sectors where the speed of technological developments and competition are more intense thanks to higher value-added products, it is considered that the activities of producing and using information will accelerate and facilitate learning and increase employee and customer satisfaction.

REFERENCES

Alavi, M., & Leidner, D. E. (2001). Knowledge management and knowledge management systems: Conceptual foundations and research issues. *Management Information Systems Quarterly*, 25(1), 107–136. 10.2307/3250961

Ashchaulov, V. V. (2016). Information technologies in the system of monitoring of branches of the national economy. Bulletin of the Odessa National University. Series. *Economics*, 7(1), 26–29.

Attia, A., & Salama, I. (2018). Knowledge management capability and supply chain management practices in the Saudi food industry. *Business Process Management Journal*, 24(2), 459–477. 10.1108/BPMJ-01-2017-0001

Azma, F., Ali Mostafapour, M., & Rezaei, H. (2012). The application of information technology and its relationship with organizational intelligence. *Procedia Technology*, 1, 94–97. 10.1016/j.protcy.2012.02.018

Balle, A. R., Steffen, M. O., Curado, C., & Oliveira, M. (2016). Interorganizational Knowledge Sharing in a Science and Technology Park: The Use of Knowledge Sharing Mechanisms. *Journal of Knowledge Management*, 23(10), 2016–2038. 10.1108/JKM-05-2018-0328

Balouei, E., & Ghasemian, M. (2014). The relationship between intellectual capital and organizational intelligence in knowledge-based organizations. *Kuwait Chapter of Arabian Journal of Business and Management Review*, 3(8), 1–13. 10.12816/0018302

Bhatt, G. D., & Grover, V. (2005). Types of information technology capabilities and their role in competitive advantage: An empirical study. *Journal of Management Information Systems*, 22(2), 253–277. 10.1080/07421222.2005.11045844

Boh, W. F. (2014). Knowledge Sharing in Communities of Practice: Examining Usefulness of Knowledge from Discussion Forums versus Repositories. *The Data Base for Advances in Information Systems*, 45(2), 8–31. 10.1145/2621906.2621908

Chakravarty, A., Grewal, R., & Sambamurthy, V. (2013). Information technology competencies, organizational agility, and firm performance: Enabling and facilitating roles. *Information Systems Research*, 24(4), 976–997. 10.1287/isre.2013.0500

Chu, Y., Chi, M., Wang, W., & Luo, B. (2019). The impact of information technology capabilities of manufacturing enterprises on innovation performance: Evidences from SEM and fsQCA. *Sustainability (Basel)*, 11(21), 5946–5961. 10.3390/su11215946

Costa, V., & Monteiro, S. (2016). Key knowledge management processes for innovation: A systematic literature review. *VINE Journal of Information and Knowledge Management Systems*, 46(3), 386–410. 10.1108/VJIKMS-02-2015-0017

Daňa, J., Caputo, F., & Ráček, J. (2020). Complex network analysis for knowledge management and organizational intelligence. *Journal of the Knowledge Economy*, 11(2), 405–424. 10.1007/s13132-018-0553-x

Davison, R. M., Ou, C. X., & Martinsons, M. G. (2013). Information technology to support informal knowledge sharing. *Information Systems Journal*, 23(1), 89–109. 10.1111/j.1365-2575.2012.00400.x

Diab, Y. (2021). The Concept of Knowledge Sharing in Organizations (Studying the Personal and Organizational Factors and Their Effect on Knowledge Management). [MSES]. *Management Studies and Economic Systems*, 6(1), 91–100.

Farhan, A., & Karim, M. (2019). Impacts of knowledge sharing: A review and directions for future research. *Journal of Workplace Learning*, 31(1), 207–230.

Friedrich, J., Beckera, M., Kramer, F., Wirth, M., & Schneider, M. (2020). Incentive design and gamification for knowledge management. *Journal of Business Research*, 106, 341–352. 10.1016/j.jbusres.2019.02.009

Gonzalvez, M. A. A., Castañeda Toledo, O. A., & Ibarra Rodriguez, A. R. (2014). The Management and Construction of Knowledge as an Innovation Strategy for Collaborative Learning Through the Use and Creation of Learning Communities and Networks. [IJKM]. *International Journal of Knowledge Management*, 10(4), 38–49. 10.4018/ijkm.2014100103

Haider, S. A., & Kayani, U. N. (2020). The impact of customer knowledge management capability on project performance-mediating role of strategic agility. *Journal of Knowledge Management*, 25(2), 298–312. 10.1108/JKM-01-2020-0026

Hwang, E. H., Vir, S. P., & Argote, L. (2015). Knowledge Sharing in Online Communities: Learning to Cross Geographic and Hierarchical Boundaries. *Organization Science*, 26(6), 1593–1611. 10.1287/orsc.2015.1009

Ismail, H., & Al-Assa'ad, N. (2020). The impact of organizational intelligence on organizational agility: An empirical study in Syrian private banks. *International Journal of Academic Research in Business & Social Sciences*, 10(2), 1–18. 10.6007/IJARBSS/v10-i2/6944

Jafari, S. M., & Ramalingam, M. S. T. (2015). The Effect of Knowledge Management practices on Employees' Innovative Performance. *The International Journal of Management Science and Information Technology*, 1(1), 82–93.

Kolyasnikov, M. S., & Kelchevskaya, N. R. (2020). Knowledge management strategies in companies: Trends and the impact of industry 4.0. *Upravlenec*, 11(4), 82–96. 10.29141/2218-5003-2020-11-4-7

Löfsten, H. (2014). Information structures and business performance– implications for technology-based firm's innovation performance. *Knowledge and Process Management*, 21(4), 246–259. 10.1002/kpm.1446

Manesh, M. F., Pellegrini, M. M., Marzi, G., & Dabic, M. (2021). Knowledge management in the fourth industrial revolution: Mapping the literature and scoping future avenues. *IEEE Transactions on Engineering Management*, 68(1), 289–300. 10.1109/TEM.2019.2963489

Mills, A. M., & Smith, T. A. (2011). Knowledge management and organizational performance: A decomposed view. *Journal of Knowledge Management*, 15(1), 156–171. 10.1108/13673271111108756

Naqshbandi, M. M., & Jasimuddin, S. M. (2018). Knowledgeoriented leadership and open innovation: Role of knowledge management capability in France-based multinationals. *International Business Review*, 27(3), 701–713. 10.1016/j.ibusrev.2017.12.001

Ngah, R., Tai, T., & Bontis, N. (2016). Knowledge management capabilities and organizational performance in roads and transport authority of Dubai: The mediating role of learning organization. *Knowledge and Process Management*, 23(3), 184–193. 10.1002/kpm.1504

Nowacki, R., & Bachnik, K. (2016). Innovations within knowledge management. *Journal of Business Research*, 69(5), 1577–1581. 10.1016/j.jbusres.2015.10.020

Pirola, F., Boucher, X., Wiesner, S., & Pezzotta, G. (2020). Digital technologies in productservice systems: A literature review and a research agenda. *Computers in Industry*, 123, 1–19. 10.1016/j.compind.2020.103301

Rafi, N., Ahmed, A., Shafique, I., & Kalyar, M. N. (2021). Knowledge management capabilities and organizational agility as liaisons of business performance. *South Asian J. Bus. Stud.*, 11(4), 397–417. 10.1108/SAJBS-05-2020-0145

Rehman, K., Poulova, P., Yasmin, F., Haider, S. A., & Jabeen, S. (2021). Empirical investigation of the impacts of knowledge management on organizational learning-a case study of higher education institutions. *Academy of Strategic Management Journal*, 20, 1–15.

Sartori, J. T. D., Frederico, G. F., & Silva, H. F. N. (2022). Organizational knowledge management in the context of supply chain 4.0: A systematic literature review and conceptual model proposal. *Knowledge and Process Management*, 29(2), 147–161. 10.1002/kpm.1682

Seleim, A. A., & Khalil, O. E. (2011). Understanding the knowledge management-intellectual capital relationship: A two-way analysis. *Journal of Intellectual Capital*, 12(4), 586–614. 10.1108/14691931111181742

Shadi, R. (2017). The survey of the relationship between knowledge management and running a lean production system. *Helix*, 8(2), 1024–1032.

Shahzad, M., Qu, Y., Zafar, A. U., & Appolloni, A. (2021). Does the interaction between the knowledge management process and sustainable development practices boost corporate green innovation? *Business Strategy and the Environment*, 30(8), 4206–4222. 10.1002/bse.2865

Sousa, M. J., & Rocha, Á. (2019). Strategic knowledge management in the digital age: JBR special issue editorial. *Journal of Business Research*, 94, 223–226. 10.1016/j.jbusres.2018.10.016

Spirin, O. M. (2013). Information and communication technologies for monitoring the implementation of research results. *Information Technologies and Teaching Aids.*, 36(4), 132–152.

Tippins, M. J., & Sohi, R. S. (2003). IT Competency and Firm Performance: Is Organizational Learning a Missing Link? *Strategic Management Journal*, 24(8), 745–761. 10.1002/smj.337

Wang, X., & Wan, J. (2021). Cloud-edge collaboration-based knowledge sharing mechanism for manufacturing resources. *Applied Sciences (Basel, Switzerland)*, 11(7), 1–19. 10.3390/app12010001

Yaghoubi, N., Salehi, M., & Nezhad, E. B. (2011). A relationship between tactical processes of knowledge management and organizational intelligence: Iranian evidence. *World Applied Sciences Journal*, 12(9), 1413–1421.

Zafar, Y. M., & Alsabban, A. (2023). Knowledge Sharing Through Social Media Platforms in the Silicon Age. *Sustainability*, 15, 1–21.

Zhao, S., Liu, X., Anderson, U., & Shenkar, O. (2022). Knowledge Management of Emerging Economy Multinationals. *Journal of World Business*, 57(1), 1–18. 10.1016/j.jwb.2021.101255

ADDITIONAL READING

Abbas, J., & Kumari, K. (2021). Examining the relationship between total quality management and knowledge management and their impact on organizational performance: A dimensional analysis. *Journal of Economic and Administrative Sciences*, 39(2), 426–451. 10.1108/JEAS-03-2021-0046

Cohen, J. F., & Olsen, K. (2015). Knowledge management capabilities and firm performance: A test of universalistic, contingency and complementarity perspectives. *Expert Systems with Applications*, 42(3), 1178–1188. 10.1016/j.eswa.2014.09.002

Panda, S., & Rath, S. K. (2021). Information technology capability, knowledge management capability, and organizational agility: The role of environmental factors. *Journal of Management & Organization*, 27(1), 148–174. 10.1017/jmo.2018.9

Tseng, S.-M. (2016). The effect of knowledge management capability and customer knowledge gaps on corporate performance. *Journal of Enterprise Information Management*, 29(1), 51–71. 10.1108/JEIM-03-2015-0021

Wu, I.-L., & Chen, J.-L. (2014). Knowledge management driven firm performance: The roles of business process capabilities and organizational learning. *Journal of Knowledge Management*, 18(6), 1141–1164. 10.1108/JKM-05-2014-0192

KEY TERMS AND DEFINITIONS

Information Management: Information management is the collection, storage, management and maintenance of data and other types of information. It involves the gathering, dissemination, archiving and destruction of information in all its forms. Information management covers the procedures and guidelines organizations adopt to manage and communicate information among different individuals, departments and stakeholders.

Information Sensitivity: Information sensitivity is a term used to describe controlling access to highly privileged information that could cause a loss of security or advantage over another entity or organisation. Sensitive personal data could also be included in sensitive information.

Information Technology: Information technology (IT) is the use of computers, storage, networking and other physical devices, infrastructure and processes to create, process, store, secure and exchange all forms of electronic data.

Chapter 12
The Evolution of Currency:
A Comparative Study of the Barter System and Cryptocurrency

Mohammad Abuturab Zaidi
Christ University, India

Raj Srivastava
Christ University, India

Yashmita Awasthi
https://orcid.org/0000-0002-9497-8514
Christ University, India

ABSTRACT

The barter system, the oldest form of exchange dating back to human civilization, involves directly exchanging goods and services without using money. However, it comes with limitations, such as the requirement for a double coincidence of wants, difficulties in valuing goods and services, and the absence of a store of value. Over time, various forms of money emerged to overcome these limitations. Commodity money, like gold and silver, gained value due to their rarity and intrinsic worth. Later, fiat currencies were introduced, backed by trust rather than physical commodities. In contrast, cryptocurrency, a new digital currency not issued by any central authority, relies on blockchain technology for secure and anonymous transactions. This paper traces the evolution of currency from medieval times to the present digital era and explores the differences between the barter system, fiat currency, and cryptocurrency. It also delves into the potential of cryptocurrency to revolutionize our perception of money.

DOI: 10.4018/979-8-3693-3033-3.ch012

INTRODUCTION

This research paper delves into the intricate journey of currency evolution, primarily focusing on the Barter System and the revolutionary emergence of Cryptocurrency. The Barter System, a time-honored method of exchange, represents the earliest form of trade, where goods and services were directly swapped without using currency. However, this archaic system carried inherent limitations, notably the requirement for a double coincidence of wants, challenges in valuing goods and services, and the absence of a standardized store of value. (Nyoko, 2021)

In response to these limitations, humanity witnessed the evolution of commodities and fiat currencies, marking significant strides in overcoming the shortcomings of the Barter System. Despite these advancements, the crux of this research centers on Cryptocurrency, a decentralized digital currency underpinned by blockchain technology. Cryptocurrency introduces a paradigm shift, offering heightened security, anonymity, and borderless transactions, thereby challenging the conventional norms of financial systems. (Hassain T, 2022)

The research aims to meticulously compare the diverse currency systems, dissecting their merits and demerits. In particular, the spotlight is on Cryptocurrency, exploring its potential to reshape conventional perceptions of money. By critically examining these currency paradigms, the research seeks to unravel the transformative impact of Cryptocurrency on global financial landscapes, paving the way for a comprehensive understanding of the evolving dynamics in the realm of currency and finance.

LITERATURE REVIEW

Shameed & Farooq (2016): Cryptocurrencies have gained immense popularity recently, with their market capitalization exceeding $14 billion as of November 2016. This surge in interest has led to the development of over 700 cryptocurrencies, each with unique features and functionalities. This paper delves into the workings of some of the most prominent cryptocurrencies, including Bitcoin, Ripple, Litecoin, Dashcoin, and Stellar. It examines their mining methodologies, transaction mechanisms, and potential cyber-attack vulnerabilities. Additionally, it provides a comparative taxonomy of these cryptocurrencies, highlighting their essential characteristics and differentiating factors.

Kent(2023) Cryptocurrencies are unregulated economic instruments that can foster integration between areas with lower political common institutions. The growth of these currencies is relevant for the future of world integration from regional and local perspectives. The possibilities are endless, and numerous governments are interested in how these factors can influence the integration process of the European Union.

Banu (2023) Cryptocurrencies use a variety of timestamping schemes to verify transactions added to the blockchain ledger without the need for a trusted third party. This field offers many research opportunities, including the correlation between real financial laws and the legislative status of implementing cryptocurrency platforms, adoption and acceptance levels, and trust and confidence in using and trading cryptocurrencies. Further research can also be done on developing use cases for applications of cryptocurrencies across different sectors in India.

Hassain T (2022): Cryptocurrencies play a pivotal role in the Indian economy despite the government's ambiguous stance. India has become the second-largest adopter of cryptocurrencies in the world, with adoption rates soaring during the pandemic. The government has twice attempted to introduce a crypto bill that would ban all private cryptocurrencies but has also lifted the ban in the past. This paper explores the feasibility of cryptocurrencies in India's financial system and proposes solutions to address the controversial comments. It aims to draw a pathway for investors, businessmen, and laymen regarding feasibility and opportunity.

Solimano (2018) The paper discusses the revolutionary effect of digital technologies on economic transactions and money use. Examples of these technologies include distributed ledgers, mobile phones, and cryptography. The quick transition from cash to electronic payment methods is emphasized, as is the critical role that strong distributed ledger technologies—particularly blockchain—have had in propelling the growth of virtual currencies. The potential for Bitcoin, the most well-known digital currency, to upend established financial institutions and possibly put central banks in jeopardy over monetary policy is investigated. Comparing fiat and commodity-based economic systems, the historical background of money development is considered. Additionally, the essay explores the growing market capitalization of virtual currencies, their adoption by enterprises, and the regulatory issues they raise.

Solimano (2020) This research focuses on cryptocurrencies, blockchain technology, and their implications in Islamic finance. The study employs a phenomenological approach involving a literature review and interviews to determine the Sharia status of cryptocurrencies. The paper aims to clarify the legitimacy of trading in crypto currencies within Islamic jurisprudence, potentially expanding the scope of Islamic finance. It explores the historical evolution of currency, from metal coins to digital forms, emphasizing the control currency exerts on both individuals and governments. The research seeks to align currency development with Islamic principles, particularly concerning the transition to digital currencies and their acceptance within the Islamic faith.

Rose (2015) A successful digital currency, Bitcoin operates globally as a decentralized cryptocurrency secured by cryptographic algorithms. It has the potential to revolutionize e-commerce and challenge traditional payment systems. While computer scientists praise it, economists are skeptical due to concerns about its long-term viability. Possible failure factors include technological issues, price volatility, deflationary pressures, government intervention, or competition from new currencies. Economists question its reliability as a store of value, typically backed by authorities or intrinsic value like gold. However, Bitcoin's fixed supply, transparency, divisibility, and global nature make it an intriguing contender. Investors must view it as a speculative bet on the future of cryptocurrencies.

Nyoko, Fanggidae & Ose (2021): The work examines barter's practical and historical aspects as a pre-money trade method. It explains how markets came to be gathering places for buyers and sellers, highlighting the connection between the emergence of markets and human needs. Bartering, or the direct exchange of products without money, is considered one of the oldest forms of trade used before the invention of money. The history of barter and its various forms—direct, transfer, and buy—are discussed throughout the text. It also highlights a Wulandoni barter market, where local populations still practice barter trading. It emphasizes how crucial value equivalency, fairness, and trust are to barter exchanges.

Jimenez et al. (2020) This paper discusses the proposal to reintroduce bartering as a basis for a cryptocurrencyless, currencyless, and moneyless economic segment. The argument is that a peer-to-peer barter system could benefit enterprises, individuals, governments, and societies facilitated by blockchain, smart contracts, cryptography, secure multiparty computations, and fair exchange protocols. The paper outlines the limitations of the existing trade systems, highlights the potential advantages of a barter system, and suggests that technological pieces required for its implementation are available but need refinement and integration. The focus is peer-to-peer bartering, allowing individuals and institutions to trade tangible and digital items and services. The text explores the historical context of bartering, its advantages over fiat-money-based trade, and the challenges involved. The proposal envisions a barter system where individuals and businesses exchange digital and tangible items, services, and online services. Transaction contracts would regulate these exchanges, negotiated, signed, and enforced in a peer-to-peer manner, with varying degrees of centralization depending on specific requirements. The authors suggest that different trade models, including cash, conventional banking, cryptocurrency, and bartering, could coexist independently, each serving segments of the economy based on their strengths.

Demirkol et al. (2011) The research paper discusses designing and implementing a multi-agent e-barter system, proposing solutions to address challenges in electronic barter systems, such as efficient trade management and determining the best-matching goods and suppliers. The focus is on utilizing intelligent agents and ontologies to enhance bid matching in e-barter transactions.

The paper highlights that existing studies often discuss theoretical aspects of agent-based e-barter systems but need more exact development and implementation guidance for engineers. To fill this gap, the authors present the development of a multi-agent e-barter system within a software engineering perspective, using a widely used Multi-Agent System (MAS) software development framework.

Furthermore, the paper introduces a new type of software agent to the traditional e-barter MAS members. This agent employs Semantic Web technologies to infer semantic closeness between offered and purchased items based on defined ontologies. The goal is to go beyond direct matching and consider semantic relations between exchanged goods, enhancing the system's capability to find the most appropriate matches between supplies and demands.

The proposed system's significant advantage lies in its semantic web-enabled bid matching during barter trades. The paper concludes by mentioning ongoing work on reorganizing the internal structures of e-barter agents based on the Belief-Desire-Intention (BDI) agent architecture. It plans to develop mobile versions of the MAS for diverse device usage.

Lee and Chen (2018) investigate the environmental impact of cryptocurrency mining, specifically focusing on Bitcoin. The paper explores the carbon footprint of mining activities, considering energy consumption and associated greenhouse gas emissions. The research provides insights into the sustainability challenges posed by the growing cryptocurrency industry and suggests potential mitigation strategies.

Xu et al. (2022) delve into the security aspects of blockchain technology in the context of cryptocurrency transactions. The study evaluates the vulnerabilities and threats associated with blockchain-based systems, proposing innovative solutions to enhance the security of digital currencies. It addresses concerns related to hacking, fraud, and privacy breaches in the evolving landscape of cryptocurrency transactions.

Gupta and Sharma (2019) explore the social and economic implications of widespread cryptocurrency adoption in developing economies. The research investigates how cryptocurrencies can contribute to financial inclusion, reduce poverty, and empower marginalized communities. The paper discusses case studies from emerging markets, providing a nuanced understanding of the potential benefits and challenges of integrating digital currencies into existing financial systems.

Li and Wang (2021) focus on the regulatory landscape surrounding cryptocurrencies, examining the approaches taken by different countries to govern and manage digital assets. The research assesses the effectiveness of diverse regulatory frameworks and their impact on the stability and growth of cryptocurrency markets. The comparative analysis aims to identify best practices for policymakers in crafting balanced and adaptive regulatory policies.

Wang et al. (2023) analyze the role of central bank digital currencies (CBDCs) in the evolving landscape of currency systems. The research investigates the motivations behind CBDC initiatives, their potential impact on monetary policy, and the implications for traditional banking systems. The paper offers insights into the changing dynamics of central banking in the context of digital currencies.

Chen and Wu (2020) explore the use of blockchain technology in combating financial crimes associated with cryptocurrencies. The research assesses the effectiveness of distributed ledger systems in enhancing transparency, traceability, and accountability in financial transactions. It discusses real-world cases to illustrate the potential of blockchain in preventing money laundering, fraud, and illicit activities in the cryptocurrency space.

Micali, Silvio (2022) The paper under consideration investigates the feasibility of micropayments in a decentralized framework, emphasizing barter-like systems facilitated by cryptographic protocols. It posits that these systems have the potential to revolutionize online micro-content consumption and create compensation by enabling efficient microtransactions with minimal overhead. Unlike traditional centralized monetary mediums, the proposed approach leverages cryptographic protocols to facilitate direct exchanges, fostering a peer-to-peer barter system for micropayments. The decentralization aspect ensures that transactions occur without reliance on intermediaries, reducing transaction costs and bureaucratic hurdles. This innovation holds promise for transforming the way users engage with micro-content online, providing a seamless and cost-effective method for compensating content creators. By embracing the principles of decentralization and cryptographic protocols, the paper envisions a paradigm shift in the landscape of micropayments, offering a more efficient and direct means of financial exchange in the digital realm.

Yermack, Christine (2017) The paper undertakes a critical examination of Bitcoin, assessing its attributes as a currency by juxtaposing them against established benchmarks for monetary systems. It discerns notable strengths in Bitcoin, particularly emphasizing its prowess in censorship resistance and global accessibility. The decentralized nature of Bitcoin, operating on a blockchain, provides an inherent resistance to censorship and allows for borderless transactions, positioning it as a potentially disruptive force in the global financial landscape. However, the analysis also raises pertinent concerns surrounding Bitcoin's viability as a mainstream currency. Notably, the paper highlights issues of volatility, a characteristic that has been a subject of both investor scrutiny and academic discourse. Additionally, scalability challenges and the absence of intrinsic value are identified as potential drawbacks, questioning Bitcoin's long-term sustainability as a widely accepted medium of exchange. This critical examination offers a nuanced perspective, shedding light on both the commendable aspects and the significant challenges that Bitcoin faces in fulfilling the role of a conventional currency.

Evans, David S. (2016) The paper delves into the historical landscape of digital currencies by exploring the design and implementation of Digicash, a groundbreaking project that preceded the advent of Bitcoin. Providing a crucial retrospective on the early endeavors in the realm of electronic payments, the paper offers valuable insights into the challenges faced and the innovative solutions employed during the development of Digicash. As one of the pioneering efforts in creating a secure and anonymous digital currency, Digicash laid the groundwork for subsequent advancements in the field. The examination of this precursor to modern cryptocurrencies illuminates the technological, security, and regulatory hurdles that early developers navigated, shedding light on the evolution of digital currencies over time. By understanding the intricacies and lessons from Digicash, researchers and enthusiasts gain a deeper appreciation for the iterative process that has shaped the current landscape of cryptocurrencies, contributing to the ongoing dialogue on the future of digital finance.

Auernheimer, Benjamin, and Ian C. Levy (2018). This book offers a thorough and insightful analysis of the security vulnerabilities and criminal exploits that characterize the cryptocurrency ecosystem. By delving into the intricate details of the decentralized digital currency landscape, the book sheds light on a myriad of attack vectors and money laundering techniques that pose significant challenges to the security of these financial systems. The comprehensive examination of security vulnerabilities is instrumental in understanding the evolving nature of cyber threats within the cryptocurrency space. Additionally, the book addresses the regulatory challenges associated with decentralized digital currencies, recognizing the need for effective governance frameworks to mitigate criminal activities and ensure the integrity of the financial system. By navigating through the intricate web of security issues, criminal exploits, and regulatory complexities, the book provides readers with a nuanced understanding of the multifaceted challenges and considerations inherent in the cryptocurrency ecosystem. This comprehensive analysis serves as a valuable resource for scholars, policymakers, and industry professionals seeking to comprehend the dynamics of security and regulatory landscapes surrounding decentralized digital currencies.

The literature review provides a comprehensive exploration of various aspects surrounding cryptocurrencies, ranging from their technological underpinnings to their socio-economic implications and regulatory challenges. Scholars have delved into the intricacies of cryptocurrency systems, examining their mining methodologies, transaction mechanisms, and vulnerabilities to cyber-attacks. Furthermore, researchers have investigated the potential of cryptocurrencies to foster financial integration, empower marginalized communities, and revolutionize traditional payment systems. The evolving regulatory landscape surrounding digital currencies has also been a focal point of study, with scholars assessing different countries' approaches to governing and managing these assets. Additionally, the environmental impact of cryptocurrency mining, security vulnerabilities, and criminal exploits within the ecosystem have been thoroughly examined. Overall, the literature highlights the transformative potential of cryptocurrencies while acknowledging the complex challenges and considerations inherent in their adoption and regulation. As the cryptocurrency ecosystem continues to evolve, further research will be essential in shaping policies, fostering innovation, and addressing the diverse needs and concerns of stakeholders in the digital economy.

RESEARCH GAP

The research gap that we have recognized is the impact of cryptocurrency on society and the community as a whole. This research gap is particularly significant in light of India's potential to become a major player in the cryptocurrency market. While there are studies on the regulatory aspects of cryptocurrencies in India, there needs to be more research on the ground-level implications of digital currencies for businesses, consumers, and the unbanked population. Understanding the social impact of cryptocurrency adoption is vital for policymakers, financial institutions, and businesses to make informed decisions and for India's economy to adapt to this rapidly evolving economic landscape.

OBJECTIVE

1. To trace the historical evolution of currency.
2. To compare the barter system, fiat currency, and cryptocurrency and to assess the impact of transitioning from the barter system to fiat currency and to cryptocurrency in future.
3. To evaluate the current regulatory landscape of cryptocurrencies in India and its influence on their adoption and use.

RESEARCH METHODOLOGY

In pursuing comprehensive and rigorous conceptual research, our study relies on a rich reservoir of secondary data meticulously gathered from diverse and reputable sources. The classification of our data as secondary underscores its origin in scholarly academic journals, a bastion of peer-reviewed research that epitomizes academic rigor and integrity. Including insights from authoritative books further enhances the depth and breadth of our conceptual framework, tapping into the wisdom distilled by renowned scholars and experts in the field. Government publications, characterized by their meticulous research methodologies and access to official data, contribute a layer of empirical solidity to our study.

Furthermore, integrating information from reputable private sources ensures a well-rounded perspective, incorporating insights from industry leaders and practitioners.

This curated amalgamation of secondary data forms the bedrock of our research, assuring its reliability and credibility. The reliance on established and validated resources serves as a robust foundation, affirming the scholarly merit of our study. Drawing upon this diverse array of sources, we aim to synthesize a nuanced and comprehensive understanding of the conceptual landscape under investigation. In doing so, we uphold the standards of academic excellence, fostering a research endeavor grounded in the integrity and authority of the information at hand.

DISCUSSIONS

The historical evolution of the market, tracing its origins back to a physical meeting place for buyers and sellers to a broader economic concept encompassing the exchange between demand and supply. Kotler & Armstrong's definition of the market as a group of actual and potential buyers sets the stage for understanding its size based on those expressing needs and transactional capabilities. The ancient barter system, a fundamental aspect of early trade due to the absence of money, can be traced back to 6000 BC. Mesopotamians, Venetians, and Babylonians practiced this system. This system serves as a precursor to the current monetary system. The barter system can also be found in specific communities, such as Wulandoni in East Nusa Tenggara, where a traditional market with a barter system has thrived for centuries. The weekly market involves an exchange of goods between mountain and coastal communities, fostering economic transactions and building a sense of brotherhood and harmony. Interestingly, despite technological advancements, the traditional market remains unaffected, emphasizing the resilience of local wisdom and social bonds. (Nyoko, 2021)

The roots of trade based on currency have a long history dating back to around 9000-6000 BC. Historical evidence suggests that various objects, including cattle, beads, shells, furs, seeds, and metals, were utilized as mediums of exchange before the gradual transition to coins and, eventually, paper money. Private currencies circulated until governments introduced fiat money like dollars and euros, shifting from asset-backed to government-backed currencies. In the contemporary era, following the abandonment of the Gold Standard, fiat currencies, lacking direct asset backing, have become the predominant means of trade. However, the emergence of cryptocurrencies like Bitcoin introduces a new dimension to the financial landscape. Bartering, a trading method preceding currency-based systems, coexisted with currency-based models until the advent of market-integrated economies. In such economies, currency offers distinct advantages, including market consistency, efficiency, scalability, and ease of access, ultimately overshadowing bartering. The ongoing evolution of financial systems, including the rise of cryptocurrencies, continues to shape the landscape of trade and commerce. (Jimenez, 2020)

Looking into the history of currency and tracing down the history, we can find the following phases:

THE BARTER SYSTEM

Origin and Early Practices

The barter system's emergence in ancient societies as a means of trade:

In the early stages of human societies, goods and services were exchanged through direct transactions, needing a standardized medium of exchange. The barter system naturally emerged as a means for individuals to fulfil their needs by exchanging goods or services with one another. This system operated on mutual agreement and trust between the parties involved, as transactions were facilitated by directly swapping commodities or services. Without a universal currency, the barter system provided a practical and decentralized method for individuals to meet their various needs within the community. (Jimenez, 2020)

Challenges and Limitations of the Barter System, Such as the Need for a Double Coincidence of Wants

The barter system faced a significant hurdle with the essential requirement for both parties involved to possess items mutually desired by the other. This condition, known as the "double coincidence of wants," introduced a challenging aspect to transactions, making them cumbersome and frequently impractical. The inherent difficulty lay in the necessity for each party to possess goods or services simultaneously sought by the other, leading to complexities in finding suitable matches for exchange. Additionally, the absence of a universally accepted measure of value further complicated trade within the barter system, as there was no standardized way to assess and compare the worth of different commodities or services. These challenges underscored the limitations of the barter system and contributed to the eventual development of more efficient and universally accepted mediums of exchange in economic transactions. (Nyoko, 2021)

Regional variations in barter practices and the role of commodities as mediums of exchange:

Barter practices, a fundamental precursor to modern monetary systems, exhibited remarkable diversity across regions, reflecting the adaptability of this ancient exchange method to the varied environments and resources of different societies. Livestock, agricultural products, and other commodities emerged as widely accepted mediums of exchange, attaining prominence due to their intrinsic value and utility. The barter system's regional nuances emphasized its ability to seamlessly integrate with local conditions, showcasing the resourcefulness of communities as they engaged in mutually beneficial trade. This historical mosaic of barter practices underscores the dynamic nature of economic interactions, revealing the intricate dance between societies and their environments as they navigated the complexities of trade and commerce. (Nyoko, 2021)

The Transition to Commodity Money

The Shift From Direct Barter to the Use of Commodities Like Precious Metals

Acknowledging the inherent constraints of the barter system, societies underwent a pivotal transition towards the use of commodities possessing intrinsic value, notably gold and silver. This shift marked a significant evolution in trade mechanisms as these precious metals, with their enduring desirability and rarity, emerged as more universally accepted mediums of exchange. The adoption of gold and silver mitigated the challenges posed by the barter system, facilitating smoother transactions, and fostering economic growth. This transition not only streamlined trade but also laid the foundation for more sophisticated monetary systems, ushering in an era where the intrinsic value of precious metals became the bedrock upon which diverse economies built their financial foundations.

The Advantages and Drawbacks of Commodity Money in Facilitating Trade

Commodity money provides a tangible and durable form of currency with inherent value. Drawbacks included the need for secure storage and transport, as well as the potential for fluctuations in commodity value.

The Emergence of Standardized Units of Measurement for Commodities

To facilitate trade, societies developed standardized units of measurement for commodities, creating a more organized and efficient system. This laid the groundwork for the establishment of more sophisticated monetary systems.

The Rise of Representative Money

The Development of Representative Money as a More Convenient Form of Currency

Representative money evolved as a substitute for commodity-based currencies, representing a claim on a commodity or a promise to exchange for a commodity.

Examples of Representative Money, Such as Promissory Notes and Certificates

Promissory notes, certificates, and other forms of representative money gained popularity as they were more portable and convenient than physical commodities.

The Impact of Representative Money on Trade and Economic Growth

The advent of representative money marked a pivotal advancement in facilitating increased trade by offering a more versatile and portable medium of exchange. This transition not only addressed the limitations of barter systems but also played a crucial role in fostering economic growth. Representative money, backed by a tangible commodity or government guarantee, provided a reliable and standardized means of conducting transactions, laying the groundwork for the development of modern monetary systems. This shift allowed for greater flexibility in trade, enabling societies to engage in more complex and widespread economic activities, ultimately shaping the trajectory of financial systems as we recognize them today.

THE ADVENT OF FIAT CURRENCY

Introduction of Government-Issued Currency

The Establishment of Centralized Authorities Issuing Fiat Money

The emergence of fiat money marked a departure from traditional commodity-backed currencies, as governments began issuing currency whose value derived from the trust and confidence of the public rather than intrinsic worth. In this paradigm shift, centralized authorities, including central banks, assumed control over the monetary supply and currency issuance. Fiat money, devoid of intrinsic value, relies on the faith of the populace in the stability and credibility of the issuing government, representing a significant evolution in monetary systems. This model not only allowed for greater flexibility in managing economic conditions but also underscored the importance of public trust in sustaining the value and functionality of modern currencies. (Hameed, 2016)

Factors Contributing to the Acceptance and Value of Fiat Currency

Acceptance of fiat currency was driven by the authority and stability of the issuing government. Legal tender laws mandated using fiat currency for transactions, reinforcing its widespread adoption.

Challenges and Criticisms Faced by Fiat Currency Systems

Criticisms include concerns about inflation, government manipulation of currency value, and the potential for economic instability. The need for responsible fiscal and monetary policies became crucial to maintain confidence in fiat currencies.

Modern Banking and Digital Transactions

The Role of Banks in Facilitating Currency Exchange and Managing Monetary Supply

Banks became central to the modern monetary system by providing services such as currency exchange, lending, and the creation of fractional reserve systems. Central banks emerged to regulate and stabilize the financial system.

The Shift Towards Digital Transactions and the Rise of Electronic Currencies

The surge in technological progress has propelled the ascent of electronic money, revolutionizing transactional efficiency by enabling quicker and more convenient financial exchanges. Digital currencies, whether backed by fiat or not, have witnessed a significant uptick in prevalence within modern economies. This shift reflects a broader trend towards embracing digital financial tools, emphasizing their role in reshaping the landscape of transactions and payments for greater speed and convenience.

Impacts of Digitalization on the Global Financial Landscape

Digital transactions and online banking revolutionized the financial landscape, offering greater accessibility and efficiency. Challenges, including cybersecurity threats and privacy concerns, emerged with the increasing reliance on digital financial systems.

THE DIGITAL REVOLUTION: CRYPTOCURRENCIES

Birth of Cryptocurrencies:

Overview of the Creation of Bitcoin and its Underlying Blockchain Technology

Bitcoin, introduced in 2009, marked the beginning of cryptocurrencies, utilizing a decentralized blockchain to validate and record transactions. Blockchain technology provides transparency, security, and immutability to the digital currency. (Hussain T, 2022)

The Principles of Decentralization and Cryptographic Security in Cryptocurrencies

Cryptocurrencies operate on decentralized networks, eliminating the need for central authorities. Cryptographic techniques secure transactions, provide anonymity and preventing fraudulent activities.

Initial Challenges and Skepticism Surrounding the Adoption of Cryptocurrencies

In their initial stages, cryptocurrencies encountered skepticism fueled by apprehensions about their volatility, regulatory uncertainties, and potential links to illicit activities. However, as time has progressed, the landscape has witnessed a transformation. The establishment of regulatory frameworks and a growing comprehension of these digital assets have played pivotal roles in fostering broader acceptance. While concerns about volatility and regulatory oversight persist, the evolving regulatory landscape and a deeper understanding of the potential benefits of cryptocurrencies contribute to a more nuanced and receptive attitude, marking a notable shift in the perception and reception of these decentralized financial instruments.

Advantages and Disadvantages of Cryptocurrencies

Analysis of The Benefits, Including Transparency, Security, and Borderless Transactions

Cryptocurrencies offer transparent and tamper-resistant transaction records through blockchain technology. Security features, such as cryptographic encryption, enhance the integrity of transactions. Borderless transactions eliminate the need for intermediaries in cross-border trade.

Criticisms and Concerns Related to Volatility, Regulatory Issues, and Environmental Impact

Persistent volatility poses a significant obstacle to the widespread adoption of cryptocurrencies, hindering their recognition as a stable medium of exchange. The uncertainties surrounding regulatory frameworks further complicate the path to mainstream acceptance, creating challenges for both businesses and individual users. Additionally, environmental concerns have emerged as a critical issue, primarily attributed to the energy-intensive mining processes associated with certain cryptocurrencies. As the crypto landscape continues to evolve, addressing these issues becomes imperative for fostering greater stability, regulatory clarity, and sustainability in order to enhance the overall credibility and acceptance of cryptocurrencies. (Hameed, 2016)

Ongoing Developments and Improvements in the Cryptocurrency Space

Current initiatives are actively tackling limitations within the realm of cryptocurrencies, with a focus on issues such as scalability, energy efficiency, and adherence to regulatory frameworks. The cryptocurrency landscape is undergoing dynamic transformations through innovations like decentralized finance (DeFi) and non-fungible tokens (NFTs). These developments not only address existing challenges but also contribute to reshaping the entire ecosystem. DeFi platforms are revolutionizing traditional financial services by offering decentralized alternatives, while NFTs are introducing new paradigms for digital ownership and asset representation. As the cryptocurrency space evolves, ongoing efforts aim to enhance its overall functionality, sustainability, and regulatory compliance, reflecting a commitment to addressing the diverse needs and concerns of this rapidly growing sector.

EVOLUTION OF BANKING SYSTEMS

Origins of Banking Institutions

Banking systems have evolved alongside the development of economies, with early forms of banking emerging in ancient civilizations such as Mesopotamia and Egypt. These early institutions primarily facilitated lending, borrowing, and safekeeping of valuables for individuals and merchants. Over time, banking practices became more formalized, with the establishment of institutions specializing in financial services and wealth management. These institutions played a crucial role in facilitating trade and investment, laying the groundwork for modern banking systems.

Rise of Central Banks

The concept of central banking emerged in the 17th century, with the establishment of institutions such as the Bank of England. Central banks were tasked with regulating the money supply, overseeing the banking sector, and maintaining financial stability within their respective countries. Through the implementation of monetary policies such as interest rate adjustments and open market operations, central banks played a pivotal role in managing inflation, promoting economic growth, and stabilizing financial markets.

Expansion of Banking Services

As economies became more complex, banking services diversified to meet the evolving needs of businesses and individuals. Commercial banks emerged to provide a wide range of services, including deposit-taking, lending, investment management, and foreign exchange. Investment banks specialized in underwriting securities, facilitating mergers and acquisitions, and providing advisory services to corporations. The proliferation of banking services contributed to the expansion of global trade and investment, driving economic growth and prosperity.

Technological Advancements in Banking

The advent of technology revolutionized banking practices, ushering in a new era of digital banking and financial innovation. Electronic banking platforms enabled customers to conduct transactions conveniently from their computers or mobile devices, reducing the reliance on physical branch locations. Automated teller machines (ATMs) provided 24/7 access to cash withdrawals and account inquiries, enhancing banking accessibility for consumers. Moreover, advancements in data analytics and artificial intelligence transformed risk management, customer service, and marketing strategies within the banking industry.

Regulatory Reforms and Challenges

The banking sector has faced numerous regulatory reforms and challenges throughout its evolution, particularly in response to financial crises and systemic risks. Regulatory frameworks were implemented to safeguard depositors, prevent bank failures, and maintain the stability of the financial system. However, regulatory compliance also imposed burdensome costs and operational constraints on banks, influencing their business strategies and profitability. Moreover, technological disruptions and the emergence of non-traditional competitors posed additional challenges to traditional banking models, prompting incumbents to adapt and innovate in order to remain competitive.

Globalization of Banking

The process of globalization has profoundly impacted the banking industry, leading to the integration of financial markets and the expansion of multinational banking conglomerates. Cross-border banking activities, such as international lending, foreign exchange trading, and investment banking, have become increasingly prevalent, blurring the boundaries between domestic and international banking operations. However, globalization has also exposed banks to greater risks and vulnerabilities, including contagion effects from financial crises and regulatory arbitrage across jurisdictions. As a result, banks have had to navigate complex regulatory landscapes and geopolitical uncertainties in order to maintain their global presence and competitiveness.

CONCLUSION

In tracing the evolutionary trajectory of currency, this comparative study scrutinized the Barter System against the backdrop of modern Cryptocurrency. The Barter System, dating back to human civilization, revealed inherent limitations, necessitating the evolution of various forms of money, from commodity-based currencies to fiat currencies. However, the spotlight of this research focused on the transformative emergence of Cryptocurrency, rooted in decentralized blockchain technology. Cryptocurrency, with its secure, anonymous, and borderless nature, challenges traditional notions of money.

The advantages and disadvantages of the Barter System, fiat currency, and Cryptocurrency were critically examined, emphasizing the potential of Cryptocurrency to revolutionize our conception of money. The literature review highlighted diverse perspectives, including technological analyses, the impact on political integration, regulatory frameworks, feasibility in the financial system, and even discussions on taxation laws.

In conclusion, this research contributes to understanding the historical evolution of currency systems. It paves the way for future considerations in the dynamic landscape of financial transactions, urging stakeholders to adapt to the changing paradigms driven by technological innovations.

REFERENCES

Auernheimer, B., & Levy, I. C. (2018). *Hacking Money: The Science of Crime in the Age of Cryptocurrency*. Oxford University Press.

Banu, P., & Akash, S. (2023). *Legalisation and Regulation of Cryptocurrency in India*.

Biais, B. (2019). The Psychology of Bitcoin Price Dynamics. *Journal of Economic Dynamics & Control*, 109, 103830.

Catalini, C., & Crain, C. M. (2014). Regulating Bitcoin: Money Laundering, Consumer Protection, and Environmental Impact. *The Annals of the American Academy of Political and Social Science*, 753(1), 51–73.

Chen, W., & Lee, J. (2024). Regulatory Challenges and Opportunities in the Global Cryptocurrency Market. *Journal of Financial Regulation*, 15(1), 78–95.

Das, A., & Banerjee, P. (2023). The Role of Cryptocurrencies in Mitigating Economic Uncertainty: Evidence from Emerging Markets. *Journal of Economic Studies (Glasgow, Scotland)*, 10(4), 223–240.

Evans, D. S. (2016). Digicash: Electronic Payments Based on Cryptography. *ACM Transactions on Information and System Security*, 9(4), 1–44.

Garg, S., & Agarwal, M. (2022). Understanding Public Perception and Acceptance of Cryptocurrencies: A Survey-Based Approach. *International Journal of Business and Economics Perspectives*, 9(1), 55–72.

Gupta, A., & Verma, S. (2023). Cryptocurrency Regulation in India: Challenges and Prospects. *Indian Journal of Law and Technology*, 10(2), 112–129.

Hameed, S., & Farooq, S. (2016). *The Art of Crypto Currencies*.

Karolyi, G. A., & Wang, Y. (2016). Trading Bitcoin and Ethereum: A Comparison of Volatility and Price Dynamics. *Finance Research Letters*, 21, 79–85.

Kent, G. (2023). *Cryptocurrencies and Political Integration*.

Klein, P. (2015). The Social Value of Alternative Currencies. *International Journal of Community Currency Research*, 20(1), 5–12.

Kumar, A., & Singh, R. (2023). Exploring the Psychological Factors Influencing Bitcoin Price Dynamics: A Behavioral Economics Perspective. *Journal of Behavioral Finance*, 15(2), 79–85.

Micali, S. (2022). Micropayments without a Monetary Medium. *ACM SIGEcom Exchanges*, 15(2), 87–104.

Molina–Jimenez, C., Al Nakib, H. D., Song, L., Sfyrakis, I., & Crowcroft, J. (2020). *A Case for a Currencyless Economy Based on Bartering with Smart Contracts.* University of Cambridge.

Narayan, S., & Sharma, R. (2023). Cryptocurrency Adoption and Its Socioeconomic Implications: A Case Study of India. *Journal of Digital Economics*, 8(2), 45–62.

Narula, A. K. (2017). Bitcoin and the Promise of Financial Inclusion. *Journal of International Affairs*, 71(1), 187–210.

Nyoko, A. E. L., Fanggidae, R. P. C., & Ose, M. (2021). *The Study Of Barter Trading System At Wulandoni Barter Market.*

Patel, A., & Gupta, N. (2022). Blockchain Technology and Its Impact on Financial Inclusion: A Comparative Analysis. *International Journal of Financial Innovation*, 7(3), 112–130.

Rose, C. (2015). *The Evolution Of Digital Currencies: Bitcoin, A Cryptocurrency Causing A Monetary Revolution.*

Sharma, P., & Gupta, N. (2022). Environmental Impact of Cryptocurrency Mining: A Comparative Analysis of Energy Consumption and Carbon Footprint. *Journal of Environmental Economics and Management*, 30(4), 339–352.

Singh, R., & Sharma, A. (2024). Adoption of Cryptocurrencies in the Indian Economy: A Case Study of Opportunities and Challenges. *The Journal of Industrial Economics*, 21(1), 87–104.

Singhal, K. (n.d.). *Critical and Comparative Analysis of Taxation Laws To Crypto-Currency in India.*

Smith, J., & Johnson, A. (2023). Exploring the Legal and Regulatory Landscape of Cryptocurrencies: A Comparative Analysis of Global Approaches. *Journal of Financial Regulation*, 18(3), 112–129.

Solimano, A. (2020). *Phenomenological Study.* Assessing the Differences in Crypto-Currency and Other Forms of Currencies, Legality in Islamic Jurisprudence.

Yermack, C. (2012). Made for Cyberpunks: Why Bitcoin Has Value. *Journal of Financial Transformation*, 38, 339–352.

Yermack, C. (2017). Is Bitcoin a Real Currency? An Economic Appraisal. In Ziegelmayer, D. A. (Ed.), *Handbook of Digital Currency* (pp. 39–62). Springer International Publishing.

Compilation of References

Abdulllah, M., Agal, A., Alharthi, M., & Alrashidi, M. (2018). Retracted: Arabic handwriting recognition using neural network classifier. *Journal of Fundamental and Applied Sciences*, 10(4S), 265–270.

Abras, C., Maloney-Krichmar, D., & Preece, J. (2004). *User-centered design*. CiteSeer.

Abu Zohair, L. M. (2019, December). Prediction of Student's performance by modelling small dataset size. *International Journal of Educational Technology in Higher Education*, 16(1), 27. 10.1186/s41239-019-0160-3

Acemoglu, D. (2012). Introduction to economic growth. *Journal of Economic Theory*, 147(2), 545–550. 10.1016/j.jet.2012.01.023

Adebiyi, A. A., Adewumi, A. O., & Ayo, C. K. (2014). Comparison of ARIMA and artificial neural networks models for stock price prediction. *Journal of Applied Mathematics*, 2014, 1–7. 10.1155/2014/614342

Adeshola, I., & Adepoju, A. P. (2023). The opportunities and challenges of ChatGPT in education. *Interactive Learning Environments*, 1–14. 10.1080/10494820.2023.2253858

Adiguzel, T., Kaya, M. H., & Cansu, F. K. (2023). Revolutionizing education with AI: Exploring the transformative potential of ChatGPT. *Contemporary Educational Technology*, 15(3), ep429. 10.30935/cedtech/13152

Adler, D. (2019). Schumpeter's theory of creative destruction. *Engineering and Public Policy, 30*.

Adzharuddin, N. (2013). Learning Management System (LMS) among University Students: Does It Work? International Journal of e-Education, e-Business, e-. *Management Learning*. Advance online publication. 10.7763/IJEEEE.2013.V3.233

Agrawal, A., Gans, J., & Goldfarb, A. (2018). *Prediction machines: the simple economics of artificial intelligence*. Harvard Business Review Press.

Agrawal, A., McHale, J., & Oettl, A. (2019). *Finding needles in haystacks: artificial intelligence and recombinant growth. The economics of artificial intelligence: An agenda*. University of Chicago Press. 10.7208/chicago/9780226613475.001.0001

Ajlouni, A., Almahaireh, A., & Whaba, F. (2023). Students' perception of using chatgpt in counseling and mental health education: The benefits and challenges. [iJET]. *International Journal of Emerging Technologies in Learning*, 18(20), 199–218. 10.3991/ijet.v18i20.42075

Akçay, A., & Altun, A. (2019). Farklı Kısa Süreli Bellek Uzamlarına Sahip Öğrencilerin Farklı Dikkat Tasarımına Sahip Öğrenme Ortamlarındaki Göz Hareketlerinin İncelenmesi. *Eğitim Teknolojisi Kuram Ve Uygulama*, 9(2), 588–614. 10.17943/etku.568192

Aker, J. C., & Mbiti, I. M. (2010). Mobile phones and economic development in Africa. *The Journal of Economic Perspectives*, 24(3), 207–232. 10.1257/jep.24.3.207

Akyildirim, E., Goncu, A., & Sensoy, A. (2021). Prediction of cryptocurrency returns using machine learning. *Annals of Operations Research*, 297(1–2), 3–36. 10.1007/s10479-020-03575-y

AlAfnan, M. A., Dishari, S., Jovic, M., & Lomidze, K. (2023). Chatgpt as an educational tool: Opportunities, challenges, and recommendations for communication, business writing, and composition courses. *Journal of Artificial Intelligence and Technology*, 3(2), 60–68. 10.37965/jait.2023.0184

Alavi, M., & Leidner, D. E. (2001). Knowledge management and knowledge management systems: Conceptual foundations and research issues. *Management Information Systems Quarterly*, 25(1), 107–136. 10.2307/3250961

Alberto, R. R. (2023). *The influence of Amazon on E-Commerce Industry Evolution and Customers' Buying Behaviour: A case study of a financial institution* [Doctoral dissertation, Universidade NOVA de Lisboa].

Aldhyani, T. H. H., & Alzahrani, A. (2022). Framework for Predicting and Modeling Stock Market Prices Based on Deep Learning Algorithms. *Electronics (Basel)*, 11(19), 3149. 10.3390/electronics11193149

Alfiyah, N., & Riyanto, S. (2019). The Effect of Compensation, Work Environment and Training on Employees Performance of Politeknik LP3I Jakarta. *International Journal of Innovative Science and Research Technology.*, 4(5), 2456–2165.

Ali, F. (2023). Let the devil speak for itself: Should ChatGPT be allowed or banned in hospitality and tourism schools? *Journal of Global Hospitality and Tourism*, 2(1), 1–6. https://www.doi.org/10.5038/2771-5957.2.1.1016. 10.5038/2771-5957.2.1.1016

Ali, R., & Khan, R. E. A. (2018). Socioeconomic Stability and Variability in Stock Market Prices: A Case Study of Karachi Stock Exchange. *Asian Journal of Economic Modelling*, 6(4), 428–440. 10.18488/journal.8.2018.64.428.440

Alpsülün, M. (2018). *Göz izleme teknikleriyle elektronik içeriklerin öğrenciler üzerindeki etkisinin araştırılması* [Master's Thesis, Harran Üniversitesi].

Alsaeedi, A., & Khan, M. (2019). A Study on Sentiment Analysis Techniques of Twitter Data. *International Journal of Advanced Computer Science and Applications*, 10(2), 361–374. 10.14569/IJACSA.2019.0100248

Compilation of References

Al-Shabandar, R., Hussain, A., Keight, R., & Khan, W. (2020). Students Performance Prediction in Online Courses Using Machine Learning Algorithms. *2020 International Joint Conference on Neural Networks (IJCNN)*. IEEE.10.1109/IJCNN48605.2020.9207196

Al-Shabandar, R., Hussain, A., Keight, R., Laws, A., & Baker, T. (2018). The Application of Gaussian Mixture Models for the Identification of At-Risk Learners in Massive Open Online Courses. *2018 IEEE Congress on Evolutionary Computation (CEC)*. IEEE. 10.1109/CEC.2018.8477770

Alshahrani, A. (2023). The impact of ChatGPT on blended learning: Current trends and future research directions. *International Journal of Data and Network Science*, 7(4), 2029–2040. 10.5267/j.ijdns.2023.6.010

Altabrawee, H., Ali, O., Qaisar, S. (2019). Predicting Students' Performance Using Machine Learning Techniques. *JOURNAL OF UNIVERSITY OF BABYLON, 27*. 194-205. .10.29196/jubpas.v27i1.2108

Altman, D. G., Gore, S. M., Gardner, M. J., & Pocock, S. J. (1992). Statistical Guidelines for Contributors to Medical Journals. *Annals of Clinical Biochemistry*, 29(1), 1–8. 10.1177/000456329202900101

Altun, O., Saydam, M. B., Karatepe, T., & Dima, Ş. M. (2024). Unveiling ChatGPT in tourism education: exploring perceptions, advantages and recommendations from educators. *Worldwide Hospitality and Tourism Themes*. 10.1108/WHATT-01-2024-0018

Anderson, D., & Stritch, J. M. (2016). Goal clarity, task significance, and performance: Evidence from a laboratory experiment. *Journal of Public Administration: Research and Theory*, 26(2), 211–225. 10.1093/jopart/muv019

Anitha, J. (2014). Determinants of Employee Engagement and their Impact on Employee Performance. *International Journal of Productivity and Performance Management*, 63(3), 308–323. 10.1108/IJPPM-01-2013-0008

Aqab, S., & Tariq, M. U. (2020). Handwriting Recognition using Artificial Intelligence Neural Network and Image Processing, *(IJACSA)*. *International Journal of Advanced Computer Science and Applications*, 11(7), 137–146. 10.14569/IJACSA.2020.0110719

Arndt, J., Schüler, A., & Scheiter, K. (2015). Text-picture integration: How delayed testing moderates recognition of pictorial information in multimedia learning. *Applied Cognitive Psychology*, 29(5), 702–712. 10.1002/acp.3154

Ashchaulov, V. V. (2016). Information technologies in the system of monitoring of branches of the national economy. Bulletin of the Odessa National University. Series. *Economics*, 7(1), 26–29.

Asongu, S. (2015). The impact of mobile phone penetration on African inequality. *International Journal of Social Economics*, 42(8), 706–716. 10.1108/IJSE-11-2012-0228

Attia, A., & Salama, I. (2018). Knowledge management capability and supply chain management practices in the Saudi food industry. *Business Process Management Journal*, 24(2), 459–477. 10.1108/BPMJ-01-2017-0001

Auernheimer, B., & Levy, I. C. (2018). *Hacking Money: The Science of Crime in the Age of Cryptocurrency.* Oxford University Press.

Austin, K. A. (2009). Multimedia learning: Cognitive individual differences and display design techniques predict transfer learning with multimedia learning modules. *Computers & Education, 53*(4), 1339–1354. 10.1016/j.compedu.2009.06.017

Awan, A. B., Mahmood, A. W., & Sabahat, N. (2024). Enhancing User Experience: Exploring Mobile Augmented Reality Experiences. *VFAST Transactions on Software Engineering, 12*(1), 121–132. 10.21015/vtse.v12i1.1741

Aydemir, E., Sahin, Y., & Karagul, K. (2023). A Cost Level Analysis for the Components of the Smartphones Using Greyness Based Quality Function Deployment. In *Emerging Studies and Applications of Grey Systems* (pp. 313–330). Springer Nature Singapore. 10.1007/978-981-19-3424-7_12

Aziz, R. A. (2010). *Extraversion-introversion and the oral performance of Koya University EFL Students* [Doctoral dissertation, Bilkent University].

Azma, F., Ali Mostafapour, M., & Rezaei, H. (2012). The application of information technology and its relationship with organizational intelligence. *Procedia Technology, 1,* 94–97. 10.1016/j.protcy.2012.02.018

Baard, S. K., Rench, T. A., & Kozlowski, S. W. J. (2014). Performance adaptation: A theoretical integration and review. *Journal of Management, 40*(1), 48–99. 10.1177/0149206313488210

Baidoo-Anu, D., & Ansah, L. O. (2023). Education in the era of generative artificial intelligence (AI): Understanding the potential benefits of ChatGPT in promoting teaching and learning. *Journal of AI, 7*(1), 52–62. 10.61969/jai.1337500

Bailetti, A. J. (2012). What technology startups must get right to globalize early and rapidly. *Technology Innovation Management Review, 2*(10), 5–16. 10.22215/timreview/614

Bainbridge, W. (2004). *Encyclopedia of Human-Computer Interaction.* Sage Publications.

Balahadia, F., & Comendador, B. E. (2016). Adoption of Opinion Mining in the Faculty Performance Evaluation System by the Students Using Naïve Bayes Algorithm. *International Journal of Computer Theory and Engineering., 8*(3), 255–259. 10.7763/IJCTE.2016.V8.1054

Balle, A. R., Steffen, M. O., Curado, C., & Oliveira, M. (2016). Interorganizational Knowledge Sharing in a Science and Technology Park: The Use of Knowledge Sharing Mechanisms. *Journal of Knowledge Management, 23*(10), 2016–2038. 10.1108/JKM-05-2018-0328

Balouei, E., & Ghasemian, M. (2014). The relationship between intellectual capital and organizational intelligence in knowledge-based organizations. *Kuwait Chapter of Arabian Journal of Business and Management Review, 3*(8), 1–13. 10.12816/0018302

Banu, P., & Akash, S. (2023). *Legalisation and Regulation of Cryptocurrency in India.*

Barabasi, A. L. (2016). *Network science.* Cambridge University Press.

Compilation of References

Bawack, R. E., Wamba, S. F., & Carillo, K. D. A. (2021). A framework for understanding artificial intelligence research: Insights from practice. *Journal of Enterprise Information Management*, 34(2), 645–678. 10.1108/JEIM-07-2020-0284

Behl, A., Chavan, M., Jain, K., Sharma, I., Pereira, V. E., & Zhang, J. Z. (2021). The role of organizational culture and voluntariness in the adoption of artificial intelligence for disaster relief operations. *International Journal of Manpower*, 43(2), 569–586. 10.1108/IJM-03-2021-0178

Bell, R., & Bell, H. (2023). Entrepreneurship education in the era of generative artificial intelligence. *Entrepreneurship Education*, 6(3), 229–244. 10.1007/s41959-023-00099-x

Bernard, H. R. (2017). *Research methods in anthropology: Qualitative and quantitative approaches*. Rowman & Littlefield.

Bhatt, G. D., & Grover, V. (2005). Types of information technology capabilities and their role in competitive advantage: An empirical study. *Journal of Management Information Systems*, 22(2), 253–277. 10.1080/07421222.2005.11045844

Bhave, M. P. (1994). A process model of entrepreneurial venture creation. *Journal of Business Venturing*, 9(3), 223–242. 10.1016/0883-9026(94)90031-0

Biais, B. (2019). The Psychology of Bitcoin Price Dynamics. *Journal of Economic Dynamics & Control*, 109, 103830.

Billon, M., Lera-Lopez, F., & Marco, R. (2010). Differences in digitalization levels: A multivariate analysis studying the global digital divide. *Review of World Economics*, 146(1), 39–73. 10.1007/s10290-009-0045-y

Bloodgood, J. M., Sapienza, H. J., & Almeida, J. G. (1996). The internationalization of new high-potential US ventures: Antecedents and outcomes. *Entrepreneurship Theory and Practice*, 20(4), 61–76. 10.1177/104225879602000405

Boh, W. F. (2014). Knowledge Sharing in Communities of Practice: Examining Usefulness of Knowledge from Discussion Forums versus Repositories. *The Data Base for Advances in Information Systems*, 45(2), 8–31. 10.1145/2621906.2621908

Borges, A. F. S., Laurindo, F. J. B., Spínola, M. M., Gonçalves, R. F., & Mattos, C. A. (2021). The strategic use of artificial intelligence in the digital era: Systematic literature review and future research directions. *International Journal of Information Management*, 57, 1–19. 10.1016/j.ijinfomgt.2020.102225

Bouwman, H., de Vos, H., & Haaker, T. (2008). *Mobile service innovation and business models*. Springer Science & Business Media. 10.1007/978-3-540-79238-3

Bratton, J. G. (2017). *Human Resource Management, 6th Edition: Theory and Practice*. London: Palgrave.

Braun, V., & Clarke, V. (2006). Using thematic analysis in psychology. *Qualitative Research in Psychology*, 3(2), 77–101. 10.1191/1478088706qp063oa

Breiman, L. (2003). Statistical modeling: The two cultures. *Quality Control and Applied Statistics*, 48(1), 81–82.

Brew, E. A., Nketiah, B., & Koranteng, R. (2021). A Literature Review of Academic Performance, an Insight into Factors and their Influences on Academic Outcomes of Students at Senior High Schools. *OAlib*, 8(6), 1–14. 10.4236/oalib.1107423

Brewer, E., Demmer, M., Du, B., Ho, M., Kam, M., Nedevschi, S., Pal, J., Patra, R., Surana, S., & Fall, K. (2005). The case for technology in developing regions. *Computer*, 38(6), 25–38. 10.1109/MC.2005.204

Brinkmann, S. (2014). Unstructured and semi-structured interviewing. *The Oxford handbook of qualitative research*. Oxford Press.

Brougham, D., & Haar, J. (2018). Smart technology, artificial intelligence, robotics, and algorithms (STARA): Employees' perceptions of our future workplace. *Journal of Management & Organization*, 24(2), 239–257. 10.1017/jmo.2016.55

Budhwar, P., Malik, A., De Silva, M. T., & Thevisuthan, P. (2022). Artificial intelligence–challenges and opportunities for international HRM: A review and research agenda. *International Journal of Human Resource Management*, 33(6), 1065–1097. 10.1080/09585192.2022.2035161

Buenaño-Fernández, D., Gil, D., & Luján-Mora, S. (2019). Application of Machine Learning in Predicting Performance for Computer Engineering Students: A Case Study. *Sustainability (Basel)*, 11(10), 2833. 10.3390/su11102833

Buil, I., Martínez, E., & Matute, J. (2019). Transformational leadership and employee performance: The role of identification, engagement, and proactive personality. *International Journal of Hospitality Management*, 77, 64–75. 10.1016/j.ijhm.2018.06.014

Büyüközkan, G., Güler, M., & Mukul, E. (2020). An integrated fuzzy QFD methodology for customer oriented multifunctional power bank design. *Customer Oriented Product Design: Intelligent and Fuzzy Techniques*, 73-91.

Campbell, J. P., & Wiernik, B. M. (2015). The modeling and assessment of work performance. *Annual Review of Organizational Psychology and Organizational Behavior*, 2(1), 47–74. 10.1146/annurev-orgpsych-032414-111427

Cantwell, J. (2009). Location and the multinational enterprise. *Journal of International Business Studies*, 40(1), 35–41. 10.1057/jibs.2008.82

Cao, L., & Tay, F. E. H. (2001). Financial forecasting using support vector machines. *Neural Computing & Applications*, 10(2), 184–192. 10.1007/s005210170010

Catalini, C., & Crain, C. M. (2014). Regulating Bitcoin: Money Laundering, Consumer Protection, and Environmental Impact. *The Annals of the American Academy of Political and Social Science*, 753(1), 51–73.

Compilation of References

Cerit, B., Küçükyazıcı, G., & Kalem, G. (2014). Quality function deployment and its application on a smartphone design. *Science Communication*, 2, 87.

Chakravarty, A., Grewal, R., & Sambamurthy, V. (2013). Information technology competencies, organizational agility, and firm performance: Enabling and facilitating roles. *Information Systems Research*, 24(4), 976–997. 10.1287/isre.2013.0500

Chandio, A. A., Leghari, M., & Hakro, D. AWAN, S., & Jalbani, A. H. (2016). A Novel Approach for Online Sindhi Handwritten Word Recognition using Neural Network. *Sindh University Research Journal-SURJ (Science Series),48*.

Chaturvedi, S., Mishra, V., & Mishra, N. (2017). Sentiment analysis using machine learning for business intelligence. *2017 IEEE International Conference on Power, Control, Signals and Instrumentation Engineering (ICPCSI)*. IEEE. 10.1109/ICPCSI.2017.8392100

Chen, L., Wang, S., Fan, W., Sun, J., & Naoi, S. (2015). Beyond human recognition: A CNN-based framework for handwritten character recognition. *3rd IAPR Asian Conference on Pattern Recognition (ACPR)*. IEEE. 10.1109/ACPR.2015.7486592

Chen, W., & Lee, J. (2024). Regulatory Challenges and Opportunities in the Global Cryptocurrency Market. *Journal of Financial Regulation*, 15(1), 78–95.

Chinonso, O. E., Theresa, A. M., & Aduke, T. C. (2023). ChatGPT for Teaching, Learning, and Research: Prospects and Challenges. *Glob Academic Journal of Humanities Social Sciences*, 5(2), 33–40. 10.36348/gajhss.2023.v05i02.001

Chong, D., & Shi, H. (2015). Big data analytics: A literature review. *Journal of Management Analytics*, 2(3), 175–201. 10.1080/23270012.2015.1082449

Chuang, H.-H., & Liu, H.-C. (2012). Effects of different multimedia presentations on viewers' information-processing activities measured by eye-tracking technology. *Journal of Science Education and Technology*, 21(2), 276–286. 10.1007/s10956-011-9316-1

Chu, Y., Chi, M., Wang, W., & Luo, B. (2019). The impact of information technology capabilities of manufacturing enterprises on innovation performance: Evidences from SEM and fsQCA. *Sustainability (Basel)*, 11(21), 5946–5961. 10.3390/su11215946

Cockburn, I., Henderson, R., & Stern, S. (2019). The impact of artificial intelligence on innovation. In *The economics of artificial intelligence: an agenda*. University of Chicago Press. 10.7208/chicago/9780226613475.003.0004

Costa, V., & Monteiro, S. (2016). Key knowledge management processes for innovation: A systematic literature review. *VINE Journal of Information and Knowledge Management Systems*, 46(3), 386–410. 10.1108/VJIKMS-02-2015-0017

Creswell, J. W. (2013). Qualitative inquiry and research design: Choosing among five approaches. *Sage (Atlanta, Ga.)*.

Dabbous, A., Aoun Barakat, K., & Merhej Sayegh, M. (2022). Enabling organizational use of artificial intelligence: An employee perspective. *Journal of Asia Business Studies*, 16(2), 245–266. 10.1108/JABS-09-2020-0372

Dai, Y., Liu, A., & Lim, C. P. (2023). Reconceptualizing ChatGPT and generative AI as a student-driven innovation in higher education. *Procedia CIRP*, 119, 84–90. 10.1016/j.procir.2023.05.002

Dalgıç, A., Yaşar, E., & Demir, M. (2024). ChatGPT and learning outcomes in tourism education: The role of digital literacy and individualized learning. *Journal of Hospitality, Leisure, Sport and Tourism Education*, 34, 100481. 10.1016/j.jhlste.2024.100481

Daňa, J., Caputo, F., & Ráček, J. (2020). Complex network analysis for knowledge management and organizational intelligence. *Journal of the Knowledge Economy*, 11(2), 405–424. 10.1007/s13132-018-0553-x

Das, A., & Banerjee, P. (2023). The Role of Cryptocurrencies in Mitigating Economic Uncertainty: Evidence from Emerging Markets. *Journal of Economic Studies (Glasgow, Scotland)*, 10(4), 223–240.

Davenport, T. H. (2006). Competing on analytics. *Harvard Business Review*, 84(5), 150.20929194

Davison, R. M., Ou, C. X., & Martinsons, M. G. (2013). Information technology to support informal knowledge sharing. *Information Systems Journal*, 23(1), 89–109. 10.1111/j.1365-2575.2012.00400.x

Day, G. S., & Schoemaker, P. J. H. (2016). Adapting to Fast-Changing Markets and Technologies. *California Management Review*, 58(4), 59–77. 10.1525/cmr.2016.58.4.59

Del Vitto, C. (2008). Cross-Cultural" soft skills" and the global engineer: Corporate best practices and trainer methodologies. *Online Journal for Global Engineering Education*, 3(1), 1.

Delen, D., & Ram, S. (2018). Research challenges and opportunities in business analytics. *Journal of Business Analytics*, 1(1), 2–12. 10.1080/2573234X.2018.1507324

Demir, M., & Demir, Ş. Ş. (2023b). Is ChatGPT the right technology for service individualization and value co-creation? evidence from the travel industry. *Journal of Travel & Tourism Marketing*, 40(5), 383–398. 10.1080/10548408.2023.2255884

Demir, M., & Demir, Ş. Ş. (2023c). Reflection of artificial intelligence applications on students' critical and analytical abilities. *Scientific Collection. InterConf*, (184), 459–467.

Demir, Ş. Ş., & Demir, M. (2023a). Professionals' perspectives on ChatGPT in the tourism industry: Does it inspire awe or concern? *Journal of Tourism Theory and Research*, 9(2), 61–76. 10.24288/jttr.1313481

Dempere, J., Modugu, K. P., Hesham, A., & Ramasamy, L. (2023). The impact of ChatGPT on higher education. *Dempere J, Modugu K, Hesham A and Ramasamy LK (2023) The impact of ChatGPT on higher education. Frontiers in Education*, 8, 1206936. 10.3389/feduc.2023.1206936

Compilation of References

Deng, J., & Lin, Y. (2022). The benefits and challenges of ChatGPT: An overview. *Frontiers in Computing and Intelligent Systems*, 2(2), 81–83. 10.54097/fcis.v2i2.4465

Dessler, G. (2017). *Human Resource Management*. Pearson International.

Diab, Y. (2021). The Concept of Knowledge Sharing in Organizations (Studying the Personal and Organizational Factors and Their Effect on Knowledge Management). [MSES]. *Management Studies and Economic Systems*, 6(1), 91–100.

Dias, S. B., Hadjileontiadou, S. J., Diniz, J., & Hadjileontiadis, L. J. (2020, December). DeepLMS: A deep learning predictive model for supporting online learning in the Covid-19 era. *Scientific Reports*, 10(1), 19888. 10.1038/s41598-020-76740-933199801

Ding, S., Zhao, H., Zhang, Y., Xu, X., & Nie, R. (2015). Extreme learning machine: Algorithm, theory and applications. *Artificial Intelligence Review*, 44(1), 103–115. 10.1007/s10462-013-9405-z

Dix, A. J. F., Abowd, G. D., & Beale, R. (2004). *Human-Computer Interaction*.

Dodeja, L., Tambwekar, P., Hedlund-Botti, E., & Gombolay, M. (2024). Towards the design of user-centric strategy recommendation systems for collaborative Human–AI tasks. *International Journal of Human-Computer Studies*, 184, 103216. 10.1016/j.ijhcs.2023.10321638558883

Dogru, T., Line, N., Hanks, L., Acikgoz, F., Abbott, J. A., Bakir, S., Berbekova, A., Bilgihan, A., Iskender, A., Kizildag, M., Lee, M., Lee, W., McGinley, S., Mody, M., Onder, I., Ozdemir, O., & Suess, C. (2023). The implications of generative artificial intelligence in academic research and higher education in tourism and hospitality. *Tourism Economics*, 13548166231204065, 13548166231204065. 10.1177/13548166231204065

Donovan, K., & Donner, J. (2010). A note on the availability (and importance) of pre-paid mobile data in Africa. *Proceedings of M4D 2010*, 263–267.

Dr. J Sirisha Devi, Mr. B. Sreedhar, et al.(2022). A path towards child-centric Artificial Intelligence based Education, *International journal of Early Childhood special Issue,14*(3).

Dung, N. T., Tri, N. M., & Minh, L. N. (2021). Digital transformation meets national development requirements. *Linguistics and Culture Review*, 5(S2), 892–905. 10.21744/lingcure.v5nS2.1536

Dutt, A., Ismail, M. A., & Herawan, T. (2017). A Systematic Review on Educational Data Mining. *IEEE Access : Practical Innovations, Open Solutions*, 5, 15991–16005. 10.1109/AC-CESS.2017.2654247

Dwivedi, U., Rajput, P., Sharma, M. K., & Noida, G. (2017). Cursive Handwriting Recognition System Using Feature Extraction and Artificial Neural Network, *Int.Res. J. Eng. Technology*, 4(03), 2202–2206.

Dwivedi, Y. K., Hughes, L., Ismagilova, E., Aarts, G., Coombs, C., Crick, T., Duan, Y., Dwivedi, R., Edwards, J., Eirug, A., Galanos, V., Ilavarasan, P. V., Janssen, M., Jones, P., Kar, A. K., Kizgin, H., Kronemann, B., Lal, B., Lucini, B., & Williams, M. D. (2021). Artificial Intelligence (AI): Multidisciplinary perspectives on emerging challenges, opportunities, and agenda for research, practice and policy. *International Journal of Information Management*, 57, 101994. 10.1016/j. ijinfomgt.2019.08.002

Dwivedi, Y. K., Kshetri, N., Hughes, L., Slade, E. L., Jeyaraj, A., Kar, A. K., Baabdullah, A. M., Koohang, A., Raghavan, V., Ahuja, M., Albanna, H., Albashrawi, M. A., Al-Busaidi, A. S., Balakrishnan, J., Barlette, Y., Basu, S., Bose, I., Brooks, L., Buhalis, D., & Wright, R. (2023). "So what if ChatGPT wrote it?" Multidisciplinary perspectives on opportunities, challenges and implications of generative conversational AI for research, practice and policy. *International Journal of Information Management*, 71, 102642. 10.1016/j.ijinfomgt.2023.102642

Dworschak, C., Heim, E., Kuhn, N., Schwager, J., Tröster, A., & Maercker, A. (2024). User-centered development of an internet-based CBT intervention for the treatment of loneliness in older individuals. *Internet Interventions : the Application of Information Technology in Mental and Behavioural Health*, 35, 100720. 10.1016/j.invent.2024.10072038328277

Eisenhardt, K. M. (1989). Building theories from case study research. *Academy of Management Review*, 14(4), 532–550. 10.2307/258557

Eisenmann, T. R., Ries, E., & Dillard, S. (2012). Hypothesis-driven entrepreneurship: The lean startup. *Harvard Business School Entrepreneurial Management Case*, (812–095). Harvard Press.

Elbanna, S., & Armstrong, L. (2024). Exploring the integration of ChatGPT in education: Adapting for the future. *Management & Sustainability: An Arab Review*, 3(1), 16–29. 10.1108/ MSAR-03-2023-0016

Ellingsen, E. F., Drevsjø, S., Volden, F., & Watten, R. G. (2019). Extraversion and focus of attention on facial emotions: An experimental eye-tracking study. *Current Issues in Personality Psychology*, 7(1), 91–97. 10.5114/cipp.2019.85413

El-Sabagh, H. A. (2021). Adaptive e-learning environment based on learning styles and its impact on development students' engagement. *International Journal of Educational Technology in Higher Education*, 18(1), 53. 10.1186/s41239-021-00289-4

El-Sawy, A., Loey, M., & El-Bakry, H. (2017). Arabic handwritten characters recognition using convolutional neural network. *WSEAS Transactions on Computer Research*, 5, 11–19.

Emam, R. M. (2023). The effect of using Chat GPT technology as one of the applications of artificial intelligence in tourism education for students of tourism and hotels institutes by using task *Technology fit model*, 7(2), 1-22. 10.21608/mfth.2023.327915

Emhardt, S. N., Kok, E., van Gog, T., Brandt-Gruwel, S., van Marlen, T., & Jarodzka, H. (2023). Visualizing a task performer's gaze to foster observers' performance and learning—A systematic literature review on eye movement modeling examples. *Educational Psychology Review*, 35(1), 23. 10.1007/s10648-023-09731-7

Compilation of References

Ergen, F. D. (2020). Artırılmış ve sanal gerçeklik teknolojilerinin Isparta ilinin kültürel miras alanlarında uygulanabilirliği üzerine bir literatür taraması. *Journal of Tourism Theory and Research*, 6(1), 62–74. 10.24288/jttr.673593

Eşel, E. (2005). Kadın ve Erkek Beyninin Farklılıkları. *Klinik Psikofarmakoloji Bulteni, 15*(3).

Evans, D. S. (2016). Digicash: Electronic Payments Based on Cryptography. *ACM Transactions on Information and System Security*, 9(4), 1–44.

Fan, S., Lau, R. Y. K., & Zhao, J. L. (2015). Demystifying Big Data Analytics for Business Intelligence Through the Lens of Marketing Mix. *Big Data Research*, 2(1), 28–32. 10.1016/j.bdr.2015.02.006

Farhan, A., & Karim, M. (2019). Impacts of knowledge sharing: A review and directions for future research. *Journal of Workplace Learning*, 31(1), 207–230.

Farmers in India are using AI for agriculture – here's how they could inspire the world. (2024, January 16). World Economic Forum. https://www.weforum.org/agenda/2024/01/how-indias-ai-agriculture-boom-could-inspire-the-world/

Ferrati, F., & Muffatto, M. (2021). Entrepreneurial finance: emerging approaches using machine learning and big data. *Foundations and Trends® in Entrepreneurship, 17*(3), 232-329.

Fleming, M. L., & Levie, W. H. (1978). *Instructional message design: Principles from the behavioral sciences.* Educational Technology. https://www.google.com/books?hl=tr&lr=&id=qr1u-iLqeE0C&oi=fnd&pg=PR3&dq=Instructional+Message+Design:+Principles+from+the+Behavioral+Sciences+%C3%96n+Kapak+Malcolm+L.+Fleming,+W.+Howard+Levie&ots=Gf_ZnjbcH3&sig=72VkdM2Oh_73MszMV1s-tzXhVB4

Fleury, S., & Chaniaud, N. (2024). Multi-user centered design: Acceptance, user experience, user research and user testing. *Theoretical Issues in Ergonomics Science*, 25(2), 209–224. 10.1080/1463922X.2023.2166623

Forman, N., Udvaros, J., & Avornicului, M. S. (2023). ChatGPT: A new study tool shaping the future for high school students. *International Journal of Advanced Natural Sciences and Engineering Researches*, 7(4), 95–102. 10.59287/ijanser.562

Formica, P. (2002). Entrepreneurial universities: The value of education in encouraging entrepreneurship. *Industry and Higher Education*, 16(3), 167–175. 10.5367/000000002101296261

Fraenkel, J. R., Wallen, N. E., & Hyun, H. H. (2012). *How to design and evaluate research in education.* McGraw-Hill.

Fraiwan, M., & Khasawneh, N. (2023). A Review of ChatGPT Applications in Education, Marketing, Software Engineering, and Healthcare: Benefits, Drawbacks, and Research Directions. *arXiv preprint arXiv:2305.00237.* https://doi.org//arXiv.2305.0023710.48550

Freudenthaler, D. (2015). Product Development for Emerging Markets: Towards a Framework for Integrating Contextual Information Into the Design Process. *Proceedings of the 2008 Academy of Marketing Science (AMS)Annual Conference*, (pp. 179–183). Research Gate.

Friedrich, J., Beckera, M., Kramer, F., Wirth, M., & Schneider, M. (2020). Incentive design and gamification for knowledge management. *Journal of Business Research*, 106, 341–352. 10.1016/j.jbusres.2019.02.009

Gansser, O. A., & Reich, C. S. (2021). A new acceptance model for artificial intelligence with extensions to UTAUT2: An empirical study in three segments of application. *Technology in Society*, 65, 1–20. 10.1016/j.techsoc.2021.101535

Gao, H., Hasenbein, L., Bozkir, E., Göllner, R., & Kasneci, E. (2023). Exploring gender differences in computational thinking learning in a vr classroom: Developing machine learning models using eye-tracking data and explaining the models. *International Journal of Artificial Intelligence in Education*, 33(4), 929–954. 10.1007/s40593-022-00316-z

Garg, S., & Agarwal, M. (2022). Understanding Public Perception and Acceptance of Cryptocurrencies: A Survey-Based Approach. *International Journal of Business and Economics Perspectives*, 9(1), 55–72.

Gerlich, M. (2023). The Power of Virtual Influencers: Impact on Consumer Behaviour and Attitudes in the Age of AI. *Administrative Sciences*, 13(8), 178–189. 10.3390/admsci13080178

Ghemawat, P. (2001). Distance Still Matters. The Hard Reality of Global Expansion. *Harvard Business Review*, 79(8), 137–147.11550630

Ghemawat, P. (2007). *Redefining global strategy: Crossing borders in a world where differences still matter*. Harvard Business Press.

Ghorbani, R., & Ghousi, R. (2020). Comparing Different Resampling Methods in Predicting Students' Performance Using Machine Learning Techniques. *IEEE Access, 8,* 67899-67911. 10.1109/ACCESS.2020.2986809

Gill, S. S., Xu, M., Patros, P., Wu, H., Kaur, R., Kaur, K., Fuller, S., Singh, M., Arora, P., Parlikad, A. K., Stankovski, V., Abraham, A., Ghosh, S. K., Lutfiyya, H., Kanhere, S. S., Bahsoon, R., Rana, O., Dustdar, S., Sakellariou, R., & Buyya, R. (2024). Transformative effects of ChatGPT on modern education: Emerging Era of AI Chatbots. *Internet of Things and Cyber-Physical Systems*, 4, 19–23. 10.1016/j.iotcps.2023.06.002

Gitongu, M. K., Kingi, W., & Uzel, J. M. M. (2016). Determinants of Employees' Performance of State Parastatals in Kenya: Kenya Ports Authority. *International Journal of Humanities and Social Science*, 6(10), 197–204.

Gligorea, I., Cioca, M., Oancea, R., Gorski, A.-T., Gorski, H., & Tudorache, P. (2023). Adaptive Learning Using Artificial Intelligence in e-Learning: A Literature Review. *Education Sciences*, 2023(13), 1216. 10.3390/educsci13121216

Compilation of References

Goar, V., Yadav, N. S., & Yadav, P. S. (2023). Conversational AI for natural language processing: An review of ChatGPT. *International Journal on Recent and Innovation Trends in Computing and Communication*, 11(3s), 109–117. 10.17762/ijritcc.v11i3s.6161

Göktaş, L. S. (2023). ChatGPT Uzaktan Eğitim Sınavlarında Başarılı Olabilir Mi? Turizm Alanında Doğruluk ve Doğrulama Üzerine Bir Araştırma. *Journal of Tourism & Gastronomy Studies*, 11(2), 892–905.

Gonzalvez, M. A. A., Castañeda Toledo, O. A., & Ibarra Rodriguez, A. R. (2014). The Management and Construction of Knowledge as an Innovation Strategy for Collaborative Learning Through the Use and Creation of Learning Communities and Networks. [IJKM]. *International Journal of Knowledge Management*, 10(4), 38–49. 10.4018/ijkm.2014100103

Gordon, S. (2024, February 12). *8 Best AI Tools for Finance Teams in 2024*. Datarails. https://www.datarails.com/best-ai-tools-for-finance-teams/

Grassini, S. (2023). Shaping the future of education: Exploring the potential and consequences of AI and ChatGPT in educational settings. *Education Sciences*, 13(7), 692. 10.3390/educsci13070692

Gravel, J., D'Amours-Gravel, M., & Osmanlliu, E. (2023). Learning to fake it: Limited responses and fabricated references provided by ChatGPT for medical questions. *Mayo Clinic Proceedings. Digital Health*, 1(3), 226–234. 10.1016/j.mcpdig.2023.05.004

Griffin, M. A., Neal, A., & Parker, S. K. (2007). A new model of work role performance: Positive behavior in uncertain and interdependent contexts. *Academy of Management Journal*, 50(2), 327–347. 10.5465/amj.2007.24634438

Griffith, D. A., & Zhao, Y. (2015). Contract specificity, contract violation, and relationship performance in international buyer—Supplier relationships. *Journal of International Marketing*, 23(3), 22–40. 10.1509/jim.14.0138

Grobelna, A. (2019). Effects of individual and job characteristics on hotel contact employees' work engagement and their performance outcomes: A case study from Poland. *International Journal of Contemporary Hospitality Management*, 31(1), 349–369. 10.1108/IJCHM-08-2017-0501

Gropper, G. L. (2015). Are individual differences undertreated in instructional design? *Educational Technology*, 55(2), 3–13.

Gruman, J. A., & Saks, A. M. (2011). Performance Management and Employee Engagement. *Human Resource Management Review*, 21(2), 123–136. 10.1016/j.hrmr.2010.09.004

Guesalaga, R., & Marshall, P. (2008). Purchasing power at the bottom of the pyramid: Differences across geographic regions and income tiers. *Journal of Consumer Marketing*, 25(7), 413–418. 10.1108/07363760810915626

Guo, L., & Xu, L. (2021). The effects of digital transformation on firm performance: Evidence from China's manufacturing sector. *Sustainability (Basel)*, 13(22), 12844. 10.3390/su132212844

Gupta, A., & Verma, S. (2023). Cryptocurrency Regulation in India: Challenges and Prospects. *Indian Journal of Law and Technology*, 10(2), 112–129.

Gursoy, D., Li, Y., & Song, H. (2023). ChatGPT and the hospitality and tourism industry: An overview of current trends and future research directions. *Journal of Hospitality Marketing & Management*, 32(5), 579–592. 10.1080/19368623.2023.2211993

Haefner, N., Wincent, J., Parida, V., & Gassmann, O. (2021). Artificial intelligence and innovation management: A review, framework, and research agenda. *Technological Forecasting and Social Change*, 162, 1–18. 10.1016/j.techfore.2020.120392

Haider, S. A., & Kayani, U. N. (2020). The impact of customer knowledge management capability on project performance-mediating role of strategic agility. *Journal of Knowledge Management*, 25(2), 298–312. 10.1108/JKM-01-2020-0026

Hailong, Z., Wenyan, G., & Bo, J. (2014). Machine Learning and Lexicon Based Methods for Sentiment Classification: A Survey. *2014 11th Web Information System and Application Conference*. 10.1109/WISA.2014.55

Haleem, A., Javaid, M., & Singh, R. P. (2022). An era of ChatGPT as a significant futuristic support tool: A study on features, abilities, and challenges. *BenchCouncil transactions on benchmarks, standards and evaluations, 2*(4), 100089. 10.1016/j.tbench.2023.100089

Hameed, S., & Farooq, S. (2016). *The Art of Crypto Currencies*.

Han, D. I. D., Jung, T., & Tom Dieck, M. C. (2019). Translating tourist requirements into mobile AR application engineering through QFD. *International Journal of Human-Computer Interaction*, 35(19), 1842–1858. 10.1080/10447318.2019.1574099

Harrigan, P. (2023, January 9). How Amazon Uses AI to Dominate Ecommerce. *Top (Madrid)*, 5.

Harris, R. W. (2016). How ICT4D research fails the poor. *Information Technology for Development*, 22(1), 177–192. 10.1080/02681102.2015.1018115

Hasan, A., Moin, S., Karim, A., & Shamshirband, S. (2018). Machine Learning-Based Sentiment Analysis for Twitter Accounts. *Mathematical & Computational Applications*, 23(1), 11. 10.3390/mca23010011

Henrique, B. M., Sobreiro, V. A., & Kimura, H. (2018). Stock price prediction using support vector regression on daily and up to the minute prices. *Journal of Finance and Data Science*, 4(3), 183–201. 10.1016/j.jfds.2018.04.003

Herodotou, C., Rienties, B., Boroowa, A., Zdrahal, Z., & Hlosta, M. (2019, October). A large-scale implementation of predictive learning analytics in higher education: The teachers' role and perspective. *Educational Technology Research and Development*, 67(5), 1273–1306. 10.1007/s11423-019-09685-0

Hertzum, M. (2010). Images of usability. *Intl. Journal of Human--Computer Interaction*, 26(6), 567–600.

Compilation of References

Hlioui, F., Aloui, N., & Gargouri, F. (2021). A Withdrawal Prediction Model of At-Risk Learners Based on Behavioural Indicators. [IJWLTT]. *International Journal of Web-Based Learning and Teaching Technologies*, 16(2), 32–53. 10.4018/IJWLTT.2021030103

Holsanova, J., Holmberg, N., & Holmqvist, K. (2009). Reading information graphics: The role of spatial contiguity and dual attentional guidance. *Applied Cognitive Psychology*, 23(9), 1215–1226. 10.1002/acp.1525

Huallpa, J. J. (2023). Exploring the ethical considerations of using Chat GPT in university education. *Periodicals of Engineering and Natural Sciences*, 11(4), 105–115. 10.21533/pen.v11i4.3770

Huang, M. H., & Rust, R. T. (2018). Artificial intelligence in service. *Journal of Service Research*, 21(2), 155–172. 10.1177/1094670517752459

Huang, W., Nakamori, Y., & Wang, S. Y. (2005). Forecasting stock market movement direction with support vector machine. *Computers & Operations Research*, 32(10), 2513–2522. 10.1016/j.cor.2004.03.016

Hudson, W. (2009). Reduced empathizing skills increase challenges for user-centered design. *Proceedings of the SIGCHI Conference on Human Factors in Computing Systems*, (pp. 1327–1330). Research Gate. 10.1145/1518701.1518901

Hu, S., Zhang, L., Guo, W., Zhang, D., Jia, Q., Yang, Z., & Guo, M. (2024). Research on the design of smart sleep aid interactive products. *International Journal of Industrial and Systems Engineering*, 46(2), 151–168. 10.1504/IJISE.2024.136413

Hussain, M., Zhu, W., Zhang, W., & Abidi, S. M. R. (2018). Student Engagement Predictions in an e-Learning System and Their Impact on Student Course Assessment Scores. *Computational Intelligence and Neuroscience*, 2018, 1–21. 10.1155/2018/634718630369946

Hussain, M., Zhu, W., Zhang, W., Abidi, S. M. R., & Ali, S. (2018). *Using machine learning to predict student difficulties from learning session data*. Artificial Intelligence Review. 10.1007/s10462-018-9620-8

Huysman, M. (2020). Information systems research on artificial intelligence and work: A commentary on "Robo-Apocalypse cancelled? Reframing the automation and future of work debate". *Journal of Information Technology*, 35(4), 307–309. 10.1177/0268396220926511

Hwang, E. H., Vir, S. P., & Argote, L. (2015). Knowledge Sharing in Online Communities: Learning to Cross Geographic and Hierarchical Boundaries. *Organization Science*, 26(6), 1593–1611. 10.1287/orsc.2015.1009

Hyönä, J. (2010). The use of eye movements in the study of multimedia learning. *Learning and Instruction*, 20(2), 172–176. 10.1016/j.learninstruc.2009.02.013

Ilgaz, H., Altun, A., & Aşkar, P. (2014). The effect of sustained attention level and contextual cueing on implicit memory performance for e-learning environments. *Computers in Human Behavior*, 39, 1–7. 10.1016/j.chb.2014.06.008

Ilomo, O., & Mlavi, B. (2016). The Availability of Teaching and Learning Facilities and Their Effects on Academic Performance in Ward Secondary Schools in Muheza-Tanzania. *International Journal of Education and Research*, 4, 571–581.

Imbesi, S., & Scataglini, S. (2021). A user-centered methodology for the design of smart apparel for older users. *Sensors (Basel)*, 21(8), 2804. 10.3390/s2108280433923514

Imran, M., & Almusharraf, N. (2023). Analyzing the role of ChatGPT as a writing assistant at higher education level: A systematic review of the literature. *Contemporary Educational Technology*, 15(4), ep464. 10.30935/cedtech/13605

Iqbal, R., Doctor, F., More, B., Mahmud, S., & Yousuf, U. (2020). Big data analytics: Computational intelligence techniques and application areas. *Technological Forecasting and Social Change, 153*(December 2017), 0–1. 10.1016/j.techfore.2018.03.024

Iskender, A. (2023). Holy or unholy? Interview with open AI's ChatGPT. *European Journal of Tourism Research*, 34, 3414–3414. 10.54055/ejtr.v34i.3169

Ismail, H., & Al-Assa'ad, N. (2020). The impact of organizational intelligence on organizational agility: An empirical study in Syrian private banks. *International Journal of Academic Research in Business & Social Sciences*, 10(2), 1–18. 10.6007/IJARBSS/v10-i2/6944

Ivanov, S., & Soliman, M. (2023). Game of algorithms: ChatGPT implications for the future of tourism education and research. *Journal of Tourism Futures*, 9(2), 214–221. 10.1108/JTF-02-2023-0038

Iyer, G. R., LaPlaca, P. J., & Sharma, A. (2006). Innovation and new product introductions in emerging markets: Strategic recommendations for the Indian market. *Industrial Marketing Management*, 35(3), 373–382. 10.1016/j.indmarman.2005.02.007

Jack, W., Ray, A., & Suri, T. (2013). Transaction networks: Evidence from mobile money in Kenya. *The American Economic Review*, 103(3), 356–361. 10.1257/aer.103.3.356

Jacob, R. J., & Karn, K. S. (2003). Eye tracking in human-computer interaction and usability research: Ready to deliver the promises. In *The mind's eye* (pp. 573–605). Elsevier. https://www.sciencedirect.com/science/article/pii/B9780444510204500311110.1016/B978-044451020-4/50031-1

Jafari, S. M., & Ramalingam, M. S. T. (2015). The Effect of Knowledge Management practices on Employees' Innovative Performance. *The International Journal of Management Science and Information Technology*, 1(1), 82–93.

James, J., & Versteeg, M. (2007). Mobile phones in Africa: How much do we really know? *Social Indicators Research*, 84(1), 117. 10.1007/s11205-006-9079-x20076776

Jarodzka, H., Janssen, N., Kirschner, P. A., & Erkens, G. (2015). Avoiding split attention in computer-based testing: Is neglecting additional information facilitative? *British Journal of Educational Technology*, 46(4), 803–817. 10.1111/bjet.12174

Compilation of References

Jarrah, A. M., Wardat, Y., & Fidalgo, P. (2023). Using ChatGPT in academic writing is (not) a form of plagiarism: What does the literature say. *Online Journal of Communication and Media Technologies*, 13(4), e202346. 10.30935/ojcmt/13572

Javaid, M., Haleem, A., Singh, R. P., Khan, S., & Khan, I. H. (2023). Unlocking the opportunities through ChatGPT Tool towards ameliorating the education system. *BenchCouncil Transactions on Benchmarks. Standards and Evaluations*, 3(2), 100115. 10.1016/j.tbench.2023.100115

Johanson, J., & Vahlne, J.-E. (2009). The Uppsala internationalization process model revisited: From liability of foreignness to liability of outsidership. *Journal of International Business Studies*, 40(9), 1411–1431. 10.1057/jibs.2009.24

Jones, M., Robinson, S., Pearson, J., Joshi, M., Raju, D., Mbogo, C. C., Wangari, S., Joshi, A., Cutrell, E., & Harper, R. (2017). Beyond yesterday's tomorrow: Future-focused mobile interaction design by and for emergent users. *Personal and Ubiquitous Computing*, 21(1), 157–171. 10.1007/s00779-016-0982-0

Junejo, K. N., & Eman, E. (2016). *Grade Prediction Using Supervised Machine Learning Techniques, 4th Global Summit on Education 2016 At: Malaysia*. http://worldconferences.net/home

K. K. Sayyad Liyakat. (2022). Nanotechnology Application in Neural Growth Support System. *Nano Trends: A Journal of Nanotechnology and Its Applications,*24(2).

Kaddoura, S., Popescu, D. E., & Hemanth, J. D. (2022). A systematic review on machine learning models for online learning and examination systems. *PeerJ. Computer Science*, 8, e986. 10.7717/peerj-cs.98635634115

Kaisler, S., Armour, F., Espinosa, J. A., & Money, W. (2013). Big data: Issues and challenges moving forward. *2013 46th Hawaii International Conference on System Sciences*, 995–1004.

Kalanick, T. (2016). Uber China Merges with Didi Chuxing. Retrieved August 9, 2019, from https://www.uber.com/newsroom/uber-china-didi/

Kamppuri, M., Bednarik, R., & Tukiainen, M. (2006). The expanding focus of HCI: case culture. *Proceedings of the 4th Nordic Conference on Human-Computer Interaction: Changing Roles*, (pp. 405–408). Research Gate. 10.1145/1182475.1182523

Kaplan, A., & Haenlein, M. (2019). Siri, Siri, in my hand: Who's the fairest in the land? On the interpretations, illustrations, and implications of artificial intelligence. *Business Horizons*, 62(1), 15–25. 10.1016/j.bushor.2018.08.004

Kar, A. K., Choudhary, S. K., & Singh, V. K. (2022). How can artificial intelligence impact sustainability: A systematic literature review. *Journal of Cleaner Production*, 1(1), 1–17. 10.1016/j.jclepro.2022.134120

Karale Aishwarya A. (2023). Smart Billing Cart Using RFID, YOLO and Deep Learning for Mall Administration. *International Journal of Instrumentation and Innovation Sciences,*8(2).

Karasan, A., Ilbahar, E., Cebi, S., & Kahraman, C. (2022). Customer-oriented product design using an integrated neutrosophic AHP & DEMATEL & QFD methodology. *Applied Soft Computing*, 118, 108445. 10.1016/j.asoc.2022.108445

Karolyi, G. A., & Wang, Y. (2016). Trading Bitcoin and Ethereum: A Comparison of Volatility and Price Dynamics. *Finance Research Letters*, 21, 79–85.

Käser, T., Hallinen, N. R., & Schwartz, D. L. (2017). Modeling exploration strategies to predict student performance within a learning environment and beyond. In: *17th International conference on learning analytics and knowledge 2017*, (pp 31–40). ACM. "10.1145/3027385.3027422

Kasneci, E., Seßler, K., Küchemann, S., Bannert, M., Dementieva, D., Fischer, F., Gasser, U., Groh, G., Günnemann, S., Hüllermeier, E., Krusche, S., Kutyniok, G., Michaeli, T., Nerdel, C., Pfeffer, J., Poquet, O., Sailer, M., Schmidt, A., Seidel, T., & Kasneci, G. (2023). ChatGPT for good? On opportunities and challenges of large language models for education. *Learning and Individual Differences*, 103, 102274. 10.1016/j.lindif.2023.102274

Kassarnig, V., Mones, E., Bjerre-Nielsen, A., Sapiezynski, P., Dreyer Lassen, D., & Lehmann, S. (2018, December). Academic performance and behavioral patterns. *EPJ Data Science*, 7(1), 10. 10.1140/epjds/s13688-018-0138-8

Kawade, D., & Oza, K. (2017). Sentiment Analysis: Machine Learning Approach. *IACSIT International Journal of Engineering and Technology*, 9(3), 2183–2186. 10.21817/ijet/2017/v9i3/1709030151

Kaya, F., Aydin, F., Schepman, A., Rodway, P., Yetişensoy, O., & Demir Kaya, M. (2024). The roles of personality traits, AI anxiety, and demographic factors in attitudes towards artificial intelligence. *International Journal of Human-Computer Interaction*, 40(2), 497–514. 10.1080/10447318.2022.2151730

Kazi, K. (2024). AI-Driven IoT (AIIoT) in Healthcare Monitoring. In Nguyen, T., & Vo, N. (Eds.), *Using Traditional Design Methods to Enhance AI-Driven Decision Making* (pp. 77–101). IGI Global. 10.4018/979-8-3693-0639-0.ch003

Kazi, S. S. L. (2023). Electronics with Artificial Intelligence Creating a Smarter Future: A Review. *Journal of Communication Engineering and Its Innovations*, 9(3), 38–42.

Kazi, V. (2023). Deep Learning, YOLO and RFID based smart Billing Handcart. *Journal of Communication Engineering & Systems*, 13(1), 1–8.

Kell, A. J. E., Yamins, D. L. K., Shook, E. N., Norman-Haignere, S. V., & McDermott, J. H. (2018). A Task-Optimized Neural Network Replicates Human Auditory Behavior, Predicts Brain Responses, and Reveals a Cortical Processing Hierarchy. *Neuron*, 98(3), 630–644.e16. 10.1016/j.neuron.2018.03.04429681533

Kendeou, P., van den Broek, P., Helder, A., & Karlsson, J. (2014). A cognitive view of reading comprehension: Implications for reading difficulties. *Learning Disabilities Research & Practice*, 29(1), 10–16. 10.1111/ldrp.12025

Compilation of References

Kent, G. (2023). *Cryptocurrencies and Political Integration.*

Khanna, T., Palepu, K. G., & Sinha, J. (2005). Strategies that fit emerging markets. *Harvard Business Review*, 83(6), 4–19.15938439

Kim, P. T., & Bodie, M. T. (2021). Artificial intelligence and the challenges of workplace discrimination and privacy. *J Labor Employment Law*, 35(2), 289–315.

Kim, S., Shim, J., & Shim, J. (2023). A study on the utilization of OpenAI ChatGPT as a second language learning tool. *Journal of Multimedia Information System*, 10(1), 79–88. 10.33851/JMIS.2023.10.1.79

Kintu, M. J., Zhu, C., & Kagambe, E. (2017). Blended learning effectiveness: The relationship between student characteristics, design features and outcomes. *International Journal of Educational Technology in Higher Education*, 14(1), 7. 10.1186/s41239-017-0043-4

Kirkman, B. L., & Rosen, B. (1999). Beyond Self-Management: Antecedents and Consequences of Team Empowerment. *Academy of Management Journal*, 42(1), 58–74. 10.2307/256874

Kiryakova, G., & Angelova, N. (2023). ChatGPT—A challenging tool for the university professors in their teaching practice. *Education Sciences*, 13(10), 1056. 10.3390/educsci13101056

Klein, P. (2015). The Social Value of Alternative Currencies. *International Journal of Community Currency Research*, 20(1), 5–12.

Kohavi, R., Rothleder, N. J., & Simoudis, E. (2002). Emerging trends in business analytics. *Communications of the ACM*, 45(8), 45–48. 10.1145/545151.545177

Kolyasnikov, M. S., & Kelchevskaya, N. R. (2020). Knowledge management strategies in companies: Trends and the impact of industry 4.0. *Upravlenec*, 11(4), 82–96. 10.29141/2218-5003-2020-11-4-7

Kong, H., Yuan, Y., Baruch, Y., Bu, N., Jiang, X., & Wang, K. (2021). Influences of artificial intelligence (AI) awareness on career competency and job burnout. *International Journal of Contemporary Hospitality Management*, 33(2), 717–734. 10.1108/IJCHM-07-2020-0789

Kopka, A., & Grashof, N. (2022). Artificial intelligence: Catalyst or barrier on the path to sustainability? *Technological Forecasting and Social Change*, 175, 121318. 10.1016/j.techfore.2021.121318

Koswara, R., & Alifin, F. I. (2024). A User-oriented UI/UX Application Design Using The Integration of Quality Function Deployment (QFD) and Design Thinking Methods. *MOTIVECTION: Journal of Mechanical. Electrical and Industrial Engineering*, 6(1), 85–100.

Krendzelak, M. (2014). *Machine learning and its applications in e-learning systems.* 2014 IEEE 12th IEEE International Conference on Emerging eLearning Technologies and Applications (ICETA), Stary Smokovec, Slovakia. 10.1109/ICETA.2014.7107596

Kumar, V., & Garg, M. L. (2019). Comparison of Machine Learning Models in Student Result Prediction. In: Kamal R., Henshaw M., Nair P. (eds) *International Conference on Advanced Computing Networking and Informatics*. Springer, Singapore. 10.1007/978-981-13-2673-8_46

Kumar, A., & Singh, R. (2023). Exploring the Psychological Factors Influencing Bitcoin Price Dynamics: A Behavioral Economics Perspective. *Journal of Behavioral Finance*, 15(2), 79–85.

Kumari, P., Jain, P. K., & Pamula, R. (2018). *An efficient use of ensemble methods to predict students academic performance*. 2018 4th International Conference on Recent Advances in Information Technology (RAIT), Dhanbad, India. 10.1109/RAIT.2018.8389056

Kuperman, V., Siegelman, N., Schroeder, S., Acartürk, C., Alexeeva, S., Amenta, S., Bertram, R., Bonandrini, R., Brysbaert, M., Chernova, D., Da Fonseca, S. M., Dirix, N., Duyck, W., Fella, A., Frost, R., Gattei, C. A., Kalaitzi, A., Lõo, K., Marelli, M., & Usal, K. A. (2023). Text reading in English as a second language: Evidence from the Multilingual Eye-Movements Corpus. *Studies in Second Language Acquisition*, 45(1), 3–37. 10.1017/S0272263121000954

Lachaab, M., & Omri, A. (2023). Machine and deep learning-based stock price prediction during the COVID-19 pandemic: The case of CAC 40 index. *EuroMed Journal of Business*, 2022. Advance online publication. 10.1108/EMJB-05-2022-0104

Lazuardy, M. A., Marie, I. A., & Salim, A. (2024). User Interface User Experience Design with User Centered Design Method On Mobile Application For Laundry KK Reservation. *Intelmatics*, 4(1), 52–58. 10.25105/itm.v4i1.18228

Lecler, A., Duron, L., & Soyer, P. (2023). Revolutionizing radiology with GPT-based models: Current applications, future possibilities and limitations of ChatGPT. *Diagnostic and Interventional Imaging*, 104(6), 269–274. 10.1016/j.diii.2023.02.00336858933

Lee, J., Song, H., & Hong, A. (2019). Exploring Factors, and Indicators for Measuring Students' Sustainable Engagement in e-Learning. *Sustainability (Basel)*, 11(4), 985. 10.3390/su11040985

Leman, K. (2009). *The birth order book: Why you are the way you are*. Revell.

Lichtenthaler, U. (2020). Extremes of acceptance: Employee attitudes toward artificial intelligence. *The Journal of Business Strategy*, 41(5), 39–45. 10.1108/JBS-12-2018-0204

Liebrenz, M., Schleifer, R., Buadze, A., Bhugra, D., & Smith, A. (2023). Generating scholarly content with ChatGPT: Ethical challenges for medical publishing. *The Lancet. Digital Health*, 5(3), e105–e106. 10.1016/S2589-7500(23)00019-536754725

Li, J., & Kim, K. (2023). Kano-QFD-based analysis of the influence of user experience on the design of handicraft intangible cultural heritage apps. *Heritage Science*, 11(1), 59. 10.1186/s40494-023-00903-w36974317

Liu, H.-C., Lai, M.-L., & Chuang, H.-H. (2011). Using eye-tracking technology to investigate the redundant effect of multimedia web pages on viewers' cognitive processes. *Computers in Human Behavior*, 27(6), 2410–2417. 10.1016/j.chb.2011.06.012

Compilation of References

Liu, Y., Al-Atawi, A. A., Khan, I. A., Gohar, N., & Zaman, Q. (2022). Using the Fuzzy Analytical Hierarchy Process to Prioritize the Impact of Visual Communication Based on Artificial Intelligence for Long-Term Learning. *Soft Computing*, 27(1), 157–168. 10.1007/s00500-022-07556-0

Liu, Y., & Vrontis, D. (2017). Emerging-market firms venturing into advanced economies: The role of context. *Thunderbird International Business Review*, 59(3), 255–261. 10.1002/tie.21900

Liyakat, K. K. S. (2023). Machine Learning Approach Using Artificial Neural Networks to Detect Malicious Nodes in IoT Networks. In Shukla, P. K., Mittal, H., & Engelbrecht, A. (Eds.), *Computer Vision and Robotics. CVR 2023. Algorithms for Intelligent Systems*. Springer. 10.1007/978-981-99-4577-1_3

Liyakat, K. K. S. (2024). Machine Learning Approach Using Artificial Neural Networks to Detect Malicious Nodes in IoT Networks. In Udgata, S. K., Sethi, S., & Gao, X. Z. (Eds.), *Intelligent Systems. ICMIB 2023. Lecture Notes in Networks and Systems* (Vol. 728). Springer. https://link.springer.com/chapter/10.1007/978-981-99-3932-9_12, 10.1007/978-981-99-3932-9_12

Lo, C. K. (2023). What is the impact of ChatGPT on education? A rapid review of the literature. *Education Sciences*, 13(4), 410. 10.3390/educsci13040410

Löfsten, H. (2014). Information structures and business performance– implications for technology-based firm's innovation performance. *Knowledge and Process Management*, 21(4), 246–259. 10.1002/kpm.1446

Lohmann, J. R., Rollins, H. A., & Joseph Hoey, J. (2006). Defining, developing and assessing global competence in engineers. *European Journal of Engineering Education*, 31(1), 119–131. 10.1080/03043790500429906

London, T., & Hart, S. L. (2004). Reinventing strategies for emerging markets: Beyond the transnational model. *Journal of International Business Studies*, 35(5), 350–370. 10.1057/palgrave.jibs.8400099

Lusk, D. L., Evans, A. D., Jeffrey, T. R., Palmer, K. R., Wikstrom, C. S., & Doolittle, P. E. (2009). Multimedia learning and individual differences: Mediating the effects of working memory capacity with segmentation. *British Journal of Educational Technology*, 40(4), 636–651. 10.1111/j.1467-8535.2008.00848.x

Lu, Y. (2019). Artificial intelligence: A survey on evolution, models, applications and future trends. *Journal of Management Analytics*, 6(1), 1–29. 10.1080/23270012.2019.1570365

Makarius, E. E., Mukherjee, D., Fox, J. D., & Fox, A. K. (2020). Rising with the machines: A sociotechnical framework for bringing artificial intelligence into the organization. *Journal of Business Research*, 120, 262–273. 10.1016/j.jbusres.2020.07.045

Makridakis, S. (2017). The forthcoming Artificial Intelligence (AI) revolution: Its impact on society and firms. *Futures*, 90, 46–60. 10.1016/j.futures.2017.03.006

Malik, N., Tripathi, S. N., Kar, A. K., & Gupta, S. (2022). Impact of artificial intelligence on employees working in industry 4.0 led organizations. *International Journal of Manpower*, 43(2), 334–354. 10.1108/IJM-03-2021-0173

Malinka, K., Peresíni, M., Firc, A., Hujnák, O., & Janus, F. (2023, June). On the educational impact of chatgpt: Is artificial intelligence ready to obtain a university degree? In *Proceedings of the 2023 Conference on Innovation and Technology in Computer Science Education* V. 1 (pp. 47-53). ACM. 10.1145/3587102.3588827

Manesh, M. F., Pellegrini, M. M., Marzi, G., & Dabic, M. (2021). Knowledge management in the fourth industrial revolution: Mapping the literature and scoping future avenues. *IEEE Transactions on Engineering Management*, 68(1), 289–300. 10.1109/TEM.2019.2963489

Marbouti, F., Diefes-Dux, H., & Madhavan, K. (2016). Models for early prediction of at-risk students in a course using standards-based grading. *Computers & Education*, 103, 1–15. 10.1016/j. compedu.2016.09.005

Marleau, J. D., & Saucier, J. F. (2002). Preference for a first-born boy in Western societies. *Journal of Biosocial Science*, 34(1), 13–27. 10.1017/S0021932002000135118142 10

Masiero, S. (2013). *Innovation and best practice in mobile technologies for development.* Economic and Private Sector Professional Evidence and Applied Knowledge Services.

Mazman, S. G., & Altun, A. (2012). Individual Differences in Different Level Mental Rotation Tasks: An Eye Movement Study. In *Towards Learning and Instruction in Web 3.0: Advances in Cognitive and Educational Psychology* (pp. 231–243). Springer. 10.1007/978-1-4614-1539-8

McHenry, J. E. H., & Welch, D. E. (2018). Entrepreneurs and internationalization: A study of Western immigrants in an emerging market. *International Business Review*, 27(1), 93–101. 10.1016/j.ibusrev.2017.05.008

Meesad, P., & Rasel, R. I. (2013). Predicting stock market price using support vector regression. *2013 International Conference on Informatics, Electronics and Vision, ICIEV 2013*, (pp. 1–6). IEEE. 10.1109/ICIEV.2013.6572570

Meira, C. D. M.Jr, Moraes, R., Moura, M., Ávila, L. T. G., Tosini, L., & Magalhães, F. H. (2018). Extraversion/introversion and age-related differences in speed-accuracy tradeoff. *Revista Brasileira de Medicina do Esporte*, 24(3), 225–229. 10.1590/1517-869220182403172690

Meyer, J. G., Urbanowicz, R. J., Martin, P. C., O'Connor, K., Li, R., Peng, P. C., Bright, T. J., Tatonetti, N., Won, K. J., Gonzalez-Hernandez, G., & Moore, J. H. (2023). ChatGPT and large language models in academia: Opportunities and challenges. *BioData Mining*, 16(1), 20. 10.1186/s13040-023-00339-937443040

Meyer, K. E. (2004). Perspectives on multinational enterprises in emerging economies. *Journal of International Business Studies*, 35(4), 259–276. 10.1057/palgrave.jibs.8400084

Compilation of References

Meyer, K. E., Mudambi, R., & Narula, R. (2011). Multinational enterprises and local contexts: The opportunities and challenges of multiple embeddedness. *Journal of Management Studies*, 48(2), 235–252. 10.1111/j.1467-6486.2010.00968.x

Micali, S. (2022). Micropayments without a Monetary Medium. *ACM SIGEcom Exchanges*, 15(2), 87–104.

Miettinen, S., du Preez, V., van Dugteren, J., Moalosi, R., Molokwane, S., & Luojus, S. (2016). *Service design with communities in Africa: the case of UFISA*. Academic Press.

Miles, M. B., & Huberman, A. M. (1994). Qualitative data analysis: An expanded sourcebook. *Sage (Atlanta, Ga.)*.

Mills, A. M., & Smith, T. A. (2011). Knowledge management and organizational performance: A decomposed view. *Journal of Knowledge Management*, 15(1), 156–171. 10.1108/13673271111108756

Mogavi, R. H., Deng, C., Kim, J. J., Zhou, P., Kwon, Y. D., Metwally, A. H. S., & Hui, P. (2024). ChatGPT in education: A blessing or a curse? A qualitative study exploring early adopters' utilization and perceptions. *Computers in Human Behavior: Artificial Humans*, 2(1), 100027. 10.1016/j.chbah.2023.100027

Molina, A. I., Navarro, Ó., Ortega, M., & Lacruz, M. (2018). Evaluating multimedia learning materials in primary education using eye tracking. *Computer Standards & Interfaces*, 59, 45–60. 10.1016/j.csi.2018.02.004

Molina–Jimenez, C., Al Nakib, H. D., Song, L., Sfyrakis, I., & Crowcroft, J. (2020). *A Case for a Currencyless Economy Based on Bartering with Smart Contracts*. University of Cambridge.

Monllaó Olivé, D., Huynh, D. Q., Reynolds, M., Dougiamas, M., & Wiese, D. (2019). A supervised learning framework: Using assessment to identify students at risk of dropping out of a MOOC. *Journal of Computing in Higher Education*. 10.1007/s12528-019-09230-1

Montenegro-Rueda, M., Fernández-Cerero, J., Fernández-Batanero, J. M., & López-Meneses, E. (2023). Impact of the implementation of ChatGPT in education: A systematic review. *Computers*, 12(8), 153. 10.3390/computers12080153

Mulani, A. (2019). Effect of Rotation and Projection on Real time Hand Gesture Recognition system for Human Computer Interaction. *Journal of The Gujrat Research Society*, 21(16), 3710–3718.

Mutlu Bayraktar, D., & Bayram, S. (2017). Evaluation of multimedia learning environment designed according to different attention types via eye tracking method. *Erzincan Üniversitesi Eğitim Fakültesi Dergisi*, 19(2), 119–138. 10.17556/erziefd.331370

Nair, R. R., Sankaran, N., Kota, B. U., Tulyakov, S., Setlur, S., & Govindaraju, V. (2018). Knowledge transfer using Neural network based approach for handwritten text recognition, *In 2018 13th IAPR International Workshop on Document Analysis Systems (DAS)* (pp. 441-446). Research Gate.

Nandal, N., Tanwar, R., & Pruthi, J. (2020). Machine learning based aspect level sentiment analysis for Amazon products. *Spat. Inf. Res.*, 28(5), 601–607. 10.1007/s41324-020-00320-2

Naqshbandi, M. M., & Jasimuddin, S. M. (2018). Knowledgeoriented leadership and open innovation: Role of knowledge management capability in France-based multinationals. *International Business Review*, 27(3), 701–713. 10.1016/j.ibusrev.2017.12.001

Narayan, S., & Sharma, R. (2023). Cryptocurrency Adoption and Its Socioeconomic Implications: A Case Study of India. *Journal of Digital Economics*, 8(2), 45–62.

Narula, A. K. (2017). Bitcoin and the Promise of Financial Inclusion. *Journal of International Affairs*, 71(1), 187–210.

Nayak, J., Dash, P. B., Naik, B., Mohapatra, S., & Routray, A. R. (2022). Deep Learning-Based Trend Analysis on Indian Stock Market in COVID-19 Pandemic Scenario and Forecasting Future Financial Drift. *Journal of The Institution of Engineers (India): Series B, 103*(5), 1459–1478. 10.1007/s40031-022-00762-2

Nazareno, L., & Schiff, D. S. (2021). The impact of automation and artificial intelligence on worker well-being. *Technology in Society*, 67, 101679. 10.1016/j.techsoc.2021.101679

Ngah, R., Tai, T., & Bontis, N. (2016). Knowledge management capabilities and organizational performance in roads and transport authority of Dubai: The mediating role of learning organization. *Knowledge and Process Management*, 23(3), 184–193. 10.1002/kpm.1504

Ngo, T. T. A. (2023). The perception by university students of the use of ChatGPT in education. *International Journal of Emerging Technologies in Learning*, 18(17), 4–19. 10.3991/ijet.v18i17.39019

Nielsen, J. (1994). *Usability engineering*. Elsevier.

Niu, Y., Ying, L., Yang, J., Bao, M., & Sivaparthipan, C. B. (2021). Organizational business intelligence and decision making using big data analytics. *Information Processing & Management*, 58(6), 102725. 10.1016/j.ipm.2021.102725

Nobel, C. (2011). Teaching a 'Lean Startup' Strategy. *HBS Working Knowledge*, (pp. 1–2). Research Gate.

Nowacki, R., & Bachnik, K. (2016). Innovations within knowledge management. *Journal of Business Research*, 69(5), 1577–1581. 10.1016/j.jbusres.2015.10.020

Nyoko, A. E. L., Fanggidae, R. P. C., & Ose, M. (2021). *The Study Of Barter Trading System At Wulandoni Barter Market*.

Ou, P., & Wang, H. (2009). Prediction of stock market index movement by ten data mining techniques. *Modern Applied Science*, 3(12), 28–42. 10.5539/mas.v3n12p28

Parente, S. L., & Prescott, E. C. (1994). Barriers to technology adoption and development. *Journal of Political Economy*, 102(2), 298–321. 10.1086/261933

Compilation of References

Park, B., Korbach, A., & Brünken, R. (2015). Do learner characteristics moderate the seductive-details-effect? A cognitive-load-study using eye-tracking. *Journal of Educational Technology & Society*, 18(4), 24–36.

Park, J., & Woo, S. E. (2022). Who likes artificial intelligence? Personality predictors of attitudes toward artificial intelligence. *The Journal of Psychology*, 156(1), 68–94. 10.1080/00223980.2021.201210935015615

Patel, A., & Gupta, N. (2022). Blockchain Technology and Its Impact on Financial Inclusion: A Comparative Analysis. *International Journal of Financial Innovation*, 7(3), 112–130.

Patterson, D. J., Sim, S. E., & Aiyelokun, T. (2009). Overcoming blind spots in interaction design: A case study in designing for African AIDS orphan care communities. *Information Technologies & International Development,* 5(4).

Pedregosa, F., Varoquaux, G., Gramfort, A., Michel, V., Thirion, B., Grisel, O., Blondel, M., Prettenhofer, P., Weiss, R., & Dubourg, V. (2011). Scikit-learn: Machine learning in Python. *Journal of Machine Learning Research*, 12, 2825–2830.

Petersen, B., Welch, D. E., & Welch, L. S. (2000). Creating meaningful switching options in international operations. *Long Range Planning*, 33(5), 688–705. 10.1016/S0024-6301(00)00076-5

Pillai, R., & Sivathanu, B. (2020). Adoption of artificial intelligence (AI) for talent acquisition in IT/ITeS organizations. *Benchmarking*, 27(9), 2599–2629. 10.1108/BIJ-04-2020-0186

Pirola, F., Boucher, X., Wiesner, S., & Pezzotta, G. (2020). Digital technologies in productservice systems: A literature review and a research agenda. *Computers in Industry*, 123, 1–19. 10.1016/j.compind.2020.103301

Pradana, M., Elisa, H. P., & Syarifuddin, S. (2023). Discussing ChatGPT in education: A literature review and bibliometric analysis. *Cogent Education*, 10(2), 2243134. 10.1080/2331186X.2023.2243134

Prinzie, A., & Van den Poel, D. (2008). Random Forests for multiclass classification: Random MultiNomial Logit. *Expert Systems with Applications*, 34(3), 1721–1732. 10.1016/j.eswa.2007.01.029

Pushpa, S. K., Manjunath, T. N., Mrunal, T. V., Singh, A., & Suhas, C. (2017). Class result prediction using machine learning. *2017 International Conference On Smart Technologies For Smart Nation (SmartTechCon)*, Bengaluru, India. 10.1109/SmartTechCon.2017.8358559

Pyo, S., Lee, J., Cha, M., & Jang, H. (2017). Predictability of machine learning techniques to forecast the trends of market index prices: Hypothesis testing for the Korean stock markets. *PLoS One*, 12(11), e0188107. 10.1371/journal.pone.018810729136004

Qadir, J. (2023, May). Engineering education in the era of ChatGPT: Promise and pitfalls of generative AI for education. In *2023 IEEE Global Engineering Education Conference (EDUCON)* (pp. 1-9). IEEE. 10.1109/EDUCON54358.2023.10125121

Quintero, A., Andrade, J. M., & Ramírez, E. (2019). *Entrepreneurship as an area of knowledge: Literature review.*

Rafi, N., Ahmed, A., Shafique, I., & Kalyar, M. N. (2021). Knowledge management capabilities and organizational agility as liaisons of business performance. *South Asian J. Bus. Stud.*, 11(4), 397–417. 10.1108/SAJBS-05-2020-0145

Rahman, A., & Hossen, M. S. (2019). Sentiment Analysis on Movie Review Data Using Machine Learning Approach. *2019 International Conference on Bangla Speech and Language Processing (ICBSLP).* IEEE. 10.1109/ICBSLP47725.2019.201470

Rahman, M. M., & Watanobe, Y. (2023). ChatGPT for education and research: Opportunities, threats, and strategies. *Applied Sciences (Basel, Switzerland)*, 13(9), 5783. 10.3390/app13095783

Rastrollo-Guerrero, J. L., Gómez-Pulido, J. A., & Durán-Domínguez, A. (2020). Analyzing and Predicting Students' Performance by Means of Machine Learning: A Review. *Applied Sciences (Basel, Switzerland)*, 10(3), 1042. 10.3390/app10031042

Rasul, T., Nair, S., Kalendra, D., Robin, M., de Oliveira Santini, F., Ladeira, W. J., & Heathcote, L. (2023). The role of ChatGPT in higher education: Benefits, challenges, and future research directions. *Journal of Applied Learning and Teaching*, 6(1), 1–16.

Rathore, B. (2023). Future of AI & generation alpha: ChatGPT beyond boundaries. *Eduzone: International Peer Reviewed/Refereed Multidisciplinary Journal, 12*(1), 63-68.

Raza, H., Faizan, M., Hamza, A., Mushtaq, A., & Akhtar, N. (2019). Scientific Text Sentiment Analysis using Machine Learning Techniques. *International Journal of Advanced Computer Science and Applications*, 10(12). 10.14569/IJACSA.2019.0101222

Rehman, K., Poulova, P., Yasmin, F., Haider, S. A., & Jabeen, S. (2021). Empirical investigation of the impacts of knowledge management on organizational learning-a case study of higher education institutions. *Academy of Strategic Management Journal*, 20, 1–15.

Rejeb, A., Rejeb, K., Appolloni, A., Treiblmaier, H., & Iranmanesh, M. (2024). Exploring the impact of ChatGPT on education: A web mining and machine learning approach. *International Journal of Management Education*, 22(1), 100932. 10.1016/j.ijme.2024.100932

Riyanto, S., Sutrisno, A., & Hapzi, A. (2017). The Impact of Working Motivation and Working Environment on Employees Performance in Indonesia Stock Exchange. *International Review of Management and Marketing*, 7(3), 342–348.

Robinson, L., Schulz, J., Blank, G., Ragnedda, M., Ono, H., Hogan, B., Mesch, G. S., Cotten, S. R., Kretchmer, S. B., Hale, T. M., Drabowicz, T., Yan, P., Wellman, B., Harper, M.-G., Quan-Haase, A., Dunn, H. S., Casilli, A. A., Tubaro, P., Carvath, R., & Khilnani, A. (2020). Digital inequalities 2.0: Legacy inequalities in the information age. *First Monday*, 25(7). 10.5210/fm.v25i7.10842

Rohrer, J. M., Egloff, B., & Schmukle, S. C. (2015). Examining the effects of birth order on personality. *Proceedings of the National Academy of Sciences of the United States of America*, 112(46), 14224–14229. 10.1073/pnas.1506451112226483461

Compilation of References

Rose, C. (2015). *The Evolution Of Digital Currencies: Bitcoin, A Cryptocurrency Causing A Monetary Revolution.*

Rudolph, J., Tan, S., & Tan, S. (2023). War of the chatbots: Bard, Bing Chat, ChatGPT, Ernie and beyond. The new AI gold rush and its impact on higher education. *Journal of Applied Learning and Teaching*, 6(1).

Russom, P. (2011). Big data analytics - TDWI Best Practices Report. *TDWI Best Practices Report. Fourth Quarter*, (August), 38.

Salekhova, L. L., Grigorieva, K. S., & Zinnurov, T. A. (2019). *Using LMS Moodle in Teaching CLIL: A Case Study.* 2019 12th International Conference on Developments in eSystems Engineering (DeSE), Kazan, Russia. 10.1109/DeSE.2019.00078

Sallam, M. (2023). The utility of ChatGPT as an example of large language models in healthcare education, research and practice: Systematic review on the future perspectives and potential limitations. medRxiv, 2023-02.

Sammaknejad, N., Pouretemad, H., Eslahchi, C., Salahirad, A., & Alinejad, A. (2017). Gender classification based on eye movements: A processing effect during passive face viewing. *Advances in Cognitive Psychology*, 13(3), 232–240. 10.5709/acp-0223-129071007

Santiago, B. J., Ramírez, J. M. O., Rodríguez-Reséndiz, J., Dector, A., García, R. G., González-Durán, J. E. E., & Sánchez, F. F. (2020). Learning Management System-Based Evaluation to Determine Academic Efficiency Performance. *Sustainability (Basel)*, 12(10), 4256. 10.3390/su12104256

Sartori, J. T. D., Frederico, G. F., & Silva, H. F. N. (2022). Organizational knowledge management in the context of supply chain 4.0: A systematic literature review and conceptual model proposal. *Knowledge and Process Management*, 29(2), 147–161. 10.1002/kpm.1682

Scheiter, K., & Eitel, A. (2017). The use of eye tracking as a research and instructional tool in multimedia learning. In *Eye-Tracking Technology Applications in Educational Research* (pp. 143–164). IGI Global. 10.4018/978-1-5225-1005-5.ch008

Schepman, A., & Rodway, P. (2020). Initial validation of the general attitudes towards Artificial Intelligence Scale. *Computers in Human Behavior Reports*, 1(1), 100014. 10.1016/j.chbr.2020.10001434235291

Schepman, A., & Rodway, P. (2022). The General Attitudes towards Artificial Intelligence Scale (GAAIS): Confirmatory validation and associations with personality, corporate distrust, and general trust. *International Journal of Human-Computer Interaction*, 39(13), 2724–2741. 10.1080/10447318.2022.2085400

Schmidt-Fajlik, R. (2023). Chatgpt as a grammar checker for japanese english language learners: A comparison with grammarly and prowritingaid. *AsiaCALL Online Journal*, 14(1), 105–119. 10.54855/acoj.231417

Schmidt-Weigand, F. (2009). The influence of visual and temporal dynamics on split attention: Evidences from eye tracking. In *Cognitive Effects of Multimedia Learning* (pp. 89–107). IGI Global. 10.4018/978-1-60566-158-2.ch006

Schweppe, J., & Rummer, R. (2014). Attention, working memory, and long-term memory in multimedia learning: An integrated perspective based on process models of working memory. *Educational Psychology Review*, 26(2), 285–306. 10.1007/s10648-013-9242-2

Schwonke, R., Berthold, K., & Renkl, A. (2009). How multiple external representations are used and how they can be made more useful. *Applied Cognitive Psychology*, 23(9), 1227–1243. 10.1002/acp.1526

Seleim, A. A., & Khalil, O. E. (2011). Understanding the knowledge management-intellectual capital relationship: A two-way analysis. *Journal of Intellectual Capital*, 12(4), 586–614. 10.1108/14691931111181742

Seo, K., Tang, J., Roll, I., Fels, S., & Yoon, D. (2021). The impact of artificial intelligence on learner–instructor interaction in online learning. *International Journal of Educational Technology in Higher Education*, 18(1), 54. 10.1186/s41239-021-00292-934778540

Shadi, R. (2017). The survey of the relationship between knowledge management and running a lean production system. *Helix*, 8(2), 1024–1032.

Shahzad, M., Qu, Y., Zafar, A. U., & Appolloni, A. (2021). Does the interaction between the knowledge management process and sustainable development practices boost corporate green innovation? *Business Strategy and the Environment*, 30(8), 4206–4222. 10.1002/bse.2865

Sharma, R., Reynolds, P., Scheepers, R., Seddon, P. B., & Shanks, G. G. (2010). Business Analytics and Competitive Advantage: A Review and a Research Agenda. *DSS*, 187–198.

Sharma, A., Malviya, R., & Gupta, R. (2022). Big data analytics in healthcare. *Cognitive Intelligence and Big Data in Healthcare*, 2015, 257–301. 10.1002/9781119771982.ch10

Sharma, P., & Gupta, N. (2022). Environmental Impact of Cryptocurrency Mining: A Comparative Analysis of Energy Consumption and Carbon Footprint. *Journal of Environmental Economics and Management*, 30(4), 339–352.

Sharma, S., & Yadav, R. (2022). Chat GPT–A Technological Remedy or Challenge for Education System. *Global Journal of Enterprise Information System*, 14(4), 46–51.

Shepherd, D. A., & Majchrzak, A. (2022). Machines augmenting entrepreneurs: Opportunities (and threats) at the Nexus of artificial intelligence and entrepreneurship. *Journal of Business Venturing*, 37(4), 106227. 10.1016/j.jbusvent.2022.106227

Silva, C., Fonseca, J. (2017). *Educational Data Mining: A Literature Review*. Springer. 10.1007/978-3-319-46568-5_9

Singhal, K. (n.d.). *Critical and Comparative Analysis of Taxation Laws To Crypto-Currency in India.*

Compilation of References

Singh, P., Phutela, N., Grover, P., Sinha, D., & Sinha, S. (2023, December). Student's Perception of Chat GPT. In *2023 International Conference on Electrical, Communication and Computer Engineering (ICECCE)* (pp. 1-6). IEEE. 10.1109/ICECCE61019.2023.10442033

Singh, R., & Sharma, A. (2024). Adoption of Cryptocurrencies in the Indian Economy: A Case Study of Opportunities and Challenges. *The Journal of Industrial Economics*, 21(1), 87–104.

Skavronskaya, L., Hadinejad, A., & Cotterell, D. (2023). Reversing the threat of artificial intelligence to opportunity: A discussion of ChatGPT in tourism education. *Journal of Teaching in Travel & Tourism*, 23(2), 253–258. 10.1080/15313220.2023.2196658

Smith, J., & Johnson, A. (2023). Exploring the Legal and Regulatory Landscape of Cryptocurrencies: A Comparative Analysis of Global Approaches. *Journal of Financial Regulation*, 18(3), 112–129.

Sok, S., & Heng, K. (2023). ChatGPT for education and research: A review of benefits and risks. *Available atSSRN* 4378735.

Solimano, A. (2020). *Phenomenological Study*. Assessing the Differences in Crypto-Currency and Other Forms of Currencies, Legality in Islamic Jurisprudence.

Sothan, S. (2019). The determinants of academic performance: Evidence from a Cambodian University. *Studies in Higher Education*, 44(11), 2096–3111. 10.1080/03075079.2018.1496408

Sousa, M. J., & Rocha, Á. (2019). Strategic knowledge management in the digital age: JBR special issue editorial. *Journal of Business Research*, 94, 223–226. 10.1016/j.jbusres.2018.10.016

Spirin, O. M. (2013). Information and communication technologies for monitoring the implementation of research results. *Information Technologies and Teaching Aids.*, 36(4), 132–152.

Sreenivasulu, D. (2022). Implementation of Latest machine learning approaches for students Grade Prediction. *International journal of Early Childhood special Issue,14*(03).

Stabile, A. J., Iribarren, S., Sonney, J., Demiris, G., & Schnall, R. (2024). Usability testing of a mobile health application to support individuals with active tuberculosis: A mixed methods study. *Informatics for Health & Social Care*, 1–13. 10.1080/17538157.2024.233337938529729

Stahl, B. C., Andreou, A., Brey, P., Hatzakis, T., Kirichenko, A., Macnish, K., Laulh'e Shaelou, S., Patel, A., Ryan, M., & Wright, D. (2021). Artificial intelligence for human flourishing – beyond principles for machine learning. *Journal of Business Research*, 124, 374–388. 10.1016/j.jbusres.2020.11.030

Stahl, B. C., & Eke, D. (2024). The ethics of ChatGPT–Exploring the ethical issues of an emerging technology. *International Journal of Information Management*, 74, 102700. 10.1016/j.ijinfomgt.2023.102700

Sudirjo, F., Dewa, D. M. R. T., Kesuma, L. I., Suryaningsih, L., & Utami, E. Y. (2024). Application of The User Centered Design Method To Evaluate The Relationship Between User Experience, User Interface and Customer Satisfaction on Banking Mobile Application. *Jurnal Informasi Dan Teknologi*, 7-13.

Sugiyama, K., & Yamanaka, T. (2023). Proposals and Methods for Foreign Language Learning Using Machine Translation and Large Language Model. *Procedia Computer Science*, 225, 4750–4757. 10.1016/j.procs.2023.10.474

Sujitparapitaya, S., Shirani, A., & Roldan, M. (2012). Issues in Information Systems. *Issues in Information Systems*, 13(2).

Sulloway, F. J. (1999). Birth order. Encyclopedia of creativity, 1, 189-202.

Tabbers, H. K., Paas, F., Lankford, C., Martens, R. L., & van Merriënboer, J. J. G. (2008). Studying eye movements in multimedia learning. *Understanding Multimedia Documents*, 169–184. 10.1007/978-0-387-73337-1_9

Taddeo, M., & Floridi, L. (2018). How AI can be a force for good. *Science*, 361(6404), 751–752. 10.1126/science.aat599130139858

Tate, M. (2002). Human computer interaction: Issues and challenges. *Online Information Review*, 26(5), 348. 10.1016/j.giq.2003.08.006

Thesmar, D., Sraer, D., Pinheiro, L., Dadson, N., Veliche, R., & Greenberg, P. (2019). Combining the power of artificial intelligence with the richness of healthcare claims data: Opportunities and challenges. *PharmacoEconomics*, 37(6), 745–752. 10.1007/s40273-019-00777-630848452

Tian, S., Jin, Q., Yeganova, L., Lai, P. T., Zhu, Q., Chen, X., Yang, Y., Chen, Q., Kim, W., Comeau, D. C., Islamaj, R., Kapoor, A., Gao, X., & Lu, Z. (2024). Opportunities and challenges for ChatGPT and large language models in biomedicine and health. *Briefings in Bioinformatics*, 25(1), bbad493. 10.1093/bib/bbad49338168838

Tippins, M. J., & Sohi, R. S. (2003). IT Competency and Firm Performance: Is Organizational Learning a Missing Link? *Strategic Management Journal*, 24(8), 745–761. 10.1002/smj.337

Tizard, B., & Hughes, M. (2008). *Young children learning*. John Wiley & Sons.

Trkman, P., McCormack, K., De Oliveira, M. P. V., & Ladeira, M. B. (2010). The impact of business analytics on supply chain performance. *Decision Support Systems*, 49(3), 318–327. 10.1016/j.dss.2010.03.007

Tschang, F. T., & Almirall, E. (2021). Artificial intelligence as augmenting automation: Implications for employment. *The Academy of Management Perspectives*, 35(4), 642–659. 10.5465/amp.2019.0062

Ülkü, A. (2023). Artificial intelligence-based large language models and integrity of exams and assignments in higher education: The case of tourism courses. *Tourism & Management Studies*, 19(4), 21–34. 10.18089/tms.2023.190402

Compilation of References

Uz, C., & Altun, A. (2014). Object Location Memory and Sex Difference: Implications on Static vs. Dynamic Navigation Environments. *Journal of Cognitive Science*, 14(1), 27–56. 10.17791/jcs.2014.15.1.27

Valuch, C., Pflüger, L. S., Wallner, B., Laeng, B., & Ansorge, U. (2015). Using eye tracking to test for individual differences in attention to attractive faces. *Frontiers in Psychology*, 6, 42. 10.3389/fpsyg.2015.0004225698993

van Gog, T., Kester, L., Nievelstein, F., Giesbers, B., & Paas, F. (2009). Uncovering cognitive processes: Different techniques that can contribute to cognitive load research and instruction. *Computers in Human Behavior*, 25(2), 325–331. 10.1016/j.chb.2008.12.021

van Gog, T., & Scheiter, K. (2010). Eye tracking as a tool to study and enhance multimedia learning. *Learning and Instruction*, 20(2), 95–99. 10.1016/j.learninstruc.2009.02.009

Vapnik, V. (1999). *The nature of statistical learning theory*. Springer science & business media.

Villegas-Ch, W., & Luján-Mora, S. (2017). *Systematic Review of Evidence on Data Mining Applied to LMS Platforms for Improving E-Learning*. In Proceedings of the International Technology, Education and Development Conference, Valencia, Spain. 10.21125/inted.2017.1510

Villegas-Ch, W., Román-Cañizares, M., & Palacios-Pacheco, X. (2020). Improvement of an On-line Education Model with the Integration of Machine Learning and Data Analysis in an LMS. *Applied Sciences (Basel, Switzerland)*, 10(15), 5371. 10.3390/app10155371

Villegas, W., Molina-Enriquez, J., Chicaiza-Tamayo, C., Ortiz-Garcés, I., & Luján-Mora, S. (2019). Application of a Big Data Framework for Data Monitoring on a Smart Campus. *Sustainability (Basel)*, 11(20), 5552. 10.3390/su11205552

Vrontis, D., Christofi, M., Pereira, V., Tarba, S., Makrides, A., & Trichina, E. (2021). Artificial intelligence, robotics, advanced technologies and human resource management: A systematic review. *International Journal of Human Resource Management*, 1(1), 1–30.

Wang, J., Yu, L., & Rong, Y. (2024). A new CoCoSo ranking-based QFD approach in Pythagorean fuzzy environment and its application on evaluating design attributes of mobile medical App. *Journal of Intelligent & Fuzzy Systems*, (Preprint), 1-24.

Wang, W., Chen, Y., & Heffernan, N. (2020). *A generative model-based tutoring system for math word problems*. arXiv preprint arXiv:2010.04.

Wang, X., & Wan, J. (2021). Cloud-edge collaboration-based knowledge sharing mechanism for manufacturing resources. *Applied Sciences (Basel, Switzerland)*, 11(7), 1–19. 10.3390/app12010001

Wells, T. S., Ozminkowski, R. J., Hawkins, K., Bhattarai, G. R., & Armstrong, D. G. (2016). Leveraging big data in population health management. *Big Data Analytics*, 1(1), 1–14. 10.1186/s41044-016-0001-5

Wijayati, D. T., Rahman, Z., Fahrullah, A., Rahman, M. F. W., Arifah, I. D. C., & Kautsar, A. (2022). A study of artificial intelligence on employee performance and work engagement: The moderating role of change leadership. *International Journal of Manpower*, 43(2), 486–512. 10.1108/IJM-07-2021-0423

Wright, S. A., & Schultz, A. E. (2018). The rising tide of artificial intelligence and business automation: Developing an ethical framework. *Business Horizons*, 61(6), 823–832. 10.1016/j.bushor.2018.07.001

Wu, J., & Shang, S. (2020). Managing uncertainty in AI-enabled decision making and achieving sustainability. *Sustainability (Basel)*, 12(21), 8758. 10.3390/su12218758

Yaghoubi, N., Salehi, M., & Nezhad, E. B. (2011). A relationship between tactical processes of knowledge management and organizational intelligence: Iranian evidence. *World Applied Sciences Journal*, 12(9), 1413–1421.

Yao, H., Lian, D., Cao, Y., Wu, Y., Zhou, T. (2019). Predicting Academic Performance for College Students: A Campus Behavior Perspective. *ACM Trans. Intell. Syst. Technol., 1*. DOI:10.1145/3299087

Yazıcı, H. (1997). *Karadeniz Teknik Üniversitesi Öğrencilerinin Kişilik Özelliklerinin Eysenck'in Kişilik Kuramına Dayalı Olarak Belirlenmesi*. KTÜ Sosyal Bilimler Enstitüsü Eğitim Bilimleri/Psikolojik Danışma ve Rehberlik.

Yermack, C. (2012). Made for Cyberpunks: Why Bitcoin Has Value. *Journal of Financial Transformation*, 38, 339–352.

Yermack, C. (2017). Is Bitcoin a Real Currency? An Economic Appraisal. In Ziegelmayer, D. A. (Ed.), *Handbook of Digital Currency* (pp. 39–62). Springer International Publishing.

Yiğit, S. (2023). Yapay Zekâ Gastronomi Eğitimine Katkı Sunabilir Mi? ChatGPT Örneği. *Journal of Tourism & Gastronomy Studies.*, 11(3), 1970–1982.

Yılmaz, M. T., & Kesici, Ş. (2014). Anne baba tutumları ve kardeş sırasının üniversite öğrencilerinin öz-anlayışlarının gelişimine etkisi. *OPUS Uluslararası Toplum Araştırmaları Dergisi*, 4(6), 131–157.

Yuan, H., Tang, Y., Xu, W., & Lau, R. Y. K. (2020). Exploring the influence of multimodal social media data on stock performance: An empirical perspective and analysis. *Internet Research*, 31(3), 871–891. 10.1108/INTR-11-2019-0461

Zafar, Y. M., & Alsabban, A. (2023). Knowledge Sharing Through Social Media Platforms in the Silicon Age. *Sustainability*, 15, 1–21.

Zhao, S., Liu, X., Anderson, U., & Shenkar, O. (2022). Knowledge Management of Emerging Economy Multinationals. *Journal of World Business*, 57(1), 1–18. 10.1016/j.jwb.2021.101255

Zhong, X., & Enke, D. (2019). Predicting the daily return direction of the stock market using hybrid machine learning algorithms. *Financial Innovation*, 5(1), 24. 10.1186/s40854-019-0138-0

Compilation of References

Złotowski, J., Yogeeswaran, K., & Bartneck, C. (2017). Can we control it? Autonomous robots threaten human identity, uniqueness, safety, and resources. *International Journal of Human-Computer Studies*, 100, 48–54. 10.1016/j.ijhcs.2016.12.008

About the Contributors

Gamze Sart was awarded the PhD degree in the field of Educational Sciences in Bogazici University in 2013. She worked as an Assistant Professor in the Faculty of Education, Yeditepe University in 2013 and Hasan Ali Yucel Faculty of Education, Istanbul University during the period 2014-2018 and as an Associate Professor in the Hasan Ali Yucel Faculty of Education, Istanbul University-Cerrahpaşa, since 2018. Her main research areas: Educational Studies, Higher Education Policies, Higher Education Management, Lifelong Learning, Sustainable Development.

***

Mustafa Alpsülün started to work as a lecturer at Harran University Siverek Vocational School in 2012. Her main research interests are: Video-based learning, Lifelong Learning, Human-Computer Interaction, Artificial Intelligence, Educational videos

Yashmita Awasthi currently holds the position of Assistant Professor at the esteemed School of Commerce, Finance, and Accountancy within Christ University's Delhi NCR Campus. Her academic journey includes the attainment of a doctoral degree in management discipline from Banaras Hindu University in Varanasi. Dr. Awasthi's academic pursuits are primarily centered around the fields of Finance, Entrepreneurship, and Strategic Business Management. She has made significant contributions to her field by publishing numerous research papers and articles in esteemed journals, thereby enriching the academic discourse and advancing knowledge in her areas of expertise.

Hasan Celal Balikçi was awarded his PhD degree in Computer Education and Instructional Technology at Gazi University in 2023. In 2014, he started to work as a lecturer at Harran University Siverek Vocational School. Her main research interests are: Video-based learning, Lifelong Learning, Human-Computer Interaction, Artificial Intelligence.

Kazi Kutubuddin Sayyad Liyakat has completed his B.E., M.E., and Ph.D. in E&TC Engineering and is nowadays working as a Professor & Head in Electronics and Telecommunication Engineering Department and also as Dean R&D. He is Post Doctoral Fellow working on "IoT in Healthcare applications". He has published more than 110+ articles in various Journals. Also published 11 books in the field of Engineering. He has 15 Indian Patents, 2 Indian copyright patents, 2 South African Grant Patent, and 8 UK Grant Patent. All patents are in the field of IoT in Healthcare. He worked as a Reviewer for Scopus Conferences and Journal also reviewer for IGI Global. Also work as Editorial Board Member for various Journals.

About the Contributors

Sowmiya K.C., an accomplished Ph.D. scholar at Sri Vasavi College in Erode, emerges as a dynamic and vibrant researcher with a rich educational background. Having laid the foundation with a B.Ed. degree and furthered her academic pursuits with post-graduation at PSGR Krishnammal College for Women, she has adeptly positioned herself at the forefront of scholarly exploration.Her commitment to advancing knowledge is exemplified through her proactive involvement in two conferences in 2023, where she not only showcased her research prowess but also actively engaged with peers and experts, fostering meaningful discussions. Notably, the recognition garnered from presenting her research findings at these conferences has resulted in the acceptance of her journal article for publication later this year. This noteworthy achievement not only underscores Sowmiya's dedication to the academic realm but also highlights her impactful contributions to the scholarly discourse. As a Ph.D. scholar, she stands as a vibrant and influential contributor to the ever-evolving landscape of research and academic exploration, leaving an indelible mark on her field.

Srishti Muralidharan is a NET qualified Assistant Professor working in the Department of Psychology in PES University, Bangalore. She is currently pursuing a Master's in Philosophy from IGNOU. She has published research papers in the areas of Mental Health Literacy and is also a practicing Psychologist. Her areas of interest are Clinical Psychology, Neuropsychology, Indian Psychology, Social Psychology, Psychotherapy and Philosophy.

Müzeyyen Bulut Özek completed her PhD in Electrical and Electronics Engineering at Fırat University in 2010. In 2021, she became an associate professor in the field of computer and instructional technologies. She is currently working at Firat University. Her main research interests are: Artificial Intelligence in Education, E-Learning, Instructional Technologies

Sabyasachi Pramanik is a professional IEEE member. He obtained a PhD in Computer Science and Engineering from Sri Satya Sai University of Technology and Medical Sciences, Bhopal, India. Presently, he is an Associate Professor, Department of Computer Science and Engineering, Haldia Institute of Technology, India. He has many publications in various reputed international conferences, journals, and book chapters (Indexed by SCIE, Scopus, ESCI, etc). He is doing research in the fields of Artificial Intelligence, Data Privacy, Cybersecurity, Network Security, and Machine Learning. He also serves on the editorial boards of several international journals. He is a reviewer of journal articles from IEEE, Springer, Elsevier, Inderscience, IET and IGI Global. He has reviewed many conference papers, has been a keynote speaker, session chair, and technical program committee member at many international conferences. He has authored a book on Wireless Sensor Network. He has edited 8 books from IGI Global, CRC Press, Springer and Wiley Publications.

SC Vetrivel is a faculty member in the Department of Management Studies, Kongu Engineering College (Autonomous), Perundurai, Erode Dt. Having experience in Industry 20 years and Teaching 16 years. Awarded with Doctoral Degree in Management Sciences in Anna University, Chennai. He has organized various workshops and Faculty Development Programmes. He is actively involved in research and consultancy works. He acted as a resource person to FDPs & MDPs to various industries like, SPB ltd, Tamilnadu Police, DIET, Rotary school and many. His areas of interest include Entrepreneurship, Business Law, Marketing and Case writing. Articles published more than 100 International and National Journals. Presented papers in more than 30 National and International conferences including IIM Bangalore, IIM Kozhikode, IIM Kashipur and IIM Indore. He was a Chief Co-ordinator of Entrepreneurship and Management Development Centre (EMDC) of Kongu Engineering College, he was instrumental in organizing various Awareness Camps, FDP, and TEDPs to aspiring entrepreneurs which was funded by NSTEDB – DST/GoI

Ashy Sebastian is currently pursuing her Ph.D in finance from Christ University, Bengaluru, India. Having finished her post graduation in commerce from Sb College, Kerala, she has work experience as a Tax Analyst in EY. Her work is majority interdisciplinary and combines AI with finance. Her areas of expertise span machine learning, deep learning,stock markets, and portfolio optimization.

Funda Hatice Sezgin completed her undergraduate education in Faculty of economics in University of Istanbul. She did master of business administration degree (MBA) in Econometrics of University of Istanbul, and doctor of econometrics in Marmara University. Her research interests are time series analysis, panel data analysis and statistical methods. She works in the department of industrial engineering at Istanbul University-Cerrahpasa.

Veerta Tantia is an Associate Professor in the School of Commerce, Finance, and Accountancy at Christ University. Her research interests span diverse topics such as service learning,finance, accountancy, teacher occupational stress, organizational culture of K-12 schools, and the impact of support systems on teacher satisfaction in online teaching.

V. Sabareeshwari currently serves as Assistant Professor in Department of Soil Science, Amrita School of Agricultural Sciences, Coimbatore. Having more than 5 years of research experience and more than 2 years of teaching experience. She got 7 awards in the field of agriculture. Her field of expertise are soil genesis, soil pedological studies as well as soil fertility mapping using advanced software like Arc GIS. She had published 22 research papers and more than 10 book chapters and books in high- impact reputed journals. She has actively participated and presented her papers in more than 20 conferences and seminars. She not only restrict her contribution only in the academic and research part, she had extension experience at farm level (lab to land) with varied crop research.

V.P. Arun is a driven and accomplished professional with a diverse educational background and extensive hands-on experience across various industries. Graduating with honors, Arun earned his Master of Business Administration (M.B.A) with a specialization in Human Resources and Marketing from the renowned Sona School of Management in Salem in 2018, where he excelled academically with an impressive 8.3 Cumulative Grade Point Average (CGPA). Before pursuing his MBA, Arun laid a solid foundation by obtaining a Bachelor of Engineering degree from Kongu Engineering College in 2014. Throughout his academic journey, Arun displayed an unwavering commitment to learning and personal growth, actively seeking opportunities to expand his knowledge and skills beyond the confines of traditional education. He sought practical experiences to complement his theoretical understanding, such as a 45-day summer internship focused on conducting a feasibility study for R-Doc Sustainability in the market. Additionally, Arun broadened his horizons through a 7-day industrial visit to Malaysia and Singapore, immersing himself in diverse cultural and professional environments.

Index

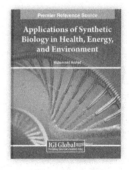

Ensure Quality Research is Introduced to the Academic Community

Become a Reviewer for IGI Global Authored Book Projects

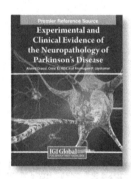
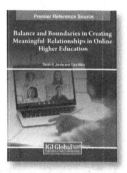

The overall success of an authored book project is dependent on quality and timely manuscript evaluations.

Applications and Inquiries may be sent to:
development@igi-global.com

Applicants must have a doctorate (or equivalent degree) as well as publishing, research, and reviewing experience. Authored Book Evaluators are appointed for one-year terms and are expected to complete at least three evaluations per term. Upon successful completion of this term, evaluators can be considered for an additional term.

If you have a colleague that may be interested in this opportunity, we encourage you to share this information with them.

Printed in the United States
by Baker & Taylor Publisher Services